Fiji

a travel survival kit

Rob Kay

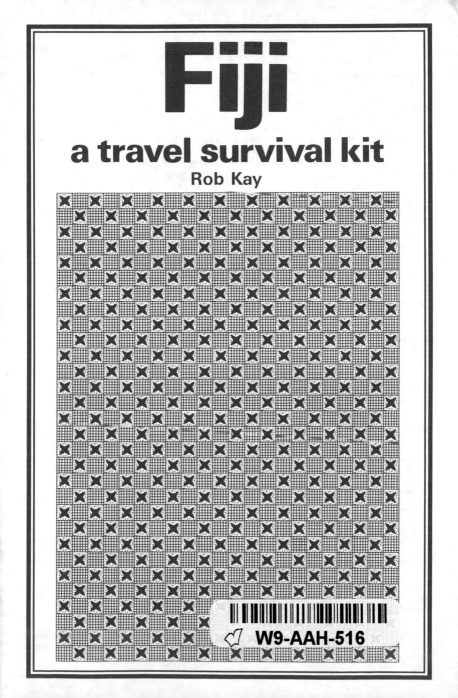

Fiji – a travel survival kit

3rd edition

Published by
Lonely Planet Publications
Head Office: PO Box 617, Hawthorn, Vic 3122, Australia
Branches: 155 Filbert St, Suite 251, Oakland, CA 94607, USA
              10 Barley Mow Passage, Chiswick, London W4 4PH, UK
              71 bis rue du Cardinal Lemoine, 75005 Paris, France

Printed by
Singapore National Printers Ltd

Photographs by
Fiji Visitors' Bureau (FVB)
Rob Kay (RK)
Ian Osborn (IO)
Tropical Dive Charters Ltd (TDC)
Jan Whiting (JW)

Front cover: Vatulele Island, Diana Calder, Scoopix Photo Library

First Published
March 1986

This Edition
March 1993

National Library of Australia Cataloguing in Publication Data

Kay, Robert F., 1953-
    Fiji – a travel survival kit.

    3rd ed.
    Includes index.
    ISBN 0 86442 177 X.

    1. Fiji – Guidebooks. I. Title. (Series: Lonely Planet travel survival kit).

919.61104

text © Robert Kay 1993
maps © Lonely Planet 1993
photos © photographers as indicated 1993

Rob Kay

After graduating from a liberal arts college in the Pacific Northwest and travelling around Europe in the mid-70s, Rob Kay, a San Francisco, California native, settled into journalism as the news director for a small radio station in the Sierra Nevada foothills. When he tired of inventing ways to make small-town news exciting, Rob caught the tradewinds for Tahiti where, between stints as a bartender, he covered French Polynesia for *Pacific News Service*, NBC radio, *New Pacific*, *Pacific Islands Monthly* and the *San Francisco Chronicle*.

Wishing to see more of the Pacific, he signed on as a tour guide for French Polynesia, Fiji, Tonga, American Samoa and Western Samoa. He liked Fiji so much, he returned for a year's stay, once again freelancing for a number of publications. The idea for his guides to French Polynesia and Fiji came about as he saw the need for comprehensive, in-depth coverage of travel and culture in these countries. Rob continues to travel frequently in the Pacific and has contributed feature articles to *Newsday*, *Los Angeles Times*, *San Jose Mercury*, *Arizona Republic*, *Philadelphia Inquirer*, *San Diego Tribune*, *San Francisco Magazine*, *Islands* and other publications. Between trips he spends his spare time restoring a Victorian home in San Francisco's Haight-Ashbury district.

From the Author

This book is dedicated to my adopted Fijian family – Waqa and Mere Nawaqatabu, and to Iliesa and Lela Duvuloco. My appreciation also goes to Fergus Clunie, former director of the Fiji Museum, for his sage advice and knowledge of old Fiji.

I was assisted in this version of the book by Tom Cooke, a longtime American expat with his soul firmly rooted in Fijian soil. Both Tom and his delightful Fijian wife, Alesi were instrumental in my research for the Viti Levu, Ovalau, Kadavu and Yasawa Group chapters. I also want to thank Australian expat Tony Anderson of Nadi, who was an invaluable source of unbiased information about Viti Levu.

For help with this edition, I would also like to express my gratitude to Susana Tuivaga of the Fiji Visitors' Bureau in Los Angeles, Joe Rayawa of the FVB in Suva, Paul Geraghty of the Fiji Dictionary Project, Professor Al Schutz of the University of Hawaii, Geoff Taylor of Savusavu, Jim Dunn of Lautoka, and Steve Yaqona, the US director of the Fiji Visitors' Bureau. Finally I must express my gratitude to John and Laura Heraty who provided me with the most incisive look at Fijian insects that I could ever hope for.

From the Publisher

This edition of Fiji was edited by Miriam Cannell. Glenn Beanland handled the mapping, design and layout.

Thanks to Frith Pike for proof reading and to Andrea Webster from Lonely Planet's UK office for her help with international airfares.

Thanks must also go to all the travellers who wrote to Lonely Planet with information, comments and suggestions. These include:

Brad Alberts (USA), Alfie Anderson (USA), John Barnett (NZ), Philippe Beck (AUS), Lisa Bedson (AUS), Mike Bidgood (UK), Mel Bloom, Simon Bourke (UK), Neil R Boyd (UK), Steve Boyle (AUS), Captain Rick Bramwell, Elliot Brown (USA), Louisa Bungey (UK), Christine Carter (C), Carolyn Caton (UK), S Cauty, B L Chamberlain (F), Rosemary Crouch (AUS), Will & Cynthia de Prado (USA), Walt Deas (AUS), L Deptuch (C), Carol Douglas, Steve Emery (C), Kent Fenton (C), Peter Fiske (AUS), John Flatt, Bob Forster, Scott Funk, David Gaughan (IRL), Brett Gordon, Susan Grinsdell (NZ), Neil & Nora Hagen (C), Ursula Haink (USA), Jack Hamm (AUS), F Harris (UK), Ian Hawkins (AUS), Bryan Heatley (UK), Colleen Henry (AUS), Laura Heraty (USA), Mark Hinton, Winona Hubbard (USA), R Hunt (AUS), Steve Hutson (AUS), Karen Jacobsen (USA), Mark Javorski (USA), Susan & Greg Johnson (USA), Jay & Margie Johnson, Craig Jung (USA), Gary Kanaby (USA), Ruth Kaufman (USA), David Kitching (UK), Edward Kosower (Isr), Rory Krauss (USA), Jan Kucera (USA), Rajend Kumar (Fij), Lucy Kunkel (USA), R T Lange, Sue Lolohem (USA), Annabel Loram (UK), Carrie Loranger, Diana Madgin (NZ), John Maidment (UK), Claudia Mangani (I), Ejvind Marteusen (DK), Neil McCrindle (UK), Lisa Mead (AUS), Frederico Medici (I), William Methven (USA), Maureen & Trevor Miller (AUS), Sue Miller (NZ), John Minson (NZ), Arvind Mishra (Fij), David Nash (USA), D A Norman (UK), Markus Nussli (S), Dennis O'Callighan, Marcus Oliver, Manfred Ossendorf (D), Michael Partington (AUS), Martine Pitts (AUS), Laurie Price (USA), Jan Price (NZ), Reila & Per (DK), Julia Richardson, David Robb (UK), John & Annette Robbins (AUS), Catherine Roberts (UK), Rod Russell (AUS), Bruce Rutherford (AUS), Brian Rutherford (AUS), Bruce Samuels (USA), Dieter Schaborak (D), Gunter Schafer (D), Glen Schleuter (AUS), Don Schuler (USA), M Slater (UK), Stephen Hansen Smythe (C), John Spurway (AUS), C Stevens (USA), John Surinchak (USA), Alisa Tasker (UK), Renate Trageiser (NL), James Trujillo (USA), Tomas Valentine, Gayle Wade, Neal Watts (UK), Linda Weil (USA), J D Williams (C), Marge Williams, Elizabeth Woolnough (C).

AUS – Australia, C – Canada, D – Germany, DK – Denmark, Fij – Fiji, F – France, IRL – Ireland, Isr – Israel, I – Italy, NL – Netherlands, NZ – New Zealand, S – Sweden, UK – United Kingdom, USA – United States of America

Warning & Request

Things change – prices go up, schedules change, good places go bad and bad places go bankrupt – nothing stays the same. So if you find things better or worse, recently opened or long since closed, please write and tell us and help make the next edition better.

Your letters will be used to help update future editions and, where possible, important changes will also be included in a Stop Press section in reprints.

We greatly appreciate all information that is sent to us by travellers. Back at Lonely Planet we employ a hard-working readers' letters team to sort through the many letters we receive. The best ones will be rewarded with a free copy of the next edition or another Lonely Planet guide if you prefer. We give away lots of books, but, unfortunately, not every letter/postcard receives one.

Contents

Map Legend

BOUNDARIES

— · — · — · — .... International Boundary
— · · — · · — .... Internal Boundary
+·+·+·+·+·+·+·+ .... National Park or Reserve
— — — — — — — .... The Equator
· · · · · · · · · · · · · · · · .... The Tropics

SYMBOLS

◉ NEW DELHI .... National Capital
● BOMBAY .... Provincial or State Capital
● Pune .... Major Town
● Barsi .... Minor Town
■ .... Places to Stay
▼ .... Places to Eat
⊠ .... Post Office
✈ .... Airport
i .... Tourist Information
⊖ .... Bus Station or Terminal
66 .... Highway Route Number
☪ ☨ ⛪ ☨ ...... Mosque, Church, Cathedral
∴ .... Temple or Ruin
✚ .... Hospital
☀ .... Lookout
Å .... Camping Area
⋒ .... Picnic Area
⌂ .... Hut or Chalet
▲ .... Mountain or Hill
⊢■⊣ .... Railway Station
▤ .... Road Bridge
+++++ .... Railway Bridge
⇒ ⇐ .... Road Tunnel
→) (← .... Railway Tunnel
⌇⌇⌇ .... Escarpment or Cliff
⌣ .... Pass
⊓⊔⊓⊔ .... Ancient or Historic Wall

ROUTES

——————— .... Major Road or Highway
– – – – – – – .... Unsealed Major Road
————————— .... Sealed Road
– – – – – – – ..... Unsealed Road or Track
══════ .... City Street
+++++++++++ .... Railway
●─●─●─●─● .... Subway
· · · · · · · · · · · · · · · · · · · .... Walking Track
– – – – – – – .... Ferry Route
++++++++++ .... Cable Car or Chair Lift

HYDROGRAPHIC FEATURES

.... River or Creek
.... Intermittent Stream
.... Lake, Intermittent Lake
.... Coast Line
.... Spring
.... Waterfall
.... Swamp

.... Salt Lake or Reef

.... Glacier

OTHER FEATURES

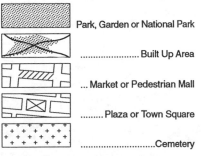

Park, Garden or National Park

.... Built Up Area

... Market or Pedestrian Mall

.... Plaza or Town Square

.... Cemetery

Note: not all symbols displayed above appear in this book

Introduction

On a press trip a decade ago, several big-league travel writers with well over a million and a half km under their belts were informally polled as to their all-time favourite destinations. Without consulting one another, each of the journalists unhesitatingly answered 'Fiji'. The man who took the poll, himself a globetrotting airline executive, was astounded. 'I've never been there. What makes it so great?' he asked. 'The people', was the reply.

After logging many more miles under my belt, I still agree with the writers polled. Chances are a visitor would not find a more tolerant, hospitable and friendly people on the planet than in the Fiji islands. It sounds like office-of-tourism hype but it's true. Fijians, who ironically were the fiercest cannibals in the South Pacific just over 100 years ago, are so gentle and kind that some visitors may even doubt the islanders' sincerity. The realisation of how ingenuous the Fijians are is more than enough to make you feel mean-spirited in comparison.

South Seas hands can talk about the aesthetic beauties of Bora Bora or the ethnological diversity of Papua New Guinea, but the final measure of the 'spirit of place', to quote Laurence Durrell, is the people who inhabit it. In this respect the Fijians are in a class of their own.

When you meet a Fijian an instant human dialogue is established. A Fijian will look straight into your eyes and an almost tele-pathic communication begins. From an early age Fijians are taught that family and friends are the most important things on earth. Children are instructed to pay attention to human beings and to understand their nature. It is not surprising that the islanders have amazing powers of observation and an intuitive sense when it comes to what people require and desire. Consistent with their comprehension of the human experience, Fijians will never forget a person they have met. Even the substance of a casual conversation will be vividly recalled over a long period of time.

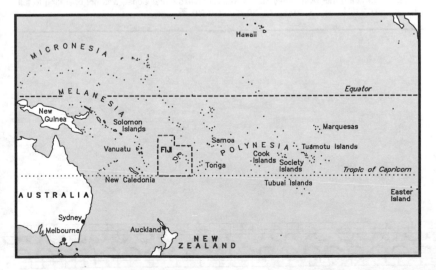

In addition, the 300 islands that make up the Fiji group offer clear blue water, fine beaches, world-class diving and snorkelling, excellent resorts, magnificent landscapes and seascapes, a varied cuisine and cultures rich in tradition.

South Pacific islands have their own slow tempo and Fiji is no exception. Things don't move as quickly as in Sydney or San Francisco and you would be wrong to expect that they should. The sun is hot, the air is humid and no-one – except a few misguided tourists – rushes around for any reason. If the bus is late (or doesn't show up at all), don't worry: there will be others. The Fiji Bitter you ordered may be slow in being served, but it will come and it will be cold. The hotel operator may not move like lightning to place your call, but he or she will place it eventually. In their own way and in their own time, people in Fiji do get things done.

When the aeroplane's rubber hits the runway at Nadi, slow yourself down and keep an open mind. If possible, soak up the sun and bask in the goodwill of these marvellous people. My hunch is that you may learn something from them and take it back with you.

A Warning on Pronunciation

There are some peculiarities in the pronunciation of words in Fijian. The letter *d*, for example, is pronounced *nd*. Similarly *b* is pronounced *mb*. Thus your aircraft lands at *Nadi* airport which is pronounced *Nandi*. And the island of *Lakeba* is pronounced *Lakemba*. This causes particular difficulties because some maps (including the ones in this book) spell things as they are spelt, others as they are pronounced. For more information see the Language section in the Facts about the Country chapter.

STOP PRESS

At the time of going to press, we received reports that Village Stays in Bukuya, a village tour operation in the Nausori Highlands on Viti Levu had gone downhill. If you're thinking of taking this tour, check it out first.

Visiting yachties should note that Lautoka's Neisau Marina complex has closed.

Finally, we heard that Man Friday Resort, on Viti Levu's Coral Coast, was not operating to full capacity, so check to see if it is open before you go there. ■

Facts about the Country

Fiji is known in the Fijian language as *Viti*. The present name came from the Tongans, who prior to the mid-18th century, called the island group *Fisi* (now *Fiji*). According to linguist Albert Schutz, early use of the name 'Fiji' by Captain Bligh and the Reverend John Davies probably reflects this Tongan influence. Some of the early spellings were 'Fejee' and 'Feejee,' which persisted well into the 19th century.

Geographically speaking, the two major features of the Fiji group are Viti Levu, the largest island, with 70% of the population; and, to the north-east, Vanua Levu, the second-largest island. Vanua Levu is also a population centre, although more sparsely settled than Viti Levu. To the south-east of Viti Levu and Vanua Levu, the majority of Fiji's other islands are scattered over 500,000 sq km of ocean. Among these islands are the Lomaiviti group, which includes Ovalau, where Fiji's original capital of Levuka is; Kadavu, south of Viti Levu and a bastion of traditional culture; and the Lau group, whose history and culture were influenced by the close proximity of Tonga.

HISTORY

The original homeland of the Pacific island peoples was South-East Asia. Early people, *Homo erectus*, reached South-East Asia about two million years ago and modern man, *Homo sapien*, arrived approximately 60,000 years ago. Although evidence of human settlement in New Guinea dates back at least 25,000 years, the Austronesian migration from South-East Asia to New Guinea 6000 years ago marked a new stage in cultural evolution. Unlike their neolithic forebears, who were hunters and gatherers, the newcomers (who eventually were to populate Fiji) had adopted sail and outrigger canoes, methods of cultivating root crops, and pig farming.

According to archaeological evidence (mostly pottery), Fiji was settled in three different waves. The earliest wave dates from about 1600 BC and the migrants settled in within a few hundred years (which, historically speaking, is fairly quickly). This is evidenced by a number of birds becoming extinct and changes in the distribution of bird life, indicating a massive environmental impact caused by a large, sophisticated population.

There is, however, new evidence suggesting that Fiji and the South Pacific may have been settled 8000 to 10,000 years ago. In an article published in the *Journal of Pacific History* (April 1986), Fergus Clunie and the late John Gibbons postulated that the oceans have risen dramatically in the last 4000 to 18,000 years due to the melting of the polar ice caps. If this is true, massive land areas that were once above the sea's surface now may be 130 to 150 metres beneath the sea. Thus, many of the sites that were settled by the first migrants to the South Pacific are inaccessible to archaeologists. Clunie and Gibbons buttress their argument with biological, archaeological and linguistic evidence.

Though scientists may disagree about exactly when the forebears of Fijians first came to roost, they submit that these people came from the New Britain area (now belonging to Papua New Guinea) and were most likely ancestors of present-day Polynesians. They practised agriculture, raised pigs and poultry, and fished.

Changes in pottery style indicate a probable second wave of migrants to the area between 400 and 100 BC. Scientists use the word 'probable' because they are not sure if the new pottery style was caused by an influx of new people or if it was simply a local development. If the changes were caused by migrants, the newcomers probably mixed with the indigenous people and perhaps dominated them.

The final settlement of Fiji (1000 to 1800 AD) was a massive movement from Melanesia. This wave of people practised a

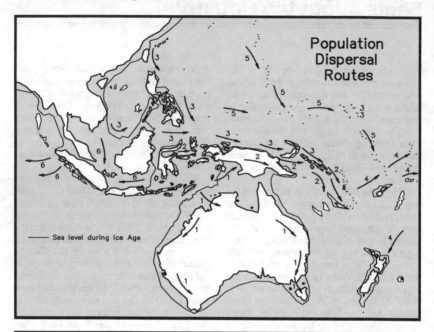

Population Dispersal Routes

— Sea level during Ice Age

1 Ancestors of Australian Aborigines (50,000 to 60,000 years ago)
2 Papuan speakers (5000 to 15,000 years ago)
3 Austronesian speakers (4000 to 7000 years ago)
4 Austronesian/Papuan mixture (4000 years ago – New Zealand settled 1000 years ago)
5 Dispersal from Japan and Philippines mixing with Polynesians (about 3000 years ago)
6 Other Austronesians migrate south-westerly, some as far as Madagascar

sophisticated form of terraced agriculture, which helped support a large population that may have risen to 200,000. People grew yams and taro, raised poultry, fished and evolved a highly developed culture.

Pre-European Contact Society

As evidenced by their advanced form of agriculture, the pre-contact Fiji islands were a highly evolved, stratified society, interlocked and interdependent through trade. Different clans were responsible for various crafts or activities such as pottery-making, mat-weaving, canoe-building and salt pro-

duction. These items were traded throughout the Fiji group of islands and even as far away as Tonga.

Women worked hard and aged early. Men did intermittent hard jobs such as breaking in land for crops. They also performed occasional social duties like warfare, house building and ceremonial *lovo* cooking in large underground ovens. In other words, the more spectacular activities were usually in the man's domain, whereas the drudgery of weeding, washing and collecting firewood was (and still is) done by women.

Fijian society was dominated by a complicated class system. Chiefs often had tremendous personal power, which was expressed in demands for tribute from conquered tribes and in many bloody human sacrifices. To outsiders, the chiefs seemed to have arbitrary and ruthless power based on 'club law'. Said one early observer:

No eastern tyrants can rule with more absolute terror than the chiefs do here; and few people are more thoroughly enslaved and trampled than are these islanders.

Each 'tribe' was broken up into several clans, each with its own function in society. There were chiefly clans, priestly clans, artisans, fishing clans and diplomatic clans whose purpose was to act as spokespeople for the chief.

Leadership in the tribal units was strictly hereditary and succession often a subject of debate. Rank was inherited through both parents, and in a polygamous society this could be very confusing. A chief might have five different sons from five different wives, each with a different political status. To complicate matters even more, rank could be inherited from one's mother's brothers, and succession was usually through brothers before it passed on to sons. There might be a number of individuals qualified as chiefly candidates, but those who became chiefs had to stand out from the group.

Because of intermarriage, incredibly complex relationships between tribes throughout Fiji were created. Tribal leaders hoping to gain political power could thus draw support from different clans throughout the islands through their blood ties, and in the process just as easily make enemies. No one chief was dominant in Fiji. The political scene was in a constant flux of changing allegiances brought about by disputes over land, property or women, by quarrels, or by the rulers' petty jealousies.

Cannibalism Cannibalism was an extremely important institution in pre-Christian Fiji, practised as early as several hundred years before the birth of Christ. According to Fergus Clunie,

former director of the Fiji Museum, it was a 'perfectly normal part of life'. The practice was a function of the religion: the great warrior-gods were cannibals and they required human sacrifice. Although some clans did not in fact eat human flesh for religious reasons (their totems were human), the practice of cannibalism was widespread throughout the Fiji group.

Victims were not just randomly selected, but were almost always enemies taken during battles. Eating your enemy was the ultimate disgrace the victor could impose, and in the Fijian system of ancestor worship this became a lasting insult to the victims' families. This explains much of the sometimes extremely vicious infighting, internecine warfare and vengeance-seeking that went on in pre-Christian times. By all accounts, violence was a way of life and an accepted form of behaviour when directed towards one's foes. Chiefs generally had a grudge against someone or were involved in a power struggle, and war could be an everyday occurrence. It was during these periods of warfare that cannibalism was practised.

Fijians were not without a gruesome sense of humour. They often got a chuckle out of cutting off a piece of some unfortunate soul's flesh (tongue or fingers for example) cooking it, commenting on how good it tasted and then offering it to the victim to eat. There are also horrifying accounts of missionaries who, in times of war, were given samples of cooked meat and were later told what they had eaten.

Eating human flesh was only one of many bloody practices in a society where extreme violence and extreme kindness existed side by side. Some examples of the darker aspects included hanging captured 'enemy' children by the feet or hands from the sail yards of war canoes; burying men alive at the post holes of new homes or temples being constructed; and strangling women at the graves of chiefs so that they could 'accompany' the chiefs into the next world.

European Exploration
European knowledge of Fiji and the other

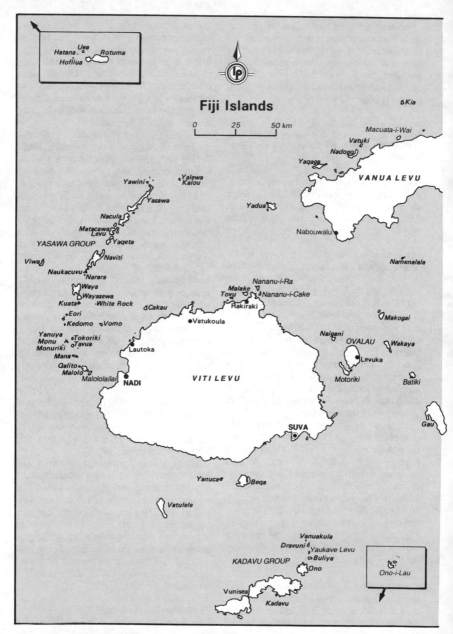

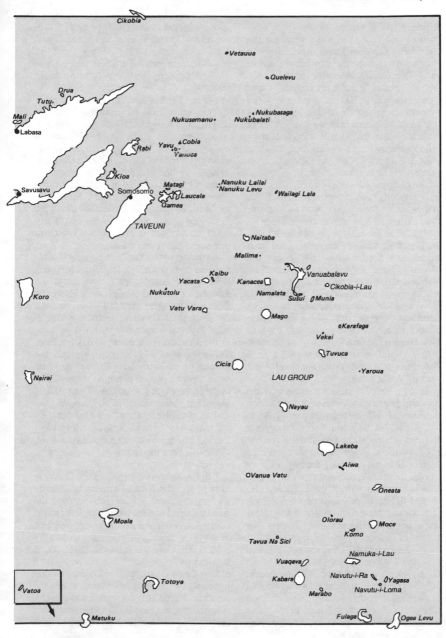

principal island groups of the south-west Pacific was a result of the search for the legendary 'Southern Land', *terra australis incognita*, which the geographers of the 16th and 17th centuries felt must exist to balance the land masses of the northern hemisphere. During the nearly 100 years when voyages were made in search of this hypothetical continent, Spaniards from the coast of South America passed to the north of Fiji and established settlements in islands farther to the west, and Dutch sailors skirted the Tongan group, little more than 300 km to the east.

The discovery of the Fiji archipelago was no organised affair, but was carried out over 200 years by navigators such as Tasman, Cook, Bligh, Wilson and Bellingshausen.

Abel Tasman, skippering two vessels for the Dutch East India Company, sailed from Mauritius in September of 1642 seeking the 'Southern Land'. He came instead upon Tasmania and later discovered New Zealand, where he skirmished with the Maoris. Unwilling to risk further troubles, he headed north and came to Tonga where he was hospitably received. He set a course towards New Guinea and on 6 February 1643 sighted a low island now known to have been Nukubasaga, a sand cay upon a circular reef west of Vanua Levu.

Tasman luckily found a passage over the reef and later sighted points of land which were probably the peaks of Taveuni, lying to the north. Naming his discovery 'Prince William's Islands', he turned north (probably in no mood to seek unknown continents in reef-infested waters), feeling his way among the reefs and islands until he passed Cikobia and so gained the open sea. He skirted the northern coasts of the Solomon Islands and New Guinea and brought his ships home to Batavia (now Jakarta, the capital of Indonesia) on 14 June 1643.

The next navigator known to have touched Fiji was Captain James Cook, who in the course of his second voyage in the Pacific sailed from Tonga and sighted a low, wooded island (Vatoa) in the southern Lau group, and a neighbouring reef on 2 June 1774. A few people were seen on the shore, but they scurried inland at the boat's approach. Cook landed and left a few nails, some medals and a knife on some rocks. Having fixed the position, he named it Turtle Island.

Bligh's discoveries in Fiji came as a direct result of the famed mutiny on the *Bounty*. On 28 April 1789, when the *Bounty* was in Tongan waters, the crew mutinied, putting Bligh and 18 loyal officers and men in a small open vessel with very few provisions and no weapons. Bligh made for the smouldering volcanic island of Tofua, which was in sight, but the island had neither food nor water. Greeted only by a party of hostile Tongans and realising he could not turn back to Tahiti, Bligh had no option but to sail for the Dutch colony on Timor. Although nearly 6000 km away, it was the nearest European settlement of which he knew.

As master of the *Resolution* during Cook's third voyage in the Pacific, Bligh had seen Fijians and heard a great deal from the Tongans of their fierce reputation. However, there was no alternative but to sail through the uncharted Cannibal Islands, which is what Fiji was known as in those days. Late in the afternoon of the second day out from Tofua (4 May 1789), Bligh sighted the islands of southern Lau. During the next three days he passed through the very heart of the archipelago sighting numerous islands including Nairai, Gau, Batiki, Koro, Wakaya and Ovalau. He eventually sailed between the two major islands, Vanua Levu and Viti Levu. Near the Yasawa group of islands on 7 May he met the first signs of unfriendly natives.

Bligh sighted two large canoes definitely in pursuit of his vessel. Fortunately he made his way to a passage in a nearby reef, but the wind dropped and the men had to take to the oars. Meanwhile, the canoes gained on them. The Fijian canoes were speedy, seaworthy craft which clearly outclassed Bligh's skiff. But luckily for the Englishman a dark squall closed down on them all, with thunder and lightning blotting out everything. When the weather cleared only one canoe was in sight. A fresh wind enabled Bligh and his crew just to hold their distance, and at sunset the canoe returned to land while Bligh's boat headed into the darkness of the open sea. On 14 June, after 41 days at sea, he was in sight of the Dutch settlement at Kupang on Timor.

Despite the distractions of foul weather, cannibals and uncharted reefs, Bligh found the time to record in great detail his numerous discoveries. To his credit, his chart of the 'Bligh Islands' is remarkably accurate.

The most notable advance in the exploration and charting of the Fiji islands was made in 1840, in the brief period of three months, by a US expedition led by Commandant Charles Wilkes. The headstrong American – whose actions in later years nearly precipitated a war between Britain and the USA – had an excellent staff of navigators, surveyors, geologists, zoologists, botanists, artists and philologists.

Wilkes' visit was not entirely serene. Though Fijians were known to be treacherous in war, Wilkes was no slouch in this department either. In June of 1840 Wilkes learned that the brother of the King of Rewa had been responsible for the 1834 massacre of the crew of the US merchant ship *Charles Dogett*. He lured the royal family aboard one of his ships and held them as hostages until the king's brother surrendered. Instead of executing the man, he was taken as a prisoner to the USA to be given proper instruction that 'to kill a white person was the very worst thing a Feegee could do'. Unfortunately the man never got a chance to return and educate his fellow Fijians on this fine point. He died shortly after arriving in New York in 1842.

In another instance, Wilkes' party went on to torch a Fijian village after a skiff was stolen by some locals. Worse was yet to come.

On Malolo in the Mamanuca group, where tourists now work on their tans, nine sailors including Wilkes' nephew, went ashore and seized a young man as a hostage. The furious islanders attacked them and several of the Americans were killed and eaten for dinner. Among the dead was Wilkes' nephew, the only son of his widowed sister. Wilkes vowed 'to inflict the punishment it merited...not by burning towns alone, but in the blood of the plotters and actors of the massacre'. In the resulting violence two villages were burned and more than 50 Fijians were killed. The next morning a line of more than 40 men and women approached Wilkes on their hands and knees, 'groaning and sighing in the most piteous and supplicating manner'. After they had sworn that the killers of the sailors were dead and had begged for clemency, Wilkes levied a fine of 3000 coconuts, plus a few pigs and yams to reprovision the ships.

The US Secretary of the Navy later congratulated the commander for his 'severe chastisement', and went on to express the hope that this action would 'deter them from similar outrages in the future'. Wilkes was also cleared by a court martial of charges by some of his officers that he had mistreated the Fijians. An excellent account of these adventures and a thorough history of the diplomatic activities of US naval officers from 1798 to 1883 can be found in David F Long's book *Gold Braid & Foreign Relations* (see Books & Maps in the Facts for the Visitor chapter).

Despite the violence, the chart produced by the expedition was a remarkable achievement and long remained the standard chart of the archipelago. Unfortunately, the originals of the artists' highly detailed renditions of Fijian life during this era were lost in a fire in the USA.

European Influence

When the first Europeans arrived, Fiji was divided into about seven different *vanua* or political confederations and the trend towards political centralisation was already under way. For a variety of reasons – primarily the introduction of arms and Christianity – this political consolidation would be greatly speeded up through the influence of the White people.

The early explorers knew Fiji to be a dangerous place, an unknown area inhabited by unpredictable cannibals and strewn with dangerous reefs – in short, a place one avoided. However, people have been known to take great risks for the possibility of economic gain, and this accounted for Fiji's first sustained contact with Europeans during the sandalwood rush of 1804 to 1810. The precious wood, prized by the Chinese, was discovered by the survivor of the shipwrecked US schooner *Argo*, Oliver Slater, who found groves of sandalwood in Bua on the southern coast of Vanua Levu. Ships soon poured into the area, bringing a variety of men including beachcombers – the first Europeans to live with the Fijians. They bartered nails and trinkets at first, but when the Fijians discovered how valuable the wood was to the Europeans they soon demanded axes, knives and whales' teeth in exchange for it.

Eventually the chiefs wanted more than goods to procure a cargo. They asked for men armed with muskets to aid them in battle, sometimes demanding this even before the crews were allowed ashore. The next several years saw the arrival of men who specialised in helping the Fijian chiefs in tribal warfare. Such were the exploits of Charlie Savage, a Swedish beachcomber/mercenary whose name became synonymous with modern warfare in Fiji and the rise of the Bauan Empire.

Savage was aboard the US brig *Eliza* when it went down in Fiji in 1808, and managed to salvage Spanish silver dollars and muskets from the wreck. The reputation of European arms grew in Fiji and Savage made his way to the tiny island of Bau, an up-and-coming political power. Savage managed to survive for five years on Bau, and acquired a number of wives for his help in subduing his host's enemies. The Swede was eventually ambushed and killed in battle and his skull preserved as a yaqona bowl.

The second stage of European influence, which lasted from the 1820s to the 1850s, came about from the bêche-de-mer (sea cucumber) trade. This had greater impact on Fiji as it was more widespread and longer lasting than the sandalwood trade and involved far more Fijians as labourers. Bêche-de-mer traders also introduced even larger quantities of guns which reinforced

the Bauans' cause, already on the ascendant without the help of foreign arms.

The Rise of Bau

In the late 18th century there were seven main confederations: Rewa, Verata and Bau in south-eastern Viti Levu; Lakeba in the Lau group (an area often controlled by Tongans); and Cakaudrove, Macuata and Bua on Vanua Levu. Of these, Bau, a tiny island off the eastern coast of Viti Levu, was a recent confederation. Until the 1760s the island, which had been home to a few fisherpeople, traders and skilled canoe builders, was a vassal to nearby Verata. The original inhabitants were later driven out by the Verata confederation and Bau was occupied by the invaders.

Through a policy of intermarriage with leading families of Rewa and Cakaudrove and utilisation of the maritime skills of the exiled fisherpeople (some of whom were allowed to live on the island), the power of Bau grew. These factors, combined with the firepower of Charlie Savage, helped Bau defeat Verata in 1808. By 1829 Bau, which was allied closely with Rewa in the southwest, controlled northern and eastern Viti Levu and had crushed the supremacy of nearby Verata.

However, a factor that differentiated Bau from other confederations was the extent to which chiefly authority was personalised (as opposed to institutionalised). This was demonstrated by Chief Tanoa, who refused to allow his warlords to capture European vessels, and especially by his son and successor Cakobau, who ruled with an iron-fisted power.

Chief Cakobau's Reign

Cakobau, a brilliant and bloody Machiavellian strategist, was certainly the most influential chief in recorded Fijian history and a central figure for nearly half a century. It was during his reign that much of Fiji became politically consolidated and was eventually ceded to Britain. His rise to influence as Chief of Bau must be understood within the context of the never-ending power struggle of Fijian chiefs and the emergence of European influence upon Fiji.

In 1849 Cakobau was described by Captain Erskine of HMS *Havannah*, who said:

It was impossible not to admire the appearance of the chief: of large, almost gigantic size, his limbs were beautifully formed and proportioned; his countenance with far less of the negro cast than among the lower orders, agreeable and intelligent; while his immense head of hair, covered and concealed with gauze, smoke-dried and slightly tinged with brown, gave him altogether the appearance of an Eastern sultan. No garments confined his magnificent chest and neck, or concealed the natural colour of the skin, a clear but decided black; and in spite of his paucity of attire – the evident wealth which surrounded him showing that it was a matter of choice and not necessity – he 'looked every inch a king'.

According to historians, warfare and women were Cakobau's prime interests. His ambition was no less than total supremacy over Fiji. Described by European observers as 'arrogant, cruel, cunning, devious, and bold,' he 'seemed to think of nothing else but war, and...to desire nothing else but power'. As with all chiefs, who were considered semi-divine, the lives of underlings meant nothing to Cakobau. As K R Howe in his excellent historical account of the Pacific wrote:

Tales of his human sacrifices and punishments are legion...at times Cakobau's anger was spontaneous, as when a chief was slow to pay tribute and was immediately clubbed to death.

On another occasion, Cakobau had the tongue of a Bauan rebel cut out which he:

...devoured raw, talking and joking at the same time with the mutilated chief, who begged in vain for the boon of a speedy death.

Cakobau certainly had his moments, but in general his behaviour was not out of character for any self-respecting chief of that day.

Cakobau's craving for power led Bau into a constant state of war throughout the 1840s and quarrels with his allies in Cakaudrove and Rewa. In 1844 a ferocious war broke out between Bau and Rewa which continued for

Cakobau

another 12 years. At the height of his power, and having gone so far as to proclaim himself 'Tui Viti' (King of Fiji), Cakobau was increasingly resented by other Fijian tribes and the growing European settlement of Levuka on the nearby island of Ovalau.

Established in the 1830s by a handful of American and European beachcombers who took Fijian wives, Levuka became one of the most important ports of call in the South Pacific for whalers and trading vessels in the latter part of the 19th century. The men who lived there acted as pilots, interpreters and traders' agents. During the 1840s their once friendly relationship with Cakobau deteriorated and the town was razed in 1841 – under Cakobau's orders, it was believed, but there was no proof.

When Cakobau was not busy at war he monopolised the bêche-de-mer trade, often committing himself to providing more of it than he could produce without resorting to arms. This was merely one of many obligations he had to assume as self-proclaimed King of Fiji.

One incident in particular with an American trader in 1849 was to plague Cakobau for years. John Brown Williams came to Fiji in 1846 as the US commercial agent. In 1849, a cannon set off during a 4 July celebration exploded and set fire to Williams' home and store. In true island style the locals helped save as much merchandise as possible but naturally 'liberated' what they had saved, keeping it for themselves. Williams called this looting and held Cakobau responsible as King of Fiji. In 1851 a US man-of-war was sent to support Williams in his claim for compensation to the tune of US$5000. Other incidents involving US property ran the figure up to US$43,000 by 1855 and the king was summoned aboard a US warship and forced to sign a promissory note giving him two years to pay.

If the 1840s were the zenith of power for the great warlord, the 1850s were the beginning of his downfall. Fighting broke out with Verata and struggles were renewed against Rewa. The European settlers in Levuka became united against Cakobau when for the second time the town was burned to the ground. Although Cakobau was not at fault (at least this time) he was blamed, and Europeans did all they could to direct shipping away from Bau and thus blockade the island.

It was clear Cakobau's authority was waning. He became ill, and as a final straw, his old allies at Kaba – an area from which he used to stage raids into Rewa – revolted. The force he sent in to quell them was thrashed and for the moment he seemed a defeated man.

The Christian Presence

The earliest Christian presence in Fiji was the London Missionary Society (LMS), which converted a chief from Oneata, near Lakeba, in 1830. The mission had a small following, but failed to convert the powerful Chief of Lakeba. In 1835 the Wesleyans, engaged in a running evangelistic war with the LMS, sent William Cross and David Cargill, along with an envoy of converted Tongans, to Lakeba. Several hundred of the local Tongans (who were under no obligation to the Fijians in matters of religion) took up Christianity. Once again the Fijian Chief of Lakeba, undoubtedly fearing reprisals from Bau if he converted, refused to be swayed.

It was an uphill battle for Cargill and Cross, who realised that the real power in Fiji lay in Bau and visited there in 1838. It was a period when Cakobau and his father Tanoa were seeking vengeance from their former enemies and not a serene time to visit. The mission was aghast at the savagery they witnessed and instead moved to Rewa where they were accepted by the Tui Dreketi, Cakobau's arch rival. Although the missionaries set up a base, they were by no means accepted by the populace.

US captain, Charles Wilkes, explained the situation in this way:

All the chiefs seem to look upon Christianity as a change in which they had much to lose and little to gain. The old chiefs, in particular, would often remark that they were too old to change their present gods for new gods, or to abandon what they considered their duty to their people; yet the chiefs generally desire the residence of missionaries among them. I was, therefore, anxious to know why they entertain such a wish, when they had no desire for their instruction. They acknowledged that it was to get presents, and because it would bring vessels to their place, which would give them opportunities of obtaining many desirable articles.

Meanwhile the war between Bau and Rewa raged and missionary activity in the area ceased. Missionary progress in other areas looked dim except for the Tongans in Lau. It was clear that the chiefs exerted a powerful influence in religious matters, and unless they were converted, the rank and file would never convert (lotu in Fijian).

Ma'afu & Tongan Imperialism

Tongans had always traded with Fiji and had lived in the Lau Islands of eastern Fiji for hundreds of years. Although they did mix with the local population, they were looked upon by Fijians as arrogant, conceited carpetbaggers. However, because of the Lau group's proximity to Tonga, the Fijians were subject to Tongan influence.

In 1847, Ma'afu, a cousin of the Tongan king and a Tongan in search of 'overseas adventure', came to Fiji in the name of protecting Christian Tongan interests. In other words, he exploited, plundered, massacred and stole whatever he pleased in the name of Christianity. His 'good' works came to the attention of the King of Tonga, and in 1853 he became governor of all Tongans in Lau – the de facto leader of the Tongan-Wesleyan cause in Fiji.

Ma'afu's imperialistic ventures into Fiji worried Cakobau, but pleased the Wesleyan missionaries, who saw the Tongan as one of their own. In 1853, under political pressure, Cakobau reluctantly allowed a missionary to live in Bau. A year later he was advised in no uncertain terms by the King of Tonga to convert and enjoy the support of Tonga or stand alone and face the dire consequences. He consulted with a missionary and his advisers and several days later converted.

Cakobau lost a great deal of influence, but soon re-established his power – at a price. Although he was still a force to reckon with in western Fiji, the Tongans clearly were the dominant influence in the east.

Despite the newfound legitimacy of Christianity, Howe explains that Fiji did:

...not become a missionary kingdom in the manner of Tahiti, Hawaii and Tonga...Christianity as an institution was not politically centralised because there was no political unification of the island group.

In spite of the influence enjoyed by Ma'afu and Cakobau, they still did not have total control over their dominions, which were presided over by local chiefs. This was an extremely important aspect in the development of the country, especially regarding the preservation of culture and tradition. Among other things, it would mean less interference by outside forces – namely missionaries – in dictating what was good or bad for Fijians and may be a primary reason for so much of

modern Fiji's culture still being intact. (See under Culture in the Facts for the Visitor chapter.)

The Baker Incident

One of the most celebrated incidents in the 'Christianisation of Fiji' was the murder of Reverend Baker, the only missionary ever to be killed by Fijians. In 1867 Baker, who had spent eight years in Fiji, set out to cross Viti Levu from the Rewa area via the upper reaches of the Sigatoka Valley, an isolated region where no missionary had ever ventured. The independent-minded residents of the area – the unruly *kai colo* (hill people) – wanted nothing to do with Cakobau, Christianity or the coastal tribes who were likely to practise this strange religion. Baker's Fijian disciples who doubled as guides were well aware of this and imparted the news to Baker.

The expedition stopped at the recently converted village of Dawarau en route to Navosa, where the hill people lived. The missionary was well treated at Dawarau but the chief refused to lead Baker personally to the Navosa area, saying it was too dangerous. Instead he selected two guides to accompany Baker. At Naqaqadelavatu, the next village, the evangelists were treated coldly. The following day the chief warned the expedition that someone was coming to kill them. Upon leaving the village the group was ambushed and Baker was murdered with a blow to the head from a steel axe. As was customary, the bodies of the slain men were cooked and since Baker was a person of rank, pieces of his body were distributed to villages throughout the district. Folklore has it that the hill people attempted to eat the missionary's shoes.

But why was Baker killed at all? The most credible answer is that the hill people, who despised Cakobau, felt threatened by Christianity, which they considered 'Cakobau's religion', and felt that the best way to rid themselves of the threat was to kill the man spreading it.

Cakobau was forced by the British consul to send warriors to avenge the killing, but his men were thrashed by the hill people. In 1903 the people from the area where Baker was killed took part in a special ceremony to atone for his killing. To this day, a sort of collective shame is still felt by the descendants of those who precipitated the crime.

European Settlement

European settlement in Fiji resulted in the almost immediate involvement of foreign powers. French, British and US war ships called regularly, often on behalf of aggrieved nationals. As the European population grew, settlers who lived under the protection and at the whim of local chiefs lobbied their respective governments in an effort to annex Fiji and establish a business-as-usual climate. Both the British and US consuls living there were deeply immersed in Fijian affairs.

As self-proclaimed King of Fiji, Cakobau offered to cede Fiji to Britain in return for the payment of his long-overdue US$43,000 debt to the USA. Four years later the offer was refused.

After the 1860s, European settlement evolved from a handful of scraggly beachcombers and vagabonds to a more orthodox settler society arriving mostly from Australia and New Zealand. Fiji became attractive because of the belief that the British were going to annex it, and economically as a cotton-growing centre for European markets which were deprived of this commodity during the American Civil War. By 1870 the European population numbered more than 2000.

Settlers purchased land, sometimes fraudulently, by selling firearms which were used in tribal conflicts. Claims and counter-claims often followed with no form of arbitration. There were also problems with labour. Men were needed to work the plantations, and the Fijians were reluctant to do so. Virtual slave labourers from the Solomons or New Hebrides were imported or 'blackbirded' to Fiji. With no set rules to govern these activities, anarchy sometimes reigned. The consensus among Fijians and Europeans was that a government was needed to sort things out.

Fiji's Foray into Government

The first attempt at a national government was a council of chiefs which met in 1865, but collapsed two years later because no-one could agree on anything. This was followed by the creation of regional governments in Bau, naturally headed by Cakobau; in Lau, run by Ma'afu (with close links to Tonga); and in Bua. Although the latter two were moderately successful in establishing some kind of order, events were moving too rapidly for the chiefs' attempts at political reform, particularly with the influx of European settlers.

Levuka was attracting more and more shipping, and the town's population, which had increased significantly by 1870, was in dire need of public amenities and law and order. The *Fiji Times* noted in 1870, 'It is not the natives that we want the government for, but ourselves'.

In the countryside the situation was also deteriorating. Disputes over land led to racial violence and as usual the tribes were at each others' throats. As if things weren't bad enough, the end of the Civil War in the USA created a depression in the cotton market, and in late 1870 terrible hurricanes destroyed the crops. More than ever, a governmental solution had to be found.

In 1871 the Cakobau government was established at Levuka. Hopes were high on all sides that it would work. However, as K R Howe noted, 'the ministers could not satisfy the irreconcilable demands of merchants, planters and Fijians. The government became universally unpopular'. Again the situation deteriorated. Talk of race war was heard, and in order to prevent anarchy and bloodshed Cakobau was forced to cede Fiji to Britain. The British, realising the responsibility they had towards the settlers and the Fijians, and not wishing the country to fall into another government's hands, accepted. On 10 October 1874 the deed of cession was signed in Nasova, near Levuka. Fiji had become a crown colony.

Indian Arrival

Fiji was now a colony, but a colony deemed in need of economic growth. Large-scale plantations seemed the obvious answer to the new rulers, but labour was scarce. Sir Arthur Gordon, the colony's first governor, and fortunately for Fiji a decent man, was dead set against using natives to work the fields. Not only did he take steps immediately to protect Fijians from being exploited as a labour force, he also made it illegal to sell land owned by indigenous Fijians. In addition, he set up a taxation system requiring Fijians to work their own land rather than that of a planter.

Thus Gordon set in motion laws that would forever benefit the Fijian people by making sure they would never be alienated from their land nor exploited as workers. Gordon, a true 19th-century romantic, took the role of protector seriously and developed an administration very paternalistic towards the Fijians.

However, the colony was still in a dilemma. The infant sugar industry did have potential, but no-one to work the fields. The planters were screaming for labour. Gordon had a plan. Having previously worked in Mauritius and Trinidad, he had seen indentured Indian labour. He convinced the planters to bring over Indians as the answer to their needs.

On 14 May 1879 the era of the Indian in Fiji began. On this day the *Leonidas* arrived from Calcutta with 463 immigrants aboard. Between May 1879 and November 1916, when the final labour transport ship arrived, 60,000 people had come to serve as 'coolies'. Of these, some 85% were Hindus, 14% Muslims, and the rest were mainly Christians and Sikhs. Most of the migrants were men 20 to 40 years of age from the poor, uneducated, agricultural castes. Life in India was never easy, and economic conditions had pushed them to accept the inducement offered by the British Empire.

In theory, workers understood that the *girmit* (agreement) was to work for five years with the option to return to India in another five years or to remain in Fiji. In reality many of the Indians recruited were often tricked by unsavoury characters or even unwillingly 'shanghaied' aboard the ships.

In Fiji, life was usually abysmal for the workers. They were housed in 'coolie lines' – barracks of 16 rooms in two rows of eight, each room measuring three metres by two metres. The rooms housed three single men, or a married couple with no more than two children. Residents of this type of accommodation called them *kasbighar* (brothels). According to Fiji-Indian scholar and leader Ahmed Ali, in these conditions 'privacy was nonexistent, marriages fragile, morality a luxury, overtasking widespread, violence, including murder and suicide, not infrequent...'

In *Fiji Times – A History of Fiji* Kim Gravelle quotes an immigrant who described the conditions of servitude:

To a man with a wife and family, who had belonged to a middle or high caste in India, his new life was a miserable one, at best that of a well-treated animal – fed, looked after if sick, driven to work, and given a stable to live in...Conditions in the factories and on the plantations in India were as bad, if not worse ...but it was not without reason that the Indians called their life on the plantations in Fiji *narak*. Hell.

After girmit ended, workers became *khula* – free but not unfettered. There were still five years to wait before getting a ticket home, and signing on for another five-year agreement was not appealing. However, there was also the small matter of survival. For people willing to work, plenty of work was available.

Most importantly, traditional differences between Muslim and Hindu, upper and lower castes were forgotten. Because the caste system had broken down, those who would have been on the bottom rungs of society in India had opportunities in Fiji they never would have had in their own country.

Free Indian settlers applied their farming skills, and 30 years after the first indentures were completed, 6500 hectares were leased to former coolies. Likewise, Indian cattle herders were raising 10,000 head of livestock and Indian entrepreneurs were opening shops around the country. Indian labour was particularly important in the sugar industry, which had become the lifeblood of the colony.

Still, as people brought over to work as beasts of burden in a strange land, the Indians were looked upon with disdain both by the Fijians and the Europeans. Fiji's Indians were not handed their human and civil rights on a silver platter: they had to fight hard for them.

The first political stirrings surfaced in 1910, when 200 Suva and Rewa Indians asked for representation in government. A year later, the British Indian Association was formed. Their first task was to ask none other than Mahatma Gandhi – who at this time was active in the struggle for Indian rights in South Africa – to send a lawyer to Fiji.

The man who responded was D M Manilal, a Gujarati lawyer from Mauritius who had built a reputation fighting against the indenture system in India. Manilal, or Manilal Doctor, as he was called, arrived in 1912 and immediately commanded a wide following. Four years later, when a pro-indenture Indian was named sole Indian representative to the legislative council, Manilal's supporters urged that their own man be considered for the job. The colonial government was not fond of the idea.

Manilal responded by railing bitterly against the government's indenture system. His publicity campaign along with anti-indenture activities in India whipped up support in that country and even persuaded the viceroy of India to announce that the indenture system would cease 'as soon as possible'. However, this was not to be the case. The colonial government in India later announced that the indenture system would continue for another five years.

Fiji's planters were happy but Indians there and in India were outraged. Protests were staged at the viceroy's office and Gandhi and his supporters worked vigorously against the indenture system. In the end, as Kim Gravelle described in *Fiji Times – A History of Fiji*, 'The economy of a tiny few sugar producing islands wasn't worth the price of Britain's self respect in India'. On 12 March 1917, all labour recruiting was stopped 'for the duration of the war (WW I) and two years after'. It would never restart. Indenture officially ended on 1 January 1920.

Although the anti-indenture forces had won a victory, there was still the matter of civil rights for Indians in Fiji. Manilal and company presented the colonial government with a list of requests which included the repeal of various taxes and discriminatory laws, and the establishment of a minimum wage. The appeal was ignored.

The potentially violent situation was aggravated by wartime inflation and a general dissatisfaction with the state of affairs. Strikes by Indians followed, and in a confrontation with police three Indians were hit by gunfire, resulting in one death. Manilal was deported and strike leaders were exiled to remote parts of the country. The strike did not appear to accomplish much at the time, but in actuality it did effect some gains for the Indians, including repeal of certain taxes and the setting up of government advisers who were to work on improving the Indians' lot. In essence, this marked the beginning of the end of Indian serfdom and absolute colonial rule.

WW I

When WW I broke out, 700 of Fiji's European residents left for the trenches. The government had instructed the colonial office not to send native Fijians, but somehow a handful made their way to the action. Among them was Ratu Sukuna, a young high chief who would later distinguish himself in government service. Sukuna, who was studying at Oxford, tried to enlist in the British army but was refused. He responded by joining the French foreign legion and winning the *Medaille Militaire*, the highest honour awarded to a soldier. Wounded three times while assaulting enemy trenches in the face of machine-gun fire, Sukuna was one of 35 men to survive out of a force of 2500.

Back in the islands a German sea raider, Count Felix Von Luckner, was on the loose. The wily count's ship, the *Seeadler* (Sea

Eagle), was disguised as a Norwegian freighter and preyed upon Allied ships by feigning friendliness until the last moment, when it unfurled the iron cross and displayed its cannon.

Stopping at remote Mopelia Atoll near Tahiti for a respite, Von Luckner's vessel was severely damaged by a freak tidal wave and the sailors were marooned. Von Luckner salvaged the lifeboat – which was christened *Cecile* – loaded it with provisions and set sail with five of the healthiest crew members in search of a ship to steal. They sailed over 1000 km to the Cook Islands, but failed to find a ship.

From there the crew of the *Cecile* made it to Katafaga in the northern Lau group. Here they found adequate food supplies in a home where the owner was absent, but still no ship. (A framed letter politely thanking the owner of the home now hangs for all to read at the Ovalau Club in Levuka.) The crew then sailed to Wakaya near Ovalau and finally found what they were looking for – a handsome three-masted schooner with all the qualifications to be the *Seeadler II*. The captain of the vessel even agreed to take them on.

Before Von Luckner got a chance to steal the ship, however, a Fijian government cattle boat called the *Amra* lowered a skiff that approached the sea raiders. Von Luckner recorded that the vessel contained 'an officer and four Indian soldiers who wore puttees and those funny little pants'. Only the officer was armed. According to Von Luckner, 'We could have easily shot them down, or thrown a hand grenade in their boat. Then we could have captured the ship and sailed away'. However, being out of uniform and a good German aristocrat who played by the old-fashioned rules, he surrendered peaceably.

The prisoners were first taken to nearby Levuka and then to Suva, where Von Luckner described their arrival as 'the event of the year. The only warlike happening that had come along to break the monotony of life on the dreary South Seas'. The count was sent to New Zealand where he commandeered a boat, stole a New Zealand army

officer's uniform and was recaptured. In the midst of his plans for another escape, armistice was signed. Meanwhile, back on Mopelia, the rest of the *Seeadler*'s crew had lured a French vessel to the island, captured her and sailed safely to Chile.

Back in Fiji, anti-German hysteria was whipped up. Longtime residents of German origin were interned and sent to camps in Australia. A few months later, the war was over.

WW II

Unlike WW I, WW II saw Fijians recruited in earnest. In the early years, men were trained and fortifications were constructed (such as the well-preserved gun emplacements at Momi near Sigatoka). With the attack on Pearl Harbor, it seemed only a matter of time until the Japanese war machine would roll onto Fiji's shores.

By the middle of 1942 the Americans had established bases on Fiji and the Japanese no longer seemed a direct threat. Americans were actually being trained under Fiji commandos whom they regarded as experts in jungle warfare. In December 1942 Fijians had the opportunity to prove their worth in the Solomon Islands. Thirty commandos were sent to Guadalcanal and on to Tenaru where Americans were holding the beachhead. The Fijians, who were later referred to as 'death in velvet gloves' by a US journalist, had the unenviable responsibility of mopping up the dug-in Japanese who had survived the US shelling. This was the first of many actions which distinguished the Fijians as among the finest fighters in the South Pacific.

With the Fijians' proven early successes the US command cabled for more soldiers, and in April 1943, 36 officers and 799 men joined the ranks of those already in the Solomons. The Fijians continued their trail of valour in Bougainville and through to the end of the war. The cost in lives had been 57.

Ratu Sukuna

In ancient times the exploits of certain chiefs became legendary and were eventually woven into a kind of mythology. Years later, the individual was deified. Had Ratu Sir Lala Sukuna lived in ancient times he surely would be a god by now.

Perhaps the greatest modern-day statesperson Fiji has ever produced, Ratu Sukuna was born on Bau on 22 April 1888, of chiefly lineage from Bau and Lau. As a child he received the education due the son of a high chief as well as tutelage in English and Latin from the age of six. He later attended Wilkenson School in Auckland and graduated from Wanganui College. He returned to Fiji and worked briefly as a government clerk, after which he sailed to England to study law and political science at Oxford. In his second year of studies, during the beginning of WW I, Ratu Sukuna dropped his schooling and attempted to join the British army. He was refused. Undaunted, he crossed the channel, joined the French foreign legion, distinguished himself in the field of battle and was awarded the highest honour the French military could bestow.

After the war Ratu Sukuna returned to Oxford, received a BA degree from Wadham College, and went on to qualify as a barrister. He went back to Fiji and started up the bureaucratic ladder, serving as district commissioner, commissioner for native reserves, adviser on native affairs, secretary for Fijian affairs and chairman of the Native Land Trust Board – the position he distinguished himself most in.

Though Ratu Sukuna's day-to-day responsibility in this capacity was sorting out land disputes for the colonial administration, he was a man of vision who did much to lay the groundwork for the modern-day government of Fiji. As an editorial in the *Fiji Times* put it, he was 'the best of interpreters of his people to those in authority, and of the affairs of government and of the outside world to the Fijian villager'.

Ratu Sukuna was instrumental in sending Fijian soldiers overseas during WW II because he believed Fijians would never be taken seriously until they had spilled blood. It would not be an exaggeration to call him the father of modern-day Fiji.

On 30 May 1958, news of a tragedy reached the country. The chief, who had catapulted his people into the 20th century and sparked the vision of an independent nation, died – 12 years before Fiji would attain the independence of which he had dreamed. He had retired from public service only a month earlier and was sailing to England for a holiday that was not to be.

The death of Ratu Sir Lala Sukuna stunned the colony. Fiji mourned and thousands attended memorial services.

Independence

Life had barely returned to normal in the years following WW II when Fijian soldiers were called to arms again. The 'Emergency', as it was called in Malaya, began in 1948. The British-Malayan negotiations for an independent Malaya were opposed by Chinese living in Malaya and by communist guerrillas. Both groups began making raids to topple the new government. Britain then began assembling colonial forces to combat the guerrillas and wanted troops experienced in jungle warfare. The King's African Rifles, Rhodesian African Rifles, the Ghurkas of Nepal and soon the 1st Battalion, Fiji Infantry Regiment, were fighting in Malaya.

The first detachment of Fijian soldiers arrived in January 1952 and saw action within 48 hours of taking up their positions. By 1954, the jungles around the Fijian camp at Batu Pahat were so safe that the first of 80 Fijian families moved in. The camp eventually included a school, and Fijian *mekes* (traditional dances) were performed for nearby villages. The Fijian battalion became one of the most decorated on and off the battlefield, collecting every sporting trophy it competed for.

Four years and four months after its first skirmish, the Fijian battalion was sent home with an enemy loss of 205 to its credit, and its own loss of 25 men. The modern Fijian reputation of ferocity in combat was still firmly intact.

In the late '50s labour unrest at home began to grow. Labour unions, flexing their new-found muscle, called a general strike in

December 1959, which eventually led to rioting by Fijians and Indians against European property. The strike was short-lived, but was followed by a huge sugar workers' strike the following year. A massive march on the capital by sugar workers was turned back at the Rewa Bridge by Fijian military forces reinforced by the New Zealand army.

The colonial government, realising that postponing independence any longer would be to no-one's benefit, set the spring of 1963 for the first popular election of the legislative council. For the first time, common Fijians and Indians would vote, and women of all races would be enfranchised. The legislative council had existed in various forms since cession to Britain in 1874, but its members were chosen by different methods according to race. Thus the European members were selected by an election amongst European men, the Fijians were appointed by the Great Council of Chiefs, and Indian members were chosen by wealthy Indians.

The next moves toward independence occurred between 1964 and 1965 when members of the National Federation Party (NFP) and the newly formed Alliance Party met in London to draft a constitution that would lead to self-government. But the parties clashed bitterly at every session and negotiations ended in a deadlock. The situation would remain that way for four years.

A ministerial system of government was introduced in 1967, with Ratu Mara appointed chief minister, and members of the executive council in the legislative council becoming the council of ministers. Negotiations began again in 1969 between the Alliance Party led by Chief Minister Ratu Mara and the National Federation Party led by A D Patel, the party's founder. The main stumbling blocks were the issues of full self-government and communal roll elections. The Patel-led Indians wanted a republic with no ties to the British Commonwealth or Crown and a one-person, one-vote electoral system. The Alliance Fijians and other races, including a minority of anti-NFP Indians, insisted on maintaining close links to the Crown and rejected any idea of a republic.

The Alliance Party was also insisting on a communal election system.

In October 1969, Patel died and was succeeded by Siddiq Koya, who had a good working relationship with Ratu Mara and was ready to compromise. In January 1970 a tentative date of 10 October 1970 was set for independence. However, there was still no constitutional agreement. A solution would not be reached until 30 April – just five months before the planned date. Incredibly, the target date was met, and 96 years to the day after Fiji's sovereignty was handed to Britain, it became an independent state in the presence of His Royal Highness, Prince Charles, representing Queen Elizabeth.

In one of the first moves after independence, the government agreed to pay F$10 million to the Colonial Sugar Refining Company for its holdings in the country's four sugar mills. This was the first step towards nationalising the sugar industry and forming the government-owned Fiji Sugar Corporation.

April 1972 saw Fiji's first post-independence election in which Ratu Mara's Alliance Party gained a 14-seat majority in the house of representatives. The following January, the paramount chief of the Fijians, Ratu Sir George Cakobau, was sworn in as governor general, succeeding Sir Robert Foster, the last governor under colonial rule.

Fiji celebrated the 100th anniversary of its link with the British Crown and the fourth anniversary of its independence in October 1974, and Prince Charles made his third visit to the country in four years. By the end of 1976 vast amounts of development work had been done and the ground was set for many other large projects such as the Monasavu hydroelectric scheme and the completion of the highway from Nadi to Sigatoka. Electricity, roads and water systems were being taken to rural areas and remote islands; tuna fishing and pine-tree planting had been introduced, tourism was growing and the country was nearing self-sufficiency in poultry, pork and beef. In addition, several new export crops such as cocoa and ginger were being developed.

Thanks to a booming tourist industry and high sugar prices, Fiji's economy grew 5% per year from 1970 to 1980. But the economic downturn in the first half of the 1980s exposed Fiji's failure to diversify its economic base. Thus, when sugar prices collapsed in 1980, the Fijian economy was sent into a nose dive. Only the continued growth of tourism, falling petroleum prices and continued foreign aid softened the blow.

Fiji's international stature, almost single-handedly shaped by Ratu Mara, grew after independence. Perhaps the most visible manifestations of the nation overseas are the Royal Fiji Military Forces. In April 1978 Fiji offered to send a battalion to Lebanon as part of the United Nations Interim Force in Lebanon (UNIFIL). The first soldiers left two months later, and in 1989, 600 troops were still on duty in that war-torn country, with only 20 Fijian soldiers having lost their lives.

Fiji sent a 24-person detachment to Zimbabwe in December 1979 as part of the Zimbabwe-Rhodesia cease-fire monitoring force. And in 1981 sent another 550 soldiers to the Middle East as part of the Camp David agreement between Egypt and Israel, which called for an international peacekeeping force to monitor the border between the two nations in the Sinai.

The 1987 Coups

Since independence, Fiji had been the shining example of democracy, multicultural harmony and development in the Pacific, and indeed a standard for the entire Third World. That was shattered on the morning of 14 May 1987, when Lieutenant Colonel Sitiveni Rabuka marched into parliament with a handful of soldiers and overthrew the government in a bloodless coup.

The event triggering the coup had occurred a month earlier when Ratu Mara's Fijian-dominated Alliance Party, which had ruled since independence, was defeated in the country's fifth election. A coalition composed of the mostly Indian NFP and the newly formed Labour Party won a stunning victory.

The Labour Party had been formed three years earlier by trade union leaders, Fijians disenchanted with the increasingly conservative policies of the Alliance Party, and Indians weary of the constant bickering and infighting of the NFP. Although the Labour Party and NFP did form a coalition heading into the election, it was the Labour Party's Timoci Bavadra who was chosen to head the new government after the election. Although Bavadra was Fijian and the majority of his cabinet was made up of non-Indians, the coalition was labelled 'Indian-dominated'.

In the month that followed the coalition's victory, racial tensions heightened considerably around the country – particularly in the Suva area. The Taukei movement, an ultra-conservative group of Fijians with the support of many Fijian chiefs, staged protests around the nation against the new government inciting fears that Fijians would lose land rights and that Indians, who already had the upper hand economically, would dominate politically as well. Many indigenous Fijians felt that this development might be the beginning of the end – the loss of control of Fijian land and the demise of Fijian culture. Taukei leaders hearkened to the plight of the Maoris and the Hawaiians – cultures that were now disenfranchised from their birthright. Perhaps it was this fear that ignited sporadic acts of violence against Indian shops and businesses during the Taukei protests.

It was into this strained atmosphere that the new government convened its first business session of parliament. In its first hour, it was toppled. At gunpoint, Bavadra and his entire cabinet were kidnapped from the floor of the parliament before the disbelieving members of the house.

Lieutenant Colonel Rabuka, third in command of the army at the time, announced to the chamber that he was taking control of the government. He suspended the constitution, the power of Governor General Ratu Sir Penaia Ganilau and formed his own council of ministers to run the country.

An astonished nation at first refused to believe it, but as word spread, radio reports confirmed the news. The governor general, who coincidentally was also Rabuka's hereditary chief, tried to regain control of the government by declaring himself in charge of the army and ordered the troops back into their barracks.

The next day, Ratu Mara, one of the fathers of democratic Fiji, announced he would serve on the new government's council of ministers. This legitimised the coup in the minds of many Fijians.

The standoff between Rabuka and Ratu Penaia continued for several days with Rabuka gaining the upper hand when he shut down the only independent radio station and closed the newspapers. Meanwhile the world reacted to the coup. Australia, New Zealand, Britain and the USA denounced the coup and suspended aid. The United Nations demanded that the former government be returned to power and Fiji was ejected from the Commonwealth of Nations. Immediately after the coup, most of the international airlines suspended services to Fiji.

The economy was shattered overnight. The tourist industry, which was poised for tremendous growth, collapsed. Sugar cane production, the number two earner of hard currency, suffered a blow when Indian farmers refused to harvest their crop. Unemployment rocketed, the Fijian dollar was devalued in the following months and the government cut back wages.

Rabuka said the purpose of the coup was to return political power to Fijian hands and demanded that changes be made to the constitution guaranteeing Fijian control of the government. The Great Council of Chiefs met and gave their support to the Rabuka regime with a mandate to amend the constitution. Bowing to international pressure, Rabuka eventually handed control of the government to the governor general. But Rabuka remained in command of the army and police.

Ratu Penaia began mediating negotiations between Ratu Mara and Bavadra to form a caretaker government to lead the country back to democracy under an amended constitution agreeable to all parties. However,

the conservative Taukei movement opposed the unification talks and demanded more radical changes to the constitution, ensuring Fijian supremacy. A Taukei protest in Suva turned violent and led to several days of rioting in Suva. Several Indian-owned businesses were looted and burned.

On 25 September 1987, Rabuka staged his second coup, claiming his actions were to quell the violence against the Indian population. At the same time he scrapped the constitution and ordered the writing of a new document guaranteeing Fijian supremacy. Twelve days later Rabuka declared Fiji a republic, naming Ratu Penaia president, and ending the 113-year tie to the British Crown. At the end of 1987 Rabuka appointed Ratu Mara prime minister of an interim government and named himself minister for home affairs in charge of the army and police.

Dr Timoci Bavadra died of natural causes on 3 November 1989.

The New Constitution

Under the new constitution, promulgated in 1990 and implemented in 1992, the posts of president, prime minister, police commissioner and civil service commissioner are

Lieutenant Colonel Rabuka

reserved for Fijians. Of 71 seats in the single-chamber parliament, Fijians are guaranteed 36 seats, of which one is for the commander of the army who is also the defence and security minister. Indians retain 22 seats and general voters – non-Fijians and non-Indians – get eight seats. The prime minister is empowered to appoint four cabinet ministers who would each be given a seat.

Ratu Mara had announced his intention to retire from politics before the elections of 1992. A new generation of leaders is now left with the formidable task of rebuilding a democratic government and instilling confidence in the nation.

That 'new generation' took power with the long-awaited elections of May 1992. Former coup leader (who was elevated to the rank of general), Sitiveni Rabuka, was elected prime minister. Rabuka formed a new government with the immense goal of restoring interracial harmony to Fiji's pluralistic society. His other important task is to re-establish international goodwill as well as trade and assistance where it was revoked upon the cessation of democracy.

Although the Indian popular majority is unhappy about the new constitution (which it finds discriminatory), the government has made assurances that the group will not be summarily banished from Fiji on a whim of nationalist frenzy. The Indians carry on with their lives and businesses in what appears to be a stable political environment.

Like the Indians, other factions of the political spectrum are not necessarily enthralled with the new constitution. The consensus seems to be that the document is less than perfect and may need amendment but can be lived with for the time being.

Fiji Today

Though the political landscape has changed, the Fijian character has not dimmed. Moreover, improved roads, air services and expanding tourist facilities are making Fiji more and more accessible to the visitor. Yet despite these developments, Fiji has been wrestling with a downturn in its economy, especially in the higher end of the tourism

sector. The economic problems are compounded by a brain drain due to the past political unrest – doctors, nurses, lawyers, engineers, bank officers, mechanics and other skilled professionals have left the country, and productivity and services have declined. In key areas such as health care, the government has hired foreign nationals to take up the slack. Fortunately for the Fijian government, most of the nations that had stopped contributing foreign aid after the coup, rethought their policies and once again provided money to the cash-strapped country.

High unemployment and a 30% devaluation of the Fijian dollar have also dented consumer spending and slowed the economy. Relations between Indians and Fijians, which previously could have been described as 'peaceful coexistence', suffered during the time of political unrest. They appear to be returning to a more benign state of being. It seems that Fijian Indians have in general accepted the political status quo and must work within the system to re-establish whatever political power they can muster.

One of the biggest challenges facing the Fijian government is to create jobs for its rapidly growing population. The lack of jobs for school graduates has resulted in increasing crime in urban centres. In the past the villages could easily absorb unemployed Fijians into the subsistence economy. This is impossible now because the numbers are too large and many Fijian youths are urban kids who have not been exposed to the discipline and structure imposed by village life.

In order to encourage employment and overseas investment, Fiji has provided tax-free zones for economic development. By providing investors with tax holidays and cheap skilled labour, it is hoped that employment ills will be cured and the country might earn much-needed hard currency.

In summary, Fiji has made tremendous strides in business and infrastructure development since independence. Despite the economic consequences of the coup, the country is slowly pulling itself up by its bootstraps. Solid growth will come with time when investors sense that Fiji is once again stable, especially with the new constitution in place.

GEOGRAPHY

The Fiji islands are in the south-west Pacific Ocean, where they occupy a central locale 2797 km north-east of Sydney, Australia, and 1848 km north of Auckland, New Zealand. Fiji lies wholly in the southern tropics, that is, between the equator and the tropic of Capricorn. The Fiji archipelago forms the eastern outpost of the chain of high volcanic islands of continental origin that extends eastward from Papua New Guinea to the Solomon Islands and Vanuatu. Fiji's closest neighbour to the east is Tonga and to the west Vanuatu (formerly the New Hebrides). Longitudinally, Fiji is where the new day begins; on the 180th meridian the International Date Line makes a special eastward bend around the island group so that all of the country keeps the same time.

The territorial waters of Fiji are defined in the deed of cession as all that area 'lying between the parallels of latitude of 15 degrees south and 22 degrees south of the equator, and between the meridians of longitude of 177 degrees west and 175 degrees east of the meridian of Greenwich'. In 1965 the boundary was extended by one degree to take in Conway Reef, extending the limit to 174° east. In latitude, the Fiji islands correspond with Tahiti, Townsville in Australia, Zimbabwe, Rio de Janeiro and northern Chile.

The area included within these limits is approximately 709,660 sq km, about 97% of which is water. The remaining 3% (18,376 sq km) is land. The Fiji archipelago includes about 300 islands (depending on how many reefs and tiny islets you take into consideration) of which about 100 are inhabited. The largest island, Viti Levu, which has 70% of the population and an area of 10,388 sq km, is the hub of the entire archipelago. On it are Suva, the largest city, the chief port and the capital; Nadi, site of the international airport; and Lautoka, the second largest city and the second port of entry.

Vanua Levu, to the north-east of Viti Levu, is the second largest island which, with an area of 5538 sq km, is slightly more than half the size of Viti Levu. Although more sparsely settled than Viti Levu, it is also a centre of population. Like Viti Levu, it produces sugar cane and also has large coconut plantations.

Taveuni lies to the east of Vanua Levu, being separated from it by the Somosomo Strait. With an area of 435 sq km, it is verdant, mountainous and agriculturally rich.

Tied with Taveuni as the third largest island in the archipelago (with an area of 409 sq km) is Kadavu, which lies to the south of Viti Levu. It is a centre of traditional Fijian culture and not often seen by tourists.

All of the remaining islands of Fiji are small and are divided into two main groups, Lomaiviti and Lau.

Lomaiviti translates as 'middle' or central Fiji, which describes exactly where this island group is on the map. It is composed of seven main islands, with smaller ones lying off the coasts. Their aggregate land area is 425 sq km. Gau, Koro and Ovalau are large, each being about 100 sq km or more in area. Ovalau derives its importance from the town of Levuka, which was the earliest European settlement in Fiji and the original capital. Gau is the largest, highest and southernmost of the group; Koro is a high, wedge-shaped island rising abruptly from deep water. Nairai and Batiki, to the east of Ovalau, are lower than their neighbours and are surrounded by extensive reefs. Makogai, north-east of Levuka, was once a leper colony serving the entire south-west Pacific. Wakaya, once a plantation, is now an exclusive real estate development. All of the islands can be seen from the old capital of Levuka on a clear day.

Lau, or eastern Fiji, the area most heavily influenced by the Tongan culture, includes numerous limestone islands and others of volcanic or composite structure, all set among widespread reefs. For administrative reasons all of Lau is one district, but it is geographically divided into four subgroups: northern Lau, central Lau and southern Lau (which together form a chain of islands stretching 432 km in a north-south direction), and the Moala group, lying to the south of Lomaiviti.

Northern Lau includes the Exploring Islands (one large island and eight small ones, all enclosed within a barrier reef) and some 14 others of which Naitauba, Kanacea, Mago and Cicia are the most important.

Central Lau includes five islands centring on Lakeba, which is the hereditary seat of the chiefs of Lau and the home of Ratu Sir Kamisese Mara.

Southern Lau comprises 16 islands as well as some clusters, most of them grouped within 100 km of Lakeba. Beyond these, in the attenuated 'tail' of the archipelago, lie Vatoa and Ono, isolated from their nearest neighbours and from one another by wide stretches of open sea. The most outlying islands of southern Lau are actually closer to Tonga than they are to Fiji.

The Moala group is composed of three islands having an aggregate area of 119 sq km and situated about halfway between Kadavu and southern Lau. Moala is the principal island; Totoya is the rim of an extinct volcano whose breached and flooded crater forms a beautiful landlocked lagoon; and Matuku is reckoned to be one of the garden spots of Fiji.

The Yasawa group, to the north-west of Viti Levu, includes six principal islands (four of them large) and many small ones, having a total area of 135 sq km. These islands, which have been compared to a string of pearls, extend across the sea for 80 km in shallow water behind the Great Sea Reef. This area is the destination for Blue Lagoon Cruises. It is a favourite of many tourists and lives up to the visitor's idea of what the South Seas 'should' look like.

Rotuma, a Polynesian outlier 386 km north-west of the Fiji group, was ceded to Britain in 1881 as part of the colony of Fiji. Although politically part of Fiji, geographically and ethnologically it has nothing to do with the islands. Most Rotumans, who are Polynesians related to the Samoans, live on Viti Levu rather than their 'home' island. Rotuma's policy is to discourage tourism.

The islands with which most visitors find themselves familiar are those of the Mamanuca group, also an archetypal 'South Pacific' locale, just offshore from Nadi and Lautoka on Viti Levu. It is here that many of the popular resorts such as Beachcomber, Plantation Island, Castaway and Mana are located.

Some of the other smaller but well-known islands are Beqa, home of the firewalkers; Vatulele, famous for its sacred prawns; and Rabi, once inhabited by Fijians, but now the adopted home of Banabans or Ocean Islanders (Micronesians) who moved there after WW II (see the Other Ethnic Groups section later in this chapter). Both Beqa and Vatulele are off the southern coast of Viti Levu, while Rabi is off the coast of Taveuni.

Political & Administrative Divisions

Politically, the archipelago is divided into four areas or 'divisions': the Northern Division which is composed of Vanua Levu and the neighbouring islands of Taveuni, Rabi and Qamea; the Western Division which consists of the western half of the main island of Viti Levu, including the Yasawa group to the north-west and Vatulele to the south; the Central Division made up of the eastern half of Viti Levu; and the Eastern Division, composed of the Lau, Kadavu and Lomaiviti groups.

Types of Islands

Sailors generally speak of 'high' and 'low' islands, but to be geologically correct there are three types of islands in the archipelago. The majority are high islands of volcanic origin and low islands which include coral and limestone varieties. The volcanic islands, of which Viti Levu is an example, have sharply defined, mountainous landscapes, ancient volcanoes and rocky outcrops and shores. Inland, the terrain is broken, with few stretches of flat land except in river valleys. In the windward areas where rains are frequent, the hills are covered with thick vegetation and are smothered almost incessantly with rain. Leeward, growth is sparse and hills are brown. Lively vestiges

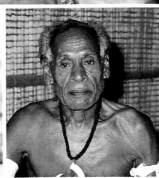

Top: Aerial view of a Fiji island (FVB)
Left: Fijian woman (RK)
Right: Village children (RK)

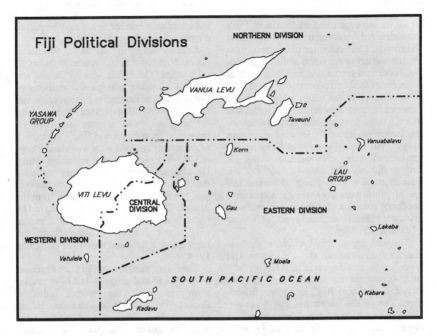

Fiji Political Divisions

of the active volcanic period are hot springs, which are always found at low elevations. The best known in Fiji are the springs at Nakama, in the old coconut-plantation town of Savusavu on Vanua Levu.

Coral islands, although low and small, have their own peculiarly Robinson Crusoesque charm. Generally located near the inner margin of a broad reef, they are usually only a few metres above sea level, are flat as a table and have beautiful white-sand beaches. Despite limited soil, they often support luxuriant vegetation including vines, grasses, broad-leaved trees and, of course, the coconut palm. A classic example is the resort on Beachcomber Island off Lautoka.

Limestone islands may also appear to be low and flat-topped, but have steep, sharp sides suggesting that they are huge masses of rock heaved up from the sea. This is exactly what they are – often surrounded by a succession of precipitous cliffs, undercut by the surf. Because the limestone erodes easily, the rock may be pitted and bristling with sharp pinnacles or cut by ravines or narrow canyons. Inland, central depressions give the islands a basin-like appearance. The depression floors are commonly cut up into rolling hills, fertile and well wooded. A good example of a typical limestone island is Vanua Balavu in the Lau group.

Of the hundreds of islands in the Fiji group, only a few may be classed as true atolls. The typical atoll, of which so much has been written in the romantic literature of the South Seas, is basically long strips of broken coral and sand ranging from a few metres to half a km forming a circular or ring-like structure that surrounds a lagoon. Perhaps the best-known example of an atoll in Fiji is Wailagilala, on the eastern side of the Nanuku Passage, the main shipping lane through the islands.

CLIMATE

Fiji has a tropical maritime climate, tempered by the ocean and trade winds. Fiji's weather is not, however, uniform throughout the islands. There is a range of climates, from the hot and dry to the warm and wet, providing conditions favourable for the growth of a variety of food and commercial crops. The leeward sides of the major islands (eg the Lautoka or Labasa areas) are dry, with clear skies, a limited temperature range and abundant sunshine. It is on the leeward or western side of Viti Levu that most of Fiji's resorts are located. Average annual rainfall there is 165 to 180 cm. The windward sides of the islands are subject to cloudy skies and frequent rains with even temperatures and moderate sunshine. Suva is an example of a windward climatic area and averages 300 cm of rainfall annually.

The cool, dry months – which are the best time to visit – are from May to October. The so-called 'winter' begins in July. During July and August the temperature may drop to between 18°C and 20°C, and lower inland. Even during the winter months, however, these relatively low temperatures are by no means constant. Spells of cloudy, cool weather with occasional rains alternate with warm, sunny days, sometimes of high humidity. The hot, wet season may begin as early as November; but the conjunction of heat and humidity that most people from moderate climates find trying occurs during the first three months of the year. During this time the temperature ranges from 23°C to 31°C, and it may rain nearly every day.

Forces of Nature

Despite Fiji's volcanic history, strong earthquakes in the region are rare. Of much greater relevance are cyclones, which have struck Fiji over the last several years with greater frequency than they have at any other time within a century. Normally Fiji gets 10 to 15 cyclones per decade, with perhaps one of hurricane intensity. Since the beginning of 1985, Fiji has suffered over a dozen cyclones, of which nearly half have had devastating hurricane-force winds. The sudden increase in cyclone activity is inexplicable,

but scientists postulate that it may be part of a meteorological cycle.

In early 1985 Fiji was hit by two hurricanes, Nigel and Eric, within 24 hours of each other. The result was 26 deaths and massive flooding that caused millions of dollars worth of damage to homes, crops and hotels, thus crippling the vital tourism sector for months. A few months later, not yet recovered from Nigel and Eric's wrath, Fiji miraculously escaped what would have been terrible destruction from Hurricane Hina. Hina had appeared to be heading directly for the country's most populated areas, but suddenly veered into the ocean, away from the islands. The hurricane had gusts of up to 160 knots (about 300 km/h), making it potentially more destructive than Tracy, the hurricane that flattened the city of Darwin in 1974.

The forces of nature in Fiji not only cause havoc to life and property but have caused problems within the tourism industry. Because the number of insurance claims have increased, insurance companies have upped the cost of premiums to resorts which in turn pass on the costs to the consumer.

FLORA & FAUNA

The indigenous flora and fauna of Fiji (and the south-west Pacific) are strongly Indo-Malayan in character. They entered the Pacific from the west, in the face of the prevailing winds and ocean currents, and as might be expected, their range and variety decreased the further they were from the source. Thus, Fiji has less range and variety than the Solomon Islands and Vanuatu, which are poorer in species than Papua New Guinea but richer than Tonga, Samoa and Tahiti. Even within the Fiji archipelago the same attenuation of species is evident, the flora and fauna of the eastern islands being much poorer than those of the large islands to the west.

Flora

When the Europeans first arrived in Fiji they found mangroves on the salt mud flats and estuaries; coconuts on the foreshores and coastal plains; rainforests, bamboos and ferns on the mountains and hills; and on the dry leeward, sides of the islands reeds, grasses, casuarinas and pandanus. More than half of Fiji's total area is still covered with forest, principally tropical rainforest occupying the windward or wet slopes of the large islands. The forested area also includes large sections of intermediate forest and some 20 sq km of mangroves. Early in the 19th century, Europeans discovered sandalwood in the dry, natural environment along the west coast of Vanua Levu and within about a decade removed most of it. Later, other indigenous woods such as *dakua*, *yaka* and *vesi* were discovered and are still exploited commercially.

Fijians had already utilised the coconut for food, drink and construction; large timber for canoe building; pandanus leaves for mats and baskets; bamboo and reeds for home building; hibiscus for twine; mangrove for firewood; kava for the ceremonial drink, *yaqona*; and mulberry bark for *masi* (tapa) cloth.

Visitors flying over Fiji will note the many pine forests that cover the mountains. The 30 sq km of introduced pine have become an important national resource and export product.

One of the best places to see Fiji's flora, as well as plants from throughout the South Pacific, is Thurston Gardens (the museum grounds) in Suva.

Fauna

Mammals Fiji's indigenous mammals are limited to six species of bat and the small grey Polynesian rat. Four of the bats are fruit bats (otherwise known as flying foxes) and the two remaining varieties are insect-eating bats. Dogs and pigs were introduced by the Polynesian immigrants to Fiji. All other mammals now in the islands have been brought here during the last 200 years.

Cattle, horses and sheep were introduced to Fiji about the middle of the last century – cattle and horses by the missionaries, and sheep by the settlers. Goats were introduced by the missionaries in the early 1800s. In 1859 several cows and a bull were introduced to the island of Wakaya for breeding purposes. The story goes that upon seeing the animals, the local people asked 'What are these?' and the reply was, 'A bull and a cow'. According to folklore, the Fijian word for cattle, *bulumakau*, was coined from this reply. This would be a convincing story for lexicographers; however, according to historian R A Derrick the first two cattle in Fiji were a couple of milking cows (no bull at all), and the word bulumakau was already in existence in pidgin talk throughout the Pacific.

Similar stories exist for pig *(puaka* or *vuaka)* and dog *(koli)*. Logically we might think the words have English derivations, koli from collie and puaka from porker.

Derrick tells us it is a pity that 'mere facts spoil a good story'. Both koli and puaka have Polynesian roots extending long before the Europeans arrived.

The mongoose, often seen darting across a road or lawn, was introduced from India during the 1880s as a means of controlling the snakes and rats which plundered the cane fields. Unfortunately mongooses also liked hens, native birds and the shellfish clinging to the mangroves. By 1890 they had become a pest and remain so today. They are restricted to the larger islands.

Birds Bird life in Fiji is varied and, for the ornithologically minded, quite interesting. There are more than 100 species of birds, which include seven varieties of parrots, several honeyeaters, a kingfisher, two fantails, owls, ducks, rails, cuckoos and large swamp fowl. Some of the most interesting are jungle fowl (wild ancestors to chickens) and fruit doves, some of which exist in astonishing colours. There are many endemic species, for bird-watchers who love to add species to their 'life lists'. The most numerous and well-known introductions to Fiji are the mynahs and bulbuls from India, which have chased many of the smaller native birds into the hills. For those interested in bird life

Kingfisher

the best book on the subject (available only in Fiji) is *Birds of the Fiji Bush* by Fergus Clunie, a former director of the Fiji Museum.

Reptiles Snakes are found on many of the islands, the most common being the harmless Pacific boa which may grow up to two metres long and feeds on rats and ground-nesting birds. The one venomous land snake in Fiji, the *bolo*, is not aggressive and is rarely seen; there is no record of death from its bite. Seasnakes, commonly seen along the coast, are highly venomous but normally very docile.

There are several varieties of lizard. The friendly gecko or house lizard, seven to 10 cm long, pays visits to hotel rooms but is a welcome guest because it preys on mosquitoes and flies. Several other varieties of lizard are often seen scurrying among the rocks and brush, but the banded iguana, which can be up to a metre long, is rarely observed.

In the past decade scientists discovered an entirely new species of lizard in Fiji, the crested iguana, on a tiny island off the coast of Vanua Levu. The original home of the iguana is South and Central America and biologists speculate that the iguanas may have drifted from the Americas on large pieces of floating vegetation and ended up in Fiji. At any rate it was too far to swim. Both species of iguanas have been successfully hatched at Orchid Island, a tourist attraction near Suva that among other things has many different exhibits of local flora and fauna on display. This is the closest thing to a zoo in Fiji and the only place where the rare reptiles may be seen.

Amphibians The giant toad was introduced from Hawaii in 1936 to help control slugs, beetles and millipedes, and has spread prolifically ever since. When the toad's natural food becomes scarce it turns cannibalistic and grows smaller, as most have in Fiji. The toads breed in still water; you can always see multitudes of black tadpoles in ditches and potholes. They come out en masse on lawns at night, or on the roads after a rain. One wit observed that the only predator the toad and the mongoose have in Fiji is the automobile.

The Fiji frogs occupy the extreme eastern outpost to which amphibian Pacific migration reached. Their appearance has been recorded on a number of islands, including Ovalau, Taveuni, Vanua Levu, Viti Levu and Beqa. These are frogs of damp, thick forests, whose eggs are attached to the surface of leaves; the frogs complete their metamorphosis inside the eggs.

Underwater Fauna Fiji's underwater attractions are manifold and magnificent. Apart from the unusually prolific filter-feeder population (soft corals, crinoids, gorgonians etc) Fiji's waters host a number of nectonics and other species such as parrot fish, trumpet fish, sea snakes, damsel fish, barracuda, sweet lips, walu and coral trout just to name a few. Perhaps the most interesting and photogenic are the clown fish and the anemone, which form symbiotic relationships. Various species of clown fish live in the protection of the poisonous sting of the anemone. The timid curiosity of the fish will delight divers and photographers.

There are also turtles (some, unfortunately, killed for their shells), lobster-like crayfish, giant clams, bêches-de-mer, trochus and the annelid seaworm called *balolo*. The balolo rises to the surface with uncanny punctuality twice a year, generally

Coral

in October and November. Freshwater prawns in the streams and rivers of most of Fiji provide a source of food.

Large pelagic and open-ocean sea creatures are found throughout Fijian waters. Sharks, mantas, dolphins, bill fish and other deep-water hunters can frequently be observed by divers.

The Fijians have in some cases developed a friendly relationship with turtles, sharks, eels and prawns, and claim to be able to call them up from the depths. In Koro turtles are called up for the benefit of tourists (with mixed results at best). Kadavu is also a spot where turtles will rise in response to a particular chant. The people of Korolevu, a village on the Sigatoka River, are said to be able to call up eels. In Vatulele, off the western coast of Vanua Levu and on Vanua Vatu in Lau, sacred red prawns can be summoned. In Lakeba individuals from certain clans can call sharks to the surface. (See the section on Lakeba in the Lau Group chapter.)

Green turtle

Insects The insects of Fiji, whether they are mosquitoes that find nourishment on the nape of your neck or huge roaches which seek refuge in your F$300 hotel, are difficult to miss. Before you instinctively raise your foot to crush a Fijian insect, take a moment to contemplate how this tiny, defenceless creature managed to arrive on such a tiny fragment of land in the midst of the largest body of water on the planet.

Of the few thousand species that probably exist on Fiji, less than 10% have been catalogued or described. Though no books have been written on Fijian insects, field guides for insects on almost any continent will help you identify the common types of butterflies, beetles, wasps and other bugs found here.

As with other fauna, the insects of Fiji are typical of those found in Papua New Guinea or Vanuatu. Many species arrived via water dispersal (rafting on vegetation) or by aerial transport. In the past, Fiji's isolation meant there were few opportunities for insects to successfully colonise the islands. Once established, each group of insects often underwent evolution independent of its ancestral counterparts which may have resulted in the formation of new species. Today, more than 80% of the species in some groups of insects are considered unique.

In more recent history humankind has acted as a major transporter of insects to the islands. Creatures ranging from cockroaches to flour beetles owe their presence to human transport of produce, ships' ballast or even luggage. In some cases, these introductions have caused serious economic problems.

The introduction of the coconut moth was the first major pest of the Fiji Islands, and at the end of the last century caused almost complete defoliation of coconut and sable palms, nearly destroying the island's copra industry. From 1925 to 1926 a parasitic fly that feeds on the moth larvae was introduced from Malaya and by 1926 control of the troublesome moth was evident in Fiji.

The biological control program was a complete success and within a few years it was difficult to even find the moth. With the decline of this creature a new pest, the coconut scale, made an unwelcome entry. A small legless insect that sucks the sap of coconut palms, the coconut scale was also becoming an economic threat.

However, help was on the way. Two minute parasitic wasps from Java and a predatory beetle from Trinidad were introduced and again, the pest was completely under control.

Since the coconut moth solution, numerous insects have been imported to control both native and introduced pests with varying degrees of success. Of these, predatory mosquitoes were introduced to control another mosquito that attacks humans, and predatory beetles and some accidentally introduced ants have helped to control the population of house flies.

On small islands, insect populations can change rapidly and are highly sensitive to perturbation. Accidental introduction of any insect or plant can result in the displacement of native species. As habitat is altered to expand sugar cane cultivation or pine plantations, the result is a net loss of native species.

Destruction of native habitat is probably one of the greatest threats to the diversity of insects on Fiji. Think again about the insect you are about to crush – it may be the last of its kind.

GOVERNMENT

Fiji became an independent nation on 10 October 1970, 96 years after cession to Britain. Until 1987 its constitution provided for a bicameral parliament modelled on the Westminster plan with a house of representatives elected by popular vote and a senate with appointed members.

Prior to the coups of 1987, Fiji was ruled by the Alliance Party headed by Ratu Sir Kamisese Mara. Ratu Mara and his party, which consisted mostly of Fijians, Europeans, Chinese and other islanders, had presided over Fiji since independence. The opposition party (National Federation Party or NFP), made up mostly of Indians, won briefly in 1977 but due to squabbling within the ranks failed to form a government. The governor general re-appointed the Alliance Party as a minority government, but it was dissolved at the first sitting. In a second election the Alliance Party won again.

Following the coups of 1987, Fiji withdrew from the British Commonwealth and was ruled by an interim government. The interim government, which lasted until 1992, was a coalition of mostly former Alliance Party members, military functionaries and powerful tribal leaders. Fiji was, in effect, ruled without a constitution. Indian representation during this period was nil.

A new constitution, promulgated in 1990 and implemented in 1992, reserved the posts of president, prime minister, police commissioner and civil service commissioner for Fijians. Of the 71 seats in the single-chamber parliament, Fijians are guaranteed 36 seats, one of which is held by the commander of the army (who is also the defence and security minister). Indians retain 22 seats, and general voters (non-Fijians and non-Indians) get eight seats. The prime minister is empowered to appoint four cabinet ministers who would each be given a seat.

In 1992 Sitiveni Rabuka, former coup leader, shed his military uniform and won a five-year term as prime minister. Rabuka, head of the SVT party (associated with the Taukei movement, a Fijian nationalist group) rules the country in a loose coalition with the General Voters Party. The other major parties in the Fijian political spectrum include the National Federation Party (NFP), consisting mostly of Indians; the Labour Party, composed of Fijian and Indian trade union members; and the ultra-nationalist National Fijian Party, with an interest in preserving traditional or 'chiefly' power.

National Symbols

Flag Fiji's flag flew for the first time on Independence Day, 10 October 1970. It includes the red, white and blue 'Union Jack' of Britain in the top left-hand corner and the shield from Fiji's coat of arms on a light blue background. The design of the national flag was selected through a competition won jointly by Mr Robi Wilcock and Mrs Murray MacKenzie, both of Suva.

Coat of Arms Fiji's coat of arms consists of the images of two Fijian warriors (one bearing a war club, the other a spear) on either side of a shield, a *takia* (Fijian canoe) at the top of the shield, and the motto *Rerevaka na Kalou ka doka na Tui* (Fear God and Honour the Queen) below the shield. The shield itself bears the image of a heraldic lion holding a cocoa pod across the top. Sugar cane, a coconut palm, a bunch of bananas and the dove of peace occupy each of the four quadrants of the shield. The dove was the flag symbol of Chief Cakobau's government, the administration of the self-proclaimed 'King of Fiji' that preceded the British colonial government in Fiji.

Provinces

Fiji also has 'provinces' which are traditional entities or fiefdoms that still define tribal land ownership, and are distinct from the government administrative areas that divide Fiji into five units (ie Northern Division, Western Division etc). However, since the coups, and the resulting expanded power of indigenous Fijians (especially the resurgence of chiefs or ratus in local politics), the provinces, as political power centres, are becoming more of a factor in political machinations. There is definitely a trend towards allowing the provinces to retain greater autonomy in decision-making on local issues.

ECONOMY

The economy of Fiji is primarily agrarian, with subsistence farming on a village level still an important way of life for much of the population. The largest earner of hard currency is tourism followed by sugar, the main export crop.

The cane fields of Fiji lie along the seaboard from the south-west to the north-west coast of Viti Levu, the largest island; and in the northern portion of Vanua Levu, the second-largest island. Cane is grown mainly on small holdings (averaging around 4½ hectares) leased by Indian farmers from communally owned Fijian land. The cane is hand-harvested and sent by truck and small-gauge railway to regional mills. It is then crushed and partially refined by the government-owned Fiji Sugar Corporation.

The system of small-holder cane farming has played an important role in the economic and social stability of the country. When Indian migration ended in 1916 and indentured labourers no longer worked the land, a new system had to be found to harvest the crop. The best alternative, which is still used today, was to break up the large estates and lease out the smaller holdings.

Aside from sugar, other hard-currency earners are gold, copra, tuna, ginger, cocoa, light industrial products and coconut oil. Timber and pine chips have gained importance as export items, but they are still dwarfed by sugar exports and tourism as a source of revenue. The government is also encouraging small-scale agricultural development, especially in traditional root crops such as taro, cassava and yams.

The aim of the government is to wean the country away from its dependence on sugar. The wisdom of this was evident during the hurricanes of 1985, which severely damaged the cane crop in Viti Levu and left farmers, who had all their eggs in one basket, with very little. Except for pine forest production, the benefits of which will not be realised until later, no large-scale attempt at agricul-

tural diversification has begun. However, the country has achieved self-sufficiency in poultry, pork and beef production.

Tourism first gained importance in the 1960s and is currently the most important sector of the economy. Despite the current lull in high-end tourism it appears that hotels will continue to be built and tourism will be the leading industry in the country for years to come.

POPULATION & PEOPLE

Fiji is perhaps the most cosmopolitan of all South Pacific nations. Its population, just over 785,000, is an amalgam of Indians (46.2%), Fijians (49.9%), 'part-Europeans' or half-castes (1.7%), Europeans (0.7%), Rotumans (1.2%), Chinese (0.7%) and other Pacific Islanders (1%). (Note that the term 'Europeans' refers to White residents of Fiji, unless specified.) The late Fijian statesman Ratu Sukuna spoke of Fiji as a 'three-legged stool' requiring the support of Fijians, Indians, Europeans and other races to keep it upright.

Fijians

Fijians, the indigenous inhabitants of Fiji, are Melanesians who possess a mixture of Polynesian blood which is very apparent in the eastern islands (such as the Lau group), but less so in the west and interiors of the main islands. Many of the present chiefly families trace their descent, through 11 or more generations, from strangers who sailed or drifted to these shores from distant islands, and who settled singly or in small groups among the Melanesian people already occupying the land.

The strong Polynesian influence, both physical and cultural, is due primarily to visiting parties of Tongans, many of whom stayed in Fiji for years or settled permanently. Eastern Fiji is thus the frontier on which two streams of migration – Melanesians from the west and Polynesians from the east – met and mingled.

Melanesians are characteristically short and dark-skinned, with fuzzy hair. Polynesians are generally tall and well built, with fair skin and straight hair. The intermingling of these two races has produced in Fiji a variety of physical types, ranging from the people of southern Lau – fair-skinned and very tall, with aquiline features – to the *kai colo* (hill people) who are dark-skinned, short and flat-nosed. Culturally the differences are not so obvious, but social organisation does differ between tribes from east and west.

Fijian customs reflect an utmost courtesy and dignity toward the visitor. There are ceremonies for every occasion, which may include the presentation of *tabua* (whale's teeth), food or other gifts, or more commonly the drinking of yaqona (kava), the national beverage.

Indians

Fiji's Indians can be divided into two broad cultural categories reinforced by physical differences. Those from the north of India – the 'Calcuttas', or 'Calcutta Wallahs' – came from Bengal, Bihar and Uttar Pradesh through the immigration point of Calcutta and spoke 'village' Hindustani. The second group was the 'Madrassis', who generally had darker skin and lacked the sharp features of those from the north. They were recruited from Madras, Malabar, North Arcot, Vizakapatnam and Tanjore in southern India and spoke Tamil, Telegu and Malayalam. From this amalgam of cultures 'Fiji Hindi' has become the lingua franca of Fijian Indians.

Europeans

European settlement in Fiji dates from the beginning of the 19th century. None of the discoverers had any but chance contact with the locals; it was the 'beachcombers' – shipwrecked sailors and deserters – who first attempted to live with the natives. Despite intermittent trade, the first 50 years of the century ended with no more than 50 White residents in all of Fiji.

The demand for cotton in Europe caused by the American Civil War and the belief that Fiji would be annexed by Britain brought entrepreneurs and planters, and by 1870 the White population had grown to 2000. The primary European settlement was Levuka, the major port and centre of commerce.

Alternating periods of economic growth and decline kept the European population – which was generally involved in cotton planting, commercial enterprises, or government service – fairly stable. It reached its peak in the 1960s at around 7000. After independence in 1970, many Europeans left seeking greener pastures in New Zealand, Australia or the USA. Today the European population numbers around 4200.

Part-Europeans

The part-Europeans, also known as *kai loma*, are a distinctive cultural group with one foot in the Fijian world and the other in the Western world. Many are descendants of White Australians, Americans or Europeans who established themselves either in Levuka, on the isolated coconut plantations of Vanua Levu or on the outer islands of Fiji during the 19th century, and took Fijian wives. One of the most famous part-European families is the Whippy family, directly descended from David Whippy, an American seaman who came to Levuka in 1824 and became that town's leading citizen. By 1881 there were around 800 part-Europeans; today there are about 13,800.

The part-European's character can be a fascinating melange of the easy-going sensibilities of the Fijian and the business acumen of the Westerner – in effect, the best of both worlds. Part-Europeans generally speak fluent English and can at least understand Fijian, if not speak it fluently. Conversations may be carried on in both languages simultaneously, with jokes made in the tongue that best suits the story. Many still make a living in communities like Levuka or Savusavu (on Vanua Levu), in the old-time professions of planter, shipbuilder or sailor. Part-Europeans proudly trace their cultural heritage on both sides and may even enjoy land rights of the family group to which the Fijian parent belonged.

Rotumans

The Rotumans, a distinct Polynesian ethnic

group, come from the island of Rotuma (386 km north-west of Fiji). The Rotumans ceded their island to Fiji in 1881 and have been governed as part of Fiji since then. They enjoy full citizenship, and many have settled on Viti Levu in order to find greater opportunity. Some have married Fijians or Chinese. Although a separate racial and cultural group, Rotumans have always assimilated easily and see themselves as an intrinsic part of the Fijian nation. Today Rotumans number about 11,500, most of whom live outside Rotuma.

Other Ethnic Groups

The Chinese, of whom there are about 5800, first came to Fiji in 1911. They have the reputation of being model citizens and generally make a living as merchants or restauranteurs. Many have intermarried with the local population.

The total membership of other ethnic groups of Pacific Islanders is about 7300. Tongans, who as traders and warriors have lived in Fiji for hundreds of years, form the largest part of this community. In the old days there was active commerce between Tonga and Fiji, and later in the history of this relationship the Fijians in the Lau Islands became vassals to the King of Tonga. One particular reason Tongans and Samoans came to Fiji was to build *drua* (large double-hulled canoes) which they couldn't build on their own islands because of the lack of proper timber.

The second most important members of this group numerically are the Banabans, who are Micronesians. Originally from minuscule Ocean Island, which lies just south of the equator near the 170th meridian of east longitude, the Banabans were employed by a British mining company to excavate the rich deposits of phosphate that covered their island home. When it became obvious in 1942 that the island was doomed to devastation by phosphate stripping, Rabi Island, near Vanua Levu, was given to the Banabans as a new home by the Great Council of Chiefs. However, before they could make any move towards occupying Rabi Island, Japanese troops landed on Ocean Island and the Banabans suffered greatly. At the war's end the survivors were gathered, some from Nauru, others from the Gilberts (now Kiribati) and the Carolines; and the process of settling Rabi Island began. There are about 3000 Banabans living on Rabi Island and throughout Fiji.

Other ethnic groups include Tuvaluans (formerly Ellice Islanders), Samoans and the descendants of Solomon Islanders. The Solomon Islanders were brought to Fiji during the 19th century by 'blackbirders' (who might politely be called labour recruiters) as labourers to work the cotton and sugar plantations. Although these islanders have by now thoroughly mixed with Fijians, they still trace their ancestry back to the Solomons.

EDUCATION

Fiji has a good system of education compared with most of its neighbours and is a centre for learning in the South Pacific. Enrolment is nearly 100% for primary-school children, and tuition for grades one to eight is free. Classes are taught in the pupil's parent tongue (the local Fijian dialect for the Fijians and Hindi or Urdu for the Indians) and in English for the first few years until students have grasped enough English to make it the medium of instruction. Thus nearly everyone – except some of the older generation – speaks English.

Fiji has 660 primary schools, 140 secondary schools, 37 vocational schools, a theological college and one university (the University of the South Pacific). Vocational training includes courses in engineering, maritime studies, telecommunications, agriculture, carpentry, hotel and restaurant management and business. The University of the South Pacific, established in 1968, has an enrolment of about 2500 students from throughout the Pacific and is funded primarily by Fiji and grants from overseas. There is also a separate Fiji School of Medicine, associated with the university.

ARTS

While other countries such as Tahiti and

Hawaii are experiencing a revival in traditional arts, Fiji has no such contemporary movement – the reason being, for the most part, that Fijians never lost their cultural heritage. Most of the folkloric crafts are practised in the villages, and village life is still the foundation of Fijian society.

Critics do point to the decreasing quality (primarily due to the commercialisation of crafts caused by the tourist trade) of wood-carving and pottery, but there are still people around who know what they are doing. Except for a few skills like traditional house-building, which will probably disappear within 15 years because village homes are not built with traditional materials anymore, the arts remain part of contemporary culture. Mat-weaving is taught to nearly every village girl, and the making of masi (tapa) cloth is widespread. Likewise, the meke (traditional dance) continues to be handed down from generation to generation and is often performed, with new mekes being created for special occasions, just as has always been done.

The closest thing to a revival has been in the Dance Theatre of Fiji, a highly praised troupe that has travelled throughout the world. Produced by Manoa Rasigatale, young chief and former Fijian rock star, the theatre has revitalised Fijian dance by re-introducing old ceremonies, choreographing them and presenting them to modern audiences.

Pottery

A craft that dates from the original settlement of Fiji around 1290 BC, pottery-making is still practised in the lower Sigatoka Valley, the islands of Kadavu and Malolo, western Vanua Levu, the Rewa Delta and the province of Ra. Each district has its own distinct signature in its pottery style. Today the technique and division of labour differ little from those of pre-European contact times. Sometimes the men dig the clay, but it is almost always the women who are the potters. The clay is first kneaded, and then sand is added to control shrinkage and to improve the texture. The mixture is left to dry for a short period before being worked into its final form.

The tools used by today's potters are also the same as those used in the past: a rounded stone, a large pebble or a wooden paddle for beating; a piece of coconut husk for rubbing the clay; a shell or stick for ornamenting; and a cushion of leaves on which to place the work during the moulding process. Pottery wheels were unknown to ancient Fijians and are still not used. Instead, a saucer-like section is shaped for the bottom of the pot or bowl and the item is progressively built up with slabs, strips or coils. The sides are shaped by beating the clay with a paddle or pebble. Considering the implements used, the Fijians achieve remarkable symmetry.

After the object is shaped and finished with moistened fingers or a smooth stone, it is dried for several days and fired for an hour in a fire made from brush, reeds or coconut fronds. Fijian pottery is not glazed – instead, certain plants are rubbed on the finished objects as a kind of varnish to improve water-holding qualities.

Mat & Basket Weaving

Whereas pottery is a skill shared by very few villages, basket and especially mat-plaiting is a universally practised art – every village girl has learned how to weave a mat or *ibe* by the time she is 10 years old. Palm fronds or the long fibrous pandanus leaves are vital construction materials in Fijian culture. The traditional *bure* (Fijian home) is constructed from plaited pandanus or palm fronds; pandanus mats are woven into floor coverings, bedrolls, fans and baskets. Almost every home in Fiji, whether in a village or town, has at least several mats for use as rugs or for sleeping on. They are considered an important element in the wealth of the Fijian family and are traditionally given at weddings, funerals or during the visits of high chiefs.

Masi

Masi and tapa are names for bark cloth. This art form is practised in many regions of the South Pacific and in several areas of Fiji. Masi has many uses, including as ceremonial dress, wall decorations and more recent innovations such as table mats and handbags. It also makes a fine souvenir for visitors.

Masi is produced from the inner bark of the paper mulberry tree *(Broussoneua papyrifera)*, which is cultivated by Fijians expressly for this purpose. The process of making the bark cloth is time-consuming and arduous work, and typically a job given to women. The bark is stripped from the tree, soaked, scraped clean and pounded with a rolling pin-like beater on a wooden anvil.

Masi can be purchased in many shops. The most inexpensive place to buy it is from villagers who make it themselves. The thicker the masi the better the quality.

Woodcarving

Woodcarving is a declining art in Fiji, no doubt another victim of the modern era. The woodcarver's role was a highly specialised one, important because of the cultural value of the items he produced. The war club, for example, was a vital part of Fijian culture. Not only was it the primary weapon in a warrior's arsenal, it was a symbol of authority used in ceremony and dance. Likewise, the *tanoa*, or yaqona bowl, also played (and still plays) an important part in Fijian society. Artist clans were so specialised that carvers in the old days only produced one particular kind of artefact – say clubs or yaqona bowls – and that was it.

Tabua

A tabua, a tooth of the sperm whale, is the highest token of respect one can receive in Fiji. While the use of yaqona is shared with other regions of the Pacific, tabua-giving is strictly a Fijian ritual. The tabua is presented to a distinguished guest – for example a high chief – or is given if a favour is requested. The tabua may be exchanged at betrothals, weddings, births, deaths or when a major contract or agreement is entered into. Likewise, tabua may also be used to make apologies after an argument. Like yaqona, the tabua has an intrinsic role in the social and economic fabric of Fijian life. The value

of each tabua is judged by its thickness and length. Taking one out of the country as a souvenir is strictly forbidden and given stricter laws protecting whales and other endangered species, it's probably illegal to bring them into the USA and other nations.

Meke

The meke is a communal dance/theatre combining singing, chanting and drumming. Traditionally it is performed in a village setting on special occasions – typically for visiting dignitaries. Today mekes are commonly presented at hotels for the benefit of tourists. However, the meke is much more than a colourful dance – it is a medium of transmission that allows important historical events, stories, legends and culture to be handed down from one generation to the next. Often the composer of a meke is unknown, but the dances are embellished and passed on by the *daunivucu* whose role it is to preserve the custom. Traditionally the daunivucu has links with the spirit world and when in communion with the spirit plane may go into a trance and begin to chant and sway. During this time the daunivucu's disciples will watch his motions, which may be added to a particular ceremony.

In the meke every motion and nuance has its significance. The positioning of the performers and even of members of the audience is extremely important. Villagers of high birth have special positions in the ceremony, and to place them in a subordinate spot would be insulting and possibly misrepresentative of the community's history.

Firewalking

Fijian firewalking is an ancient ritual, which according to legend was given by a god only to the Sawau tribe of the island of Beqa off the south coast of Viti Levu. The skill is still possessed by the Sawau (who live in four villages on the southern side of Beqa), but in special cases members of other tribes adopted by the Sawau can also perform this mystifying ceremony. Nowadays firewalking is performed occasionally for Fijians, but most often for the benefit of tourists at

various resorts. The performances for the visitors are generally less steeped in custom than the one described here, but the demonstration of firewalking is just as genuine.

Traditionally, several male representatives are chosen from each village. All are immediate family of the *bete*, the traditional priest-cum-master of ceremonies. For two weeks before the event the participants must observe two strict rules: there must be no contact with women (an act of true sacrifice for most Fijian men) and eating coconuts is forbidden. Failure to observe these taboos may result in severe burns.

In preparation for the firewalking a circular pit a metre or more in depth and four to five metres wide is dug. It is lined with large, smooth stones a third to half a metre in diameter and covered with large logs. Six to eight hours before the ceremony a huge bonfire is built. The burning logs are later removed by men with long green poles who chant *O-vulo-vulo* and clear the way for the participants. A long tree fern, said to contain the spirit of God, is laid across the pit in the direction of the bete. Large vines are then dragged across the stones, levelling them for the actual firewalking.

When the stones are finally in position, the bete jumps on them and takes a few trial steps to test their firmness. He then calls for bundles of green leaves and swamp grass, which are placed around the edge of the pit. Finally, the position of the tree fern is adjusted at the command of the bete; the firewalkers will approach the pit from the direction in which it points. Meanwhile, the village men who have prepared the fire take their positions surrounding the pit, leaving a gap for the entry of the firewalkers.

The bete surveys the scene and when satisfied, shouts *vuto-o*, the signal for the firewalkers' approach. They appear from their place of concealment and walk briskly towards the pit. The tree fern

is removed and the firewalkers walk single file across the red-hot stones around the circumference of the pit. The devotees jump out of the pit and the bundles of grass and leaves are spread out on the stones, which steam in the fiery heat. The performers re-enter the pit amid the clouds of steam and squat for a few minutes in their version of a Turkish bath. After this they walk off the stones unscathed by the ordeal. At this time, if the ceremony is held at a resort, the inevitable sceptic will cautiously approach the pit and place the palm of his hand over the stones. He or she will then walk away convinced it was no charade.

How do they do it? No-one has the definite answer but scientists point to the power of suggestion, especially when the religious element of the ceremony is considered as well as the fact that an insulating film of moisture on the skin may act as a protective layer.

Members of the British Medical Association came to several conclusions after witnessing a ceremony. First, the skin of the participants was neither thicker nor tougher than that of anyone else accustomed to walking barefoot all their lives. Second, there was no evidence of oil or any other substance applied to their feet, nor were the participants under the influence of opiates. Finally, the performers reacted normally to painful stimuli such as burning cigarettes or needles jabbed into their feet before and after the firewalking.

Those who claim the performers may be in a trance-like state are also incorrect. Get close enough to the firewalkers during a performance and you may hear them crack jokes. One reliable witness told me he saw a participant pull a cigarette from behind his ear, light it on a red-hot stone and have a leisurely smoke!

Even with its tourist trappings, the firewalking experience is definitely worth seeing. Firewalking may be seen at Pacific Harbour's Cultural Centre (☎ 450 045); telephone them or check *Fiji Magic*. The express bus to Pacific Harbour costs F$2 and the 'show' is around F$10. Firewalking can also be witnessed at the annual Hibiscus Festival in Suva at the Civic Centre in August or September. Tickets for the events are on sale at Morris Hedstrom a week before the festival begins.

CULTURE

The visitor to Fiji with even the vaguest perception cannot help but notice the pride of the indigenous people, which comes across in their way of looking you squarely in the eye and their respect for tradition, manifest in their hospitality. While other South Pacific cultures are dying or long dead, Fiji's way of life remains strong and resilient in the face of outside influence. What accounts for this?

The reasons can be traced to Fiji's recent history. Just prior to cession, during the early period of settlement, Fiji hovered on the brink of a race war. Settlers and the indigenous people fought over land, and the nation, which was primarily ruled by feudal chiefs, was near anarchy. The country was voluntarily handed over to the British by the chiefs under terms and conditions that would protect the Fijian people. A basically benign, paternalistic sort of colonialism was provided by rulers who wanted to prevent a race war (like that which was already occurring in New Zealand) and to make sure no other power would step in and take advantage of the situation.

Fortunately for Fiji, the first governor Sir Arthur Gordon was a 19th-century romantic who saw himself as a head Fijian chief. He was anxious to see that Fijians were not exploited and took the role of protector quite seriously. He realised that the best way to govern the country was to let the Fijians govern themselves in the manner they always had – with the chief as the authority. He also set into motion the protection of Fijian lands so that the Fijians would never be alienated from them, and laid down laws that prohibited Fijians from being used as labour for the White people's plantations.

Realising that somebody had to work the fields, Gordon set up the indentured labour system which opened the floodgates to Indian workers. After Gordon there were some governors who had planters' interests at heart and who perhaps would have liked to loosen the laws prohibiting the use of Fijian labour, but the scheme developed by Gordon held fast. Also, thanks to Gordon's foresight more than 80% of the land is still held communally by Fijians.

Thus in answer to the original question of what accounts for the strength of Fijian culture, the Fijians never really lost their land nor their leadership. The chiefs have always held political sway and were always recognised by the colonial government, which was in itself often loosely based on a traditional Fijian system. The colonial government merely put an end to political bickering and warfare. In this way, communities weren't disrupted by men being forced into labour. Fijians were left to live as they always had; there was no reason to change and they didn't.

Aside from Gordon's assistance, Fijians have always had a tremendous reverence for tradition and an innate conservatism. Today we see this reflected in the sanctity of the yaqona-drinking ceremony and other customs. People still operate entirely on a traditional system or methodology when in the village. Despite modern education's trend towards individualism – the direct opposite of traditional society – and the preponderance of material and pop culture imported from the USA and Europe, Fijians generally remain deeply entrenched in and psychologically committed to the old ways: respect for chiefs and respect for the system.

Fijian Life

On the surface, Fijian life – especially in the traditional village setting – appears idyllic. People are almost always friendly and generous to a fault. The climate is pleasant, though humid by European standards. Food is plentiful, vicious tropical diseases like malaria are virtually nonexistent, and culture is rich in ceremony and tradition. Society and environment seem to be in a kind of gentle harmony.

The visitor whose head is filled with images of the way the South Pacific should be, may feel Fiji is paradise. The verdant landscape is coloured by tropical flowers, the sound of guitars fills the air, and the gentle night breeze caresses the skin. Watching the muscular virility of even the average Fijian man and the graceful ambling stroll of women (who seem akin to fertility goddesses) adds to the ubiquitous sensuality.

However, pure sweetness and light exist nowhere except in people's minds. Even in paradise, day-to-day life must be faced; bills must be paid and people go to hospital.

Today's Fiji is a society of two main ethnic groups, the indigenous Fijians and the Indians. No two peoples could be more different. The Fijian is easy-going, communal in orientation towards family and society, and most importantly, tied to the land. On the other hand, the Indian is intense, harder to know, enterprising, and landless. Families are tightly knit because Indians had to break with the past to get to Fiji, but kinship groups are small. Like the overseas Chinese or the Jew, the Indian is a stranger in his or her own land and compensates for landless insecurity by working harder and valuing material gain.

The goals of the two races were different in earlier years when the Indian simply worked the estates and the Fijian lived undisturbed in the village. However, with the emerging industrial age and an economy based on money, the goals have become the same. The Indian long ago ceased to be the simple farmer content to cut cane and tend goats. Indian children have become educated and better off materially than the previous generation, and they continue to work hard in the hope of an even brighter future. Likewise, the village life of the Fijian no longer interests many of the young people who have seen discos, fancy hotels and flashy clothing. Increasingly, urban areas are becoming crowded with migrants who have drifted from the villages in search of employment or at least excitement.

With jobs and resources becoming ever more scarce, the peaceful coexistence the two races always enjoyed has become strained. Both groups are competing for the same jobs and both want as complete an education as possible for their children and the material prizes the 20th century has to offer.

The government's task and indeed the key to Fiji's future, will be to accommodate harmoniously the aspirations of both races. ■

Fijian Communal Life

Traditional Fijian society is based on communal principles derived from village life. People in villages share the obligations and rewards of community life and are still led by a hereditary chief. They work together in the preparation of feasts and in the making of gifts for presentation on various occasions; they fish together, later dividing the catch; and they all help in communal activities such as the building of homes and maintenance of pathways and the village green.

The great advantage of this system is an extended family unit that allows no-one to go hungry, uncared for or unloved. Ideally it is an all-encompassing security net that works very effectively not only as a caretaking system, but also by giving each person a sense of belonging and identity. On the negative side, the communal system can be restrictive for the individual, who has no choice but to toe the line. Ambition and any kind of entrepreneurial instinct are quickly stifled, sometimes by jealous relatives if someone actually gets too far ahead. This means one can't really be too different or rebel too much.

Prior to independence there was a move on the part of the government to incrementally change or 'modernise' the village system by dispensing with some communal obligations. At times these changes, combined with a societal transformation in general, were not positive. The slackening of obligations combined with the outside influences of tourism and money coming in from new jobs sometimes meant more diversions and less chiefly authority. The results were higher consumption of alcohol, disrespect for traditional values and a general breakdown of the social fabric. Elders decided it best to go back to the more traditional way of doing things, and many villages have reinstated the old ways that had been thrown out just a few years ago.

Although some individuals have broken away from the village to set up a business and/or a separate identity in town, there are always family obligations that cannot be ignored. The concept of communal property, in which anything that belongs to you can be claimed by friends or relatives, is still very strong. When someone says *Kerekere...* (which translates roughly as 'Please may I have...') it would be socially unacceptable to ignore such a request. Due to commitments to friends and relations, Fijian businesses often go under.

One will never grow rich in the village, but there is stability. Land ownership and the security of village life have provided Fijians with a 'safety net', but this has been a burden as well. In a sense, it has prevented Fijians (who own more than 80% of the land) from competing with the Indians, who have never had the luxury of land ownership. The communal life has put Fijians at a disadvantage with people whose lot has always been to struggle and make the most of what little they have; in the transition from a communal, subsistence-farming society to a capitalist money economy, Fijians have had to adjust much more than the Indians.

Indian Families
Although Fijian Indians come from a variety of subcultures and religious groups, they are seen as a people who share a common way of life, and for political and administrative purposes they have always been lumped together. Early migrants coming to Fiji were carriers of Indian culture only in a limited sense. Most were young, illiterate peasants whose connections with India ended the day their ship left port. Once in Fiji, social groups based on caste

disappeared for the most part; and because of a shortage of women, migrants were compelled to marry across religious lines. In addition, communal kinship patterns found in the traditional Indian village gave way to more individualism due to the breakdown in social structure and heightened demands for personal survival.

Yet Fijian Indians are still distinguished by their institutions of family and marriage. Although individuals have more free will to choose their partners today than in times past, relatives continue to have influence in this realm. Arranged marriages are more common in rural areas, and marriage occurs mainly within subcultural categories and religious groups. Strict marriage ties are especially observed by the more clannish Gujaratis and Punjabis (Sikhs).

Today the trend is towards nuclear-family households but in many areas, both urban and rural, the joint-family household persists. Financial and domestic arrangements may differ from home to home, but families may consist of parents, grandparents and both married and unmarried siblings residing under the same roof. Sons are given a freer rein than daughters, who are traditionally kept under very strict supervision.

Thus, despite a diverse cultural background, Fijian Indians are generally united through the common experience of indenture, the use of Fiji Hindi as their lingua franca, family organisation, cuisine and interests in sports and Indian movies.

The exceptions are the Gujaratis and the Punjabis, who arrived as free migrants from north-west India. They came as traders and merchants, and today own most of the shops and businesses in Fiji's urban centres. Generally the Gujaratis and Punjabis have much stronger kinship ties and attachments to India.

Yaqona Drinking
We have slept through the night and day now dawns
The sun is high in the heavens
Go uproot the yaqona and bring it...
Prepare the root and proclaim it!
The acclamation rose skywards,
Reaching distant lands!

Perhaps nothing reflects the Fijians' reverence for tradition like yaqona (kava) drinking. Visit any Fijian village or home, particularly on a weekend, and you will probably come upon the spectacle of a family sitting on the floor around a large wooden bowl filled with a muddy-coloured liquid, drinking the contents from half a coconut shell. You will then be asked, *E dua na bilo?* ('Try a cup?').

You definitely should try a cup, though don't expect ambrosia. The drink is prepared from the pulverised root of *(Piper methysticum)*, a plant from the pepper family, and has a tingly numbing effect on the tongue. The taste, not unpleasant, takes some getting used to and from a visitor's point of view it is de rigueur at least to *Tovolea mada* ('Try please').

The most important aspect of yaqona drinking is psychological. Sitting around a bowl in the village, exchanging *talanoa* (conversation, chat) and listening to the guitars hammer away is a very pleasant experience. Most importantly, the act of sharing a bowl creates an invisible bond between the participants. The visitor feels a warmth and acceptance among complete strangers that is normally associated with family or close friends. It is no accident that in Fiji many business deals and social contracts are consummated around a yaqona bowl.

Yaqona is a Fijian link to the past, a tradition so inextricably woven into the fabric of culture that life without it is unimaginable. Fijians would scarcely be Fijians without their national beverage. It is consumed ritually when welcoming visitors, sending village members on journeys, christening boats, laying the foundations of homes, casting magical spells, making deals, settling arguments and, as is usually the case, chatting. It is also presented as a *sevusevu*, a traditional gift offered by guests to the host, or as a token of respect to visitors of higher rank in official ceremonies.

Yaqona drinking was an ancient custom when the first Europeans arrived, and its use today is still an accurate reflection of their observations. Basil Thomson, a 19th-century ethnologist, said:

The chief's yaqona circle supplied the want of newspapers; the news and gossip of the day were related and discussed; the chief's advisers seized upon the convivial moment to make known their view; matters of policy were decided; the chief's will, gathered from a few careless words spoken while drinking, was carried by mouth throughout his dominions.

Legend has it that yaqona was derived from the Fijian god Degei (whose name means 'from heaven to the soil and through the earth'), who asked his three sons where they wanted to live and what they wanted to do with their lives. They replied with where they wanted to dwell and what they thought their tasks should be. Degei was pleased but told his sons that although they had power and strength, they lacked the wisdom to make decisions. He gave them two sacred crops, yaqona and *vuga* (a type of tree) from which to draw wisdom. The sons in turn gave them to the people and to this day, goes the legend, the crops grow where the Fijian descendants live.

A nonalcoholic beverage, yaqona has varying effects on the individual, ranging from a fuzzy-headedness to mild euphoria. The drink always acts as a diuretic and has been used as such by pharmaceutical manufacturers.

Early explorers spoke in awe of yaqona's effects, but no-one knows for sure if their accounts were exaggerated or if the 'grog' was more potent in those days. One theory postulates that because the root was chewed (by young virgins) before mixing, the saliva somehow reacted with the active ingredients to intensify the effect. Another more plausible theory is that additives – possibly hallucinogenics such as 'angel's cap' and 'yaqoyaqona' *(Piper puberulem)* – were added to the mix. C F Gordon Cumming, a noted travel writer who lived in Fiji from 1875 to 1880, noted that:

Its action is peculiar, inasmuch as drunkenness from this cause does not affect the brain, but paralyses the muscles, so that a man lies helpless on the ground, perfectly aware of all that is going on. This is a condition not unknown to the British sailor in Fiji.

Even though the chemical make-up of yaqona is known, organic chemists haven't figured out the specific active ingredient(s). A pharmacologist from the University of the South Pacific, Yadu Singh, has made an extensive study of the drug and believes the kick comes from recently discovered compounds known as *alpha pyrones*. Said Singh:

Their nature is not like a stimulant such as cocaine, but cannot be described as a depressant either. Yaqona has a calming effect somewhere in between.

Although yaqona is used primarily as a social drink, local healers have cured ailments ranging from tooth decay and respiratory diseases to gonorrhoea with it. Excessive yaqona drinking causes a host of disorders including loss of appetite, bloodshot eyes, lethargy, restlessness, stomach pains and scaling of the skin. The latter condition, known as *kanikani* by Fijians, is fairly common among heavy drinkers who may consume up to half a dozen litres or more in the course of a day.

In villages the brew is generally consumed by men in a home or community bure, but occasionally women gather in the kitchen and drink among themselves. On other occasions an older woman may join the men and imbibe in an area that is usually all male. A woman visitor will generally be offered a bowl with no compunction; however, unless she is someone of rank, a man will be given the first opportunity to drink. In the cities where yaqona drinking is not so segregated according to sex, men and women can freely take a bowl together.

While some missionaries discouraged yaqona, which they referred to as a 'filthy preparation', some of the more enlightened students of culture saw its merits. Basil Thomson questioned the wisdom of the Wesleyan missionaries who denied Fijians their yaqona. He wrote:

The path of virtue for the native has been made dull enough already by the prohibition of all his ancient heathen distractions...

Thomson felt that, denied their grog, the Fijians would inevitably be swayed by the Catholic missionaries, whose policy was to make the lives of the Fijians 'as joyous as they dare'.

Thomson also recognised yaqona as a cure for the 'great temptation' that afflicted his fellow Englishmen in lonely tropical climes – alcoholism. Yaqona, he claimed, when substituted for spirits, satisfied the craving for liquor without producing intoxication. 'In this respect,' he wrote, 'it is a pity that yaqona cannot be acclimatised in Europe.'

Today, although yaqona is central to the Fijian culture, it is controversial in terms of how healthy it is for economic growth. Whereas in the old days grog was strictly used for ceremonial purposes by chiefs or priests, today it is drunk copiously in villages, often to the detriment of gardening, fishing or other 'productive activities'. Because of the negative side effects of this drinking, which certainly do not promote hard work, some Fijian officials have asked if excessive grog drinking is good for the country.

The kava plant, used to make yaqona, is cultivated like any other crop and is big business in Fiji. It thrives at altitudes of between 150 and 300 metres and grows to a height of 3½ metres at full maturity. Kava can be harvested after a year's growth, but the longer it grows the more potent the brew. Potency also varies with geographic location, subspecies and method of preparation. Generally the dried root is used in making grog, but on occasion the green root or stem is utilised. The retail market price is from US$9 to US$12 a kg and it can be purchased as a dried root or pre-ground. Both forms are suitable as gifts and should certainly be considered when visiting a village or a household.

No-one knows the origins of the plant but botanists believe it may have come from Java via India; from Java it was transplanted throughout the South Pacific during various migrations of islanders. Whatever the origins, kava is or has been used in the majority of the central and eastern Polynesian societies as well as in areas of Melanesia and Micronesia. Its use is documented as far north as Hawaii, as far south as Tonga, as far west as New Britain and as far east as the Gambier group.

In Fiji yaqona drinking was and is the social cement that bonds society. The importance of its use today can be illustrated by an incident at the University of the South Pacific campus in Suva.

During a weekend beer-drinking bout, the age-old rivalry between Tongans and Fijians surfaced and a Tongan and a Fijian got into a fist fight. The Fijian got the short end of it, and the next day the offending Tongan was severely thrashed by a group of Fijians. The other Tongans on campus took retribution and a vicious cycle was set in motion. Soon no Tongans were safe on the school grounds and all had to be moved to another location.

One day the authorities got wind that both sides were going to meet en masse and police were summoned to prevent any bloodshed. However, instead of tribal warfare, the police found Tongans and Fijians sitting peacefully next to a yaqona bowl, where they played guitar and sang into the wee hours of the night.

Both cultures so respected the 'peace pipe' represented by yaqona that the score was settled over a bowl of grog and a public confession by the protagonists. The war was over.

Avoiding Offence

To show up at a village uninvited and simply start wandering around is very rude – something akin to wandering around the suburbs of Los Angeles, entering strangers' backyards and perhaps peeping in their bedroom windows. It just isn't done.

What you also shouldn't do is take advantage of the Fijians' hospitality. I have nothing but contempt for travellers who stay with villagers and do not have the decency either to contribute food or to pay the villagers F\$5 per day for accommodation and at least F\$10 per day if they are being fed. I have received too many letters describing how some travellers have lived off Fijians without so much as offering to assist them. This type of behaviour is inexcusable, and unforgivable. People who carry on in this manner are anathema to the spirit of the road.

It's important to realise that the Fijians' culture dictates that they should always invite a stranger into their home, whether they can afford to feed that stranger or not. I know personally of a family who couldn't send their child to school for a term because they spent her tuition money taking care of an uninvited guest who stayed for a month.

Yaqona Ceremony Should you be fortunate enough to be invited into a village (a likely circumstance if you become friendly with the locals), there are certain rules of etiquette to be observed. Prior to the visit, if you have the opportunity, buy a kg of kava root (which can be purchased at any outdoor market or from local proprietors for F\$9 to F\$15 per kg) as a sevusevu – a traditional gift offered by guests. This will surely start you off on the right foot and show your hosts you care about their tradition. Your host will gladly accept the gift and may perform a welcoming ritual that in effect says your visit is officially recognised by the village. In the course of the ceremony you will be offered a *bilo* (coconut shell) full of yaqona, which of course you should accept and drink (in one big gulp rather than sips).

After the initial ceremony you may be asked to sit with the gang around the tanoa (yaqona bowl) and chat (talanoa). This is the best way to get to know Fijians. Drinking yaqona is a sacramental ritual with Fijians and cements friendships with strangers. After drinking a while, perhaps your host will offer you something to eat or show you around the village. Children will inevitably be curious about your presence and will surround you as though you are the Pied Piper, asking innumerable questions. They will probably ask you to take their photo.

Photography The visitor wishing to take photos of village life is free to do so, but is best accompanied by an adult or youngster from the community. Always ask permission when taking photos (which will almost always be granted), and as obvious as it sounds, never casually wander into someone's bure and start shooting. During the yaqona ceremony do not stand upright and indiscriminately take snapshots without having asked permission beforehand. This is a solemn occasion, not a press photo opportunity.

Dress Dress modestly when visiting a village. Men should not be bare-chested and women should wear slacks or a below-the-knee dress. Women should definitely not be in shorts or a bathing suit. Scanty clothing is disrespectful and might be construed as a moral reflection on the hosts. For women it would also send the wrong message to the village Lotharios. Another item to remember is that when entering a village, take off your hat.

Note: Given that visitors should respect Fijian sensibilities regarding the wearing of modest attire in villages, it's equally important never to swim or bathe in the nude at a beach or river that may be frequented by locals.

Staying in a Bure When invited inside a bure, remove your shoes, place them outside the doorstep, and stoop slightly when entering. Avoid standing fully upright inside – it's bad manners.

As your parents hopefully told you, good manners will get you everywhere. Fijians are perhaps the politest and in many ways the most civilised people on the planet. They display good manners, which should be reciprocated. They sense this respect and will go out of their way for a person they like.

If you are spending the night and are offered sleeping room in a bure, accept the accommodation rather than pitch a tent outside the home. Should you camp outside someone's home, the message advertised is that the host's house is an unpleasant place to sleep.

Try to avoid ostentatious displays of wealth. Remember that most villagers could never hope to own the kind of cameras, tape decks and other goods that we take for granted. Aside from bringing kava to a village it's not a bad idea to pick up groceries such as powdered milk, sugar, bread, tea, for your hosts. Chances are these staples will be appreciated as much or more than kava.

Sport
Like most South Pacific Islanders, Fijians are sports fanatics. Soccer and rugby contests between major clubs and overseas tournaments are listened to religiously. Fiji has facilities for golf, tennis, basketball, volleyball, track and field, swimming, soccer, cricket, boxing, lawn bowling and of course rugby, which is the closest thing to a national sport. Over the years Fijians, who have the build and stamina ideally suited for rugby, have excelled at the game, often winning in international competition.

Golf has been popular in Fiji for years with the British – many of the courses were actually laid out to meet the recreational needs of the old Colonial Sugar Refining Company. The finest course in the country is the facility at Pacific Harbour Resort, which was designed by Robert Trent Jones. The only other 18-hole course in Fiji is the Fiji Golf Club in Suva. There are also nine-hole courses at Nadi, Lautoka, the Fijian Resort Hotel, Naviti Beach Resort, Reef Hotel and Taveuni Estates on the island of Taveuni.

RELIGION
Fiji is a meeting ground of three of the world's great religions – Christianity, Hinduism and Islam – which are all practised here in tolerance of each other. Surveys indicate that almost all of Fiji's inhabitants belong to some type of organised religion. Church attendance is generally high and pastors and priests wield a great deal of power over their flock. Approximately 51% of the population are Christians, 40% Hindus and 8% Muslims. Of the Christians the majority, Fijians, are Methodists, followed by Roman Catholics, Seventh Day Adventists, members of the Assembly of God, Anglicans, Presbyterians, Mormons and other Christian groups.

Ancient Fijian Religion
The old Fijian religion contained a myriad of gods and spirits. Along with the same gods worshipped in different parts of the country, each clan might have its own deities. The core of the system was ancestor worship in

which people paid homage to their forebears, particularly the illustrious ones. Each clan had its own temples dedicated to one god or goddess – an ancestor with a specific role. Thus one ancestral spirit, perhaps descended from a great warrior, would be dedicated to warfare and cannibalism; others, perhaps descended from an agriculturalist, would be concerned with crop productivity; and others might be concerned with fishing or some other activity. Gods thus reflected the society they sprang from.

Deification of chiefs went on right into the last century. This was evidenced on the battlefield, when warriors were reluctant to kill chiefs because they were seen as demigods – people who stemmed from the gods and had the potential to become gods. When a chief fell in a battle, the ranks broke and the enemy was for all practical purposes vanquished. This aspect was not lost on unscrupulous chiefs who hired European mercenaries to shoot enemy chiefs on sight. Perhaps this explains why a small group of Europeans backed by a strong 'conventional' Fijian army could wreak havoc upon armies of thousands of Fijian warriors.

Christianity

Although the priesthood and many of the ruling elite were at first reluctant to accept Christianity, Fijians in general embraced the new religion once their leaders had done so. They saw that the Christian god was powerful: he could produce incredible things like guns, ships and other technology. He was certainly a god to be reckoned with, but by their thinking he was only one of many gods.

During the introduction of Christianity some Fijians were so impressed they built temples to the Christian god even before the missionaries attempted conversion. They saw little difference between the Christian god and their own deities except that the Christian god didn't like them to worship other gods.

In post-coup Fiji the Methodist church, which is as close to an 'official' religion as Fiji has, has gained considerably more influence. One reason is that the church has a

good friend in Sitiveni Rabuka, who is a fervent believer. The church is also very sympathetic to the nationalist leanings of the current government. Perhaps the most obvious influence of the Methodist church is its strict support of 'desecularising' Sunday – making it devoid of any commercial activities.

In Fiji there is a church or denomination for just about everyone (see the following list of Christian churches and services). Visitors are always welcome to a Fijian service, and participating in one – particularly in a village – is a wonderful Fijian experience.

Methodist
Suva
Centenary Church (10 am, 7 pm Fijian); Dudley Church (10 am Hindi, 5 pm English); Wesley Church (8, 9.30, 10.45 am, 7 pm English)
Sigatoka
Prem Methodist (10 am English); Olosara (7.30 pm at private home); Nasigatoka Village (10.30 am, 7.30 pm Fijian)
Korolevu
(10.30 am, 7.30 pm Fijian)
Nadi Airport
Bethany Church, Nakavu (10.30 am, 7.30 pm English)

Anglican
Suva
Suva Cathedral, Macarthur St (7.30 am Eucharist, 10 am sung Eucharist, 5 pm Evensong); St Matthew's, Samabula (8.30 am every Sunday except third Sunday of month, 5 pm) (☎ 25 316); St Luke's, Laucala Bay, (7.30 am Holy Communion, 7 pm Evensong)
Sigatoka
Church of the Good Shepherd (9 am Holy Communion)
Nadi Airport
St Christopher's Church, off London Ave (10 am Holy Communion)

Roman Catholic
Suva
Sacred Heart Cathedral, Pratt St (7, 8.30, 10 am, 7 pm English; 5 pm Fijian)
Nadi
St Mary's Martintar (7.30, 9.30 am English; 5.30 pm Fijian)

Bethany Assembly of God Church
Suva
    391 Grantham Rd, Samabula (10.45 am, 6.30pm)
Nadi
    AOG Balevu Fijian Branch, past Mocambo turn-
    off towards airport (11 am, 8 pm Fijian)

Evangelical Fellowship Church (Baptist)
Lautoka
    7 Wainunu St (10.30 am, 7.30 pm)
Nadi
    Northern Press Laundry Rd (10.30 am, 7.30 pm)

Church of Jesus Christ of Latter Day Saints
Suva
    29 Des Voeux Rd (9 am to noon, 2 to 5 pm Fijian);
    29 Helsen St, Samabula (9.30 am to 12.30 pm
    English)
Nadi
    Northern Press Rd (9.30 am to 12.30 pm)

Presbyterian
Suva
    St Andrew's Church, on the corner of Gordon and
    Goodenough Sts (10 am)

Indian Religion

Basically the same religions (with the exception of Buddhism) exist in Fiji as in India,
but several generations of separation from
India have made the Fijian Indian a bit less
orthodox in his or her practice. Less orthodox does not mean less religious; most
Hindu homes have shrines where the family
worships together. Although the caste
system essentially ended for the Indians who
arrived in Fiji, it still carries weight with
Hindus in the realm of religion. 'Pundits' or
priests who officiate at weddings and the like
must be of the Brahmin caste.

The Hindu Fijian Indians, who make up
about 80% of the Indian population, cele-
brate Diwali, Holi and the birth of Lord
Krishna. Diwali is the colourful 'Festival of
Lights', which occurs in October or November and resembles Christmas in the West.
Houses are decorated ornately to welcome
Lakshmi, the goddess of wealth and prosperity. Traditionally it is a time when businesses
end their fiscal year, paying up their accounts
and opening new books.

Holi, held in February or March, is a
spring festival. During this time *chautals*
(holy songs) are sung and people amuse
themselves by squirting coloured water at
each other in the streets.

Sikhism, an offshoot of Hinduism, is an
eclectic monotheistic religion. Sikhs have
their own temples *(gurdwaras)* where they
carry out prayer meetings and read their holy
book.

The Muslims, who make up about 15% of
the Indian population, worship in numerous
mosques throughout Fiji. The major holidays are the fasting period of Ramadan, the
two Eids and the Prophet Mohammed's
birthday.

Firewalking Firewalking in Fiji is also practised by Indians at an annual purification
ritual called Trenial. It is performed at the
Mariamman Temple in Suva and other locations in July or August. Hindu firewalking
differs from the Fijian custom (see the earlier
Culture section) in that the Indians walk
across a shallow trench of burning embers
whereas the Fijians stroll across a large pit of
hot stones. Trenial is accompanied by the
placing of *theresual* (three-pronged forks,
tridents) into cheeks, hands, ears, nose and
tongue prior to walking over the red-hot
coals.

During the 10-day period of preparation,
devotees must sleep on the hardwood floor
of the temple where the firewalking will
occur; eat two meals a day of bland food (not
the usual spicy Indian fare which is associated with lust and bodily satisfaction); bathe
in cold water twice a day; abstain from
alcohol, tobacco and sex; wear a minimum
amount of clothing; devote time to prayer,
confession and holy scriptures; and refrain
from ill-feelings towards each other. If that
isn't enough, the faithful must submit to the
disciplinary whip of the priest. Whippings
are held in the morning and evening, following prayer.

The idea of this self-denial is to make the
devotees forget their 'body consciousness'.
According to one religious authority, Pujari
Rattan Swami:

All of us are conscious of our body...We are not prepared to leave our self body consciousness, therefore whipping and self-control methods make the devotees at least temporarily semi-conscious.

The firewalkers go through a host of other activities, including soaking their clothing in turmeric water (which acts as a germicide and insect repellent to keep the mosquitoes away from their more exposed and therefore more vulnerable bodies) and smearing themselves with ash from burnt cow dung to illustrate that if one conquers one's weaknesses, one will become pure. In this same respect the devotees ritually crack open coconuts, meditating on the three layers (outside layer, fibrous layer and shell) which symbolise a person's three weaknesses – ego, ignorance and attachment. (The last is hardest to crack literally and figuratively.)

On the day of the event, a ritual bath is taken in a nearby river followed by chants and drum beating. The participants are whipped into a trance-like state and may pierce their tongues, cheeks and skin on the forehead with sharp needles. They walk back to the temple chanting 'Govinda', the name of God. Upon returning to the temple the chief priest works the firewalkers into another trance and leads them across the glowing embers, once more shouting 'Govinda'.

LANGUAGE

Fijian, Hindi and English are the three main languages. Urdu, Tamil and Chinese are also spoken, as well as other dialects derived from these languages.

FIJIAN

When the earliest inhabitants of Fiji arrived 3500 years ago, they brought with them the language of the homeland they had set sail from – an island in Vanuatu, or possibly the Solomons (but certainly not Africa!).

That language has changed and splintered over the years into a multitude of different 'communalects' now numbering more than 300. This is because language divides naturally as people spread out, and there may

have been some additional input from more recent immigrants from other islands lying to the west.

The Fijian 'communalects' belong to the enormous Austronesian language family, which means they are related to thousands of other languages spanning the globe from Malagasy in the west to Rapanui (Easter Island) in the east, from Aotearoa (New Zealand) in the south to Hawaii and Taiwan in the north. The family includes such important national languages as Tagalog (Philippines) and Malay. After Fiji had been settled, the flow of population continued north and east. The languages of Polynesia (such as Maori, Tahitian, Tongan, Samoan and Hawaiian), the language of the tiny island of Rotuma to the north of Fiji, and of course their speakers, all originated in Fiji more than 3000 years ago. These relationships can be clearly seen in the following table of selected words.

The early missionaries had a keen appreciation of the importance of using local language in their work, and by 1840 had already devised an excellent spelling system for Fijian as well as published a number of books in different 'communalects'. When the need for a standard language became apparent, they selected the language of Bau, the tiny island off the south-east coast of Viti Levu which was, and in some ways still is, the seat of the major power in Fijian politics. Nowadays the spoken Fijian of the towns and the Fijian used in books and newspapers are both known as 'Bauan', even though neither is quite the same as the language of the island of Bau.

While many of its Pacific relatives, such as Hawaiian and Maori, have been struggling for survival, Fijian has never been in serious danger of extinction, even though it was ignored for a long time in schools. The vast majority of Fijians have always used it as their everyday language, and most Indians understand at least some. In rural communities like Levuka, Taveuni and Savusavu, the Indians all speak Fijian fluently. In general, however, English is the lingua franca in Fiji.

Selected Words

	Indonesian Malay	Nggela Solomons	Standard Fijian	Rotuman	Tongan	Maori
ear	telinga	talinga	daliga	faliga	telinga	taringa
eye	mata	mata	mata	mafa	mata	mata
fish	ikan	iga	ika	i'a	ika	ika
two	dua	rua	rua	rua	rua	rua
six	enam	ono	ono	ono	ono	ono
liver	hati	ate	yate	afe	'ate	ate
skin	kulit	guli	kuli	'uli	kili	kiri

Since independence in 1970, Fijian has also been increasingly used on the radio, in books and newspapers, and in the schools. To ensure that future evolution of the language has a sound base, the government has set up a department to research and develop the Fijian language. The department's first major task is to compile a dictionary of Fijian for Fijians, with all definitions and other information in Fijian, which when completed will be the first of its kind in the Pacific.

Fijian Alphabet

Fijian spelling will come as a surprise to visitors because it uses some familiar letters in an unfamiliar way. Upon arriving in Fiji, you will soon realise that 'Nadi' is pronounced 'Nandi' (rhyming with candy). As linguist Albert Schutz in his very fine primer *Say It In Fijian* explains, the reason for this alphabet system was 'due neither to any perversity on the part of the first linguists, nor to chance'. Instead, David Cargill, the missionary who devised the alphabet especially for Fijian students learning to read, found that they considered it simple and satisfying.

The result of Cargill's work is a spelling system that is economical and, more importantly, regular. This second quality is extremely significant to the learner of Fijian because it means there is a good chance the student will pronounce the words correctly when he or she reads them. Contrast this system with the English language, which is riddled with exceptions.

Pronunciation

Consonants Most of the consonants other than b, d, q, g and c hold no surprises, but there are some differences from the way the English counterparts are usually pronounced. Like the combination 'dr', the letters b, d and q are pronounced with a nasal sound in front of them – like 'ndr'. 'R' is rolled or trilled, as in Spanish. 'Y' has not nearly as much glide quality to it as does the English 'y', as in 'yes'.

The consonant letters that seem unusual to English speakers are:

b as 'mb' in member
d as 'nd' in Monday
q as 'ng' plus 'g' in finger
g as 'ng' in singer
c as 'th' in father

Vowels The following is a guide to the pronunciation of vowels:

a as in father
e as in day, without glide at end
i as in see, without glide at end
o as in go, without glide at end
u as in zoo, without glide at end

Some Useful Words

yes
io
(ee-oh)

no
  sega
    (sayngah)
work
  cakacaka
    (thaka-thaka)
bad
  ca
    (tha)
beer
  bia
    (bee-a)
big, many
  levu
    (layvu)
bird
  manumanu vuka
    (mahnumahnu vukah)
boy, male
  tagane
    (tahng-ahnay)
cassava, tapioca
  tavioka
    (tav-i-oh-kah)
child
  gone
    (ngonay)
comb
  i-seru
    (ee-seru)
cup
  bilo
    (bee-low)
eat
  kana
    (kahna)
fish
  ika
    (ee-kah)
food
  kakana
    (kakahna)
girl, female
  yalewa
    (yah-lay-wah)
handsome, beautiful
  totoka
    (toe-toe-kah)

happy, satisfied
  marau
    (mah-rau)
house
  vale
    (va-lay)
kava
  yaqona
    (yang-go-nah)
kava bowl
  tanoa
    (tah-noah)
man
  tagane
    (tahng-ahnay)
man
  turaga
    (tu-rahng-ah)
matches
  masese
    (mah-say-say)
money
  ilavo
    (ee-lah-vo)
pot
  kuro
    (koo-row)
sleeping house
  bure
    (bur-ay)
small
  lailai
    (lie-lie)
smart
  matai
    (mah-tye)
stone
  vatu
    (vah-too)
stupid or crazy
  lialia
    (lee-ah lee-ah)
taro
  dalo
    (dahlo)
tobacco
  tavako
    (tah-vak-o)

today
nikua
(nickuah)
toilet
vale lailai
(vah-lay lie-lie)
tomorrow
ni mataka
(ni mahtahka)
tree
vu ni kau
(vu ni cow)
village
koro
(koro)
whale's tooth
tabua
(tam-boo-ah)
woman
marama
(mah-rah-mah)
yesterday
nanoa
(na-noa)

Some Useful Concepts

killing time, fooling around
moku siga
(moku singah)
wandering around
gade
(gan-day)
go slowly, take your time
vaka malua
(vaka-mahluah)
eat heartily
kana vaka levu
(kahna vaka layvu)
taboo, forbidden
tabu
(tamboo)
exclamation of regret
isa, isa lei
(ee-sah, ee-sah lay)
ashamed, shy
madua
(man-doo-ah)
go ahead and try
tovolea mada
(toe-vo-lay-ah mahndah)

a request
kerekere
(kerri-kerri)

Some Useful Phrases

Where are you going? (Interestingly enough there are no literal equivalents for 'How are you?' Instead, Fijians might ask a friend they see on the street this, which is as much a greeting as it is a question.)
O sa lako ki vei?
(o sa lahko kee vay)

Good day (a polite greeting and one of the first Fijian phrases you will hear).
Nibula.
(nimbula)

A less formal greeting (literally 'health' and 'life').
Bula.
(mbula)

Good morning.
Ni sa yadra.
(ni sah yandra)

Goodbye/Good night (literally, 'sleep').
Ni sa moce.
(ni sah mothay)

Come here.
Lako mai eke.
(lahko my kay)

Good/Thank you.
Vinaka.
(vinahka)

Thank you very much.
Vinaka vaka levu.
(vinahka vaka layvu)

Where do you come from?
O ni lako mai vei?
(o ni lahko my vay)

I come from New Zealand.
Au lako mai Niu Siladi.
(ow lahko my new silandi)

What's this?
A cava oqo?
(ah thava ongo)

It's a...
E dua na...
(ay do-ah nah...)

Phrasebooks
Those interested in further studies of Fijian will find Albert Schutz's *Say It In Fijian* (Pacific Publications, Sydney, 1979) an excellent introduction to the language. The book is available in Fiji. Likewise, Schutz's *Spoken Fijian* (University Press of Hawaii, Honolulu, 1979) is a good primer for more advanced studies. My experience in Fiji has been that even the most minimal attempt at learning a few words or phrases will be amply rewarded with kindness and a greater respect for the visitor.

FIJI HINDI
The language of the Fijian Indians is generally called Hindi or Hindustani, but it is quite different from the Hindi spoken in India. Fijian Indians call their language Fiji Bat (literally, 'Fiji Talk') or simply Fiji Hindi. This lingua franca of Fijian Indians is a hybrid of many Indian languages, dialects and borrowed words from Fijian and English. As Jeff Siegel, author of *Say It In Fiji Hindi* aptly puts it, 'Fiji Hindi reflects the diverse origins of the Fiji Indians as well as their unique new culture which has developed in Fiji'. Linguists and scholars may argue about the legitimacy of this dialect, but there is no doubt that it is a living language with its own special grammar and vocabulary suited for Fiji.

The history of the language mirrors the history of the Indian experience in Fiji. The Indians who settled here were a diverse group – Hindus, Sikhs, Muslims and Christians from numerous castes and subcastes. Some people came from the northern districts of India speaking Urdu or Hindustani and dialects such as Bhojpuri, Awadhi, Bagheli and Maithili. From the southern regions some spoke unrelated languages

from the Dravidian family such as Tamil, Telugu and Malayalam.

However, passage on the vessels to Fiji and later plantation life necessitated living at close quarters. This quickly resulted in the breakdown of caste taboos regarding food and work. The coming together of all the different Indian cultures also demanded a common language so that everyone could communicate. Thus Fiji Hindi was conceived. Siegel theorises that Fiji Hindi possibly evolved out of a 'Bazaar Hindustani' that already existed in India with many words and features of the various Indian languages. The influences of English and Fijian were later incorporated.

The vast majority of Fijian Indians speak Fiji Hindi, but some still speak a different language at home such as Gujarati, Tamil, Telugu or Punjabi. Some of these languages are taught in school, but mostly Indian Standard Hindi or Urdu are taught for use in connection with religion, literature or formal occasions. English is taught in all Fijian schools and is the lingua franca of the nation. The average Fijian Indian may thus speak Tamil at home, Fiji Hindi with the neighbours, the local Fijian dialect with the villagers, English at work and Standard Hindi at a religious gathering.

Scholar Richard Barz informs me that students of Fiji Hindi will be interested in knowing that the first play ever to be published in that language, *Adhura Sapna* (A Shattered Dream) by Raymond Pillai, is featured (along with an English translation) on pages 221-255 in *Language Transplanted: The Development of Overseas Hindi* (Otto Harrassowitz, Wiesbaden, 1988), edited by Richard Barz & Jeff Siegel.

Hindi – Hindustani – Urdu
It's all very confusing. Hindustani is the language used in parliamentary debate yet Hindi is designated as the official language of Fiji Indians. The Fiji broadcasting system uses Hindustani but newspapers are in Hindi. According to a government survey, nearly 90% of Fijian Indian households speak Hindustani, but Hindus learn Hindi in

school, while Muslims learn Urdu. How do we make sense out of this?

First of all, we must distinguish between spoken and written languages. Hindustani usually refers to the spoken language of northern India. It evolved from the classical Indian language of Sanskrit (which is studied much like Latin in the West) but utilises a lot of borrowed Persian words. A formal style of Hindustani is used on the radio. Fiji Hindi is a colloquial form of Indian Hindustani.

Formal Hindi is a literary form of Hindustani utilising Devanagari script (the same writing as Sanskrit), but replaces the borrowed Persian words with Sanskrit. Urdu is also a written or literary form of Hindustani using Arabic script and Persian as well as Arabic words rather than Sanskrit ones. There are also important religious distinctions between Hindi and Urdu. Urdu, used exclusively by Muslims, developed from the Persian court language spoken by India's Moghul conquerors who were Muslims. Hindi, of course, is used by Hindus.

The bottom line is that Hindi and Urdu are very different in their formal and written forms but are almost the same spoken language.

Greetings & Civilities

Only rarely will the visitor encounter a Fijian Indian who does not speak English. Just the same, Indians will appreciate the visitor who extends him or herself by learning a few commonly used expressions.

Many greetings are used but the most heard is 'Namaste', meaning both hello and goodbye. Another common greeting, corresponding to the English 'How are you?' is 'Kaise?' The answers might be:

I'm fine.
Thik hai.
(teak high)

Right/OK.
Rait.
(right)

Well/Good.
Accha.
(ach-cha)

Some Useful Phrases

What's your name? (formal)
Ap ke nam ka hai?
(app kay nam key-yah high)

What's your name? (familiar)
Tumar nam ka hai?
(too-mar nam key-ya high)

My name is...
Hamar nam...hai.
(hah mar nahm...high)

I didn't understand.
Ham nhii samjha.
(hahm anh-hee sahm-jah)

Please say it again.
Fir se bolna.
(fear say boll nah)

I don't know.
Pata nahi.
(patah na-hee)

What's happening?
Ka hue?
(key-yah who-way)

What happened?
Ka bhay?
(key-yah ba-hay)

I'm tired.
Ham thak gaya.
(hahm-tahk gah-hay)

I like...
...accha lange
(...ach-cha la-gay)

Eating Out

The food is very good.
Khana bahut accha hai.
(kana bahoot ach-cha high)

Just a little.
Thora thora.
(tora tora)

Enough!
Bas!
(bahs)

Finished.
Khalas.
(kalas)

My stomach is full.
Pet bhar gaya.
(pet bahar gah-yah)

I'm drunk.
Nasa ho gaya.
(nah-dah ho gah-yah)

Shopping
How much is it?
Kitna dam hai?
(kit-nah dahm high)

very expensive
bahut mahaga
(ba-hout mah-ha gah)

I can get it cheaper there.
Huwa sasta mili.
(who-wah sas-tah mill-li)

Knock down the price.
Dam thora kamti karo.
(dahm tora kam-ti car-ro)

Lower it more.
Aur kamti.
(our kam-ti)

Just looking.
Khali dekhta.
(kali deck-tah)

Phrasebooks
Visitors interested in Fiji Hindi would be
well advised to pick up a copy of *Say It in
Fiji Hindi* (Pacific Publications) which is
available in local bookshops.

Facts for the Visitor

VISAS

Visitors who do not need visas can get permits on arrival to stay for up to four months; these may be extended to up to six months. You must have a valid passport, an onward or return air ticket and adequate funds for your stay. To renew visas you must go directly to the immigration office in Suva – don't expect to accomplish this task over the phone from your hotel.

Visas are not required for citizens of Commonwealth countries, or for nationals of Austria, Belgium, Denmark, Finland, France, Greece, Iceland, Indonesia, the Republic of Ireland, Israel, Italy, Japan, Liechtenstein, Luxemburg, Nauru, the Netherlands, Norway, Philippines, South Korea, Spain, Sweden, Switzerland, Taiwan, Thailand, Turkey, Tunisia, the USA, Germany and Western Samoa.

Nationals or citizens of other countries require visas unless their stay in Fiji does no exceed three hours.

Passports and visas are not required by people who transit Fiji directly by the same ship or aircraft. (The term 'ship' does not include yacht.)

The conditions for a visitor's permit are (according to a government pamphlet):

...that while in Fiji he will not behave in a manner prejudicial to peace or good order, will not engage in any business, profession or employment whether for reward or not, except with the approval of the Permanent Secretary of Home Affairs, and will not engage in any religion, vocation, or research without the Permanent Secretary's approval. Permit may be subject to other conditions which the Permanent Secretary may impose.

Work Permits

Those wishing to reside and work in Fiji should be advised that work permits are nearly impossible to get. The only exceptions are for visitors with skills the government thinks are worth the permission to stay. The best procedure in this case is to apply in writing to the Permanent Secretary for Home Affairs, Government Buildings, Suva, prior to entering the country. In practice, it's usually only your employer who can obtain a work permit for you, after agreeing to hire you (assuming you have a locally-rare skill).

CUSTOMS

You may bring the following items into Fiji duty free: 200 cigarettes or 250 grams of tobacco; one litre of liquor or two litres of wine or two litres of beer; and other durable goods not exceeding F$30 per passenger.

Meat, dairy products, plants, seeds and flowers are prohibited from being brought in without necessary licences from the Ministry of Agriculture.

MONEY
Currency

The currency used in Fiji is the Fiji dollar (F$). Notes come in denominations of F$1, F$2, F$5, F$10, and F$20. Coins are in amounts of 1, 2, 5, 10, 20 and 50 cents. Despite Fiji's withdrawal from the Commonwealth, the Queen's countenance shines brightly from Fijian currency. Traditions die hard.

Always carry plenty of small change, especially small bills (which are called 'notes' here). It never ceases to amaze me how often taxis seem to be short of the proper change and expect you to make up the difference. The same scenario might occur when bargaining for an item at a craft market.

You will find that travellers' cheques are readily cashed in any Fiji bank and in most hotels and duty-free shops.

Avoid changing money on the black market. You may think you will get a better deal than from the banks, but you will inevitably get screwed.

Exchange Rates

US$	=	F$1.56
A$1	=	F$1.08
UK£1	=	F$2.44
C$1	=	F$1.23
NZ$1	=	F$0.81
1DM	=	F$0.98

Consumer Taxes

Though longtime visitors may feel reassured that the Queen's visage still graces Fiji currency, they may not be so happy to discover that there is now a 10% 'value added tax' (VAT) on all transactions associated with tourism. This includes car rentals, meals, rooms and other major (and minor) items. Visitors, however, should not feel persecuted. The new tariffs are also tacked onto goods and services that apply to locals.

Credit Cards

Major credit cards are accepted in Fiji at many shops, restaurants, car-rental agencies and most hotels. There are representatives in Fiji for three of the major credit cards:

Diners Club
6 Pratt St, Suva (☎ 300 552, 320 838)
MasterCard
LICI Building, Butt St, Suva (☎ 301 821)
American Express
ANZ House, 25 Victoria Parade, Suva
(☎ 302 333)

VISA cardholders can get cash advances from correspondent banks in Fiji – very handy for itinerant authors and travellers in general. The American Express office will quickly replace travellers' cheques or lost cards, but the Fiji representative doesn't seem to offer the other much-vaunted cardholder services.

Banks

Fiji has six banking groups, most of which have head offices in Suva and other branches around the country. They are: Australia & New Zealand Banking Group (ANZ), about 35 outlets; Bank of Baroda, 12 outlets; Westpac, 17 outlets; National Bank of Fiji (NBF), about 15 outlets; Bank of Habib, one outlet; and Merchant Bank of Fiji, three outlets. Banks open Monday to Thursday from 10 am to 3 pm; to 4 pm on Friday. Westpac has a 24-hour currency-exchange service at Nadi International Airport.

WHAT TO BRING

Dress in Fiji is usually casual and, because of the warm climate, it's easy to subscribe to the adage 'travel light'. Unless you plan to travel in the high mountains, you can be certain it will always be warm, even at night. So clothing should be light. Bathing suit and shorts (for men and women) are practical and always fashionable around resorts, but scanty clothing should never be worn outside these areas, especially in or near a Fijian village. Cotton shirts and dresses are also necessary, as are sandals, a waterproof jacket or coat for the odd tropical downpour, a light sweater, a hat to shield you from the intense rays, sun block, sunglasses, insect repellent and perhaps small souvenirs or toys for Fijian children. Guitar strings and T-shirts make fine gifts for villagers, as do framed photos to thank a family after you return home for hospitality extended.

TOURIST OFFICES

The main information office for the Fiji Visitors' Bureau (also known as the FVB) is in a quaint colonial-style building (formerly the customs house) in central Suva. There is a large desk occupied by helpful, patient Fijians with maps and brochures.

Local Tourist Offices

Suva
Scott St, GPO Box 92 (☎ 302 433)
Nadi
PO Box 9217, Nadi Airport (☎ 722 433, 723 064)

Overseas Reps

Australia
38 Martin Place, Sydney, New South Wales 2000
(☎ 231 4251)
Japan
Embassy of Fiji, 10th Floor Noa Building, 3-5, 2-chome, Azabudai, Minato-ku, Tokyo (☎ 03 587 2038)

New Zealand
    Room 605, Tower Block, Canterbury Arcade, 47 High St, Auckland; PO Box 1179 (☎ 732 133/4)
UK
    Marketing Services (T&T) Ltd, 52-54 High Holborn, London WC1V 6RL (☎ 071 242 3131)
USA
    Fiji Visitors' Bureau, 5777 West Century Blvd Suite 220, Los Angeles, California 90045
    (☎ 1 800 YEA FIJI)
Canada
    1275 W 6th Ave, Vancouver, BC V6H 1AG (☎ 604 731 3454; fax 604 736 1760)

BUSINESS HOURS & HOLIDAYS

Government and business offices are open five days a week. The usual hours are from 8 am to 4.30 pm (4 pm on Fridays), with at least an hour for lunch between 1 and 2 pm. Most shops and commercial outlets (including the public markets) are open five days a week and Saturday mornings which is traditionally the biggest shopping day of the week. After 10 pm virtually all restaurants begin closing down, even in Suva, so eat early. For those craving food in the wee hours there are a few takeaways open but these are not easy to find. If you really are starving its best to ask the taxi driver where to go – they know these things.

Almost no shops are open on Sundays (and holidays). However, Sunday morning service stations are often open and sometimes sell cigarettes and other 'essentials'. Bakeries may be open at certain hours on Sundays and in major towns a chemist shop is also open. In Suva, the Le Pain de Mie bakery is always open, and sells milk and newspapers along with wonderful baked goods. Licensed restaurants are open from noon until 2 pm and from 7 to 10 pm.

'Fiji time' does not necessarily coincide with the split-second punctuality you may be used to back home. Social and even business appointments tend to be later than scheduled, so if someone is late in appearing, don't fret. Late arrivals and even no-shows are endemic to this part of the world. This can be very frustrating to the uninitiated, but there is nothing that can be done except to adopt the same behaviour.

As a footnote to this latest edition regarding the vagaries of 'Fiji time', my associate Tom Cook tells me that times are really changing. Some businesses and government offices in Fiji are actually beginning to expect 'Western' punctuality.

Before listing the various public holidays, it should be mentioned that since the change in government, activities on Sundays have been curtailed. The 'desecularisation' of Sundays is probably the most visible change from the old Fiji to the post-coup era. Once the clock strikes midnight on Saturday, most commercial activities are forbidden by law for 24 hours. This means most restaurants, shops or pharmacies are closed. There is, however, public transport and taxi services. Whereas immediately after the coup all Sunday activities (except going to church) were forbidden, Fijians now are permitted to visit the beach, or play golf, tennis or any other similar recreational activity – though organised team sports are still forbidden (paradoxically, however, they can be watched on television without restriction). Resorts seem to be relatively immune to the 'Sunday bans,' so they could be a good place to be on Sundays if you must optimise your time in Fiji.

Sunday restrictions on public transport and the sale of goods may be more stringent in rural areas. Check with the locals for details.

Public holidays in Fiji include:

January
    New Year's Day
March/April
    Easter (Friday, Saturday, Sunday, Monday, Tuesday)
April
    Auckland to Suva Yacht Race
June
    Queen's Birthday
June
    Ratu Sukuna Day
July
    Constitution Day
August/September
    Hibiscus Festival – Suva
September
    Sugar Festival – Lautoka
October
    Fiji Day

Top Left: Suva Market, Viti Levu (RK)
Top Right: Mending nets, Vanua Levu (IO)
Bottom: Spear fishing off Seashell Cove, Viti Levu (IO)

Top: Sigatoka Valley, the 'salad bowl' of Fiji, Viti Levu (RK)
Left: Wild-pig hunter, Nausori Highlands, Viti Levu (RK)
Right: Fijian woman (RK)

October/November
   Diwali (Indian Festival of Lights)
November
   Prince Charles' Birthday
November/December
   Prophet Mohammed's Birthday
December
   Christmas & Boxing Day

POST & TELECOMMUNICATIONS
Post
Fiji's postal system is generally efficient. Because of numerous international flights to and from Australia and North America, delivery time to destinations outside the country is usually no longer than a week.

Those wishing to receive mail at the post office may do so at the general delivery window. American Express clients can pick up mail from the American Express representative, 4th Floor, ANZ House, 25 Victoria Parade, Suva.

Telegrams and phone calls can also be made from any post office.

Telephone
Telephone services in Fiji have improved since the telephone company's recent privatisation, and the phone system now gets a pass grade. In the last few years, services have been overhauled and most of the outer islands can now be dialled direct from overseas. Just a few years ago one had to go through the Suva operator.

Although public telephones for local calls are available in post offices, the main problem seems to be a lack of functioning public phones. In an emergency a shopkeeper or neighbour will always oblige. The cost for a local call is about 20 cents.

The long-distance service is quite adequate: Fiji is linked with every country in the world via satellite. Calls can be placed at post offices or from any hotel. To make a long-distance call or send a telegram in Suva, the best idea is to visit the modern Fiji International Telecommunications (FINTEL) office on Victoria Parade, near the public library.

TIME
Fiji skirts the International Date Line (180th

meridian), so arrivals from the west coast of the USA will find upon landing that they have lost a day: Sunday becomes Monday, Tuesday becomes Wednesday – you get the idea. When you go in the opposite direction a day is gained.

Fiji is two hours ahead of Australian Eastern Standard Time, 12 hours ahead of GMT and 20 hours ahead of US Pacific Standard Time – so when it is noon Monday in Fiji, it is 10 am Monday in Sydney, midnight Sunday in London and 4 pm Sunday in Los Angeles. Once in Fiji you realise it doesn't matter what the clock hands or digital read-outs say. Fijians have a time standard of their own, regulated by 'Fiji time' – which is usually slower than the time you're used to.

ELECTRICITY
Throughout Fiji the current is 240 V, 50 cycles AC. Most hotels have 110-V converters for razors. Outlets are in the Australian/ New Zealand mode – a three-pronged configuration. Adapters are available in the numerous duty-free shops and in electrical supply stores around the country.

BOOKS & MAPS
Travel Guides
There are comparatively few books (guides or otherwise) written about Fiji, especially when you compare what is available on Hawaii or other South Pacific destinations. Some of the more popular books are listed here.

How to Get Lost & Found in Fiji (Waikiki Publishing, Honolulu, 1978), by John McDermott, was the only guide to Fiji available in North America for years. It's the best of McDermott's Lost & Found series, although now a bit dated. The book contains a lot of useful nuts-and-bolts-type information and good observations on the character of the people, but you have to wade through a lot of verbiage and chitchat.

Fiji Islands Handbook (Moon Publications, 1990), by David Stanley, is solidly aimed towards the low-budget visitor, and offers detailed information and good maps.

Fiji Handbook & Travel Guide (Pacific Publications, Sydney, 1980), edited by John Carter, is the ultimate book of facts about Fiji, covering everything from banking to weather. It reads like an encyclopaedia rather than a guidebook, and is therefore dull but still full of useful data. It could also do with an update.

Suva – A History & Guide (Pacific Publications, Sydney, 1978), by Albert Schutz, is a very fine booklet (52 pages long), painstakingly researched and well written. Schutz, who is a professor of Polynesian languages at the University of Hawaii, details virtually everything you ever wanted to know about Suva and its environs, including the people behind the street names and the history of every neighbourhood. Although more a historical work than a guidebook, it is a must for the serious Fijiphile.

The Fiji Explorer's Handbook (Graphics Pacific, Suva, 1985), by Kim Gravelle, is a very fine road guide covering Viti Levu and Ovalau. This is the book to get for the serious driver – it has good maps.

History
Where the Waves Fall (George Allen & Unwin, Sydney, 1984), by K R Howe, is subtitled 'a new South Seas history from first settlement to colonial rule' and is thus not strictly a work about Fiji. Howe's perspective is 'new' in that he brings the islanders themselves into the centre of the picture and interprets how their lives were affected by the intrusion of the Europeans rather than how the islanders affected imperialistic concerns. It is a scholarly but very readable tome and one of the best books available on the exploration and settlement of Fiji and its South Pacific neighbours.

Howe goes all the way back to the actual settlement of the Pacific by the Polynesians and Melanesians and utilises the latest historical and archaeological information. In areas where historians differ in opinion – for example the method by which early Polynesians discovered the islands – the author explores the varying theories so that all points of view are touched upon.

Fiji – A Short History (George Allen & Unwin, Sydney, 1984), by Deryk Scarr, is a very thorough work by a leading Fiji historian. Unfortunately, the writing style is heavy-handed and almost unreadable.

Fiji Times – A History of Fiji (The Fiji Times & Herald, Suva, 1979), by Kim Gravelle, is a collection of 50 stories originally published in a newspaper series by the *Fiji Times*, Fiji's oldest publication. It is probably the most entertaining historical account available, but its newspaper-like format spotlights only particular areas and thus is limited. It is available only in Fiji.

A History of Fiji (Government Press, Suva, 1946), by R A Derrick, is a seminal work on Fijian history written by an educator who was considered an all-time authority on the subject.

Gold Braid & Foreign Relations (Naval Institute Press, Annapolis, Maryland, 1988), by David F Long, has only a few pages dedicated to Fiji, but is a thorough work which sheds light on the diplomatic activities of US naval officers from 1798 to 1883 in the Pacific and throughout the world. It is considered the definitive reference work on US naval diplomatic history.

Matanitu (University of the South Pacific, Suva, 1985) by David Routledge is, according to the experts, one of the very best books to date on Fiji's history. It is an extremely comprehensive book, concentrating chiefly on the years up to cession. The title translates as 'Confederation of States', a term that incorporates both the old and new systems of government. The book is very readable, but available only in Fiji.

Sir Philip Snow, who now resides in Britain, was a highly respected civil servant in Fiji's colonial government from 1938 to 1952. A fluent speaker of Fijian and Fiji Hindi, he has an intimate knowledge of Fiji as well as other islands of the Pacific and has written a number of books.

The People From the Horizon, An Illustrated History of the Europeans Among the South Seas Islanders (Phaidon, Oxford & McLaren, London, 1979, 1986), by Philip Snow & Stefanie Waine, details the exploration, settlement and development by Europeans in the Pacific. It also discusses the problems that arose regarding the contact between the indigenous and foreign cultures. Fiji features prominently in this book written by Sir Philip and his daughter.

Bibliography of Fiji, Tonga & Rotuma (Australian National University, Canberra, 1969; Miami University Press, Coral Gables, 1969), by Philip Snow, is a large volume containing over 10,000 entries. Sir Philip is currently working on a second volume of the bibliography and his memoirs.

Best Stories of the South Seas (Faber, London, 1967) and *Stranger & Brother: A Portrait of Lord Snow* (MacMillan, London, 1982; Scribner, New York, 1983) are more titles by Philip Snow.

People & Society

On Fiji Islands (Penguin Books, 1987), by Ronald Wright, captures the spirit of Fiji in a way I've not encountered in any other book. Mr Wright, a polished writer with a background in anthropology, does not miss a nuance. His book is a distillation of a sojourn to Fiji which took in everything from the cane fields to the cocktail bars. His real gift is providing insight by weaving a modern chronicle of Fiji in with its history and culture. Wright's anecdotes, which recreate conversations with Fijians of every stripe, are true to life and often very amusing. If you were to purchase one book as a supplement to this guide, I would recommend this one.

Tin Roofs & Palm Trees – A Report on the New South Seas (University of Washington Press, Seattle, 1977) by Robert Trumbull, is a serious socioeconomic/historical overview of the South Pacific nations with a particular emphasis on their emergence into the 20th century. Trumbull, a former *New York Times* correspondent, has distilled a great deal of useful background information into his Fiji chapter.

Under the Ivi Tree (University of California Press, Berkeley & Los Angeles, 1964; Routledge & Kegan Paul, London, 1964), by Cyril S Belshaw, is an exhaustive socioeconomic study of the Fijian people drawn from the author's obviously considerable personal experience in the islands.

Although put together in the late '50s and early '60s, this look at the interplay of individuals and the society that surrounds them is still right on target in discussing the limitations of economic growth faced in Fiji, particularly with regards to the indigenous population. Belshaw, a former colonial administrator and professor of anthropology at the University of British Columbia, demonstrates great sensitivity for the Fijian people and their culture. Though much of the book deals with economic models and village structure, there are many very practical gems of insight for the average reader if you are willing to wade through the verbiage. The book is highly recommended for the serious student of Fiji.

Flora & Fauna

Birds of the Fiji Bush (Fiji Museum, Suva, 1984), by Fergus Clunie, describes birds of Fiji with illustrations by Pauline Morse. It's the best book on the subject. Alas, a planned companion volume on birds of the coast and sea was never completed.

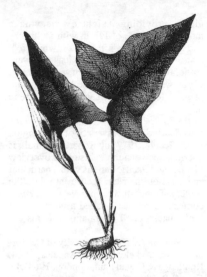

Fiji's Natural Heritage (Southwestern Publishing Co, Auckland, 1988), by Paddy Ryan, is quite readable, authoritative and interesting. It's the only book available on the subject of Fiji's non-avian fauna.

Mai Veikau: Tales of Fijian Wildlife (Dick Watling, 1986), by Dick Watling, is a book of essays on Fiji's fauna. Though an excellent resource, it is poorly produced.

Fiji Literati

Alas, this is virtually a barren section. A number of great writers did drop in, namely Rupert Brooke, Jack London, Mark Twain, Rudyard Kipling and Somerset Maugham, but none of their visits resulted in exceptionally good literature. The 'great Fiji novel' remains to be written. Kipling did write a short poem about the old capital of Levuka and Twain did comment on his short stay in Fiji in *Following the Equator* in 1897, but these are miniscule compared to the volumes of literature set in other parts of the Pacific. London wrote a short story called 'The Whale Tooth' which appeared in his *South Sea Tales* and was probably based on the killing of Reverend Baker, but it is not one of his best. Perhaps the best book yet written

about Fiji by a major author is Leonard Wibberly's contemporary account *Fiji: Islands of the Dawn* (Ives Washburn, New York, 1964). Although out of print, it is worth looking for. The book is a wonderfully written account of one man's experiences in Fiji within a historical context. That is, the author alternates between chapters dealing with his own encounters and an entertaining history of Fiji. Wibberly, author of *The Mouse that Roared* and other books, has keen powers of observation and a wit to match. Unfortunately, he seems to be the only writer of stature in modern times to have drifted into Fiji and left us with something in print. The dearth of literature on Fiji makes his book all the more important.

If you are a Michener fan, he wrote an essay on Fijian-Indian relations called 'Fiji' which was at best a subjective if not vituperative blast at Indians. Likewise, his short story 'The Mynah Birds' portrayed Indians in an ugly and racist manner. Both pieces appeared in Michener's *Return to Paradise*. To his credit Michener apologised about his untoward remarks years after the publication of the book.

Bookshops & Libraries

There are quite a few bookshops in Fiji, but selection is generally poor and prices range from high to astronomical.

Desai Bookshops have two locations in Suva: on the corner of Pier and Thomson Sts, and Dominion House on Thomson St. Other booksellers in Suva are the Suva Book Shop on Greig St, which has interesting children's and health-food sections; Xenon Ltd in Vanua House on Victoria Parade; Wheeler's (Tapa) Bookclub of Fiji, Carnarvon St, which specialises in children's books; City Bookshop, 15 Nina St; Coconut Frond, 8 Disraeli Rd, which is a book exchange; Lotu Pasifika Productions (publishing arm of the Pacific Conference of Churches) at 7 Thurston St, which sells its own publications on Fiji and other Pacific island topics; Kevat's Book Centre at 97 Cumming St; Morris Hedstrom department store on Thomson St (specialising in romance novels and cookbooks); and Methodist Book Shop, Epworth House on the corner of Stewart and Thomson Sts, which specialises, of course, in Methodist books.

Other towns around the country have branches of some of these same bookshops or independent shops. Titles tend to be identical regardless of which shop you enter (except for the speciality sections).

The Pacific Conference of Churches, at 4 Thurston St in Suva (near the Fiji Broadcasting Commission offices), also has a library-cum-bookstore with a good selection of reference books about Fiji and the South Pacific.

For avid readers staying any length of time, the best bet is to obtain a library membership at the Suva Public Library or better yet, enquire about using the University of the South Pacific Library, which has an excellent Pacific collection and the best general collection of books in the South Pacific. The opening hours are from 8 am to 4.30 pm at the university. Better yet, bring your own books. If you leave them behind when you depart, be assured that they will be read and passed around many hands until they fall apart or get eaten by cockroaches.

MEDIA
Newspapers & Magazines
Fiji is served by two daily English-language newspapers – the *Fiji Times*, founded in 1869, and the *Daily Post*, just a few years old. The *Fiji Times* group also publishes a weekly Fijian paper, *Nai Lalakai*; and *Shanti Dut*, a weekly Hindustani publication. The *Fiji Times* is the more conservative of the two, usually echoing government opinion, while the *Daily Post* is often the rebel voice (but less cautious with verification of facts). It is a widespread feeling that truth frequently lies somewhere between the two.

If you require a major overseas newspaper, the Suva Travelodge sells the *Sydney Morning Herald* only a few days late, and very expensive.

A bimonthly publication *Fiji Magic* is free of charge in many hotels, shops and travel agencies. It is commercial in nature, but includes quite a bit of valuable information for the traveller, including events, tours, accommodation, restaurants, cruises, shopping guides and miscellaneous information. *Fiji Magic* is published by George Rubine Ltd.

Another publication to come out of Fiji is *Islands Business News*, a monthly South Pacific-oriented news and business journal. This magazine would be of interest to business people as well as visitors who wish to understand what's going in this region.

Other magazines such as *Pacific Islands Monthly (PIM)* and *Pacific* are also available. *PIM*, published in Sydney, is an excellent regional publication and a venerable institution in the Pacific, oriented mostly toward the old British colonies. *Pacific*, (formerly *New Pacific*), published in Honolulu, is a younger upstart that also covers the Pacific basin, but has better reportage of former US trust territories and current dependencies than its rival. The old stand-by, the Pacific edition of *Time*, is sold here, as is a hybrid which combines *Newsweek* and Australia's *Bulletin*.

Radio
The government-owned Fiji Broadcasting Commission (FBC) operates three national networks of AM transmitters: Radio Fiji 1 (which broadcasts in Fijian), Radio Fiji 2 (in Hindi), and Radio Fiji 3 (in English). Radio Fiji 3 also broadcasts on FM. Programming includes US, Fijian and Indian pop music, sports, locally produced news, international news from the Australian Broadcasting Corporation (ABC), Voice of America and the BBC, British soap operas and panel shows, as well as locally produced educational and quiz shows.

In 1985 a privately owned radio station, FM 96, opened up the airwaves for the first time to a non-government enterprise. FM 96, which broadcasts in the Suva and Nadi areas, is modelled after a US or Australian pop music station. It provides entertaining listening, playing a variety of rock, R&B and, occasionally, Fijian or Indian tunes. It also broadcasts sports, news and the occasional interview.

TV

In late 1991, the government allowed an experimental TV broadcast of a sports event. It proved so overwhelmingly popular that 'temporary' was extended until regulations and a permanent operation – Fiji One – could be established. At the time of this writing, the project is in infancy and will probably undergo numerous changes.

For the past few years the nation has been swept by a video craze. On practically every corner there is a video-tape rental shop and nowadays it is a common sight to see Fijians of all ages huddled before a colour TV, watching a C-grade Hollywood movie or a pirated television show from the USA or Australia, often an umpteenth-generation copy which is virtually unwatchable by my standards. In general, Fijians seem to be winding up with the poorest, most socially unredeeming videos that Hollywood has to offer. Hopefully, the government's new TV project will continue to bring quality television to the people of urban Fiji, who have eagerly seized the opportunity to become TV junkies.

FILM & PHOTOGRAPHY

No self-respecting traveller or journalist comes to Fiji without a camera. Should you need them, film and photographic accessories are readily available in Suva and, thanks to duty-free prices, are probably the most inexpensive in the South Pacific.

There are several labs where a same-day service is available for colour prints – Caines Photofast Services, on the corner of Victoria Parade and Pratt St; Fiji Color Lab at 40 Cumming St; and Brijlal's Photo Service at Vanua House, Victoria Parade. Expect to pay about F$25 to develop and print a roll of film with 36 exposures. Film is about F$10 to F$12 per roll of 36.

Keep in mind that daylight is much more intense in the tropics, so if in doubt when shooting film, underexpose. That is, if you really want that photo, shoot according to what your normal meter reading dictates and then shoot one third to one full stop under. For best light conditions it's also a good idea

to take photos at dawn or dusk – the midday sun is usually too harsh.

Always keep film dry and cool, and upon your return have your camera cleaned if exposed excessively to the elements – the humidity and salt air can ruin sensitive photo equipment in no time. If your travel plans are likely to take you through customs at airports frequently, it's advisable to buy a laminated lead pouch for film, available in any photo shop. If you're planning an extended visit, be aware that a vicious tropical fungus grows on the coatings of lenses, ruining them. This will not be a problem if your stay is only a few weeks; but for longer visits, protect expensive lenses (including binoculars etc) with silica gel (available from chemist) in an airtight container. The fungus will not continue to grow after you return home to a temperate climate.

When taking photos of locals, smile and ask permission first. People will be happy to let you photograph them 99% of the time, but on other (rare) occasions some folks may not want to be part of your future slide show. (See Photography under Avoiding Offence in the Facts about the Country chapter.)

HEALTH

Travel health depends on your predeparture preparations, your day-to-day health care while travelling and how you handle any medical problem or emergency that does develop. For those who have never been in the South Seas, the extreme changes in humidity, the heat, torrential rains, food, mosquitoes and other conditions may tax the system. The best advice is to take it easy for the first few days until you are acclimatised.

While the list of potential dangers can seem quite frightening, with a little luck, some basic precautions and adequate information few travellers experience more than upset stomachs.

Travel Health Guides

There are a number of books on travel health:

Staying Healthy in Asia, Africa & Latin America
(Volunteers in Asia, Stanford California, 1988),

by Dirk G Schroeder, is probably the best all-round guide to carry as it's compact but very detailed and well organised.

Travellers' Health (Oxford University Press, Oxford, 1986), by Dr Richard Dawood, is comprehensive, easy to read, authoritative and also highly recommended although it's rather large to lug around.

Where There is No Doctor (Hesperian Foundation, Palo Alto, California, 1977), by David Werner, is a very detailed guide intended for someone wanting to work in an undeveloped country (eg a Peace Corps volunteer), rather than for the average traveller.

Travel with Children (Lonely Planet Publications, Hawthorn, 1990), by Maureen Wheeler, has basic advice on travel health for younger children.

Predeparture Preparations

Health Insurance A travel insurance policy to cover theft, loss and medical problems is a wise idea. There are a wide variety of policies and your travel agent will have recommendations. The policies handled by STA or other student travel organisations are usually good value. Some policies offer lower and higher medical expenses options but the higher one is chiefly for countries like the USA with extremely high medical costs. Check the small print:

1. Some policies specifically exclude 'dangerous activities' which can include scuba diving, motorcycling, even trekking. If these activities are on your agenda you don't want that sort of policy.
2. You may prefer a policy which pays doctors or hospitals direct rather than you having to pay now and claim later. If you have to claim later make sure you keep all documentation. Some policies ask you to call back (reverse charges) to a centre in your home country where an immediate assessment of your problem is made.
3. Check if the policy covers ambulances or an emergency flight home. If you have to stretch out you will need a second seat and somebody has to pay for it!

Medical Kit A small, straightforward medical kit is a wise thing to carry. In many countries if a medicine is available at all it will generally be available over the counter and the price will be much cheaper than in the West. If you forget to take anything, there are plenty of pharmacies in Fiji which stock all the medicines and accessories you are likely to need.

A possible medical kit could include the following:

1. Aspirin or panadol — for pain or fever
2. Antihistamine (such as Benadryl) – useful as a decongestant for colds, allergies, to ease the itch from insect bites or stings or to help prevent motion sickness
3. Antibiotics – are useful if you're travelling well off the beaten track, but they must be prescribed and you should carry the prescription with you. Ideally antibiotics should be administered only under medical supervision and should never be taken indiscriminately. Overuse of antibiotics can weaken your body's ability to deal with infections naturally and can reduce the drug's efficacy on a future occasion. Take only the recommended dose at the prescribed intervals and continue using the antibiotic for the prescribed period, even if the illness seems to be cured earlier. Antibiotics are quite specific to the infections they treat, so stop taking them immediately if there are any serious reactions and don't use them at all if you are unsure if you have the correct one.
4. Kaolin preparation (Pepto-Bismol), Imodium or Lomotil – for stomach upsets
5. Rehydration mixture – for treatment of severe diarrhoea, this is particularly important if you're travelling with children
6. Antiseptic, mercurochrome and antibiotic powder or similar 'dry' spray – for cuts and grazes
7. Calamine lotion – to ease irritation from bites or stings
8. Bandages and Band-aids – for minor injuries
9. Scissors, tweezers and a thermometer – note that mercury thermometers are prohibited by airlines
10. Insect repellent, sun block, suntan lotion, chapstick and water purification tablets

Your Health Make sure you're healthy before you start travelling. If you are embarking on a long trip make sure your teeth are OK, there are lots of places where a visit to the dentist would be the last thing you'd want to do.

If you're shortsighted bring a spare pair of glasses and your prescription. Losing your glasses or contact lenses can be a real problem although in many places you can get new spectacles made up quickly, cheaply and competently.

If you require a particular medication take an adequate supply as it may not be available locally. Take the prescription, with the generic rather than the brand name which may not be locally available, as it will make getting replacements easier. It's a wise idea to have the prescription with you to show you legally use the medication, it's surprising how often over-the-counter drugs from one place are illegal without a prescription or even banned in another.

Note that Fiji is malaria-free, but if you plan to visit a malaria-infected area before or after Fiji, make sure you seek advice from your doctor about malarial prophylactics.

Immunisation These days vaccination as an entry requirement is usually only enforced when you are coming from an infected area – yellow fever and cholera are the two most likely requirements. Nevertheless, all vaccinations should be recorded on an International Health Certificate which is available from your physician or health department.

Plan ahead for getting your vaccinations since some of them require an initial shot followed by a booster while some vaccinations should not be given together. Most travellers from Western countries will have been immunised against various diseases during childhood, but your doctor may still recommend booster shots against measles or polio, diseases still prevalent in many developing countries. The period of protection offered by vaccinations differs widely and some are contraindicated if you are pregnant.

In some countries immunisations are available from airport or government health centres. Travel agencies or airline offices will tell you where. The possible list of vaccinations includes:

Cholera Fiji requires cholera vaccination if you are coming from an infected area. However, protection from the vaccination is not very effective, only lasts six months and is contraindicated for pregnancy.
Tetanus & Diptheria Boosters are necessary every 10 years and protection is highly recommended.
Typhoid Protection lasts for three years and is useful if you are travelling for long in rural, tropical areas. You may get some side effects such as pain at the injection site, fever, headache and a general unwell feeling.
Infectious Hepatitis Gamma globulin is not a vaccination, but a ready-made antibody which has proven very successful in reducing the chances of hepatitis infection. Because it may interfere with the development of immunity, it should not be given until at least 10 days after administration of the last vaccine needed and as close as possible to departure because of its relatively short-lived protection period of six months.
Yellow Fever Fiji requires vaccination only if you are coming from an infected area – chiefly Africa and Latin America. Protection lasts 10 years. Vaccination is contraindicated in pregnancy, but if you are going to a high-risk area it is probably advisable.

Basic Rules

Care in what you eat and drink is the most important health rule; stomach upsets are the most likely travel-health problem, but the majority of these upsets will be relatively minor. Don't become paranoid, trying the local food is part of the experience of travel after all.

In Fiji the most basic rule of thumb is be very careful about drinking water in villages. If in doubt, boil it or treat it with water-purification tablets. Water is safe and plentiful in most other areas, but for the skittish there is always Coca Cola or Fiji Bitter beer.

Salads and fruit should be washed with purified water or peeled where possible. Thoroughly cooked food is safest, but not if it has been left to cool or if it has been reheated. Take great care with shellfish or fish and avoid undercooked meat. If a place looks clean and well run and the vendor also looks clean and healthy then the food is probably safe. In general, places that are packed with travellers or locals will be fine, empty restaurants are questionable.

In hot climates make sure you drink enough, don't rely on feeling thirsty to indicate when you should drink. Not needing to urinate or very dark yellow urine is a danger sign. Always carry a water bottle with you on long trips. Excessive sweating can lead to loss of salt and therefore muscle cramping.

Readers should note, however, that in Fiji (and most of the Pacific island nations), there's no need to consider adding salt to your food, as there is enough salt in the local diet.

Many health problems can be avoided by taking care of yourself. Wash your hands frequently, it's quite easy to contaminate your own food. Clean your teeth with purified water rather than straight from the tap. Avoid climatic extremes, keep out of the sun when it's hot, dress warmly if it's cold. Avoid potential diseases by dressing sensibly. You can get worm infections through bare feet or dangerous coral cuts by walking over coral without shoes. You can avoid insect bites by covering bare skin when insects are around, by screening windows or beds or by using insect repellents. Seek local advice, if you're told the water is unsafe due to jellyfish, crocodiles or bilharzia, don't go in. In situations were there is no information, discretion is the better part of valour.

Medical Problems & Treatment

Self diagnosis and treatment can be risky, so wherever possible seek qualified help. In Fiji medical care is available and you should not hesitate to see a doctor but, unfortunately, the standard medical care in Fiji is not as high as in Europe, the USA, Australia or New Zealand. You should be aware of this, especially when dealing with local hospitals. That does not mean that there are not good local doctors available or that the hospitals are not safe dealing with minor afflictions. Your best bet when ill is to get a recommendation from the management of a hotel, your embassy or consulate, or a friend. And as always, do not hesitate to ask questions. Many people assume that doctors are gods, and therefore accept any treatments given by a doctor, even when they suspect that a diagnosis or treatment is incorrect. You are ultimately responsible for your own good health. On the recommendation of trusted expatriates I have suggested the name of a local clinic in Suva. (See the Medical Services section in the Viti Levu Chapter.)

Sunburn

No matter how hot it feels on a given day in the tropics, the sun is less filtered by the atmosphere than in other climes and is much more potent. You can get sunburnt surprisingly quickly even through cloud. Damage can be done to skin and eyes, so take heed. Use a sun block and take extra care to cover areas of your body which don't normally see sun – your feet for example. Tanning can still occur with sunscreen. A hat provides added protection and use zinc cream or some other barrier cream for your nose and lips. Remember that you will only peel that much sooner if you burn. A bad burn can ruin a vacation, and a severe burn will require medical attention.

A minor burn can be treated with a cool shower or compresses, soothing cream or calamine lotion. An aspirin two or three times a day will also ease the pain. Some folks are allergic to ultraviolet light, which will result in redness, itching and pin-sized blisters. For these unfortunates, clothing is the only answer. Fair-skinned people beware in the tropics.

Prickly Heat

Prickly heat is an itchy rash caused by excessive perspiration trapped under the skin. It usually strikes people who have just arrived in a hot climate whose pores have not yet opened sufficiently to cope with greater sweating. Keeping cool by bathing often, using a mild talcum powder or even resorting to an air-con room may help until you acclimatise.

Heat Exhaustion

Dehydration or salt deficiency can cause heat exhaustion. Take time to acclimatise to high temperatures and make sure you get sufficient liquids. Salt deficiency is characterised by fatigue, lethargy, headaches, giddiness and muscle cramps and in this case salt tablets may help. Vomiting or diarrhoea can deplete your liquid and salt levels. Anhidrotic heat exhaustion, caused by an inability to sweat, is quite rare and unlike the other forms of heat exhaustion is likely to strike people who have been in a hot climate for some time, rather than newcomers.

Heat Stroke

This serious, sometimes fatal, condition can occur if the body's heat-regulating mechanism breaks down and the body temperature rises to dangerous levels. Long, continuous periods of exposure to high temperatures can leave you vulnerable to heat stroke and you should avoid excessive alcohol or strenuous activity when you first arrive in a hot climate.

The symptoms are feeling unwell, not sweating very much or at all, high body temperature (from 39 to 41°C). Where sweating has ceased the skin becomes flushed and red. Severe, throbbing headaches and lack of co-ordination will also occur and the sufferer may be confused or aggressive. Eventually the victim will become delirious or convulse. Hospitalisation is essential, but meanwhile get the victim out of the sun, remove clothing, cover the person with a wet sheet or towel and then fan continually.

Fungal Infections

Humidity not only means discomfort, but the possibility of rashes caused by yeasts and fungi which thrive in a warm, moist environment. Hot-weather fungal infections are most likely to occur on the scalp, between the toes or fingers (athlete's foot), in the groin (jock itch or crotch rot) and ringworm on the body. You get ringworm (which is a fungus infection, not a worm) from infected animals or by walking on damp areas, like shower floors.

To prevent fungal infections keep as cool and dry as possible. Wear loose-fitting, comfortable clothes, preferably made of cotton, avoid synthetic fibres. Open-toed sandals are also a good idea are open-toed sandals. Wash frequently and dry yourself carefully. To reduce chafing, talcum powder or corn starch can be applied to body creases (under arms, on necks, under breasts etc). If all else fails, medications are available to combat fungal and yeast rashes (as usual, the most potent ones are available only by prescription).

If you do get an infection, wash the infected area daily with a disinfectant or medicated soap and water, then rinse and dry well. Apply an antifungal powder like the widely available Tinaderm. Try to expose the infected area to air or sunlight as much as possible and wash all towels and underwear in hot water and change them often.

Colds

If your constitution is one that normally is susceptible to catching whatever cold is currently making the rounds, you will be wise to bring along an ample supply of your prefered cold medicines. Not only will you probably be coming to an entirely unfamiliar climate, but you will also be coming to a horde of unfamiliar germs. General good habits and nutrition are your best protection against catching a cold. But it's probably inevitable that one will get you if you're here for very long. So don't let it ruin your vacation. Nearly all health centres stock big bottles of nasty green cough elixir. But come prepared with decongestant/antihistamine tablets. Your favourite brand may not be sold locally (and depending upon where you are, cold tablets may not even be sold at all.)

Motion Sickness

Eating lightly before and during a trip will reduce the chances of motion sickness. If you are prone to motion sickness try to find a place that minimises disturbance – near the wing on aircraft, close to midships on boats, near the centre on buses. Fresh air usually helps, reading or cigarette smoke doesn't. Commercial motion-sickness preparations, which can cause drowsiness, have to be taken before the trip begins; when you're feeling sick it's too late. Ginger is a natural preventative and is available in capsule form.

Diarrhoea

A change of water, food or climate can all cause the runs, but more serious is diarrhoea due to contaminated food or water. There are several things you can do to guard against this:

1. Make sure meals are cooked properly. Virtually all organisms that thrive at body temperature are killed in the cooking process.
2. Water in Fiji is nearly always potable (the only exception being in the villages), but if you have the slightest fears, drink bottled water or soft drinks.
3. Peel or thoroughly wash any fruit or vegetables purchased in a market. Peeling fruit yourself is always a good idea.
4. Avoid swimming, walking barefoot or collecting seafood from beaches or lagoons directly in front of settlements. Raw sewage is often dumped or piped into the nearest convenient grounds – the beach that forms the villagers' front yard.

Despite all your precautions you may still have a bout of mild travellers' diarrhoea, but a few rushed toilet trips with no other symptoms is not indicative of a serious problem. Moderate diarrhoea, involving half a dozen loose movements in a day, is more of a nuisance. Dehydration is the main danger with any diarrhoea, particularly for children, so fluid replenishment is the number one treatment. Weak black tea with a little sugar, soft drinks allowed to go flat and diluted 50% with water or soda water are all good. With severe diarrhoea a rehydrating solution is necessary to replace minerals and salts. You should stick to a bland diet as you recover.

Lomotil or Imodium can be used to bring relief from the symptoms although they do not actually cure it. Only use these drugs if absolutely necessary, if you *must* travel for example. For children Imodium is preferable, but do not use these drugs if you have a high fever or are severely dehydrated. Antibiotics can be very useful in treating severe diarrhoea especially if it is accompanied by nausea, vomiting, stomach cramps or mild fever. Three days of treatment should be sufficient and an improvement should occur within 24 hours.

Giardia

The intestinal parasite *Giardia lamblia*, which causes giardiasis, is present in con-taminated water and the symptoms are stomach cramps, nausea, a bloated stomach, watery, foul-smelling diarrhoea and frequent gas. Giardiasis can appear several weeks after you have been exposed to the parasite, the symptoms may disappear for a few days and then return; this can go on for several weeks. Metronidazole known as Flagyl is the recommended drug, but should only be taken under medical supervision, antibiotics are no use.

Dysentery

This serious illness is caused by contaminated food or water and is characterised by severe diarrhoea, often with blood or mucus in the stool. There are two kinds of dysentery. Bacillary dysentery is characterised by a high fever and rapid development; headache, vomiting and stomach pains are also symptoms. It generally does not last longer than a week, but it is highly contagious.

Amoebic dysentery is more gradual in developing, has no fever or vomiting, but is a more serious illness. It is not a self-limiting disease, but will persist until treated and can recur and cause long-term damage.

A stool test is necessary with dysentery but if no medical care is available tetracy-cline is the prescribed treatment for bacillary dysentery, metronidazole for amoebic dys-entery.

Viral Gastroenteritis

Viral gastroenteritis is not caused by bacteria but, as the name suggests, by a virus and is characterised by stomach cramps, diarrhoea, sometimes vomiting, sometimes a slight fever. All you can do is rest and drink lots of fluids.

Hepatitis

Hepatitis A is the most common form of hepatitis and is spread by contaminated food or water, the symptoms are fever, chills, headache, fatigue, feelings of weakness and aches and pains. This is followed by loss of appetite, nausea, vomiting abdominal pain, dark urine, light-coloured faeces and jaundiced skin; the whites of the eyes may turn yellow. In some case there may just be a feeling of being unwell, being tired, with no appetite; having aches and pains and the jaundiced effect. You should seek medical advice, but in general there is not much you can do apart from rest, drink lots of fluids, eat lightly and avoid fatty foods. People who have had hepatitis must forego alcohol for six months after the illness: hepatitis attacks the liver and it needs that amount of time to recover.

Hepatitis B, which used to be called serum hepatitis, is spread through sexual contact, especially male homosexual activity; through skin penetration, for example through dirty needles; and through blood transfusions. Avoid having your ears pierced, tattoos done or having injections where you have doubts about the sanitary conditions. The symptoms and treatment of type B are much the same as type A but gamma globulin as a prophylaxis is only effective against type A.

Worms

These parasites are most common in rural, tropical areas and a stool test when you return home is not a bad idea. The worms can be present on unwashed vegetables or in undercooked meat and you can pick them up through your skin by walking in bare feet. Infestations may not show up for some time, and although generally not serious, can cause severe health problems if left untreated. A stool test is necessary to pinpoint the problem and medication is often available over the counter.

Bilharzia

Bilharzia is carried in water by worms which attach themselves to the intestines or the urinary bladder, where they produce large numbers of eggs. The larvae infect certain varieties of snail at one cycle in their life and are found in streams, lakes and particularly behind dams. They enter through the skin and the first indication is a tingling and sometimes a light rash around the area where the worm entered. Weeks later, when the worm is busy producing eggs, a high fever

may develop. A general feeling of being unwell may be the first indication but once the disease is established, abdominal pain and blood in the urine are other signs.

Avoiding swimming or bathing in fresh water where bilharzia is present is the main method of preventing the disease. Even deep water can be infected and if you do get wet dry off quickly and dry your clothes as well. Seek medical attention if you have been exposed and tell the doctor your suspicions, as bilharzia in the early stages can be confused with malaria or typhoid. If you cannot get medical help immediately, Niridazole is the recommended treatment.

Tetanus

This potentially fatal disease is found in undeveloped tropical areas and is difficult to treat, but is preventable with immunisation. Tetanus occurs when a wound becomes infected by a germ which lives in the faeces of animals or people so clean all cuts, punctures or animal bites. Tetanus is known as lockjaw and the first symptom may be discomfort in swallowing, stiffening of the jaw and neck, then painful convulsions of the jaw and whole body.

Sexually Transmitted Diseases

Sexually transmitted diseases are rampant in Fiji. Sexually adventurous visitors should take the same precautions they would take anywhere else on this planet. Use condoms. Although few cases of AIDS have been reported in Fiji, there are no really accurate statistics on this disease, so visitors should be wary.

Gonorrhoea and syphilis are the most common of these diseases; common symptoms are sores, blisters or rashes around the genitals, and discharges or pain when urinating. Symptoms may be less marked or not observed at all in women. The symptoms of syphilis eventually disappear completely, but the disease continues and can cause severe problems in later years. Treatment of gonorrhoea and syphilis is by antibiotics.

There are numerous other sexually transmitted diseases for most of which effective treatment is available. There is no cure for herpes and there is also currently no cure for AIDS. Using condoms and avoiding certain sexual practices such as anal intercourse are the most effective preventatives.

AIDS can also be spread through infected blood transfusions, or by dirty needles – vaccinations, acupuncture and tattooing can potentially be as dangerous as intravenous drug use if the equipment is not clean. If you do need an injection it may be a good idea to buy a new syringe from a pharmacy and ask the doctor to use it. All blood used in Fiji hospitals and clinics is screened for HIV.

Dengue Fever

Dengue fever (pronounced 'deng gee') is a mosquito-spread disease for which there is no prophylactic; the main preventative measure is to avoid daytime mosquito bites. A sudden onset of fever, headaches and severe joint and muscle pains are the first signs before a rash starts on the trunk and spreads to the limbs and face. After a further few days, the fever will subside and recovery will begin. Serious complications are not common, but a new haemolytic strain of dengue has appeared in Fiji. It causes dangerous internal bleeding and requires immediate medical attention if blood appears in vomit or stools. In any case, dengue's discomfort is such that sufferers often wish they could just die quickly; so when epidemics are reported, avoid mosquito bites.

Cuts & Scratches

Skin punctures can easily become infected in hot climates and may be difficult to heal. The tropics are a prime breeding ground for staphylococcal bacteria, a common bacteria found on the skin. These bacteria multiply rapidly under the right tropical conditions, especially if there is a cut, blister or insect bite on the skin releasing the fluids they thrive on. (Tropical ulcers are the very common consequence of a mosquito bite or other 'insignificant' wound becoming infected; they sometimes leave ugly black scars.) Treat any cut with an antiseptic solu-

tion and mercurochrome. Where possible avoid bandages and Band-aids which can keep wounds wet. But do take necessary measures to keep flies away from healing cuts. Coral cuts are notoriously slow to heal as the coral injects a weak venom into the wound. Avoid coral cuts by wearing shoes when walking on reefs and clean any cut thoroughly. An old but effective remedy is to wash fresh coral cuts with kerosene (which is commonly available in rural shops and villages).

Bites & Stings

Jellyfish Local advice is the best way of avoiding contact with these sea creatures with their stinging tentacles. Stings from most jellyfish are simply rather painful. Dousing in vinegar will deactivate any stingers which have not 'fired'. Calamine lotion, antihistamines and analgesics may reduce the reaction and relieve the pain.

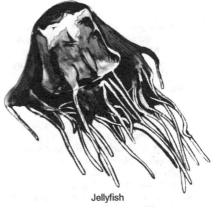

Jellyfish

Insects & Spiders Bee and wasp stings are usually painful rather than dangerous. Calamine lotion will give relief or ice packs will reduce the pain and swelling. There are some spiders with dangerous bites, but antivenenes are usually available. Scorpions often shelter in shoes or clothing and their stings are notoriously painful. Centipedes (not millipedes) in leaf litter will sometimes bite intrusive feet/hands. Bites can be anaesthetised remarkably quickly with the juice of the ubiquitous Mile-a-minute vine *(wabasucu)*; just crush a few leaves and apply as a poultice.

Bedbugs & Lice Bedbugs live in various places particularly dirty mattresses and bedding. Spots of blood on bedclothes or on the wall around the bed can be read as a suggestion to find another hotel. Bedbugs leave itchy bites in neat rows. Calamine lotion may help.

Lice all cause itching and discomfort and make themselves at home in your hair (head lice), your clothing (body lice) or in your pubic hair (crabs). They get to you by direct contact with infected people or sharing combs, clothing and the like. Powder or shampoo treatment will kill the lice and infected clothing should then be washed in very hot water.

Women's Health

Gynaecological Problems Poor diet, lowered resistance due to the use of antibiotics for stomach upsets and even contraceptive pills can lead to vaginal infections when travelling in hot climates. Good personal hygiene, wearing cotton underwear and skirts or loose-fitting trousers will help prevent infections.

Yeast infections, characterised by a rash, itch and discharge, can be treated with a vinegar or even lemon-juice douche or with yoghurt. Nystatin suppositories are the usual medical prescription. Trichomoniasis is a more serious infection with a discharge and a burning sensation when urinating. If a vinegar-water douche is not effective, medical attention should be sought. Flagyl is the prescribed drug. Male sexual partners must also be treated.

Pregnancy Most miscarriages occur during the first three months of pregnancy so this is the most risky time to travel. The last three months should also be spent within reasonable distance of good medical care as quite serious problems can develop at this time. Pregnant women should avoid all unneces-

sary medication, but vaccinations and malarial prophylactics should still be taken where necessary. Additional care should be taken to prevent illness and particular attention should be paid to diet and nutrition.

WOMEN TRAVELLERS

Fiji is still a terrific place for solo women travellers; rape is rare in Fiji. However, taking precautions is prudent, especially if you are by yourself late at night in Suva. Women should also understand that when a man asks you out, chances are he expects more than a good-night kiss – even on the first date. Likewise, an invitation to a midnight stroll on the beach implies more than gazing at the stars and holding hands.

In the same vein, women should realise that though bikini tops and lots of exposed skin may be the norm on the streets of Waikiki, in Fiji, anywhere except on the beach or in resort areas it is not the norm. Women wearing (what locals would construe as) overly 'sexy' clothing may as well wear a flashing green light.

Should a solo woman traveller accept an invitation from a family to stay with them? More often than not it will be a great experience, especially in a village setting. However, one solo woman traveller, Lucy Kunkel of Ithica, New York, remarks that in the more well travelled areas of Viti Levu, 'perhaps families were not as innocent as they once were'. Her experience on several occasions was that invitations 'carried strings'. In one instance after accepting an invitation to stay at a family home she was immediately shuttled to a store and given a laundry list of what to purchase. Her conclusion:

This happens, I'm sure, because travellers have taken advantage of them in the past, but I felt very uncomfortable, and don't recommend solo females accept any such offers. This is also because of the rude way a woman travelling alone is treated. Wear a wedding ring and make up stories...it saves a lot of hassles.

Finally, I've had letters from several women, including a Peace Corps volunteer with years of experience, who suggest that I bring up the subject of 'peeping toms'. My Peace Corps reader tells me that this behaviour is relatively common throughout the South Pacific. Without probing the socio-cultural aspects of this practice or judging whether or not it is innocuous behaviour, just be fore-warned that 'they' are out there, and visitors are fair game.

DANGERS & ANNOYANCES
Theft
In recent years locals have shaken their heads sadly when speaking about the rise in crime and lack of respect among Fijian youth. This may be true by Fijian standards, but compared with that in the rest of the world, crime in Fiji is still minimal. This is also despite the fact that many people live in what Western-ers would call 'poverty'.

However, petty theft is on the rise, even on the outer islands, and visitors should be aware of that. If you are in an area where there is a lot of foot traffic, avoid leaving your clothing on the clothes line for long periods of time – it may well be gone when you return. Shoes, particularly expensive hiking boots and the like, are also prime targets for casual thieves; it might be wise not to leave them unattended. Valuables should always be stored in a safe, if one is available. Guest houses are often the target of local thieves and I've heard especially worrying reports of petty theft in Somosomo (Taveuni). Perhaps the best thing one can say is that violent crimes are still rare.

Venomous Creatures
Snake bites are virtually unknown in Fiji. Highly-venomous black and white banded sea snakes, which are often found along Fiji's shores or swimming in lagoons do not bite, unless severely provoked. In the evenings sea snakes will venture on land and I have even observed them come into my room. Despite their disturbing appearance, these creatures are docile and I have seen Fijians pick them up and handle them (though this is rare). For cultural reasons (perhaps through superstition) Fijians will

never purposefully kill, much less touch, these serpents.

The bolo, another venomous species, is so rare that even herpetologists cannot find it, and it's not aggressive anyway. Pacific boas are the most common land snakes (on the islands where they haven't been extermi-nated by mongoose) but are not venomous or aggressive. If you are lucky enough to see a boa (usually in a tree), enjoy the sight.

Certain cone-shell creatures found in Aus-tralia and the Pacific can give a dangerous or even fatal sting. There are various fish and other sea creatures which can give dangerous stings, bites or be dangerous if you eat them. Again taking local advice is the best sugges-tion. Reef walkers might consider asking locals about the presence of stone fish. Also, many sea creatures are endangered and should not be harvested for ecological reasons (doing so is sometimes also against the law).

Dangers in the Sea
As a general rule, inexperienced snorkellers and swimmers should be extremely careful about plunging into areas of the sea with strong currents. There are no warning signs in Fiji for areas with dangerous currents or for hazardous swimming areas; every year novices drown. If you have the least hesita-tion about swimming or snorkelling, ask about local conditions before you get your feet wet. (See also Diving & Snorkelling later in this chapter.)

ACTIVITIES
Village Visits
Many travellers visit Fijian villages or Indian settlements, which certainly provide an insight into traditional life. While cultural exchange is the essence of travel, uninvited guests and trekkers who suddenly show up in a community can be extremely disruptive and, what's more, the government actually encourages the community to frown upon interlopers. Fijians, being generous people, will provide the visitor, even the uninvited freeloader, with their last spoonful of instant coffee or last tin of jam without uttering a

peep. There is no question that when visitors are around, the normal routine of the village changes. Gardens do not get weeded, chores are put off and the attention goes to the entertainment of the guest. Visitors may not even realise the burden they can become.

Fijian culture dictates that the stranger be treated with the utmost hospitality and unfortunately some people take advantage of this. You should realise that although Fijians are rich in spirit, they are often very poor materially. You should always match your host's generosity by purchasing groceries and practical gifts if you plan to stay for a while. (See the Avoiding Offence section under Culture in the Facts about the Country chapter for more information.)

Trekking

Trans-island trekkers or visitors to outer islands where there are no visitor facilities should not camp unless permission is given by the village. Nor should you assume that you can automatically stay in a village. Villages are simply not equipped to handle guests nor to provide guides if someone wanders in looking for the right trail. Thus, even the best-intentioned visitors can become a nuisance. The government is reacting to this type of activity by considering ways of limiting backpackers to certain rural areas.

Aside from possible disruption of village life, hiking in the bush can be dangerous to the uninitiated and unprepared. Monsoon-like rains often wash out trails and it is easy to get lost in the rainforest. Backpackers have often been stranded, sometimes with injuries, in remote areas awaiting rescue from villagers or government officials – certainly not the way to spend a vacation. When in doubt about camping or hiking, always enquire at the Lands & Survey section of the Ministry of Lands (☎ 211 516) in Suva, or the Forestry Department (☎ 301 611).

Diving & Snorkelling

Most of Fiji's islands are bounded by reefs where tropical fish of every colour and description thrive. Those in the know say

that three of Fiji's dive locales – Beqa Lagoon, Astrolabe Lagoon and Taveuni – are world-class in calibre. What accounts for this? Just several hundred km from Fiji is the Great Tongan Trench where upwelling waters rich in nutrients nourish Fiji's ocean life. This steady food supply provides for an abundance of sea life. Locals say the sharks are not a problem for divers in the area, although for me sharks are always a concern. But that's my problem.

If you are a weak swimmer or a novice at snorkelling you have much more to fear from strong currents than creatures of the deep. Inevitably a visitor to Fiji drowns each year, but not because of shark attacks. Rather, the visitor has literally jumped off the plane and into the water, unprepared for a strong current or a riptide. There are absolutely no warning signs in Fiji for hazardous currents or surf so if you feel your safety is in doubt, ask someone first. As David E Robb, a reader from London aptly put it, 'Do not go snorkelling alone without fins or local knowledge.'

Dive-shop owners in Fiji point out that because Fiji is a relatively remote destination, thousands of km of its reefs are as yet unexplored by divers. Despite the remoteness of the destination, Fiji's reefs are more accessible for Australians than the Great Barrier Reef and cheaper for North Americans than Hawaii. However, you need not be a scuba diver to appreciate the fish – snorkelling is also excellent and easily learned. Nor should you feel that because you don't know how to dive this should prevent you from learning in Fiji. The warm waters of Fiji (which average about 28°C annually) are more conducive to learning than the frigid waters of the US west coast. Visibility can exceed 60 metres on a good day, but can be reduced to 20 metres or less when the water is turgid or on days with heavy plankton bloom.

The best time of the year to visit for diving purposes is from April to November, when trade winds blow more favourably, the water is clearer and the fish are more active. Divers are advised to bring their own regulator, mask, snorkel and fins. If you don't have or don't want to bring gear, most operators have equipment that can be rented. To be sure about rentals, check ahead of time. Keep in mind that spearfishing in Fiji is prohibited for conservation reasons. Also, as electrical standards are 240 V, underwater photographers and night divers should bring converters to assure proper charging of their gear.

Expect to pay F$325 to F$450 (plus tax) for an open-water certification course approved by the Professional Association of Diving Instructors (PADI). This should include all equipment such as tanks, regulator, fins, snorkels etc. Note that some dive operators such as Aqua-Trek specialise in teaching, whereas others such as Dive Taveuni are simply underwater tour guides.

Those who wish to take a resort course or an open-water certificate course must bring a medical certificate stating that they are fit to dive. If you don't have the document in hand (and you are not able to see a local doctor) forget about diving with a legal dive operator. They will not touch you for fear of legal repercussions.

As a point of interest, Fiji now has a diver recompression chamber in Suva. This apparatus is for treating a scuba diver who gets the 'bends' which may occur if the unlucky individual ignores the standard safety procedures and stays below too long or rises too fast. There is also a nationwide set-up to provide medvac and recompression for

diving accidents. Sally Cammick of Sea Fiji recommends that any visitors intending to dive should obtain insurance which will cover costs for recompression if any injuries occur.

For those interested in researching dive sites and resorts in Fiji and other areas I recommend *Undercurrent – the private, exclusive guide for serious divers*, a newsletter published in Sausalito, California. This publication accepts no paid advertising and sends out reporters to visit and assess dive resorts and dive sites anonymously. The cost is US$39 per year. Write to PO Box 1658 Sausalito, CA 94965, USA for more details.

Should you be interested in a 'live-aboard' dive trip, your dive tour operator in Australia or the USA should be able to book you on the 18.5-metre *Matagi Princess*, which operates in the Taveuni area, or the 35-metre *Pacific Nomad* which visits the Astrolabe Reef and northern Lau.

Snorkelling Sites Just as diving conditions may vary according to microclimatic conditions (such as rainfall), season and other factors, so it goes with snorkelling. Some of the better areas that readers have recommended include: Namotu Island, better known as 'Magic Island', which is very close to Tavarua (the surfing resort) about 12 km off Momi Bay in the Mamanuca group; Natadola Beach, about 54 km from Nadi Airport; the deep channel off Tagaqe village, about 12 km east of Hideaway Resort; Plantation Hideaway, on Kadavu; Nananu-i-Ra off Rakiraki in Viti Levu; and Leleuvia off Ovalau. There are dozens of other spots; your best bet is to ask around. Normally local divers will know where to go. Dive operators often take snorkellers to excellent offshore sites when space permits in their boats; ask at dive centres.

Snorkelling Safety Tips My good friend and fellow traveller Sophia Banerji suggested that those new to snorkelling and underwater activities in general, should keep this cardinal rule in mind – do not touch. Unfortunately, the most brilliantly coloured and attractive creatures can be those which could give a nasty, if not fatal, sting or poison. Coral cuts should always be cleaned thoroughly, as warm climates encourage infection. Keep in mind the following tips:

1. Use a water-resistant sun block and/or wear a T-shirt. Those rays are potent, especially to the fair-skinned. Protection should cover all the same spots that clothes cover, otherwise, serious sunburn is the likely result. And don't forget the sensitive backs of your knees.
2. Practise and test your equipment in shallow water. Don't snorkel without fins. Currents can be very strong.
3. Don't snorkel alone and if you are inexperienced and/or don't know the area, ask about the local conditions.

Dive Sites Dive sites can be found throughout the islands. The following list covers the main sites.

Nadi The principal dive operation in the Nadi area is at the Sheraton Resort. Tropical Divers (☎ 723 435; fax 701 818) at the Sheraton, provides PADI-approved training for beginning divers and advanced/refresher courses for those already certified.

Dive sites are scattered around Namotu Island which is about 20 minutes by boat from Viti Levu. Nutrients from the open ocean outside the Malolo Barrier Reef (which surrounds the nearby Mamanuca group off the coast of Nadi and Lautoka) supply food for filter feeders like soft corals and crinoids. Also found in the waters around Namotu are abundant growths of hard corals and the numerous fish that live and feed in hard-coral gardens. Since Namotu Island is so close to the shore of Viti Levu, some interference in the natural development of the ecosystem is caused by run-off and construction (roads, hotels etc). As you venture further away from Viti Levu, this problem diminishes. Underwater visibility can exceed 35 metres.

Mamanuca Group The Mamanuca group is a cluster of a dozen or so large islands and numerous tiny islets just off the western side of Viti Levu. It is Fiji's most popular resort area and includes such favourite hotel destinations as Beachcomber, Plantation Island, Mana, Musket Cove, Matamanoa, Club Naitasi, Castaway and others. Though populated by hordes of tourists and within easy access of Nadi, the underwater habitats have not been terribly disturbed. These islands sit on top of 'coral pillars' which, over thousands of years, have grown from the ocean floor towards the sunlight. Because the local underwater ecosystems in the area have remained relatively untouched, abundant life still exists within these coral canyons. Divers can witness a full biosystem of nectonic reef fish as well as numerous filter feeders from soft coral to gorgonians. Outside the Malolo Barrier Reef, visibility can exceed 35 metres, and pelagic fish such as dolphin, mantas, humphead wrasse and others can be observed.

Diving in the Mamanucas is expertly handled by Aqua-Trek's Ocean Sports Adventures on Mana; Mamanuca Divers at Musket Cove on Malololailai; and Dive Centre Fiji Ltd on Beachcomber and Treasure islands. Aqua-Trek is the only dive operation in the South Pacific with wholly owned dive-travel services in the USA and Australia. Aqua-Trek is a PADI teaching facility and has full equipment rentals, including underwater photography gear. Instructors are available for students of all skill levels, from beginner to advanced, and will match your skills to the proper dive site. Of all the dive operations in Fiji, this is among the best.

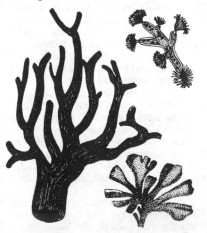

Yasawa Group There are now two resorts in the Yasawa Group where diving is featured – Yasawa Island Lodge and Waya Island Adventures. Though the area has long been visited by tourists, few divers have ventured into the Yasawas. Reports are that the diving is spectacular. Waya Island sites include underwater caves, a shark dive and plenty of virgin territory.

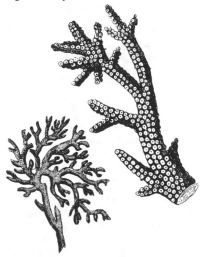

Coral Coast Diving along the outer reef of the Coral Coast is good for flora, fauna and reef fish but lacks the open-ocean pelagics found in less-visited waters. Because dive sites are generally closer to shore than in other areas, the high-powered speed boats used by operators in other parts of Fiji are not necessary. Reef boats will get you to dive sites where there are minimal current problems, excellent visibility (seasonal) and the opportunity to hand-feed fish.

The main dive operator on the Coral Coast is Sea Sports Fiji which handles diving at the Fijian Resort, the Warwick, Naviti, Hideaway, the Reef Hotel, Tubukula and the Crow's Nest. Transport is available from other resorts along the Coral Coast. Sea Sports is a PADI-approved facility, and its instructors are seasoned professionals.

Taveuni & Vanua Levu The 'North' as it is known in Fiji is composed of the country's second largest island, Vanua Levu; Taveuni, the 'Garden Island'; and a number of other smaller islands and atolls. These are among the more remote dive sites in Fiji, hence instructional programmes and gear hire are more limited. Resorts in this area are smaller, more intimate and geared to couples. The two primary dive operators are Dive Taveuni on Taveuni, and H20 Sportz, which handles diving at Na Koro, Matani Kavika and Namale (Savusavu), Qamea Beach Resort, Fiji Forbes and Matagi. Boats are spacious and reliable, and tanks and weights are provided. Despite this, the best bet is to bring your own gear.

With Fiji's rapid tourist development, however, many new dive operations are springing up, including one in western Taveuni at Vuna Lagoon.

Diving in the 'North' is considered the best in Fiji. This area is fed by nutrient-rich currents emanating from the Great Tongan Trench. The ecosystem supports abundant soft corals, gorgonians and numerous reef fish. Because the area is relatively underpopulated, overfishing is not a problem and the reefs are relatively untouched. Unfortunately, some pelagics are not as numerous here or anywhere else in Fiji as in former times. Ric Cammick, from Dive Taveuni, says that at one time, great schools of tuna could be seen in the waters off Savusavu. These were wiped out due to overfishing by Japanese fleets.

Currents in this area can be very strong, and are best dealt with by experienced divers. Neophytes should be extremely careful.

Suva Beqa Diver, Dive Centre Fiji, and the new Marlin Bay Resort are the main operators in Beqa Lagoon. Accommodation is provided at Pacific Harbour Resort, Marlin Bay and other smaller properties in the immediate area. Because of the large amount of rainfall (more than 250 cm annually) on this side of Viti Levu, the dive sites close to shore often suffer from poor visibility. The exceptional dive site in this region is Beqa Lagoon, which is far enough away from shore that rainwater run-off and human interference from the nearby populated area offer no problems. Beqa Lagoon provides divers with breathtaking trenches and undercuts. Sights include soft corals, moorish idols, coral trout, damsels, butterfly fish and other creatures.

Beqa Diver offers full instructional programmes and gear hire as well as a spacious, fast dive boat. Dive Centre Fiji also operates from Suva.

Kadavu Kadavu is the newest area to open up and features some of the best diving in Fiji. Diving on a regular basis was established there only in 1988, so visitors are sure to see virgin territory in the Astrolabe and Barrier reefs. The low-end resorts in the region (Reece's Place, Kini's Bure Resort, Albert's Place and Nukubalavu) all have dive operations. The resort favoured by wholesalers is, not surprisingly, the most up-market – Dive Kadavu Matana Resort. All operators in Kadavu feature PADI instruction as well as diving in the Astrolabe Reef.

Dive Specialists Information on diving in Fiji is available from the Fiji Visitors' Bureau office in the USA and should be available in Australia and New Zealand as well. Some of the listings are dive operators, such as H20 Sportz, who serve a number of resorts. Other listings, such as Dive Taveuni, are affiliated with one resort; and still others, such as Sea Fiji or Nuku Baluvu Dive Centre are travel agencies that specialise in booking dive vacations. Keep in mind that the prices listed in this book are apt to change so write to the individual resorts for further information. Some of the larger dive operators like Aqua Trek have offices in the USA and Australia which specialise in arranging hotel/air/dive packages.

If you visit the more remote areas such as Kadavu, plan on paying for diving with cash or travellers' cheques; Kadavu has no banks.

It's probably a good idea to find out ahead of time what the preferred form of payment is and prepare accordingly. Dive specialists (resorts, agents and dive operators) are listed below:

Aqua-Trek
Mana Island, Nadi. This is one of the premier dive operations in Fiji and is also the dive concessionaire at the Regent of Fiji. Aqua-Trek's close attention to instruction and equipment has done a tremendous amount to upgrade the quality of diving in Fiji. They specialise in PADI certification of divers and have recently opened a new dive shop in Nadi at 2/465 Queens Rd. It's a full retail dive store which also services regulators and other gear. Aqua-Trek can also arrange for sightseeing, hotel accommodation and, of course, diving excursions (☎ 661 455; 800 541 4334 in the USA; fax 665 088).

Astrolabe Divers
PO Box Naqara, Ono, Kadavu. This no-frills operation works from Kini's Bure Resort, on Ono Island and features PADI open-water courses for F$350, as well as advanced instruction. A one-tank boat dive is F$50; two dives are F$90. Prices include tanks and weight belt. Bures at Kini's are F$50 per day per person (☎ 302 689/746).

Castaway Diving
Castaway Island Resort. This operation provides certificate courses as well as other diving activities. Costs are F$50 per dive (☎ 661 233; fax 665 733).

Dive Centre Fiji
PO Box 3066, Lami and 4 Matua St, Walu Bay. Facilities include scuba instruction, air-filling station, equipment sales, equipment repairs and diving excursions (☎ 300 599, 311 614).

Garry 'Hook' La Roche
PO Box 5202, Lautoka. Garry, who has dived around the world for seven years, runs the only dive operation on Tavewa in the Yasawa group. Diving is very new to Tavewa, and a great deal of the area is yet to be explored. There are a number of soft corals and pelagics in the region, and one doesn't have to go far or deep to see them. Garry has gear for a group of four divers, and offers four-day, five-dive PADI certification courses for F$300, and advanced courses for F$200. One-tank dives are F$45, two-tank dives F$70. Snorkelling trips can also be arranged.

Dive Kadavu Matana Resort
This is the most up-market dive operation in Kadavu. It has two beachfront bures, two oceanview bures and a budget bure with four double bedrooms. There are hot showers (a rarity on Kadavu), flush toilets and an abundance of fresh water. Diving is fairly close to shore and not much time is spent on boats. The resort has a PADI instructor and open-water certificate courses are available. Prices are F$45 per dive (☎ 311 780; fax 303 860).

Dive Taveuni
PO Box Matei, Taveuni. This is a top-rated outfit with its own accommodation, equipment rentals and excursions to the famous Rainbow Reef. Prices are US$1571 for a week's stay, which includes five dive days and seven nights' accommodation, ground transport from the airport and all meals (☎ 880 441).

Garden Island Resort
PO Box 1, Waiyevo, Taveuni. This is a mid-range resort on Taveuni with a 'full service' dive operation called Rainbow Reef Divers run by expat Australian, Dave Dickenson. Activities includes everything from certificate courses to excursions to the Rainbow Reef aboard a newly built vessel, the *Rainbow Diver* which can comfortably accommodate 12 divers. Rates are F$90 for two dives, F$255 for a six-dive package or F$400 for 10 dives. An introductory resort course is F$90, a resort dive is F$75 and F$60 for a night or dawn dive (reputedly a mystical experience). A five-day PADI open-water course is F$400, and a three-day PADI advanced course F$325 (☎ 880 288; 800 660-0310 in the USA; fax 880 286).

H20 Sportz
PO Box Savusavu, Na Koro Resort, Namale Plantation, Matani Kavika. This high-quality operation specialises in the Vanua Levu area, but also operates the dive concession at Seashell Cove, near Sigatoka on Viti Levu. It also has dive shops at Westpoint Arcade in Nadi, and at the Copra Shed Marina in Savusavu. It offers resort courses, PADI certificate courses, advanced speciality courses and night diving. The certificate course at Seashell Cove is F$275, while the same course in Savusavu is F$300. Two-tank dives are F$60 at Seashell, and F$85 in Savusavu (☎ 86 156/7).

Inner Space Adventures
PO Box 9535, Nadi. Run by Ron and Sharyn Naidu (formerly with Plantation Island Resort), this is perhaps the newest dive operation in Fiji. Inner Space will pick up divers from resorts in the Nadi area and transport them to Nadi Bay (in front of Traveller's Beach Resort) where they will proceed by boat to the dive spots in the Mamanucas. The cost for a one-tank dive is F$40, two-tank dives are F$70. Open-water certificate courses are F$325 (an extremely competitive price) and there are also speciality courses in night diving, deep diving, and search and salvage diving for F$150 (☎ 723 883).

Islands in the Sun
These resorts (Beachcomber and Treasure Island) have PADI instruction as well as deep dives (☎ 666 738; fax 664 496).

Marlin Bay
This is a new luxury resort on the island of Beqa run by Americans George and Dorothy Taylor (PO box 1147, Gresham, OR 97030 USA). According to a rave review in *Skin Diver*, diving is first class and equal to anything else in Fiji. Dive sites include shallow areas with huge coral heads and soft coral mazes as well as sheer walls dropping thousands of metres. Food and accommodation are also reportedly excellent. The price for a two-tank dive is US$65 (☎ 304 042; 1 800 542 FIJI in the USA).

Matagi
PO Box 83, Waiyevo, Taveuni. This exclusive resort near Taveuni has a PADI-certified dive master, but offers no instruction. Rates for two-tank dives are F$99 per person for one to four days, F$443 per person for five days, F$519 for six days and F$724 for eight days. Boat, guide, weight belts, tanks and tank refills are provided. Matagi also runs the 18-metre, live-aboard *Matagi Princess* which has four-day cruises (☎ 880 260; fax 880 274).

Naiqoro Divers
This is the name of the dive operation at Albert's Place (formerly Plantation Hideaway), also in eastern Kadavu. Albert's Place is a low-end, budget resort. Single-tank dives are F$35, double-tank dives F$65. Prices include tanks and refills, weight belt, and boat trip. Regulators, buoyancy vests, fins, masks and snorkel are F$15 per day. Divers are advised to bring their own gear (with the exception of tanks and weight belts) because of limited equipment on hand. You'll need cash or travellers' cheques for payment (☎ 302 896 in Suva).

Namena Island
This island (Namenalala) is about 30 km from Savusavu and has a very comfortable, well-regarded and very remote up-market resort. Though not strictly a dive operation, diving is reportedly excellent (☎ 813 764).

Nananu-i-Ra Island Divers
This is a new dive operation on Nananu-i-Ra run by Ken MacDonald from MacDonald's Beach Cottages. Single dives cost F$40, two dives F$70, and there are also six-dive packages for F$200 and ten-dive packages for F$300. A four-day PADI certification course is also available (☎ 694 633).

Nukubalavu Dive Centre
PO Box Naleca, Kavala Bay, Kadavu. This is a small, no-frills dive resort in eastern Kadavu that has received good reviews (☎ 311 075).

Sea Fiji
Run by Curly Carswell, this is an experienced agency based in Savusavu that specialises in putting together dive packages throughout Fiji (☎ 850 345; fax 850 344).

Sea Sports Ltd
PO Box 65, Korolevu. It has the Fijian and Warwick resorts, and PADI-approved certificate courses. Diving sites are close to either resort (☎ 500 598, 500 555).

Scuba Hire Ltd, Beqa Divers Fiji
PO Box 777, 75 Marine Drive, Lami. This is the oldest dive company in Fiji, and while much of its business is now commercial diving, it still offers training, dive trips from Suva (and Beqa Lagoon through Beqa Divers), and equipment sales and service. Two-tank dives cost F$105 on the *Beqa Diver* or *Fiji Diver* from Pacific Harbour (☎ 361 088; fax 351 017).

South Sea Divers
PO Box 718, Nadi (between the Regent and Sheraton resorts). South Seas specialises in accommodating the needs of photographers, but also offers a full selection of courses. A one-tank dive costs F$60, a two-tank dive F$90 (☎ 722 988).

Subsurface Fiji Ltd
This company operates from Lautoka, and runs the dive concession at Beachcomber as well as working with Captain Cook Cruises. (Captain Cook runs a huge yacht to Waya Island in the Yasawa Group and offers diving as part of its activities.) Diving in the Yasawas is exponentially better than on Beachcomber (☎ 664 422, 666 028).

Sun & Sea Dive
PO Box 6, Vunisea, Kadavu. Sun & Sea operates from Reece's Place, a low-end place to stay on Galoa Island in Kadavu. It has resort courses and an open-water certificate course (☎ 315 703; 02 665 6335 in Australia; 025 972 105 in New Zealand).

Tropical Divers
This group handles the diving for the Sheraton Fiji Resort. A one-tank dive, including equipment is F$81, two tanks cost F$106 (☎ 723 435; fax 701 818).

Undersea Expeditions
This is a San Francisco-based tour wholesaler specialising in sending people to Fiji's 'North'. Call or write to 291 Geary St, Suite 619, San Francisco, CA 94102-1863, USA (☎ 1 800 669 0310; 415 398 2189).

Yasawa Island Lodge
This is an up-market resort featuring PADI certificate courses and trips to dive sites. Prices start at F$70 for a one-tank dive (☎ 663 364; fax 665 044).

In addition to these dive specialists, the major resorts are affiliated with dive services and can arrange for dive excursions and equipment for their clients.

Besides the dive shops, you can check with the British Sub Aqua Club (BSAC) which organises dives for BSAC-licensed divers and will sometimes take snorkellers on expeditions if there is room. Contact any of the dive shops for information about the BSAC.

Surfing

Next to diving, surfing is the up-and-coming recreational sport in Fiji. Fiji is considered by experts to be one of the world's prime, newly discovered surfing spots – a fact which has been greatly publicised in the surfer magazines. In particular, there is fine surfing near the exclusive island resort of Tavarua which is south of the Mamanuca Islands off Viti Levu's western side. However, in the past few years budget surf camps have appeared in Fiji, and there is plenty of room for more.

According to the *Surf Report*, a first-rate newsletter which calls itself a 'monthly summary and forecast of worldwide surfing conditions', there are at least 19 documented surfing areas in the Fiji Islands. Of those, only one area (near Club Masa) is a beach break. A few others may be relatively close to shore, but most entail use of a boat for getting in and out of the surf. The biggest hazard, according to the newsletter, is infection from coral cuts. It's a given that since nearly all of the good surfing in Fiji is in and around reefs, dealing with coral is an issue. Other potential problems are boating accidents as well as treacherous currents, sharks and sea snakes. But not to worry...

Geographically, the breakdown of surfing spots goes like this: four are in the area near fabled Tavarua Island; six are off the Coral Coast area, near Club Masa or in a 30-km vicinity; five are near the capital of Suva; one is near Beqa; one is off Kadavu; one is off Kabara in the Lau Group and one is near Kia Island in the far north of Vanua Levu, near Labasa. Practically speaking, most surfers would stick around Viti Levu where most of the 'proven' sites exist rather than going further afield.

Though Tavarua is considered the primo spot, good waves are not limited to this area. The Coral Coast also has excellent surfing according to Andrew Wade, manager at Hideaway Resort (☎ 500 177), who is also an avid surfer. Most people agree that there are probably numerous as yet undiscovered sites on Fiji where surfing is also first class.

One of the newest surf developments is Club Masa (PO Box 10, Sigatoka), situated at the mouth of the Sigatoka River and in the shadows of the famous Kulakula Sand Dunes. Club Masa is a funky, low-end, homestead-like scene that specialises in catering to surfers; it's the only place in Fiji with a beach break. Windsurfing is also excellent here.

Surftrek Reef Surfing Fiji (☎ 790 435) formerly known as Trekkers Reef Resort, is the other new establishment devoted to hard-core surfers. Other than Tavarua, it is the

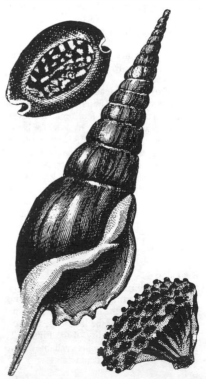

only surf camp dedicated to the breaks at Namotu and Wilkes reefs. It's on a 4.8 hectare property adjacent to Momi Bay, beneath the Momi Guns emplacement amid rolling hills and cane fields, 28 km south of Nadi. This is not a lavish affair but is a notch or two up on the comfort scale when compared to the other surf camp, Club Masa.

Those staying at Seashell Cove are also near some excellent surfing and snorkelling (☎ 790 100/393 for information about surf trips). Day trips are available to the reef.

Finally, there is Yanuca Island, near Beqa – a lush, sparsely inhabited jewel a half-hour's boat ride from Pacific Harbour. The surf camp is operated by a small local company called Frigates Surf Riders in conjunction with Rosie Travel Service (☎ 722 755), a well-established local tour company. Day trips are available, but most visitors opt for four-day packages. The surf spot is about a half-hour's boat ride from Yanuca to an area called Frigates Passage, which is on the south-western edge of Beqa Lagoon. The wave is a left-hander, and with the south-east trade wind blowing offshore, is a very consistent break.

The *Surf Report* recommends taking two boards – a short board about six feet in length and a longer one, six feet eight inches to seven feet two inches as a back-up for larger surf. They say a wetsuit is not necessary though suggest a vest or nylon jersey to keep off the sun. Naturally you would want to bring some heavy-duty sun block and mosquito coils. For more detailed information from this excellent publication, back issues on the Fiji edition (Vol 7 No 12) are available for US$5 or US$5.50 for overseas orders. Write to the Surf Report, PO Box 1028, Dana Point, CA 92629, USA (☎ 714 496 5922).

Kayaking

Ocean kayaking is a small, but growing sport in Fiji. Like surfing or diving, a kayaking holiday combines the best elements of Fiji – the natural beauty of the landscape and seascape and the hospitality of the Fijians. To my knowledge, kayaking is available on two islands – Taveuni and Kadavu.

Those interested in exploring the Taveuni coast and some of its offshore islands should contact Ringgold Reef Kayaking (☎ 880 083; 415 344 2953 in the USA). Run by Keni Madden and his Californian wife TC Donovan, Ringgold offers overnight kayak camping tours from June to September, as well as hiring kayaks for day trips all year-round (from next to Beverly Camping near Matei).

For overnight tours, guides are provided, as well as tents. A six-metre support boat is used on tours, should any trouble arise. The eight kayaks, seven of which are about five metres long (the eighth is three metres long), are the sit-on-top variety (made by Ocean Kayaks), with hatches to stow gear for overnight trips, though they can be used for day trips and even surfing.

Rates are F$8 per hour (up to two hours), F$30 for half a day, and F$45 for a full day. At the time of writing, Ringgold has not established exact pricing for overnight trips, but I'm told tariffs will be about F$80 to F$120 per person per day. For more information, write to Ringgold Reef Kayaking at Matei or Taveuni in Fiji, or in the USA at 539 West Poplar Ave, San Mateo, CA 94402.

A second Californian company, Paddling South (☎ 707 942 4796 in the USA), perhaps the most experienced kayaking tour operation, has led tours to Kadavu for the last few years. They specialise in visiting the Astrolabe Reef, combining camping and kayaking in the Ono Island area of Kadavu. Led by Trudi Angell and Douglas Knapp, Paddling South offers three, 10-day excursions in September and October for US$1495 plus airfares. They use two-person folding kayaks (Klepper/Folbot) which provide ample room for gear such as tents, camp kitchen etc. The kayaks are reportedly easy to paddle and safe. A deposit of US$300 is required to reserve a place. For more information, write to Trudi at 4510 Silverado Trail, Calistoga, CA 94515, USA.

ACCOMMODATION

Accommodation in Fiji is divided into four basic categories; camping, bottom-end guest houses and hotels, government guest houses, and hotels and resorts.

Visitors should note that Fiji has a new 10% VAT tacked on to the cost of all accommodation, meals, excursions, car rentals and virtually every other item associated with hotel expenses.

Camping

Camping in Fiji without permission is prohibited on village land, but there are camping sites on private property in Ovalau at the Ovalau Holiday Resort and some of the offshore island resorts; Seashell Cove Resort, (Sigatoka); Reece's Place and Plantation Hideaway (Kadavu); and Lisi Camping, Tom's and Beverly Beach (Taveuni). Camping in some recreational areas such as Nadarivatu on Viti Levu is legal, but you must have permission from the Lands & Survey Section of the Ministry of Lands (☎ 211 516 in Suva). If in doubt, ask a local who the owner of the land is and then offer the owner some type of compensation. Never set up camp without permission. Though Fijians are tolerant people, squatters are not well liked.

Guest Houses & Hotels

Inexpensive guest houses or hotels catering to local traffic or the 'backpacker' crowd may range from quiet, spartan but clean hotels and rooming houses to raucous, shabby dives frequented by locals seeking a hideaway for liaisons. Prices range from US$6 to US$20 for a single. Some of the better examples of this category are the Traveller's Beach Resort (Nadi) or Tanoa House (Suva).

Government Guest Houses

Government guest houses are a very specialised from of accommodation, generally for use by government workers in the field. These guest houses are either on the outer islands or in remote areas of Viti Levu or Vanua Levu. Although mostly utilised by the civil service, visitors can occasionally also use them providing government officials are not already occupying them.

Always check first with the local district office to see if there is a vacancy. The cost is usually from F$5 to F$7 per night.

Hotels & Resorts

The moderately priced hotels and resorts are mostly for tourists but are sometimes occupied by locals. These may represent the best bargains for visitors who want a modicum of luxury, but do not feel they need the most expensive hotel in order to enjoy their vacation. Amenities may include air-con rooms, pool, restaurant, bar, beach frontage and gift shop. Prices range from US$25 to US$80 for a single. An example in this category is the Crow's Nest (Sigatoka).

The top-end or up-market resorts are generally on the Coral Coast or Nadi-Lautoka area on Viti Levu, but are sometimes also on very remote islands. They are luxurious and aimed exclusively at the high-rolling visitor. These facilities usually include beach frontage, air-con, pool, bar, restaurant, gift shop, free use of snorkelling gear, bicycles, transport to and from the airport, and sometimes tennis courts and golf. Prices for this type of accommodation start at US$70 to US$110 for a single and go up to US$250 and more. Typical hotels in this league are the Regent (Nadi) or the Fijian (Coral Coast).

FOOD

There are four types of cuisine in Fiji: 'local' or Fijian, European, Chinese and Indian.

Fijians are fond of eating heavy, starchy foods (such as cassava, yams and taro) and love their beef and pork. Meat or fish is often fried in oil, and many dishes are prepared with coconut milk, which is extremely rich. Fijians also put down massive quantities of food in one sitting. A typical Fijian meal at any given time might consist of beef or fried fish, boiled taro leaves topped with coconut cream, and starchy boiled cassava or taro on the side. Visitors may find this variety of cuisine (which is not unlike the food eaten in other South Pacific cultures) heavy. Seasoning is mostly limited to salt, lemon juice or hot chillies, typically applied by you after the dish is served. Greens are also consumed, but more so in a village setting than in urban areas. Traditional Fijian feasts are always prepared by men in a *lovo* (underground oven), in which the foods are wrapped in banana leaves and placed on red-hot rocks to steam for six to eight hours.

Some of the more common food words and dishes include:

bele – a green, always boiled
bu – green coconut, for drinking
bulamakau – beef
chicken – toa
dalo – taro, usually boiled and used much like potatoes are in the West
ika – fish
ivi – Fijian chestnut, taste and texture akin to European chestnut
jaina – banana
kokoda – fish marinated in lime juice or vinegar with chilli and onions
kumala – sweet potato
kuwawa – guava
lolo – coconut milk
maqo – mango
niu – brown coconut, grated and squeezed to get coconut milk

ota – a young fern, boiled and served with lolo
palusami – taro leaves baked in a lovo with tinned beef, onions and lolo, very rich
pork – puaka
rourou – boiled taro leaves (looks like spinach)
tavioka – cassava root, a starchy white root, generally boiled and eaten like potato
ura – freshwater prawns, usually prepared in a lovo
uto – breadfruit, usually baked, cooked in a lovo, or boiled
uvi – yam
vivili – shellfish
vudi – plantain

Note that although turtle *(vonu)* is still considered a delicacy by Fijians, there are strict laws and regulations regarding the capture of turtles. To preserve their numbers, turtles may only be caught at certain times of the year.

'European' cooking in Fiji is that bland variety of food – overcooked steak, potatoes and vegetables – so many of us have grown up with and don't find particularly exciting in Fiji or anywhere else. ('European' here refers to Australia, the USA and Britain, rather than continental Europe.) Again, seasoning is minimal, with over-salting common. Excellent Chinese and Indian food is well represented in Fiji, though the Indian style may be a bit spicy by European standards. Both cuisines make extensive use of local vegetables and an array of exotic spices. Note that vegetarians who visit Fiji are better off sticking to Indian cuisine which has a vegetarian tradition, rather than Fijian cuisine, which is very much meat-oriented.

Modern supermarkets and local outdoor markets feature a variety of locally grown and imported high-quality fruit, vegetables, meat, poultry and every other conceivable household item. Those used to vegetables such as tomatoes, green onions, potatoes and the like, need not fear they will be lost in a sea of exotic local food – there is always plenty of familiar fare to be had. Mutton, pork, chicken and beef are abundant as well. Imported, canned goods are available but tend to be expensive. There is also fine locally produced cheese, milk and other dairy products. Locally grown fruit you might enjoy includes pineapples, guavas, mangoes, oranges, limes, papaws, avocados and bananas.

If you purchase fresh fruit at the market, be sure to wash it thoroughly before eating it. There are a plethora of nasty, tropical micro-organisms that may not agree with your system, so don't give them a chance to develop. Peeling the skins from vegetables and fruit is always a good idea.

The best good news for avid restaurant-goers is that the quantity and general quality of eateries has increased, especially in the Suva area. Moderately priced Chinese, Indian, Indonesian, Japanese and seafood restaurants have considerably brightened a previously bleak gastronomic landscape.

ENTERTAINMENT
Cinema
There are cinemas in every major town in Fiji and 10 in Suva alone. The theatres are divided into two categories: the standard houses showing English-language films from the USA and other countries, and the 'Indian' theatres featuring Indian-made movies exclusively. Many of the US movies are trashy B-grade 'shoot 'em up' or 'karate 'em up' clones, but those with more discriminating tastes will find that some good flicks actually make it to Fiji. The admission price is F$2 and schedules are shown in the daily papers.

THINGS TO BUY
Duty-Free Shopping
The most obvious thing about Fiji, even to the visitor who has just got off the plane, is the plethora of duty-free shops in the country and the sometimes overly aggressive touts who work there. The most popular items are photographic equipment, tape recorders and VCRs, perfumes, razors, telescopes, binoculars, sporting goods, radios, watches, liquor, tobacco and film. Duty-free shops can provide bargains for this merchandise, but buyers beware, all imported items sold in the so-called 'duty-free shops', with the exception of photo equipment, carry at least the 10% VAT.

If you're still interested, visit different shops, examine the merchandise and take a price survey. The best way to walk into a shop is to know exactly what you want and what its approximate retail market value is in your own country. Only then can you assess whether it is worthwhile to purchase the item. Some merchandise may in fact be more expensive in Fiji than where you come from.

In most stores the price is negotiated bazaar-style; the seller names a price and the buyer makes a counteroffer and so on until a bargain is struck. Don't be intimidated or afraid to drive a hard bargain. The seller will certainly not be afraid to relieve you of your money if he or she gets the chance. If you have local friends ask them to recommend a shop – or better yet, take a local along. There always seem to be local and tourist prices and you may benefit from this without excess haggling. As a general rule, forget shopping when a ship is in port; many prices rise even for locals on those days.

Make sure that you get a docket and warranty to receive service on the goods purchased when you return home. Also, try to watch the item you've purchased being wrapped in front of you and, if applicable, insist that it be given a trial run. With electronic gadgets keep in mind the possible differences in electrical standards in your country and in Fiji. Be positive that the thing will work when you get back home.

Although the huge duty-free shopping complex at Nadi Airport is in fact duty-free, it may or may not be less expensive than the duty-free stores in town. Again, the buyer should know his or her merchandise to be really sure. Prices at the airport are always fixed, so for those not interested in dealing with the bazaar method, the airport duty-free shops are the best places to buy.

For those who want to bargain but don't wish to deal with the hard sell, my experience is that the merchants outside Nadi and Suva are certainly the nicest. Try your luck in the outlying communities of Lautoka and Sigatoka and you will readily note the difference.

Any complaints can be addressed to the Fiji Visitors' Bureau or you can contact the Consumer Council of Fiji at 21 Stewart St, Suva (☎ 300 792), Labasa (☎ 812 559) and Lautoka (☎ 664 987).

Arts & Handicrafts

Art and craftwork can be purchased from three different sources – private craftspeople, duty-free shops and the government crafts centre. The cheapest source is generally the individuals, but these people are hard to find. Sometimes villagers augment their income by selling mats, carvings, pottery or masi cloth and you can always enquire. Duty-free shops are also a source of handicrafts, but quality varies.

The official government crafts centre at Ratu Sukuna House in Suva has some very fine items, but they tend to be expensive as the centre deals only with the best artisans and craftspeople. It may be wise to browse here first, to acquire a 'standard' for judging crafts you find elsewhere. The handicraft centre near the Suva municipal market has a wide variety of items, but you must check the stalls for goods and bargain. Beware of crafts handmade somewhere else (Asia, for example). There is also a handicrafts shop at Pacific Harbour, which is expensive but has good merchandise. Outside Suva, the craft centre at the Lautoka public market has some good bargains in varied items.

Keep in mind that you get what you pay for. Those interested in artefact-type replicas should first go to the Fiji Museum in Suva and carefully examine the relics therein. These are the models for the reproductions you are buying.

When considering small useful gifts to bring home, don't overlook Fiji spices (check your returning customs restrictions before buying). Spices are available in many shops; attractive gift packages in local pottery or other containers are sold at the government craft centre and other outlets. Locally grown spices include pepper, ginger,

Sword Sellers

The travel experience is not complete without being approached by at least one 'sword seller'. These Fijian capitalists peddle souvenir 'swords' on the street. They may start a conversation and upon finding out your name immediately carve it onto the 'sword' and ask for a 'small' charge or donation. If you are approached on the street by a local carrying a backpack or a small canvas bag, chances are, the individual may be a sword seller. Though not illegal, this practice is frowned upon by the Fiji Visitors' Bureau.

The swords are about as Fijian as rap music, but might make the perfect tacky gift for that special relative you don't want to spend too much money on. There is no set price for the swords, but I wouldn't pay more than F$5 for one. The sword sellers can be a nuisance but a simple *Sega vinaka* ('No thank you') will send them on their way. The fact that your name is on one of their swords is, if unauthorised by you, their problem, not yours; you have no obligation to buy. ∎

cinnamon and cardamom. (Strangely, although a lot of vanilla is grown in Fiji, it is almost impossible to buy here.)

Tailored Goods

Work done by tailors in Fiji can be quite good and very inexpensive. A Hawaiian-style shirt can be made for under US$15 for labour, and a fairly good array of fabric is available. The best bet is to bring to the tailor a shirt whose pattern you wish copied, along with material. Should you lose your suit on the aeroplane, South Seas Tailors (☎ 300 725), at 155 Victoria Parade, Suva, can replace it in 24 hours. A locally made Hawaiian style shirt (you supply the material) costs F$10.

Clothing

The national costume for men and women is the *sulu*, a rectangular piece of cloth about two metres long. It can be tied a number of ways, but is most popularly wrapped skirt-like around the waist and worn in combination with a T-shirt. For formal occasions men wear a kilt-like garment called a *sulu vakataga* and women wear a two-piece, ankle-length dress called a *sulu-i-ra*. Like a sarong in Asia many men soon find that in Fiji's often humid clime it is a practical item of clothing to wear. Get hooked and you will find yourself bringing a few sulus back home. They come in a variety of colours and patterns and in several grades of quality. Informal sulus can also be made while you wait for only a dollar or two, after you choose material from thousands of patterns available in hundreds of shops; most shops that sell cloth will also sew up a few seams for you.

Stamps

Like many smaller nations, Fiji earns a substantial income from its stamps. Collectors can purchase special sets from the Philatelic Bureau in the Ganilau building, across the street from the main post office in Suva. In addition to stamps from Fiji, the bureau also sells sets from Tuvalu, Western Samoa, Kiripati, Solomon Islands and Pitcairn Island. Orders can be paid for in cash and with American Express, Visa, MasterCard and Diners Club cards. The bureau is open from 8 am to 1 pm and 2 to 4 pm Monday to Thursday and closes at 3.30 pm on Friday. Any enquiries should be addressed to Postmaster, Philatelic Bureau, GPO Box 100, Suva, Fiji.

Getting There & Away

AIR

The vast majority of international flights land at Nadi International Airport. Although major airlines often market Fiji as a destination in its own right, it is actually an intermediate stop between major destinations in North America and Australia or New Zealand; most passengers on flights to Fiji are onward bound. Fiji is also linked to Hawaii, most of the major Pacific islands and Japan, but not South America.

Carriers to Fiji include Air New Zealand, Qantas, Air Pacific, Japan Airlines, Canadian Airlines International, Polynesian Airlines, and Air Nauru.

Round-the-World Tickets

With Round-the-World (RTW) fares two or more airlines link together to offer a service around the globe using their combined routings. The RTW ticket they jointly market allows you to fly around the world with stopovers at the various cities they serve. A number of these ticket possibilities can include Fiji.

There are often restrictions on these tickets – apart from the limitation that they only apply to services of the two (sometimes three) airlines that get together to offer them. There may be limits to the number of stopovers you are permitted, pre-booking requirements, penalties or additional charges if you change your routing, a maximum or minimum period of validity and so on. The end result, however, should be a useful saving over other methods of getting to the places you want to go.

RTW tickets that can fly you through Fiji include the Qantas-TWA ticket which costs A$3199 and allows you to fly through Fiji between Australia or New Zealand and Honolulu on Qantas services. There are also Qantas-Air Canada and Qantas-British Airways combinations at the same cost.

With Canadian Airlines International you can fly via Fiji on their Vancouver to Australia services. They have a variety of combinations with Alitalia, Cathay Pacific, Philippine Airlines, KLM and Singapore Airlines which start at around A$3199. You can also, at additional cost, add Canadian Airlines International's South American services to these round-the-world routes.

Purchased in the UK, RTW tickets through the South Pacific typically cost from around UK£1000. Possibilities include British Airways-Qantas for UK£980 (low season), UK£1520 (peak season); or Air New Zealand-British Airways-Qantas for UK£1130 (low season), UK£1515 (peak season). London bucket shops will put together their own RTW combinations at lower costs – see the To/From Europe section later.

Circle Pacific Tickets

As with RTW fares, Circle Pacific tickets involve two airlines joining to offer a route around the Pacific – which will usually mean travelling one way from Australia or New Zealand to the USA via the South Pacific and the other via Asia.

As with RTW fares there will usually be restrictions on booking, stopovers and period of validity. Most Circle Pacific tickets give you either four or five stopovers, additional stopovers cost around US$50 each.

Examples of Circle Pacific fares going through Fiji include Canadian Airlines International with Cathay Pacific or Malaysian Airlines System for A$3220 in the low season. Qantas and Northwest Orient get together for the same fare.

Pacific Air Passes

Polynesian Airlines flies to Sydney in Australia, Auckland in New Zealand, Western Samoa, Tonga, the Cook Islands and American Samoa. Polynesian Airlines has a 'Polypass' which allows you to fly on the airline's route network for 30 days for US$999. The ticket can only be purchased in

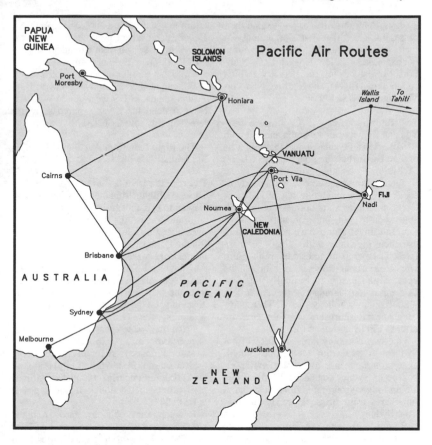

Australia and is not valid via New Zealand or in December and January.

Polynesian Airlines also has a 'Pacific Triangle Fare' that is very reasonable in price (US$448) and is good for visiting Tonga, Western Samoa and Fiji. The trip can begin from any of those destinations, and returns to the island you started from. The pass is good for 30 days and you must stay a 24-hour minimum in one destination.

Air Pacific has a similar 'Pacific Air Pass' for US$449. It originates in Fiji and is good for Apia (Western Samoa), Tonga, and Port Vila (Vanuatu). The only problem is that

after visiting any of the destinations you must return to the hub in Fiji before being able to fly on to the next destination. The Pacific Air Pass is good for 30 days from the date of commencement of travel. In order to qualify for the pass, travel must originate in North America, and the ticket must be issued there.

Solomon Airlines and Air Vanuatu (☎ 800 677 4277 in the USA) also have passes ('Discover Pacific Pass' and 'Paradise Pass' respectively) valid on any two sectors or the same sector on a round-trip basis for US$399. Passes for both carriers are good for

30 days. Solomon Airlines will extend their passes for more than two destinations (or sectors) for an extra US$100 per destination. For example, on Solomon you may fly Nadi-Port Moresby-Nadi for US$399 (which counts as two flights) and Nadi-Honiara-Port Vila-Nadi for US$499.

To/From Australia

You can fly between Australia and Fiji with Air Pacific and Qantas. Fares that might be of interest include regular one-way fares, excursion fares and group-return fares. Excursion fares require a minimum stay of six days, up to a maximum stay of 120 days. Group-return fares are normally only available if you're going on an organised package tour, but travel agents have been known to use their ingenuity with respect to these fares. The excursion fares and group-return fares are seasonal – low season is most of the year, high season is basically most of December and January – the Australian school summer holiday period. There have been special short-term bargain fares on offer to Fiji from time to time.

One-way economy fares are A$694 from Sydney, A$843 from Melbourne. Return excursion fares are available from Melbourne or Sydney for under A$750. There are no longer group fares from Australia to Fiji. Fares from Brisbane are the same as from Sydney.

Return fares, taking in Fiji as a stopover between Australia and North America, are also a consideration. Canadian Airlines International and Qantas fly this route and can include Fiji. A return excursion fare from Sydney or Melbourne to Los Angeles with Fiji as a stopover is around A$1600. Keep in mind that from season to season there are nearly always special fares available from the carriers so the above prices are not cast in stone.

The flight time from Sydney to Fiji is 3¾ hours, from Melbourne it's 4½ hours.

To/From New Zealand

Air New Zealand and Air Pacific fly from Auckland to Nadi. With Air Pacific, the return low-season fare is NZ$831. With Air New Zealand, advance-purchase return fares vary with the season from around NZ$850 to NZ$1000. There is no minimum stay period and you can stay for up to 12 months.

Fiji can also be a stopover between New Zealand and the US west coast. With Air New Zealand the advance-purchase return fare starts as low as NZ$1799 in the low season.

The flight time from Auckland to Nadi is 3¾ hours.

To/From the USA & Canada

There are flights from the US west coast and Hawaii to Fiji, most using Fiji as a stopover en route to Australia or New Zealand. Airlines operating between North America and Fiji are Qantas (out of Los Angeles and San Francisco), Air New Zealand (out of Los Angeles) and Canadian Airlines International (out of Vancouver). The flight time from the west coast to Fiji is about 12 hours depending on the carrier. From Honolulu it's six hours.

From the west coast to Fiji, the least expensive round-trip APEX (14-day advance purchase) fare for all carriers during the low season (from April to July) is around US$1100. A round trip on Canadian Airlines International on the Honolulu-Nadi segment is US$904.

Regular return economy fares from the west coast to Australia range from US$1100 to US$1300. Again, this price varies from season to season. Stopovers are permitted on any of these fares. It is often possible to get slightly more attractive fares from consolidators: check the travel ads in papers like the *Los Angeles Times*, *New York Times*, *San Francisco Examiner* or *Toronto Globe & Mail*.

To/From Europe

Few people are going to go all the way around the world from Europe simply to go to Fiji, but it can make an interesting stopover en route to Australia or New Zealand. The various RTW fares covered earlier permit you to slot Fiji in, or there are numer-

Top: Downtown Suva (RK)
Left: Fijian man, Suva (RK)
Right: Sigatoka market, Viti Levu (IO)

Top: Viani Beach, Vanua Levu (RK)
Bottom: Navluvatu village, Viti Levu (IO)

ous special fares offered in London or other European cheap-ticket centres.

In London you can check the travel ads in the *Times, Time Out, Business Traveller* or in giveaways like *Southern Cross* and *TNT*; or try ticket specialists like Trailfinders and STA. A typical ticket might take you to Australia via North America and Fiji, and back through Asia for around UK£980 in the low season, UK£1450 in the peak season. One-way fares to Australia via Fiji are available from around UK£400 (low season) if you shop around. Most agencies can be trusted, but there is the occasional wily operator: *Time Out* and *Business Traveller* give some useful advice on precautions to take.

To/From Asia

Apart from Japan Airlines there are few direct flights to Fiji from Asian nations: with most airlines you have to connect via Australia. One exception is Air Nauru, the airline of the tiny but wealthy island of Nauru, which can connect you to Fiji via Nauru. However, it involves an overnight stopover in Nauru which is not highly recommended. (Nauru is a phosphate-mining island which has been ecologically and culturally ravaged by mining activities.) From South-East Asia the only possibilities are via Australia or New Zealand.

To/From Other Pacific Islands

There are numerous connections between other Pacific islands and Fiji. Pacific airlines which fly into or out of Fiji include Polynesian Airlines, Air Nauru, Solomon Airlines, Air Caledonie and Air Vanuatu.

Two of Fiji's domestic carriers also serve neighbouring South Pacific nations. Air Pacific (which is the main carrier shuttling passengers from Suva to Nadi) has flights on 737s to Apia, Western Samoa; Auckland, New Zealand; Brisbane, Melbourne and Sydney, Australia; Vila, Vanuatu; Honiara, the Solomon Islands; Tokyo, Japan; and Tonga.

Package Tours

Package tours may not appeal to many budget travellers, but they are the way most visitors travel to the South Pacific. In Australia and the USA there are countless package tours available to Fiji resorts and any good travel agency can give you armfuls of colourful brochures. Costs depend upon the season, the resort and the length of time, but typically a week stay on a twin-share basis (from the USA) begins at US$800 to US$900 including airfares.

In other countries there may not be such a wide selection of Fiji packages, but an agent should be able to answer questions such as: Does the hotel have a mountain or ocean view? Will your accommodation be over the water, on the beach or in the garden? Is the hotel a super-deluxe one or more moderate? How far away is the beach? A specialist will be familiar with the tour packages available and should be able to answer these questions so that there are no unhappy surprises. A competent agent should also be able to prepare a tailor-made itinerary for the person who has special interests such as golf, diving, bird-watching etc. Last but not least, a reputable agency can save you money.

SEA
Ship

Unfortunately, the romantic days of catching a tramp steamer and working your way across the Pacific are gone forever. It is possible to book passage on a freighter by consulting an experienced agency or by contacting Freighter Travel Tips, a firm that has specialised in this type of travel for years. Local shipping agents can also refer you to the shipping lines that visit Fiji.

Once in Fiji, however, it is impossible to jump on a freighter to some other destination without having made previous arrangements. Freighter skippers simply do not want to deal with passengers and will refer you to a shipping agent, who will probably just shrug his shoulders.

Yacht

It is possible to hitch rides on yachts leaving Fiji, or heading there from ports on the US west coast or in Australia. To find the boats headed in this direction, you must do some sleuthing at your favourite marinas, and place notices on bulletin boards at yacht clubs and marine supply shops. The Lonely Planet newsletter once had some advice on hitching a yacht – from a yachtie:

Yachts are almost always crewed by couples or men only and are short of crew for the longer passages. No experience is necessary, just taking turns in keeping lookout for big ships (call your skipper when in doubt). Yachts travel with the trade winds preferably and also in warm climates. This means they go west. Most land travellers go via Boeing 747 and go east. Here might be a conflict.

How to find yachts? Cruising yachts generally have the following characteristics (nice when you are looking around in Los Angeles): foreign flags, wind-vane steering gear, a generally sturdy appearance and laundry of the people who live on board hung out to dry.

Cost? Share food costs. This seems normal. I charged US$50 a week for food and lodging and took care of all harbour dues, oil, propane etc. Some people still think this is expensive. (Nobody realises that with depreciation, insurance, maintenance and operating expenses my boat ends up costing US$50 a day.)

The best way to approach a skipper is to state that you're not the seasick type (check this out) and have money to share food and money to travel home in case of emergency. Show your proof in travellers' cheques. Generally be helpful with work, cooking etc on board. With a bit of luck a good skipper will teach you the ropes as well as navigation. Go for a week's trial if the route and time permit.

Leave the boat at the appointed end of your joyride. The ship is also the skipper's home and, as you will experience, affords little privacy. Boating is the last

freedom left but hassles with official permits, paperwork, visas etc are getting worse, especially in the so-called 'free world'. Still it is beautiful to share the experience. And we do need more ladies out here (adventurous types naturally).

There have been various other letters about hitching yacht rides. The letters from yacht owners generally back up these statements – that they're only too happy to take on crew. The letters from hitchers generally expressed amazement at how easy it was to pick up a ride – it's all a matter of luck.

WARNING

This chapter is particularly vulnerable to change – prices for international travel are volatile, routes are introduced and cancelled, schedules change, rules are amended and special deals come and go. Airlines and governments seem to take a perverse pleasure in making price structures and regulations as complicated as possible and you should check directly with the airline or a travel agent to make sure you understand how a fare (and ticket you may buy) works. In addition, the travel industry is highly competitive and there are many lurks and perks. The upshot of this is that you should get opinions, quotes and advice from as many airlines and travel agents as possible before you part with your hard-earned cash.

The details given in this chapter should be regarded as pointers and are not a substitute for your own careful, up-to-the-minute research.

Getting Around

The Fiji group is served by an extensive network of air routes, inter-island boats and an efficient bus system along its roads. Visitors will find that this infrastructure makes travelling within the larger islands and around the archipelago relatively easy. In addition, transport is very reasonably priced, especially for Americans who have the benefit (at least for the time being) of a strong dollar. Despite the 'mañana' attitude that pervades Fiji, planes, ferries and buses generally run on time.

Many visitors to Fiji never leave the western side of the country, finding the hotels a self-contained vacation. They may venture only by local tourist bus or rental car to nearby attractions. However, those wishing to go to Suva or other parts of Viti Levu have the options of flying from Nadi or taking the 'scenic' route via rental car, local bus (which generally makes quite a few stops and takes four to five hours), or the express coach primarily for tourists (which makes few stops and takes about three hours from Nadi to the capital). It is highly recommended that the first-time visitor travel overland (along Queens or Kings Rds) rather than by air, to get at least a cursory look at the Fijian coast and countryside.

AIR
Nadi International Airport
Although a bit provincial by international standards, Nadi International Airport lacks nothing in the way of official services and amenities.

The airport branch of the Fiji Visitors' Bureau (☎ 722 433, 723 064) is open during all aircraft arrivals and intermittently during the daytime (when there are no arrivals). It can be extremely helpful and usually has up-to-date information on all activities and accommodation.

First-time visitors should note that there is also a list of all the local accommodation prominently displayed in the customs area;

the list includes nightly rates and taxi fare from the airport.

The airport bank is a branch of Westpac and is the only 24-hour, seven-day-a-week bank in Fiji. It is not, however, a full-service bank; it operates only for currency exchange, even if you have an account with it.

Those looking for a post office in the terminal will be hard-pressed to find one because it is across the road, near the cargo building. You can also send telegrams from this agency.

There is also plenty of duty-free shopping at the airport; however, it's only for 'last chance' outbound travellers who are either in transit or about to board their planes. Shoppers need not fear; there are plenty of shopping opportunities in and around Nadi, Lautoka, Sigatoka and Suva. Despite the 'duty-free' label, prices at the terminal are nothing to get excited about.

The airport has lockers and a storage area for your belongings. The cost is 20 cents per day. There's also a storage area for larger items like bicycles and large containers, near the gift shop; the rates are also reasonable.

Nadi Airport also has a number of airline offices, car-rental agencies, resort offices and tour agencies. Airline offices include:

Air Nauru (☎ 722 795)
Air New Zealand (☎ 722 922)
Air Pacific (☎ 722 499)
Canadian Airlines (☎ 722 400)
Fiji Air (☎ 722 521)
Polynesian Airlines (☎ 722 599)
Qantas (☎ 722 880)
Sunflower Airlines (☎ 723 016)
Turtle Airways (☎ 772 988)

Tour agencies and resort offices include:

Atlantic & Pacific Fiji Tours (☎ 722 074)
Hunt's Travel (☎ 722 852)
Musket Cove/Dick's Place (☎ 722 773/488)
Rosie Tours (☎ 722 935)
Sun Tours (☎ 22 666)
Tapa International/American Express (☎ 722 100)

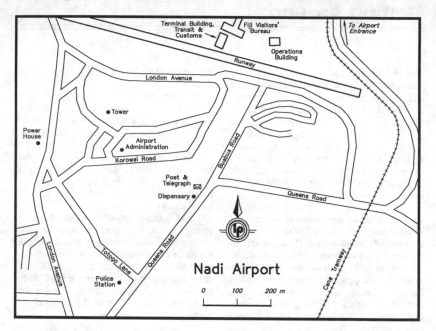

Nadi Airport

Thomas Cook (☎ 722 377)
Turtle Island Lodge (☎ 722 780)
United Touring (☎ 722 811)
Yanuca Tours (☎ 722 809)

Car rental agencies at Nadi Airport are:

Avis (☎ 722 233)
Budget Rent-a-Car (☎ 722 735)
Central Rent A Car (☎ 722 771)
Hertz Rent-a-Car (☎ 722 146)
Khans Rentals (☎ 723 506)
Letz Rent A Car (☎ 722 803)
National Car Rental (☎ 722 267)
Roxy Rentals (☎ 722 763)
Satellite Rentals (☎ 722 219)
Skyline Rentals (☎ 723 980)
Thrifty Car Rentals (☎ 722 935)
UTC Rent a Car (☎ 722 811)

Departure Tax Upon leaving Fiji you must
pay an airport departure tax of F$10. The tax
is payable in Fiji currency at the airline
counter. This is usually a good time to get rid
of your silver.

Domestic Airports
Both Nadi International Airport and Nausori
Airport, near Suva, serve as domestic hubs
for inter-island flights. Sunflower has its hub
at Nadi, while Fiji Air, which has more
extensive domestic services, has its hub at
Nausori. Sunflower has services to most of
the major tourist/dive destinations from Nadi
including Vanua Levu, Taveuni, Kadavu and
Malololailai.

For most outer-island destinations, visitors must first fly to Suva (via Air Pacific or
Sunflower Airlines) in order to connect with
Fiji Air, the major domestic carrier. Fiji's
other major domestic carrier, Sunflower Airlines, has two daily flights to Suva, while Air
Pacific has seven.

Fiji's domestic carriers fly to every island
where there is tourist accommodation and to
many where there are no facilities. If you
wish to explore the non-touristed islands,
you will need an invitation from a local
friend. It's not advisable to drop in and

assume there will be some facilities. In one case – the former prime minister's home island of Lakeba – it's not only ill-advised to visit without permission, it's illegal.

Aside from their regularly scheduled service, Fiji Air and Sunflower Airlines will charter planes for special groups or individuals. There are also two charter helicopter services, Pacific Crown Aviation (☎ 790 410 in Nadi, 361 422 in Lami), and the Island Hoppers (☎ 790 410) which offers 'flightseeing' tours.

Air Pacific Though most of Air Pacific's services are international, the carrier averages about seven flights daily between Nadi and Suva for F$52. Air Pacific operates one 747, a 767 and a 737. Its main ticket offices are in central Suva on Victoria Parade (☎ 304 388), at Nadi International Airport (☎ 722 499), and in every community served by the airline.

Sunflower Airlines Sunflower Airlines has a fleet of Britten Norman Islander Aztec twin-engined aircraft, four-engined Herons and Twin Otter aircraft which use Nadi as a hub and operate every day. One of their biggest tourist destinations (eight flights daily) is Malololailai (in the Mamanuca group) to the resorts of Plantation Island and Musket Cove. Sunflower Airlines also flies to Suva twice a day. The airline has offices at each of its destinations, but the main contact is at Nadi Airport (☎ 723 016/408; fax 790 085). Sunflower's office in downtown Suva (☎ 315 755) is on Pier St.

Fiji Air Fiji Air, with a fleet of Twin Otters, Harbin Y-12s (an 18-passenger Otter 'clone' built in China), and Britten Norman Islander aircraft, operates out of Suva and flies to 13 domestic and one international destination, covering more areas than any other local carrier.

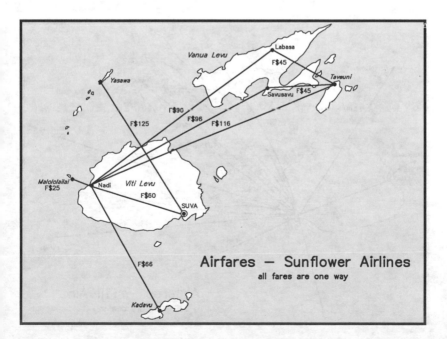

Airfares – Sunflower Airlines
all fares are one way

Visitors might want to take advantage of Fiji Air's discount air package, the 'Fiji Islands Pass' which enables the traveller to visit four major islands (Vanua Levu, Taveuni, Kadavu and Ovalau) during a 30-day period for the price of F$180. Unfortunately, only a few seats per flight are allotted for this service, and thus space may be scarce. If you have some flexibility in your itinerary, this may be a good way to get around. The four-island air pass can only be bought in Fiji. Enquire at Fiji Air's Nadi Airport office (☎ 722 521) or at its headquarters in Suva (☎ 313 666; fax 300 771).

Similarly, Fiji Air has a special stand-by fare which is considerably less than the regular tariff. It's a great deal if you get on, but the hassle and expense of going back and forth to the airport if you don't get on, may not be worth your while. (As several readers have mentioned, if you go to Nausori Airport hoping to save F$10 going stand-by, you may waste more money having to go back to Suva in a taxi costing F$15 and still have to pay full fare to avoid repeating your experience.) Check with Fiji Air personnel for information – rules and regulations are subject to change.

Fiji Air has four daily flights from Nadi Airport to Malololailai, and day tours are also available to the island at a lesser price than the normal round-trip ticket. Day tours are also available to Levuka for F$54. The package includes breakfast and a light lunch at the Royal Hotel and a guided walking tour. When you purchase this fare, make sure the Levuka Fiji Air office is advised of your arrival so the guided tour and meals can be arranged. Stand-by fares to Levuka are also available.

Fiji Air also recently increased its service between Suva and Nadi from 14 to 24 flights per week, making it the dominant carrier on this route. The fare is F$52.

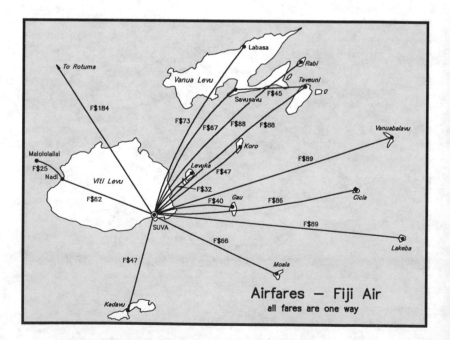

Airfares – Fiji Air
all fares are one way

BUS

While many locals have cars, the majority of the population depends on buses and trucks, which are the main means of transport even for those in very remote areas. The buses, whose bodies are manufactured in Fiji, are noisy, smoke-belching dinosaurs with open windows sealed from foul weather by means of a tarpaulin, which is communally rolled down at the appropriate time. Although time-consuming, travel by bus can be rewarding for the visitor because it encourages mixing with the local population. On the outer islands where rental vehicles are scarce, visitors may find that local buses and taxis are the only form of transport. Buses are very inexpensive (figure on approximately F$1 per 20 km), run regularly and can be caught at roadside bus stands. In more rural areas they may be hailed like taxis.

Express Bus

There are several bus companies that offer express air-con bus services between Suva and Nadi on Queens Rd and one firm that has services between Lautoka and Suva on Kings Rd. These are comfortable and speedy, but are not necessarily the most interesting buses to take.

Queens Coach (☎ 313 543 in Suva, 722 036 in Nadi) This service leaves Nadi Airport at 7.30 am and proceeds to the Regent Hotel, Nadi Hotel, Fijian Resort, Sigatoka town, Reef Hotel, Naviti Hotel, Warwick Fiji, Pacific Harbour and Orchid Island, arriving at the Tradewinds Hotel outside Suva at noon. On the return leg it leaves the Tradewinds Hotel at 5 pm (stopping at the same points) and arrives at Nadi Airport at 9 pm. The one-way fare between Suva and Nadi is around F$10.

Pacific Transport Ltd (☎ 304 126 in Suva, 700 044 in Nadi, 500 088 in Sigatoka, 660 499 in Lautoka) Express buses leave daily (except Sundays) from Nadi Airport at 7 am, 12.40 and 6 pm. In the other direction, buses leave Suva at 6.45, 9.30 am, 12.10 and 5.30 pm. The trip from Nadi Airport to Suva takes about 4½ hours. There are five other daily departures of ordinary buses that stop at every village along Queens Rd stretching from Suva to Lautoka. If in doubt about where to catch a bus, the best bet is simply to ask. If you are in

a remote area it's always easy to flag down a bus on the side of the road.

Sunbeam Transport (☎ 382 122/704 in Suva, 662 822/292 in Lautoka) This is the only bus company with an express service on Kings Rd. Daily express buses from Lautoka to Suva leave at 6.30 am, 12.15 and 4.30 pm, with three other local buses departing at various other times. In the other direction, buses leave Suva for Lautoka at 6.45 am, 1.30 and 5.15 pm, with three other local buses in the mornings. The express stops include Ba, Tavua, Vaileka, Korovou and Nausori. The fare from Lautoka to Suva is about F$10.

TAXI

Generally, taxis are an inexpensive way to get around in Fiji. A crosstown fare in Suva, for example, averages F$3. Many taxis in rural areas do not have meters, so it's wise to negotiate or at least ask the driver what the cost will be. There is also a strange law that dictates a taxi driver who has dropped off a passenger and is returning to his stand can only charge a fraction of the normal fare. This works in your favour. Whether you are travelling across town or across the island, a return taxi is a great bargain. For example a 'return' taxi within Suva only costs around 40 cents while a return taxi between Nadi and Suva is only about F$10 per person. Taxis that have come a long distance, say from Suva to Nadi and are looking for passengers, gather in a special area of town (usually near the bus stand). The idea is to stuff their cars with as many passengers as possible to make up for the crummy tariffs. In Suva, if you are looking for a ride to the western side of the island (Nadi, Lautoka, Ba, Tavua etc) go to the parking lot on Straun St, off Robertson Rd, near Morris Hedstrom. Likewise, if you are in Nadi or Lautoka and want to go to Suva, ask at the market or the bus stand where the 'return' taxis station themselves.

Keep in mind that on Sundays in the Suva area taxis are available but hard to come by, while in the Nadi area, because of the tourist trade, taxis are much easier to find on Sundays. In Suva, getting a taxi in the evenings can also be a problem. There has been an increase in taxi-related robberies, and drivers, especially Indian drivers, are wary about venturing into the Suva night.

CAR

Fiji has about 3300 km of roads, over half of which are bitumen sealed. Most of the sealed highways are on Viti Levu, which has a 500-km road that circles the island. After many years of claiming that the highway will be finished 'next year', construction on the road around the island has finally been completed.

The road is generally well engineered, but drivers must contend with cattle, horses and goats that feed on the edge of the highway and may wander across at night, as well as the occasional pothole that is on next month's schedule to be refilled. Motorists should also be aware of villagers who sometimes walk dangerously close to passing vehicles or sit in groups at the edges of roads that pass through communities. Likewise, drivers have very little 'driver's education' and will do things like pass on blind curves or tailgate unnervingly close. The driver's motto should be 'Watch out for everything – human, beast or machine'. Also beware of the speed bumps across the road at some villages. They are bigger than they appear, and the posted speed warnings should be obeyed literally, lest you rip out the undercarriage of your vehicle. In the Nadi area these are found prior to entering Nadi town from the airport and in Viseisei village, between Nadi and Lautoka.

Car rental agencies have sprung up like mushrooms over the past few years and every major hotel has a rental desk. Generally, the larger agencies keep the cars in good shape, but it's always a good idea to give the prospective vehicle a spin around the block before you take it out in earnest. Even big-name agencies can have maintenance lapses and the cars may lack minor things like working brakes or pressure in the tyres. Rates vary a bit, but on the average, expect to pay at least F$70 per day for unlimited travel. Book early for car rentals because some agencies may deny there are less expensive autos available in order to steer you towards the more expensive vehicles. Both UTC and Budget Rentals have 4WD Suzuki jeeps.

One reader found Khans Rentals, which has a 24-hour office at Nadi Airport, the cheapest. What's more, if you phone in advance (before reaching Fiji) and book a car they will give you an additional 10% discount. Prices start at about F$15 per day and 16 cents per km for the smallest models. (See the earlier Nadi International Airport section for a list of car rental agencies at the airport.)

To drive a rental vehicle visitors need only a valid driver's licence from their own country to qualify. North Americans should note that in Fiji you drive on the left side of the road. Travellers should also note that there are service stations near all major towns, but in some of the rural areas they are practically nonexistent. If you get caught on a backroad with a nearly empty tank, it might be wise to ask in village shops, which frequently sell fuel from drums.

BICYCLE

I'm told that Fiji is unsung cycling paradise. Roads are not too busy and traffic naturally slows down for a cyclist, perhaps because cycling is still a novelty. The biggest hazards are the unruly, smoke-belching buses which don't slow down on unsealed roads and cover cyclists with a layer of dirt. Another danger is dehydration. The heat in Fiji is a factor you can't ignore so be prepared to consume gallons of water. Locals are generally very happy to provide nourishment to thirsty cyclists along the road. Be sure to travel light, and bring a mountain bike if you have one. You'll need a sturdy two-wheeler to negotiate Fiji's potholed, unsealed roads. Finally, you can always safely stash your bicycle at storage area at Nadi or Nausori airports for under F$1 per day.

HITCHING

Hitching is tolerated in Fiji, and in many rural areas, is virtually the only way you can travel besides walking, as there are few if any buses. It is, however, culturally frowned upon for locals to do it, even though many can ill afford to take a bus. For foreigners, it is generally fairly easy to get a ride, and I suppose it's still enough of a novelty not to upset the authorities. Fortunately, visiting hitchhikers have not yet overwhelmed Fiji, but if they ever became a nuisance, be assured that the government would pass a law banning hitchhiking.

BOAT

Although air transport has become the preferred mode of long-haul travel, inter-island vessels remain a vital link for local travellers and cargo to the outer islands. In many instances, inter-island ferries, copra boats and small skiffs are the only way to reach isolated communities. For visitors with time on their hands who don't mind roughing it, inter-island boats are a great way to travel and meet the locals. Voyages on these vessels may range from several hours to several weeks and are generally very inexpensive.

Schedules are not posted; the best way to find out dates of departure is to call the various shipping companies listed under the following Copra Boat section. Keep in mind that shipping companies frequently give out inaccurate information regarding departure times and space availability. If you are determined to see the outer islands by boat, it is wise to check personally with the captain when the vessel is in port. He has the final say as to who goes. Half a kg of kava or a bottle of booze just may ensure your berth. This is almost mandatory for boats bound for Rotuma.

Copra Boat

Copra boats go to the outermost reaches of the archipelago, and while these boats are basically freighters, they will also take some passengers. (Note that inter-island ferries also carry freight, but are primarily used to transport people and vehicles.) The quality of accommodation varies from vessel to vessel, as does the space available – sometimes cabins can be had, sometimes only deck passage. Deck passage means just that – sleeping, eating and drinking on deck with the islanders who have chosen the economy

route. Likewise, each ship has different eating arrangements. You may have the option of bringing your own food along, or you might share regular meals with the crew.

There is something very basic about journeying on a copra boat; in a way, it is stepping into the past. You must have patience and the ability to weather minor inconveniences like choppy seas, diesel fumes, seasickness, engine noise, cockroaches and rain. On the other hand, the camaraderie, adventure, salt air, drifting and dreaming are hard to beat.

For information regarding schedules, call the following shipping firms:

Bula Ferry Service
Its vessel, *Ana Tupou*, calls at Levuka and Suva (☎ 312 794, 313 478).
Consort Shipping Co
Its vessel, *Spirit of Free Enterprise (SOFE)*, calls at Suva, Koro, Savusavu and Taveuni (☎ 313 344, 311 888; fax 303 389).
Emosi's Shipping
Vessels call at Suva, Levuka and Leleuvia (☎ 312 445, 304 619).
Patterson Brothers Shipping Co
Its vessels, *Ovalau II, Jubilee* and *Ashika*, call at Natovi, Nabouwalu, Savusavu, Labasa, Levuka, Lautoka, Ba, Tavua, Nadi, Rakiraki and Ellington Wharf (☎ 315 644, 313 088).

Whippy's Ferry Service
Its vessel, MV *Gurawa*, calls at Suva and northern Kadavu (☎ 340 015, 312 426).

Inter-Island Ferry

Several shipping companies also have inter-island ferry services. The vessels include the *Jubilee*, *Ovalau* and *Ashika* run by Patterson Brothers, and the *Sprit of Free Enterprise* run the by the Consort Shipping Co. The *Spirit of Free Enterprise* can carry 450 economy-class passengers and 24 cabin-class passengers. Emosi's Shipping and Bula Ferry Service both offer daily services to Levuka.

These vessels ply the waters between Viti Levu, Vanua Levu and Ovalau. They are fairly modern, speedy and offer you the option of bringing your own car along.

The cost for shipping a car (and driver) to Ovalau, Vanua Levu and back to Viti Levu is around F$150. Passengers are charged standard fares. For individuals without cars, Patterson Brothers provides transport from the communities it serves to and from all its terminals. Rental cars for the voyage can be obtained through any of the agencies. Note that some of the Patterson Brothers' vessels depart from Natovi Landing (about 1½ hours by bus from the Suva GPO). Most other departures are from Princes Wharf in Suva, or from the Government Jetty in nearby Walu Bay.

I have also been told that auxiliary cargo ships operated by the Fiji government are also an excellent way to travel. They are very inexpensive, provide meals, showers, padded benches for bunks, are safe and visit many of the outlying islands. There are, however, no set schedules and to find out about their comings and goings its best to ask at the Fiji Visitors' Bureau in Suva.

Warning The shipping schedules listed here are intended as a guide only. Schedules are notorious for being altered. Under no circumstances depend on written schedules. When in Suva it's best to go to the Patterson Brothers offices in Epworth House on Nina St (☎ /fax 315 644), or to telephone one of

its other offices (☎ 661 173 in Lautoka, 812 444 in Labasa, 440 125 in Levuka). The Consort Shipping Co's office (☎ 302 877; fax 303 389) in Suva is in the Dominion Arcade on Thomson St near the Fiji Visitors' Bureau.

Consort Shipping Co The *Spirit of Free Enterprise* (or *SOFE*, pronounced 'sofie') provides services to Koro, Taveuni and Savusavu from Suva. The ferry leaves Saturday at 3 pm from Princess Wharf and arrives in Savusavu (via Koro Island) at 4 am Sunday morning. The return voyage departs 6 pm Monday evening and arrives in Suva at 7 am, Tuesday morning. The Wednesday sailing (also via Koro) departs Suva at 5 am and arrives in Savusavu at 6 pm the same day. *SOFE* departs Savusavu at midnight and arrives in Taveuni at 6 am Thursday. The ferry departs Taveuni at noon on Thursday, returning to Savusavu at 5 pm the same day. *SOFE* departs at 6 pm Thursday evening for Suva (via Koro), arriving in the capital at 7 am Friday.

The fare from Suva to Savusavu is F$29.70, and from Suva to Taveuni is F$34.10. The Suva to Koro fare is F$25.30. Cabins are also available for F$66 to Taveuni, F$55 to Savusavu and F$44 to Koro.

Patterson Brothers Shipping Co The Patterson Brothers' *Ovalau* or *Jubilee* depart daily (except Sundays) for Levuka. To catch the boat you must take the Patterson Brothers' bus which departs from the Suva GPO at 1 pm, arriving at Natovi Landing at 3 pm. The ferry departs from Natovi Landing at 3.30 pm and arrives at Buresala (on Ovalau) at 4.15 pm. The bus (which is also ferried over) continues to Levuka, arriving at 5 pm. On the return trip the bus leaves Levuka at 4 am and arrives at Buresala at 5.30 am. The ferry leaves Buresala at 6 am and arrives at Natovi Landing at 6.45 am. From there the bus continues on to Suva, arriving at the capital at 9 am in time for breakfast. The fare is F$27 one way.

Note that those leaving Levuka for Suva

also have the option of travelling to Nabouwalu or Labasa on Vanua Levu simply by staying on the same vessel (as opposed to getting off at Natovi Landing and continuing to Suva). See the next paragraph for details.

Patterson Brothers has a daily (except Sunday) ferry service to Nabouwalu which connects with a bus to Labasa. The bus departs from the Suva GPO at 5 am, and arrives at Natovi Landing at 6.30 am. The ferry departs for Nabouwalu at 7.15 am, arriving about four hours later. You continue via bus for the sugar town of Labasa and arrive another 3½ hours later at around 2.30 pm. To catch the ferry back to Suva take the bus from Labasa at 6.30 am which arrives in Nabouwalu at 10 am. The ferry leaves Nabouwalu at 11 am, and reaches Natovi Landing at around 3 pm. From there a bus leaves immediately for Suva. The fare from Suva to Nabouwalu is F$29.70, and from Suva to Labasa it's F$34.10.

Patterson Brothers also provides a bus service from Nadi to Lautoka, and on to Ellington Wharf (near Rakiraki) where you can catch a direct ferry to Nabouwalu. From Nabouwalu you go by bus to Labasa. The bus leaves Nadi at 3.30 am, arrives in Lautoka at 3.50 am, departs for Ellington Wharf at 4 am and arrives there at 6.30 am. The ferry departs from Ellington Wharf at 7 am, arriving in Nabouwalu at 10.30 am. The bus to Labasa leaves at 11 am and arrives at 2.30 pm. On the return trip the bus leaves Labasa at 6.30 am and arrives in Nabouwalu at 10 am; the ferry leaves Nabouwalu at 11 am and reaches Ellington Wharf at 2.30 pm; the bus leaves Ellington Wharf at 3 pm and arrives in Lautoka at 5.30 pm. From there the bus arrives in Nadi at 6 pm. Phone Patterson Brothers in Levuka (☎ 440 125) to confirm schedules and fares.

Patterson Brothers' *Ashika* has a weekly service from Suva to Koro in the Lomaiviti group as well as to Savusavu and Taveuni (on the same run). The vessel departs on Mondays at midnight from Old Millers Wharf in Walu Bay. The fare is F$30.80 from Suva to Savusavu or Koro and F$35.20 from Suva to Taveuni.

The *Ashika* also does a run to Kadavu via Suva on Thursdays (F$34.10). The ferry leaves Suva at midnight and arrives at Vunisea, Kadavu the next day at 8 am. It leaves Vunisea around 9 am and stops at Kavala Bay (for an extra F$5) which is very close to Ono Island and the nearby resorts. The vessel then returns to Suva. Kavala Bay lacks a deep-water wharf so the *Ashika* must anchor offshore. Upon arrival she is met by a number of smaller boats which service all of the local resorts and villages. It's easy to board these vessels and get where you have to go.

Buca Bay Service There is a small company that provides service to and from Buca Bay on Vanua Levu and Taveuni for F$10 on weekdays. A bus leaves Savusavu bus stand at about 11.30 am and connects with the boat at Natuvu on Buca Bay at about 1 pm, arriving in Waiyevo (on Taveuni) at around 4 pm. The ferry leaves Waiyevo at about 8.30 am, 'Fiji time'. Make sure you bring your dramamine on this 2½-hour trip – it can be rough. Travellers should realise that once they are deposited at the landing in Buca Bay there may be a long wait for the bus to Savusavu (there are two a day); the other option is to hire a carrier to Savusavu for about F$30.

Emosi's Shipping A new company, Emosi's Shipping (☎ 440 057 in Levuka) also services the Suva-Levuka route from Monday to Saturday. Though the terminus is Levuka, the route (Suva-Bau Landing-Leleuvia-Levuka) takes a different course from the Patterson Brothers, departing by bus from Suva to Bau Landing (instead of Natovi) and stopping at the popular backpackers' resort of Leleuvia. The bus departs from Suva bus station at 11 am, stopping at Bau Landing where it connects with the boat, and you arrive in Levuka early in the afternoon. The vessel retraces its steps and returns to Suva the same day. Buy your tickets at Shop No 8 at Union Plaza, Suva (☎ 312 445, 304 619). The fare is F$12 one way for Suva-Leleuvia and F$15 for Suva-Levuka.

Bula Ferry Service Also a new company, Bula has Monday-to-Saturday services to Levuka via Natovi Landing. A bus leaves at 8 am from the Suva bus station and transfers passengers to the *Ana Tupou* at 10 am. The vessel arrives at Levuka Wharf at noon. A second trip departs from the Suva bus station at 1.30 pm, arriving at Levuka Wharf at 5.15 pm. Returning voyages leave Levuka at 7.30 am (arriving in Suva at 11.30 am) and at 1 pm (arriving in Suva at 4.45 pm). The fare is F$17. You can purchase tickets in Suva at Jina Bros (☎ 312 794), a hair salon in the Metropole Building, Shop No 1 on Scotts St, or at Talanoa Bookshop at the bus station. In Levuka see Mr Koroi Ramusu near the post office.

Whippy's Ferry Service Whippy's (☎ 340 015, 312 426) also provides transport from Suva to several resorts in northern Kadavu. Its vessel, the MV *Gurawa* departs from Suva at 7 am Tuesday and Friday, returning to Suva on Wednesday and Saturday. Prices are F$37.20 from Suva to Albert's Place and Nukubalavu, and F$35.20 from Suva to Vabea and Naqara.

Chartered Schooner *La Violante* is the answer for those whose dream vacation to the South Pacific cannot be fulfilled without an excursion on a tall-masted schooner with sails billowing in the trade winds. This private yacht is available for charter for up to six people in three private cabins, and includes everything except alcoholic beverages. You can choose deserted beaches, remote villages, diving, whatever your dream demands. But it doesn't come cheap: the cost is F$175 per day per person, which includes food and soft drinks. Book with Stardust Cruises Ltd (☎ 662 215 in Lautoka), which are based on Malololailai (Plantation) Island.

Viti Levu

Viti Levu, which translates as 'great Fiji', is the largest and oldest island in the archipelago. Roughly oval in shape, it measures 146 km long and 106 km wide and has an area of 10,389 sq km. When compared with other Pacific islands, it is exceeded in size only by New Caledonia and Hawaii. With a population of approximately 544,000 it is also the most populous island in Fiji.

Commensurate with the island's size is its importance. Viti Levu's rich river valleys support the country's densest population centres. Extensive sugar lands lie on its western and northern coasts. Gold mines, dairy farms, light manufacturing and the most important industry – tourism – contribute to its wealth. In addition, the island is the hub of air and sea communications in the south-western Pacific.

Geography

Viti Levu has evolved geologically into its present form through a long and complex series of events. During protracted periods it lay deep beneath the sea; at other times much of it was buried under massive amounts of lava and other volcanic materials. The land was tilted, broken and pushed every which way, yet it emerged as a symmetrically shaped island with a mountain barrier forming a roughly north-south axis or backbone.

The island lies in the path of the prevailing trade winds, resulting in a heavy rainfall over the windward slopes of the east, and leaving the countryside to the west generally sun-drenched and dry. The transition from the wet to the dry zones is abrupt, and can best be seen from the air. In general, the area of the island east of the north-south mountain axis is dense and green with vegetation, while the area to the west is light yellow-green or yellow and brown, according to the season.

Orientation

Viti Levu has one main road around its perimeter. Most of this road is well maintained, especially the stretches between Sigatoka and Nadi, and Suva and Pacific Harbour, which make up a comparative superhighway. Lesser utilised portions of the road may be in a poorer state of repair, due to flooding, hurricanes or whatever natural disasters may have just occurred.

The highway circling the island is actually divided into two sections: Queens Rd, which covers the southern coast from Suva to Lautoka; and Kings Rd which includes the northern coast, also from Suva to Lautoka. Of the two, Queens Rd is the shorter route to Suva (221 km). A leisurely driving time is about three hours. The northern route is in poorer shape, longer (265 km) and certainly less travelled by tourists. Both roads are now completely sealed around the perimeter of the island.

In theory the island could be circled in a day, but this would involve maniacal driving and certainly wouldn't be any fun. The best suggestion is to take your time and do it in two, three or even four days, stopping along the way to see all the points of interest and chatting with the local villagers. There are some interesting inland and coastal turn-offs mentioned in this guide, but do not expect sealed roads on these detours. Inclement weather (not unusual in Fiji) may make them even worse, so be forewarned. Drivers should also keep a lookout for locals walking along the edge of the highway and ubiquitous stray livestock at any time of the day or night.

The inland routes described in this chapter represent only a few of the options. Explorers may want to pick up a copy of Kim Gravelle's *The Fiji Explorer's Handbook* which has an excellent selection of trips and can be purchased at any bookstore in Fiji.

This chapter is organised beginning with descriptions of Nadi and Lautoka in the west, then moving east along Queens and Kings Rds and ending with Suva. The reason for

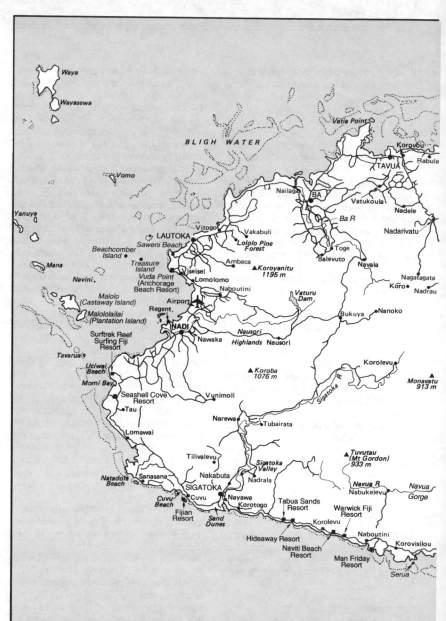

this is that 99% of visitors arrive at Nadi International Airport first, and begin their journey there before heading east.

GETTING THERE & AWAY

See the Getting There & Away chapter for information about flying to Fiji.

Nadi International Airport and Nausori Airport (near the capital of Suva) are the two major hubs of air travel throughout Fiji. Visitors heading to the more remote islands by plane or boat will find it necessary to travel to Suva in order to catch the right flight or vessel. Otherwise, the majority of tourist destinations can be reached from Nadi. See the Getting Around chapter for details on domestic flights and sailings, or see individual sections for details of air and sea transport to and from Viti Levu.

For a list of the international airlines represented at Nadi Airport, see the Getting Around chapter. In Suva, some of the major airlines are:

Air Nauru
    Victoria Parade (☎ 313 731)
Air New Zealand
    Queensland Insurance Centre, Victoria Parade
    (☎ 313 100, 312 444)
Air Pacific
    CML Building, Victoria Parade (☎ 384 955)
Canadian Airlines International
    Thomson St (☎ 311 844)
Fiji Air
    Victoria Parade (☎ 314 666)
Japan Air Lines
    Air Pacific Office, CML Building,
    Victoria Parade (☎ 385 955)
Pacific Crown Aviation (Helicopter Charters)
    Lami Airport (☎ 361 422)
Qantas
    CML Building, Victoria Parade (☎ 313 888)

GETTING AROUND
To/From the Airport

Fiji's international airport is at Nadi, but there is a second international airport (with flights to a few countries in the Pacific) at Nausori, about 20 minutes' drive from Suva on the Kings Rd.

To get to Nausori Airport from Suva, you can take a regular taxi, or a minibus from the CML building (near the Air Pacific office). A taxi will cost around F$15, while the fare for the bus is F$2. Buses leave weekdays at 6.30, 7.30, 9, 10 and 11.30 am and at 12.30, 1.30, 2.30 and 5 pm. Schedules differ slightly on weekend afternoons, so call the bus office (☎ 312 185) for more information. make sure you get to the CML building 15 minutes ahead of departure time. The bus does have the slight disadvantage of having no scheduled runs for early morning flights, in which case you have to take the taxi. If you enquire at a hotel about the CML bus and no-one seems to know about it, don't believe them. (They are probably getting a percentage of a taxi drive's fare.) Visitors lucky enough to have a car will find the new road to Nausori (which begins at Princes Rd in Suva and terminates shortly before the Nausori Bridge) is the quickest route.

Bus

Suva and Lautoka have the largest bus terminals on Viti Levu.

Around Suva, the truly budget-minded visitor can ride the buses which, though noisy and smoke-belching, are charming and cheap. A fare across town costs about 50 cents. Buses depart from the terminal next to the market.

See the Getting Around chapter for more general information on local buses, as well as timetables and fares for the express buses which operate on Viti Levu.

Taxi

Lautoka bus station is the largest taxi terminal on the western side of Viti Levu and a good place to find cabs to share, headed for Suva or other destinations on the island.

Around Suva, taxis are superabundant and cheap. At the most, a fare around Suva or its environs will be about F$3 or less, and certainly not over F$4.

Taxis in Fiji have what's called a 'return fare' system, meaning that after a taxi has dropped off a fare and is returning to its stand, the price for the fare is only five cents above the bus fare for the same route, as long as the driver does not have to go out of his way. At this point a taxi will stop to pick up all the passengers it can, to make up the loss. Most Suva taxis have meters that work, but this is not the case in rural areas. Always make sure of the price or at least the approximate price when boarding a taxi with no meter. In the case of a return fare, verify at the outset that it is indeed a return taxi (experience will help you to identify them more easily on the road. In the beginning, you could ask a local to help). Often they will stop for passengers in bus shelters. Note that Fiji law requires all front-seat passengers to wear seat belts; please comply with this law (and possibly save the driver a $40 fine or even save your own life).

For more information on taxi transport on Viti Levu, see the Getting Around chapter.

Car

For car hire on Viti Levu, note that there are several car rental agencies in and around Nadi, including Sheik's (☎ 723 535), Rental Cars Fiji (☎ 723 922) and Sharmas (☎ 701 055).

In the Suva area, the main car rental companies are:

Avis
    Corner of Thomson & Usher Sts, Suva
    (☎ 313 833)
Budget
    123 Foster Rd, Suva (☎ 315 899)
Hertz
    Lami (☎ 361 866)
Hertz
    Ratu Mara Rd, Nabua (☎ 383 411)
Central
    293 Victoria Parade, Suva (☎ 311 908)

Boat

In Suva, boats can be moored either at the Royal Suva Yacht Club (RSYC) (☎ 312 921), or at the Tradewinds Hotel, a 10-minute drive outside town. Weekly rates at the RSYC are F$20 per yacht with two or more people aboard, F$10 per week for solo yachts. Pontoon anchorage is '1.25 times the overall length of a boat per week' – call the RSYC to specify exactly what that means. There are toilets and solar-heated showers.

Poste restante mail is kept in the office. Telephones and laundry service are also available. RSYC office hours are from 8 am to 1 pm and 2 to 5 pm on weekdays. The office is usually staffed on Saturdays as well.

After registration at the office, each crew member receives honorary membership, which entails use of the bar/restaurant and social activities. The club is well maintained and the whole scene is very pleasant.

You can buy admiralty marine charts at Carpenters Shipping, 1st Floor, Harbour Centre Building, Thomson St.

Tours

For general information on tours, cruises and what they cost, it's not a bad idea to consult *Fiji Magic*, a comprehensive, bimonthly tourist rag available at the FVB, any hotel or agency.

Day Trips The vast majority of day trips on Viti Levu are on the western side and visit the many resort islands of the Mamanucas. While they are not 'adventure travel', they are fun if you've never been to a small island, and if you're travelling alone they are a fine way to meet people. For visitors with an unplanned day at their disposal, a day trip would be a good thing to do. The trips range from half-day to full-day excursions and cost from F$29 to F$49.

Sigatoka Valley Victory Tours (☎ 700 243/662) has a full day Nadi/Sigatoka Valley road tour that leaves from the Nadi area and is recommended for the individual who doesn't want to drive, but would like to see outlying rural areas not well served by public transport. It explores the rarely visited Sigatoka Valley via the Nausori Highlands.

I've also heard especially good things about a Sigatoka Valley tour run by Highland Tours (☎ 520 285) which has a full-day bus tour of the valley and the highlands. Pick-ups are available from all Coral Coast hotels for F$64 including barbecue lunch at a village, plus morning and afternoon teas. The air-con bus is a 25-seat, all-terrain vehicle and commentary is provided by Tui, a local with what one reader described as an 'inexhaustible knowledge' of the area. The tour runs daily except Sunday.

Likewise, Rosie Tours (Roadtours of Fiji ☎ 722 935) has a Sigatoka Valley drive that takes the visitor through cane land and the verdant Sigatoka Valley, the 'salad bowl' of Fiji. The drive continues into the mountains through the planted pine forests above Sigatoka, passing several villages. The varied landscape on this drive is breathtaking and unlike anything else in the South Pacific. For the benefit of shoppers, the tour stops in Sigatoka town to check out the duty-free stores. The cost for the all-day drive is F\$45, not including lunch.

Rosie Tours also has an all-day tour to the Emperor Goldmines, which takes in the cane towns of Ba and Tavua along the Kings Rd.

If you're down Sigatoka way (either staying at the Fijian Resort or nearby), the Baravi River cruise (☎ 500 155) up the **Sigatoka River** is an alternative way to see the 'salad bowl' of Fiji and catch a bit of local colour. There is a pick-up from the Fijian Resort or you can simply get to Sigatoka Jetty at 9.30 am or 2.30 pm for the twice-daily cruises. There are great views of Fijian villages; you'll see people fishing or collecting freshwater shellfish and watch produce-laden *bilibilis* (bamboo rafts) ply the waters to town. Twenty minutes after the vessel's departure, you call on **Naroro village** for a traditional yaqona ceremony and meke. The price is F\$16.50 per person.

Nausori Highlands Victory Tours (☎ 700 243/662) runs a Nausori Highlands tour which begins in the sugar cane lands past farmhouses and mosques, progresses to rolling hills and culminates in the craggy green mountains overlooking the sea. The road is bumpy but you will see bucolic countryside that hopefully developers won't get to.

'Village Stays in Bukuya' is run by a Fijian named Peni Rokolaqa who brings visitors to his home in the Nausori Highlands. From all reports, this is a wonderful experience and an opportunity learn about Fijian village life

first hand while contributing to a local community's financial well-being. When he is not entertaining guests, Peni hangs out at the Four Patinas Restaurant in Nadi's Westpoint Arcade. Using the restaurant as an informal office, he rounds up visitors (a maximum of 15) and organises a carrier to take them to Bukuya in the highlands, roughly a two-hour ride from Nadi. You can also book the tour at the Nadi Bay Motel, Hotel Kennedy and Club Fiji.

Peni and his associates have built several traditional bures, each of which sleeps two or three guests on mattresses; the bures are spartan but clean. Prices are F\$160 for three nights, F\$165 for four nights and F\$10 for each extra night. The deal includes transfers, food, accommodation and most activities. On Sundays the village prepares a lovo or underground oven for a special feast and every few days there's a barbecue. During the week guests have the option of eating Fijian or local food which, from all reports, is good and plentiful.

Aside from eating, other activities include swimming and fishing in the river, visits to a spectacular waterfall (about an hour's hike away), trekking, a visit to the local school (to teach a class), a look at a village plantation, horseback riding, yaqona drinking and even wild pig hunting (which at F\$20 is the only activity that costs extra).

Electricity will soon be installed in the village and nearby there is a small medical clinic staffed by an Indian doctor. Note that visitors who know precisely when they wish to return to Nadi should double check with Peni and/or their carrier/taxi to ensure that transport back to 'civilisation' will not be a problem. There have been reports of some guests who were inadvertently stranded.

Scenic Flights For those who prefer air travel to boats, there's a day trip to the Plantation Island and Musket Cove resorts on Malololailai – a good way to check out the resorts. Flights depart at 9 and 10 am on Fiji Air (☎ 723 521); Sunflower Airlines (☎ 723 555) has flights at 8.30 and 10.30 am. Both carriers depart from Nadi Airport, and both charge F$25 for the one-way fare. A variety of water sports including windsurfing, snorkelling and water-skiing are available at the resorts, but you must pay extra to rent the gear.

One reader wisely recommended taking the 10-minute flight to Malololailai rather than the *Island Express*. Why? The latter, although quite a fast catamaran, takes anywhere from 50 to 75 minutes because of the distance, and depending on the weather, the trip can be rough.

Cruises South Sea Cruises (☎ 722 988) has a half-day, four-island, sightseeing cruise with pick-ups at 8 am and noon from all Nadi hotels. The boats depart at 9 am and 1.30 pm respectively from Regent Jetty, and stop at Plantation Island, Musket Cove, Castaway Island, Club Naitasi and Mana Island. As the trip is just a shuttle to drop off and pick up guests, you can't actually get off unless you plan to stay. However, the trip does give you a chance to at least see the various resorts and perhaps decide which island appeals aesthetically for a long-term visit. Pack your own lunch on this trip. Drinks are served on board. The boat is the *Island Express*, a speedy catamaran with a sun deck and aircon level below. The price is F$29.

If don't want to just look at resorts, try the 'Combo Cruise' also offered by South Sea Cruises. Here you go only to Plantation Island Resort and check out the wonders of the deep in a semi-submersible craft. You return on a 26-metre, twin-masted schooner, the *Seaspray*. The cruise costs F$49 per person including lunch and hotel pick-up.

South Sea Cruises also offers the 'Mana Island Cruise', which is aboard the *Island Express*, but you get off at Mana Island, which might be considered a first choice because it has the best beach in the Mamanucas. Pick-up is at 8 am from all Nadi hotels; you'll depart from Regent Jetty at 9 am and stay a full day at Mana. The cost is F$53 per person including lunch and transfers. Passengers are dropped off by launch.

The 'Beachcomber Cruise' (☎ 661 500) is one of the most popular excursions because it was originated by Dan Costello, one of the pioneers of modern tourism in Fiji. The pick-up from Nadi hotels is between 8.30 and 9.30 am and the boat leaves Lautoka Wharf at 10 am for the 90-minute trip to Beachcomber Island. This is the only budget resort island on Viti Levu's western side and is extremely popular with young travellers. Activities include snorkelling, diving, windsurfing, water-skiing, canoeing and carousing. The beach here is nice, there are free glass-bottom boat rides and lunch is a sumptuous buffet. The price with lunch is F$50, for children under 16 it's F$25. Scuba diving is F$50 for a one-tank dive. If you are considering staying at Beachcomber, the day trip is an opportunity to give it the once-over.

'Daydream Island Cruise' (☎ 723 314) is a nice day trip to take for people who would rather spend more time on an island than on a vessel getting to one. The island destination is 2.4 hectares in area, studded with coconut palms and fringed by a white-sand beach. Except for one building, the island is totally undeveloped and offers good snorkelling, sunbathing and swimming. The *Adi Litia*, a sturdy 35-metre, 1950s 'cruiser', leaves from Newtown Beach and takes an hour to reach the island. The price is F$59 including a barbecue lunch and transfer from your hotel.

'Paradise Island Resort Day Trip' (☎ 665 222) visits tiny Paradise Island, off Lautoka. The cost is only F$25 which includes lunch and transport. Water sports are the main attraction at this low-end resort; reports have been OK.

Captain Cook Sailing Safari (☎ 701 823; fax 780 045) is a relatively new three-day, two-night cruise combining the best of several worlds – visiting a Fijian village (Yalobi) and Plantation Island Resort. It visits the Mamanucas at the southern end of the Yasawa group. The 33-metre yacht *Ra Marama* is a square-rig brigantine built from planked teak in 1950 for Fiji's governor general. Visitors are bivouacked at a deserted beach in tents (rather than staying on board), and all meals, bedding etc are provided.

Facilities at the beach include showers, toilets and a 'community hall' *bure*. Aside from visits to the village and the resort, most activities are water-oriented ie snorkelling and swimming. The cruise departs from Nadi at 10.30 am every Monday and returns at 4 pm on Wednesday. Reports on the sailing safari have been very positive, and it is expected that one more trip per week will be added to the schedule. The price is F$299 (plus tax) which includes food, accommodation and virtually everything except the booze that may be consumed at Plantation Island (Malololailai).

Adventure Tours Those opting for more adventure and the 'local' touch might be interested in a guided bilibili (bamboo raft) trip through **Waiqa Gorge**. Depending on the level of water in the river this can be an exciting, two-hour, boulder-dodging experience, or a leisurely cruise. This is a favourite of the Rucksack Club (to contact them, ask at the FVB in Suva) or write c/o Ratu of Naitauvoli Village, Naitasiri Viti Levu for information.

You start at **Naitauvoli** (several hours by bus from Suva and a short hike) where villagers put you up at local homes, feed you,

---

Eco Tourism in Fiji

No man is an island and no island can remain immune to the predations of man. Fiji's greatest asset, aside from its people, is its pristine environment. The largely insular, provincial Fiji tourism industry is finally realising that large-scale hotel complexes which destroy mangroves and harm the reef system are no way to entice tourists. At least I think they are learning these lessons. Even if they aren't fully ecologically conscious, many of the mid-range tour operators, hoteliers and other village entrepreneurs catering to travellers are acutely aware of the importance of cultural exchange as well as low-environmental impact travel.

The need for developing environmentally and culturally correct tourism in the Pacific has given rise to an organisation called Ecology Pacific based in Nadi. Ecology Pacific is a multi-disciplinary consultancy providing services to international and domestic tour operators throughout the Pacific region. Ecology Pacific is committed to the concept of ecologically sustainable development and offers guidance in economic evaluations, feasibility studies, site management planning, environmental impact studies, eco-tourism planning, market analysis and sourcing of environmentally sound products. It's staff consists of experts in management consulting, marine biology, public relations, marketing, architecture, engineering and other skills.

The founders of Ecology Pacific, Tony Anderson and Greg Inglis, told me that the organisation would like to raise ecological consciousness among tourist plants throughout the Pacific to ensure that they develop in an environmentally 'sound manner'. They envision hotels of the future that impact little on the ecosystem, use solar or alternative energy sources and bring employment to the local economy. According to Tony, an economist by training, the 'seed has been planted' and most Pacific islanders realise it is in their best interests to develop tourism with an eye to protecting the environment.

Over the past few years I've had a number of letters voicing particular concern over the problems of litter and waste disposal in Fiji. Though attitudes are slowly changing, Fijians of every stripe tend to toss litter out of buses or cars, and even dump their rubbish into the sea. In the days of old, when most waste was biodegradable and would simply decompose in the tropical heat, this was not a problem. With the preponderance of glass, plastics, and all the other non-biodegradable wonders of the late 20th century, this is obviously no longer an option.

The problem, however, is not confined to 'uneducated' villagers or insensitive tourists; some of the smaller resorts have been known to dump their trash into the sea.

What can the eco-sensitive visitor do? For one thing, make your feelings known to the resort operators or villagers themselves. Travellers who visit villages might even consider taking all of their non-biodegradable litter back with them for disposal in town and explain why they are doing so. Providing this type of 'ecologically responsible' example to Fijians will do more to educate them than all the theory in the world. The other options are to contact Ecology Pacific (PO Box 1211, Nadi, Fiji), or to report any incidents of rubbish dumping by resort operators to me. I have confronted the owners of properties who operate in this manner and will continue to do so. ∎

build your rafts and then guide them down the river for about F$20. Figure on spending F$30 to F$50 for the whole day (adding travel expenses, accommodation, gifts etc). The money is distributed throughout the village (it doesn't go to the people you stay with) so bring something extra (money or food) to give to the family. There are two daily buses to the village: one departs early in the morning and one late in the afternoon. You can disembark from the rafts either at the fork of the Walqa and the Walminala rivers, or get off two hours later at Serea Landing. In either case be prepared to get very wet and make sure everything is covered with plastic. Bring warm clothing because nights are cold in Naitauvoli (it's at an altitide of 1300 metres), and make absolutely sure the villagers are forewarned of your arrival – they need time to build the rafts.

Another option for the more adventurous is Roaring Thunder (☎ 780 029; fax 780 351), a day-long white-water rafting expedition down the **Ba River**. The tour takes the traveller by 4WD to the river's headquarters deep in the bowels of Viti Levu. At that point the rafts are inflated and the visitor is given instruction by seasoned pros on paddling and safety procedures. While the crew prepares a picnic, visitors may either swim or rest in readiness for the next part of the journey. Those who participate are guaranteed to get wet, so a change of clothing, towel and sun protection are in order. The cost is F$70, including lunch. Tours depart from Roaring Thunder's Nadi office (513 Queens Rd) daily at 8.30 am and return at 5 pm.

Trekkers will be happy to know that Rosie Tours (☎ 722 755; 800 551 2021 in the USA or Canada; 800 445 0190 in California only), now has six, eight and 10-day central highland treks through the interior of Viti Levu. The journeys entail four to six hours a day of hiking (with a backpack) in a group of no more than 15. Though most travel will be on foot, carriers or boats will occasionally be used. The trek winds through the hinterlands of Ra Province, beginning at Nananu village (about 70 metres above sea level) and descending to Nalalawa. The 50-km trek is the same course followed by the missionaries in 1849. Accommodation and meals will be provided in Fijian villages en route. All guides are local Fijians who will be in a position to enlighten the visitor on aspects of culture, tradition, herbal medicine, religion etc. The cost per person for a group of one to four is F$88 per day; for five to 10 people it's F$82; and for 11 to 15, F$77 per day.

Similar tours to Rosie's, at half the price, are run by Eli Naboso and his daughter, who call their family operation Inland Safari Tours (☎ 362 314). They offer high-country tours for F$40 per person per day, all-inclusive. The treks are not too strenuous and reviews have been very good. For more information write to PO Box 2185, Government Buildings, Suva.

Nadi & Lautoka

Nadi International Airport is where the overseas visitor will land, and Nadi town, about a 10-minute ride from the airport, will probably be the visitor's first exposure to an 'urban' Fijian environment.

Though Lautoka is only 19 km from Nadi, you get the feeling that it has existed quite a while without the tourist trade. In my opinion it is perhaps a bit friendlier than Nadi and a better place to go duty-free shopping. The merchants seem much more relaxed and the touts aren't grasping at your arm, trying to pull you into their shops.

Accommodation

You will have more accommodation choices on this side of the island than anywhere else in Fiji. All prices (meals, rooms, excursions, car rentals etc) are subject to the 10% 'value-added tax' (VAT). Accommodation in the areas around Nadi and Lautoka can be divided into five general categories: town hotels, airport hotels, beach hotels, beach resorts and offshore island resorts.

In recent years, the western side of Fiji – Nadi, Lautoka and the offshore resorts in particular – has been battered by more than its normal share of hurricanes. Damage has been particularly severe on the outer islands. Despite the destructive toll the storms have taken, the positive side of the picture is that most of the tourist places in the Nadi-Lautoka area have been completely rebuilt.

The main issue in finding accommodation in the Nadi-Lautoka area is making sure there is room at the place to stay you choose. This can be easily ascertained by calling and finding out for yourself.

Note that there is no camping in the Nadi area.

Town Hotels This is my own term for the inexpensive 'local' accommodation available in Nadi, Lautoka and Sigatoka. These hotels are always on the spartan side, full of world travellers, clean, and easy on the finances. On the other hand, they may be crowded, dingy and noisy due to street traffic or to unruly nightclubs next door. Given the choice between a 'town hotel' and an 'airport hotel', I'd go for the latter.

Airport Hotels This type of accommodation ranges from 1st to economy class and is close to the airport, often in the midst of cane fields. Most of the hotels have the usual amenities, particularly the good ones like the Mocambo or Travelodge, but with exception of a few, they often have the disadvantage of not being close to the beach.

Beach Hotels Over the last few years a new breed of hotel has sprung up in Nadi. These are the budget hotels located on or very near the beach, including properties such as Horizon Beach Motel, Newtown Beach Motel and the Traveller's Beach Resort, all of which are within a few metres of each other on Wailoaloa Rd. Backpackers should also check out Club Fiji, another place on Wailoaloa Beach. Though more of a mid-range hotel, it has excellent dorm units as well. The Nadi Bay Motel also falls into this category. Though not on the beach (it's about a km from the ocean) it matches or super-sedes anything in its class. Those planning to

shell out a fortune to stay at the Sheraton or Regent might well consider checking out Club Fiji at one-third of the price.

Beach Resorts These are often (but not always) opulent, self-contained resorts with water sports, tennis courts, boutiques, fine restaurants and, of course, excellent access to the beach. Many visitors who end up in these hotels (such as the Regent) never go too far from its confines. Exceptions to the 'opulence' rule include Club Fiji, Hideaway, Seashell Cove, Tabua Sands and others, which cater more to the 'world traveller' than to the tourist. Such resorts usually have self-contained units with refrigerators, cooking facilities, cutlery etc, as opposed to expensive restaurants. Thus at these lower end 'resorts' (which usually have less expensive restaurants) visitors generally have more options regarding where, what and how they are going to eat.

Offshore Island Resorts Off the coast of Lautoka are a group of tiny islands known as the Mamanucas where there are many island resorts. The islands are an hour or two's sailing from the coast, and offer accommodation ranging from moderate to luxurious. Their isolation provides a genuine 'South Pacific' ambience, with great beaches, excellent snorkelling, diving and deep-sea fishing. Food is often buffet-style, well prepared and in great quantity. For single people looking for company these island resorts are a good place to meet others – after all, there's nowhere else for guests to go. In general these islands are a good place to wind down and forget about the rest of the world. Some, like Beachcomber, are aimed at singles, while others are for couples. A third variety, such as Plantation or Mana islands, is better for families.

NADI

Once a small community of farmers and shopkeepers, Nadi has mushroomed into a duty-free gadget-selling megalopolis of 9500 inhabitants – Fiji's third-largest city. The area surrounding Nadi – a patchwork of sugar cane fields – has the highest concentration of hotels and resorts in the entire country. This is where most visitors spend a lot of their time, not only because of its proximity to the airport, nine km from the town, but because of the fine weather.

Nadi is a hot, dry town, little more than one long main thoroughfare, Queens Rd, which separates one row of duty-free shops from the other row on the opposite side. Touts, who populate the streets of Nadi like flies, can be a pain in the neck. Just ignore them. If you have the feeling that Nadi lives almost exclusively off the tourist trade, you are right. Except for shoppers, Nadi has little for the visitor except perhaps the local outdoor market which, as in every town, is adjacent to the bus station.

Despite Nadi's seemingly vacuous nature, the surrounding countryside is rolling and verdant, the beaches are relatively unpopulated, and the mountainous region (known as the Nausori Highlands) to the east is nothing short of spectacular. Seeing the cane country is easy – just hop on a local bus or take any of the local tours. Seeing the Nausori Highlands is more difficult. Roads can be rough and/or muddy and car rental agencies wouldn't be happy if they knew you had plans to explore remote areas. You can rent 4WDs through UTC and Budget Rentals, and one company, Rosie Tours, offers a tour of this marvellous area. (See the earlier Tours section for more information.)

Having a large Indian population, Nadi is a religious centre for Muslims and Hindus. There are two mosques: the Nadi Mosque, near the Nadi Muslim Primary School in Navakai; and the Amadiya Mosque on the Nadi College grounds. The major place of worship for Hindus is the Nadi Kalima Temple near the Nadi Bridge.

Nausori Highlands Rd
The turn-off to the Nausori Highlands is not too difficult to find. The access road is called the 'Nadi Back Rd' and it branches off the Queens Rd about three km south of Nadi Airport in an area called Nawaka, adjacent to a school playing field. It can also be

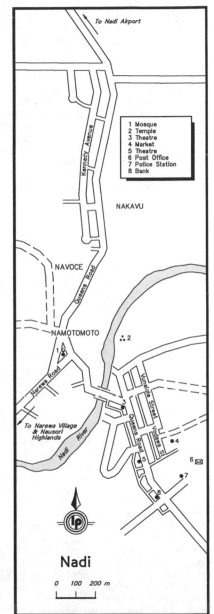

1 Mosque
2 Temple
3 Theatre
4 Market
5 Theatre
6 Post Office
7 Police Station
8 Bank

NAKAVU

NAVOCE

NAMOTOMOTO

Kennedy Avenue

Queens Road

Vunalole Street

Vodewa St

Queens Road

Narewa Road

To Narewa Village
& Nausori
Highlands

Nadi River

To Nadi Airport

Nadi

0   100   200 m

accessed on the southern edge of Nadi town. It's a bit more difficult to find from the Nadi end but it can be done. Before leaving, call the Public Works Department (☎ 700 389), the police (☎ 700 222) or the Forestry Department (☎ 661 085) to get a report on the current road conditions in the mountains.

To get to the highlands road, take the Queens Rd as far as Nawaka and turn inland; or from Nadi go east from Nadi's main street. If uncertain, ask a police officer – chances are other people will shrug their heads. Allow a day for this trip and take a picnic lunch. The road will be rough, but the scenery will be fantastic and well worth the drive.

There are several options for travelling the highlands road, depending on how adventurous you are. You can go as far as the major junction at Bukuya and then go on to Ba in the north and connect with Kings Rd. This is a long and tortuous route (about a three-hour drive) ideally suited for a 4WD. The highlight is passing through **Navala village**, deep in the mountains. The bures in this settlement are almost exclusively traditional thatched-roof homes, which are becoming a rarity in Fiji. To see this magnificent village perched on the side of a river valley is worth the trip. The village does, by the way, take in visitors for a set daily fee. There are also fees for photographing the village. You can also reach Navala via a 1½-hour bus ride from Ba three times daily.

The second option is to take the highlands road to its eastern extremity at Bukuya village and continue south 60 km along the Sigatoka Valley and eventually to Sigatoka town. The condition of the road is apt to be much better on this route. Make sure you stop at **Nakabuta village** along the Sigatoka Valley road, to purchase pottery. This is also a lovely route, but at least a three-hour drive.

A third option is to go as far as you feel comfortable, eat your picnic lunch and head back to Nadi. The scenery along the way begins with rolling hills studded with cane. About 15 to 20 km inland you get into mountains which tower over deep cleft valleys. Much of the land has been planted with

Caribbean pine, which is already yielding valuable building material and, in the form of wood chips (visible in an immense pile at Lautoka Wharf), is also a major export product. Deeper into the interior the landscape becomes more rugged, precipitous and wet.

The inhabitants of the occasional villages are poor, eking out a living from their dalo and cassava patches. It is not unusual to see them walking along the road, bush knives at their sides, on their way to the family *teitei* (vegetable patch) or perhaps leading a pair of oxen. Some residents of the area, mounted on horses, hunt wild pigs using only bush knives and dogs. After school, children will be making the often long trek back to their homes. Perhaps you will see them toting their books, or village women with prawn nets heading for a stream.

Wailoaloa & Newtown Beaches

These are great places to jog or have a picnic if you're staying near the Dominion International Hotel, the Nadi Bay Motel, Traveller's Beach Resort, Horizon Beach Resort or the Newtown Beach Motel. From the airport head south about five km and turn right at Wailoaloa Rd, which is about 100 metres past the Dominion. Continue past the Nadi Bay Hotel about three km and follow the road straight to the beach. A vast reach of sand stretches to your left and your right. If you continue to the right a few km (down the beach) you will arrive at Newtown Beach where Traveller's, Horizon and Newtown beach accommodation is located. If you don't want to walk to Newtown from Wailoaloa Beach, turn right from Nadi Bay Rd onto Enamanu Rd and follow it to the end. The public access at Newtown Beach stretches northwards from the Turtle Island Airways 'terminal'.

Regent Beach

Another beach worth exploring is called Regent Beach, near the Regent Hotel – the most expensive and luxurious hotel in the country. Take the Regent Hotel turn-off (just before the bridge on the Nadi River, eight km from the airport) past Sunseekers and turn left onto a (signposted) sandy road at the edge of the Regent Hotel grounds. The point of land where the resort is situated is also the departure point for cruises to Castaway Island, Plantation Island, Musket Cove and Naitasi. From Queens Rd to the beach is about four km.

Garden of the Sleeping Giant
This garden, which contains a collection of 30 to 40 varieties of Asian orchids and cattleya hybrids, is not just for horticulture enthusiasts. It's a combined commercial nursery and fantasy garden at the foot of the **Sabeto Mountains**, in the shadow of the ridge known as the 'Sleeping Giant'. The garden was once the private collection of US actor Raymond (Perry Mason) Burr. Burr has gone into partnership with another enterprising American and opened his garden to the public.

The highlight of the garden tour (☎ 722 701), however, is not just the orchids. Of equal interest is a meandering stroll on a canopy-covered boardwalk through gorgeous landscaped grounds, across lily ponds up to the edge of a densely vegetated jungle. The turn-off to the garden is about five km from Nadi Airport, on your right as you head towards Lautoka. Take this sideroad for about two km. You could take a bus and hoof it from the main road, but it's naturally easier if you have a rental car. Admission is F$8.50 for individuals, F$16 for couples, F$4 for children under 15, and F$20 for families.

Guns of Lomolomo
Past Nadi Airport the rugged hills of the Sabeto Mountains end almost at the foot of Queens Rd. At this juncture (about 8½ km from the airport) watch for a set of railway tracks and turn right onto the dirt road. There is a school building about 400 metres up the lane on the left. You have to go through private property to get to the gun site so be polite when doing so. It might be better taking the track to the left of the school rather than the one on the right, which will lead you to the base of the bluff and is a tougher climb

to the top of hill. Unlike the battery at Momi Bay, this site has not been taken over by the National Trust and thus has been left in the state in which it was abandoned after the war. The view from the top of the gun emplacement is outstanding. For those travelling by bus, the Lomolomo site is easier to reach than Momi Bay. Take a Lautoka or Viseisei bus from Nadi and ask the driver to let you off at the school.

Viseisei
Around the bend from Lomolomo and on your left is Viseisei, 9½ km from the airport. Legend has it that this village is the oldest settlement in the country. Fijians say their ancestors first came to Fiji in great ocean-going canoes and landed at nearby Vuda Point.

Speed humps have recently been installed in the vicinity of the village to ensure that passing cars move very slowly. This came about after a villager was run over by a speeding vehicle. This also should remind motorists that they should take care when driving in Fiji – pedestrians are not as wary of cars as they should be and can put themselves in dangerous situations.

There is a crafts centre at the Nadi side of the village. You can stop there and ask if someone can take you to see the centennial (1835-1935) monument marking the arrival of the missionaries. Opposite the monument is the bure of the chief or *tui vuda*. In the middle of the village is a large Methodist church with a monument commemorating the arrival of the missionaries. Usually a small tip to the person who has shown you around the village is proper. Incidentally, after having visited this village you'll be in good company. Queen Elizabeth II, Princess Margaret and Prince Charles have also visited Viseisei.

The huge, brand-new looking bure to the left of the road belonged to Dr Timoci Bavadra, the late, deposed prime minister of Fiji.

Vuda Point
The turn-off to Vuda Point and the Anchor-

age Beach Resort is on the left near the top of the first steep hill along the Queens Rd. About three km down, you pass several large oil storage tanks and then the road becomes very sandy. The beach is a short walk away (through a cane field between two freshwater ponds). This is traditionally where the first Melanesians landed. There is not much to see, but the point is a popular picnic spot for families in the area. Vuda Point is about 12½ km from Nadi Airport.

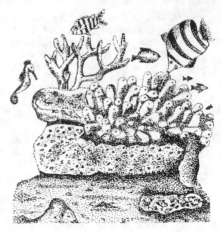

Activities

Clubs For a minimal fee, swimmers and golfers may use the facilities at the Airport Club, a private organisation near Newtown Beach. It has an 18-hole golf course and a large hall for parties. Call the clubhouse (☎ 722 413) for more information.

You also might want to check out the Farmer's Club, off the main drag in Nadi town, which has cheap beer, snooker tables and a nice ambience.

Golf This can be played at the Lautoka Golf Club (☎ 613 411), which has a nine-hole course. Green fees are under F$5.

Diving & Snorkelling For those interested in diving in the Nadi area, both Aqua-Trek (☎ 780 413) and H20 Sportz have shops in downtown Nadi selling diving gear. They can advise visitors on various dive trips and other water-oriented activities, as well as accommodation. Aqua-Trek's shop is on Queens Rd near Jack's Handicrafts, while H20 Sportz is at the Westpoint Arcade, just off the main drag.

Surfing You may have heard that Fiji has world-class surfing and it's true. There is the exclusive surfing resort of Tavarua off Nadi but it's expensive. So what do you do if you are a world-travelling surfer and can't afford US$125 a day? There are several options available.

Tavarua Island Resort takes surfers out to the breaks adjacent to Tavarua Island. Known as 'Magic Island' it is a left-hander which at times provides excellent waves up to 10 feet. One km across the passage, Wilkes Pass is a sectioning right-hander which breaks up to eight feet, and when lined up, offers a ride of 200 metres.

There are two other major surfing spots in southern Viti Levu. The Sigatoka River mouth, at Club Masa, is Fiji's only wave which breaks on sand. The river mouth at the far eastern end of the beach has been known to produce some terrific left-handers when conditions are right.

At Hideaway Resort, about 20 minutes further down the road towards Sigatoka, you'll find a classic right-hand barrel. You'd better be in good shape for this baby. The paddle out to the break takes 20 minutes and the wave breaks into approximately three feet of water.

Surftrek Reef Surfing Fiji, formerly known as Trekkers Reef Resort, is the other new establishment devoted to hard-core surfers. Apart from Tavarua, it's the only surf camp dedicated to the breaks at Namotu and Wilkes reefs. It's 28 km south of Nadi, on 4.8 hectares adjacent to Momi Bay. This is not a lavish affair but is a notch or two up on the comfort scale when compared to the other surf camp, Club Masa.

Finally, there is Yanuca Island, near Beqa – a lush, sparsely inhabited jewel that is a half-hour's boat ride from Pacific Harbour. The surf camp is operated by a small local company called Frigates Surf Riders in conjunction with Rosie Travel Service. Day trips are available but most visitors will probably opt for the four-day packages. The surf spot is about half an hour by boat from Yanuca to an area called Frigates Passage, which is on the south-western edge of Beqa Lagoon. The wave is a left-hander and has the advantage of being 'offshore' in the south-east trade wind which makes it a very consistent break.

Places to Stay – bottom end

Nadi Sunseekers Hotel (☎ 700 400; fax 780 047) is just outside Nadi town, several hundred metres from the junction of Queens Rd and the road leading to the Regent and Sheraton hotels. It has more of a dorm than a hotel feel about it and has the advantage of being close to town (Nadi town is a 10-minute walk away). However its 21 rooms, including five 10-bed dorms, are becoming less and less appealing. Compared to some of the newer dorm and inexpensive motels in Nadi it's quite shabby, and because of the intense traffic on the road, it is noisy. I have also heard horrific reports of bedbugs. Even without these creatures you can simply get better value for your money by going elsewhere. Amenities include air-con, pool and outdoor patio, hot and cold water, and a large inexpensive eating area. Prices are F$22/27 for singles/doubles, F$33/35 with air-con. Dorm facilities are F$7 per night, and credit cards are accepted.

If *Sunny Holiday Motel* isn't out of business by the time this book goes to press, it should be avoided. The carcass of a decomposing minivan (the first thing you see when you drive in the front yard) is an apt metaphor for this ramshackle motel. From the flimsy beds and the peeling paint on the walls to the holes in the mosquito screens and the marauding ants, your stay at the Sunny Holiday is guaranteed to be memorable. If the above description is not enough, I was told by one traveller that although this accommodation purports to be a member of the YHA, they did not honour her card. I've

also been told that upon arrival visitors will immediately be pressured into visiting the Kon-Tiki Resort on Nananu-i-Ra.

At the other end of the spectrum, the *White House Visitors Inn* (☎ 70 022; fax 780 468) at 40 Kennedy Ave, was a pleasant surprise. About a 10-minute walk from downtown Nadi, it is clean, reasonably priced and the management aims to please. The two-storey unit, in a residential neighbourhood, is very quiet. Dorm beds are F$8, private 'dorm' rooms F$10, and singles/doubles F$25/30. There is a F$5 surcharge for air-con. Though you can find cheaper dorm-style places, the White House is worth looking at.

Sandalwood Inn (☎ 722 044; fax 790 103), next to the Dominion Hotel, is an old Nadi stand-by. Quality and cleanliness is good here, and I noted during my last visit that the rooms have had a new coat of paint. Air-con, hot and cold water and satisfactory food is available. Costs are F$26/32 for singles/doubles, F$38/44 for triples/quadruples. If you need private bath and air-con the price is F$40/46 for a single/double. Credit cards are accepted. There are 25 rooms (most with four bunk-style beds), and a small pool.

At the time of this writing the *Bridge Hotel* on the edge of Nadi town (turn right at the bridge) may be closed for similar reasons as the Sunny Holiday, and is not recommended.

The *Melanesian Hotel* (☎ 722 438, 790 425) used to be known as a rowdy local hang-out and rendezvous point. Despite having a restaurant known as the Jolly Jumpbuck Room it appears to be quite tame nowadays and perhaps the best thing about it are the dorms. An older establishment that shows its age, it is relatively clean and quiet, and has a pool and bar. Prices are F$10 for a dorm bed, F$38/49 for singles/doubles. It's on Queens Rd, about two minutes' drive from the airport.

Nadi Bay Motel (☎ 723 599; fax 790 092) is on Wailoaloa Beach Rd, a two-minute walk from Queens Rd and opposite a cane field. When the sun goes down the palm trees are silhouetted and the cane resembles stalks of corn – it's enough to bring a tear to the eye of any Iowan. The Nadi Bay Motel is roughly across Queens Rd and down the street from the Dominion Hotel. It is an antiseptically clean, modern hotel more in the fashion of a US 'motel' than anything I've ever seen in Fiji. You would not feel uncomfortable sending your parents there and they would be happy with the prices.

It is newish in a tacky sort of way but has fine, self-contained facilities with a kitchen, air-con, bar, restaurant, pool and laundry. Prices begin at F\$9 for a dorm bunk, F\$25/35 for standard singles/twins with shared bath. The dorms are new, very clean and have fans. Rooms with a private toilet (and shared bath) are F\$35/45; deluxe air-con rooms with private bath and toilet are F\$45/55. The deluxe apartment units with kitchenettes and air-con go for F\$55/65 for a single/double. The hotel also has a policy that allows visitors who stay four nights to get the fifth night free of charge (credit cards accepted). All prices include breakfast, even for dorms. Speaking of food, fare at the Nadi Bay Motel is excellent. There is a small restaurant/patio area where food and drinks are served. The chef, formerly of the Dominion Hotel is very capable, especially with Indian dishes. Prices for dinner range from F\$5 to F\$7. Happy hour, from 6 to 7 pm daily, features half-price drinks. There is a big 'travellers scene' at the restaurant, and it's a good place to meet people.

Just down the dirt road from the Nadi Bay Motel is Wailoaloa Beach, great for evening jogs and weekend picnics.

Traveller's Beach Resort (☎ 723 322; fax 790 026) is on Newtown Beach, about 10 minutes' drive from Nadi Airport. It's one of three inexpensive beach hotels for world travellers and in my opinion is worth the extra few dollars. By taxi is the only way to get there, and the fare from the airport costs about F\$3.

The resort is a one-storey, white cinder-block complex with eight small, clean, air-con rooms and four four-bed dorms. The furnishings are simple – double and single beds, faded sheets, hot plate, refrigerator, sink and small closet. All rooms have private bath. There is also a bar/restaurant and picnic tables facing the beach. Like most places in Fiji it's quite informal. (This hotel was a favourite weekend getaway for the best reporter in Fiji, Richard Naidu, before he unfortunately had to leave Fiji during the unsettled post-coup period.) Prices start at F\$10 in the dorm, and F\$25/30 for a single/double. Add another F\$5 if you want air-con; credit cards are accepted. As in all the accommodation near Nadi Airport, there is some noise from incoming jets, so be warned.

Just down the street from Traveller's Beach on Wailoaloa Rd is one of the newest faces on the accommodation scene, *Horizon Beach Resort* (☎ 722 832), also on Newtown Beach. This two-storey building has 14 units, including two dorm rooms, and is run by Gopi Chan, a former health inspector for Nadi town, and his hip son Arvin. It is one of the cleanest places I've ever seen. The dorm has 10 bunks but is split into two spacious chambers rather than cramming everyone into a single room. There is a double shower and laundry facility in an adjoining room, and a lounge. The cost is F\$9 per person. Private rooms with bath are F\$24/28/35 a single/double/triple or F\$29/38/45 with air-con. There's also a restaurant, but it was not completed at the time of writing.

Also new on the scene is the *Newtown Beach Motel* (☎ 723 332) which is just a few metres from Horizon and Traveller's on Wailoaloa Rd. Its seven rooms are also very clean and well maintained, and cost F\$25/30 for a single/double with fan and private bath. Family rooms with a double and single bed cost F\$40. Unlike Horizon and Traveller's, Newtown Beach Motel is not on the beach, but is just metres away.

Nadi Hotel (☎ 700 000), just off the main drag in town, could use a major face-lift or even a fresh coat of paint. Walk into the rather threadbare lobby and you will see at least three generations of water stains on its ugly indoor/outdoor carpet. The best feature about the hotel is the new dorms (separate for men and women) which have old but sturdy military-style bunks for F\$8.80 per person including breakfast. The other nice feature is the garden/pool area. The Nadi Hotel has 22 rooms (air-con in some), hot and cold water, refrigerator, restaurant and bar. The service is slow to bearable and food at the restaurant is mediocre. Unless you are a very sound sleeper, avoid getting a room on the side of the hotel adjacent to the Kings Nightclub especially on Thursday or Friday nights. Prices start at F$25/30 for a single/ double; add F$10 for air-con.

Nadi Town Motel (☎ 700 600), not to be confused with its namesake the Nadi Hotel, is also kind of dumpy. I used to like this place but after visiting again, I can't figure out why. It just feels shabby. Prices start at F$5/8/11 for a dorm/single/double. Air-con costs an extra F$4, and a room with cooking facilities costs F$17. The rooms are relatively clean, but as with the Nadi Hotel, rooms in the wing near the Kings Nightclub will hear the sounds of the 'restless natives' in the evenings. Likewise, the dorm room near the window facing the street is rife with the sounds of automobiles and other select street noise.

This hotel is also an agency for all accommodation on Nan-i-Ra. However, the hotel will no doubt want you to take their own transport to the island which costs around F$21. Though this is more convenient, it is also more expensive than making your own way down there via shared taxi or bus.

Coconut Inn II (☎ 701 011), formerly Fong Hing Private Hotel, is now under the same ownership as the Coconut Inn in Suva. This old two-storey concrete structure, just off the main drag in Nadi town, has had a new coat of paint, and the owners have replaced the vanities, the linen and the fridges. Though clean, I found the dorm rooms rather stuffy – there are no windows and thus little circulation. It has 22 rooms (each with private bath) and four four-bed dorms. Prices are F$38.50/38.50 for a single/double and F$10 for a dorm bed. The food at Fong Hing's accompanying restaurant is OK and reasonably priced.

Kon Tiki (☎ 722 836) is perched on a hill overlooking cane fields on the inland road which passes the Travelodge and Mocambo. This is perhaps the nicest thing about the hotel. Relatively clean, it is a basic, low-end place with beds consisting of sheets draped over foam padding. There is a pool and modest restaurant on the premises (though the latter hadn't yet opened when I was there). Dorm beds are available for F$5, and singles/doubles are F$15/20. More expensive rooms with air-con are available. The major disadvantage of Kon Tiki is that it's at least two km from the nearest grocery store or restaurant.

Club Fiji (☎ 780 189; fax 780 324) is the newest beachside resort in Viti Levu and one of the best-value places in the low to mid-range class. If you need to stay near the airport area, or want to be on the beach in an isolated resort setting with the sea on one side and cane fields on the other, you may well consider Club Fiji. The resort includes a pool and a huge canopy-enclosed dining area, and a bar which is open to the sea breezes. There are 24 bure-style duplex units on a wide grassy area facing the sea. Each has polished hardwood floors, overhead fans, fridge, louvre windows, balcony, private bath, and two single beds with a settee. One of the bures is dedicated to dorm bunks – each half of the duplex has eight bunks with shared bath. Prices are F$45/45 for singles/doubles in the regular units, F$10 in the dorm. The restaurant has a selection of Fijian dishes including *palusami* (baked taro leaves with corned beef) and *kokoda* (fish marinated in lime juice with chilli and onions) as well as European and Chinese cuisine such as steak, curry, spaghetti and chop suey. Prices range from F$3.80 for sandwiches to F$10 for steaks. Water sports are very big at Club Fiji and include windsurfing, paddle boarding, catamaran sailing, water-skiing and snorkelling. Horse riding is also available.

On the downside, there are no cooking facilities and the nearest restaurants are a few km away so there's no choice for travellers on a really tight budget. The hotel does, however, provide occasional free shuttle service to town and the airport. A second drawback is that the beach here (as with Traveller's Beach, Horizon and Newtown Beach accommodation) is not your classic powdery, white-sand wonder. It is rather grey in hue, and at low ebb resembles a tidal flat.

For those wishing to stay near town, particularly seniors or business travellers concerned about comfort and security, you won't do better than the *Hotel Kennedy* (☎ 780 360; fax 780 218) on Kennedy Ave, just outside Nadi town. To find it, look for the logo on the bay side of Queens Rd, about a km before the Nadi Bridge. The hotel, completed in 1991, is a two-storey structure with 16 well-appointed, comfortable rooms, as well as two self-contained family units. Each room has air-con, rattan furniture and phones with international direct dial (IDD). There's also a restaurant, a boutique, beauty salon and a chiropractor who has set up a practice at the hotel. Prices are F$40/45/50 for singles/doubles/triples.

Places to Stay – middle

Dominion International (☎ 722 255; fax 790 187), about 10 minutes from the airport on Queens Rd, has everything that the expensive hotels have except the stiff prices. Under new management, the hotel is being refurbished, and plans include an all-weather tennis court, jogging track and three-hole golf course with a driving range. A business centre is also being installed. The best thing about the hotel is the staff, who are among the friendliest I have found anywhere in Fiji. The Dominion has 85 rooms, pool, restaurant, bar, gift shop and dancing. Prices begin at F$77/82 for a single/double, including airport transfers.

The Dominion is a 10-minute jog from Wailoaloa Beach, which is usually deserted. Rosie Tours has a first-class agency at the hotel's tour desk. Annabelle's is a small shop run by Joseph, one of the best hair stylists in Fiji. He charges F$10 for a very fine cut and is a charming guy who seems to know everyone. (He may share some of his immense knowledge of the place if you ask the right questions.)

The *New Westgate Hotel* (☎ 790 044; fax 790 071), about 50 metres down the road from the Dominion, is another relatively new addition to the Nadi scene. This mid-range hotel features better than average furnishings, and manicured grounds. Its 62 rooms are decorated in tan tones with white-tiled floors and louvre-style windows. There's a bar, restaurant, pool and boutique, as well as Jessica's Disco, billed as the 'hottest adult disco in the west'. Prices start at F$40/50 for standard singles/doubles, up to F$70/80 for deluxe accommodation.

Rosie's Serviced Apartments (☎ 722 755), run by Rosie Tours, is three km from Nadi Airport on Queens Rd. This clean and modern complex offers studios as well as self-contained one and two-bedroom units. Though on the pricey side, these are serviced daily like hotels and may be a good bet for families because of the capacity to accommodate a large of number of people. The studio is priced at F$88 and can sleep up to four; the one-bedroom unit costs F$113 and sleeps five; and the two-bedroom unit (F$138) can accommodate up to eight.

Skylodge Hotel (☎ 722 200; fax 790 212) was one of the first airport hotels to be constructed, and is an inexpensive and unpretentious middle-range hotel. There are 53 rooms and self-contained family units, as well as the usual amenities like pool, restaurant and live music. The outdoor buffets are very good and the management is responsive to the needs of the visitor. Prices begin at F$80/90 for a single/double.

Raffles Gateway (☎ 723 077; fax 790 163) is so-named perhaps because it is literally at the doorstep of the airport. The clientele seems to be mostly young. It was revamped a few years ago, but is in need of renovation again. It has a pool, gift shop, live music, outdoor bar and overpriced food. Of late, the airport paging system has been 'wired' into the hotel's paging system so that imbibers will not miss their flights. Prices begin at F$83/91 for singles/doubles.

The *Metro* (☎ 790 088), also new on the Nadi scene, is a tacky and expansive complex, just a few metres from the Dominion. When I visited, it was on the verge of completion. Rooms appear to be well appointed and some are self-contained. Facilities include restaurant, bar, pool, games bure, gift shop, and business services centre. Singles/doubles are F$65/75.

Adjacent to the Raffles Gateway is a relatively new place called the *Tokatoka Resort* (☎ 790 222; fax 790 400). An expansive, ultra-modern property, it has an outdoor restaurant that is a popular watering hole on weekends. The complex is divided into numerous condo-like blocks or town houses. All units feature luxuries like four-channel video, IDD phones, built-in radio alarm, fridges, and other high-tech touches. The grounds are well manicured with embellishments like a waterfall and a water slide for the kiddies. Tokatoka also boasts Fiji's largest private swimming pool. The resort falls somewhere between mid-range and top end. Prices begin at F$95 for a modest studio (single or double) and go up to F$165 for a 'suite deluxe'.

Places to Stay – top end

Mocambo (☎ 722 000; fax 790 324) and its neighbour *Travelodge* (☎ 790 277; fax 790 191) share honours as the premium airport hotels. With 132 rooms, Mocambo is slightly larger than the Travelodge (with 114 rooms), but there's very little difference in amenities (which include fine restaurants, gift shop, pool, tennis courts etc) and the stiff price. Because of the frequency of hurricanes, both hotels have gone through millions of dollars' worth of renovation and improvement. Both offer excellent accommodation, are extremely close to the airport, and have some of the best dance bands in the Nadi area. Prices for the Mocambo begin at F$140/145 for singles/doubles. Rates at the Travelodge are F$125 for a single or double.

Regent of Fiji (☎ 780 700; fax 780 259) is one of two up-market beach resorts in the Nadi area and is considered by many to be the finest hotel in Fiji. It has 300 rooms, four bars, four restaurants and all the luxury you could want. Prices begin at F$230 per room for a single or twin. Amenities include a boutique, general store (which stocks everything from newspapers to pharmaceuticals), hair salon and resident nurse on call.

The nearby ocean provides access to water sports such as water-skiing, diving, paddleboating, catamaran sailing, windsurfing and snorkelling (which is complimentary). Water-skiing, diving and snorkelling can be arranged at the tour desk. Also available are archery, a pitch-and-putt course and a pool. Tennis enthusiasts have the services of John Newcombe's Tennis Ranch (with six grass and four all-weather courts) right next door for professional instruction. In addition, the hotel provides the largest convention facility in Fiji. The Regent is a headquarters for deep-sea fishing, too – South Sea Cruises operates the 13-metre *Fleet Lady* and five other vessels for cruising and fishing trips.

Sheraton Fiji (☎ 701 777; fax 780 171), adjacent to the Regent of Fiji, is the newest up-market hotel in Fiji. As it was the first major hotel constructed in Fiji since 1978, it still lacks the luxuriant vegetation that surrounds the Regent. Sheraton Fiji is a huge, rambling complex of coral-coloured stucco buildings built near the beach. The area is elaborately landscaped – filled with pools, trees, plants and flowers. The lobby is huge and airy, featuring couches, chairs, sculptures and dozens of up-market boutiques. Like the Regent, Sheraton Fiji provides all the creature comforts – pool, sun deck, recreation centre, diving facilities, sailing, windsurfing and good dining. Rooms begin at F$295 for a single or double.

Sonaisali (☎ 790 411; fax 790 392) opened in 1991, making it one of the newest up-market island resorts in Fiji. To get there, take the Queens Rd from Nadi town and after about 10 minutes, turn right at Nacobi Rd just past Korovutu Secondary School. Continue on for another seven or eight minutes and you'll reach a marina, where you can get a boat to the resort. Sonaisali has a large selection of single and twin rooms for F$195, as well as very spacious bures that sleep up to six people for F$245. There are also two restaurants, and a pool with a swim-up bar.

Places to Eat

In Nadi most people tend to eat in their hotels. However, there are a few good 'no-frills' restaurants which serve less expensive fare than the hotels. There are also several bakeries which provide good, inexpensive buns, scones and bread. In this latter category try *Hot Bread Shoppe* next door to the Fiji Development Bank, or *Hot Bread Kitchen* across from the post office; both are on Nadi's main drag.

Maharaj, in Namaka on the main highway 10 minutes from the airport towards Nadi town, gets a three-star rating. It is the best Fiji Indian eatery in Nadi, providing a pleasant atmosphere along with better than average Indian food. The fare includes curries, Chinese food and seafood dishes ranging from F$6 to F$10.

While Maharaj provides good local-style Indian food, *Kababish* (☎ 723 430), one of the newest and perhaps the best restaurants in the Nadi area, provides the genuine thing – authentic Indian, Afghani and Pakistani fare. Just walk in and note the décor which is a cut or two above the average restaurant's. The owner, Rafiq, an effusive Pakistani, tells me that his restaurant is unlike any other Indian restaurant in Fiji because he imports his own spices and prepares food the way it's done on the Indian subcontinent. He considers 'Fiji Indian' food to be an adulteration of the 'real' thing and indeed, his food is different from anything I've ever had in Fiji. With prices in the F$8 to F$20 range, Kababish is pricier than the average Indian restaurant, but well worth it. Specialities of the house are tandoori chicken and a variety of briyanis including beef, chicken and lamb.

Also new on the scene in Nadi town is *Cardo's Chargrill Restaurant & Bar* (☎ 780 029), which is more of a watering hole than a restaurant. It represents a kind of milestone for Nadi, the first thoroughly civilised 'local' bar, other than a conventional 'hotel' bar. Though unpresumptuous in décor, it is definitely the hang-out for the Nadi cognoscenti – the hip, young local Europeans, expats, kai loma (part-Europeans) and well-heeled Fijians. The owner, Richard Cardo, has been active on the local tourism scene for many years and is quick-witted, urbane and fun to be around. He also has a rafting business, Roaring Thunder (see the earlier Tours section). For those so inclined, his restaurant has a good selection of steaks and some seafood. Prices are F$8/10 for prime sirloin, F$10 for T-bone steaks, F$8/10 for rib eye fillet, F$7.50 for barbecue chicken and F$6.50 for smoked marlin or smoked chicken salad.

Poon's is on the main street of Nadi town, upstairs in the Nadi Tower building. I find its Chinese food passable by Fiji standards (which, incidentally, are not the same as those in San Francisco) and prices range from F$6 to F$9.

Curry Restaurant, on Clay St in Nadi (not to be confused with the Indian Curry House on the main street), specialises (as you may have guessed) in curries and Indian food. If you have a weakness for this type of cuisine, this is where to go. Prices average around F$4 to F$6.

Namaka Inn, on Queens Rd between the airport and Nadi town, is a favourite of locals on their lunch break. Its speciality is curry and other basic Indian dishes. Figure on spending F$6 to F$9.

Mama's Pizza, on Queens Rd, is the pizza joint and place-to-be-seen among the hip Nadi locals and the savvy visitors. It has a good ambience, and is a good place to catch up on gossip. The pizzas, which range from F$6 to F$10, are not too bad either.

Entertainment

For avid nightclubbers the western side of Viti Levu will be rather quiet. The hotels provide most of the entertainment around here and generally there just isn't that much. The best live bands will either be at the *Mocambo*, *Travelodge* or *Ed's Cocktail Bar* across the road from the Dominion Hotel. The action is definitely on the weekends, though Thursday or Friday nights may be better than Saturdays because the 'Sunday curfew' is strictly enforced when the clock tolls midnight on Saturday. It's always good to ask the locals (the taxi drivers are usually

Top: Levuka Public School, Ovalau (RK)
Left: Catholic mission, Taveuni (RK)
Right: Chapel, Taveuni (RK)

Top: Fijian youth, Suva (IO)
Left: Catching sea fish, Vuruwai River, Vanua Levu (IO)
Right: Fijian seascape (RK)

Beach scene, Mamanuca Islands (RK)

Top: Mixing yaqona, Taveuni (RK)
Bottom: Warriors in traditional yaqona ceremony, Savusavu, Vanua Levu (RK)

a good source) which hotel is currently the most popular. The music scene changes from time to time and what's in one month may be passé the next.

The major hotels all have the traditional dance shows – mekes – and some have firewalking exhibitions.

If you are in town and want a quiet drink, check out *Cardo's* opposite the Mobil station in Nadi town, or take a taxi down to the *Sheraton*. Near the airport, the *Tokatoka Hotel* has an outdoor, patio-style bar. A quiet drink can also be had at the *Dominion*. There are also three cinemas. Check the *Fiji Times* for listings.

LAUTOKA

Lautoka is 24 km north of Nadi Airport. With a population of around 31,000, it is Fiji's second-largest city and its second most important port. From here most of the vessels sail not only for foreign ports but to the outer islands and the resort areas. Lautoka is also a quintessential sugar town, with reputedly one of the largest sugar mills in the southern hemisphere. Although tourism is important to the region, sugar is still king here and the sugar industry is the largest single employer in the district.

Tradition has it that within the bounds of today's Lautoka city limits there lived two tribes. One day a fight broke out between the tribes' chiefs at a spot known today as Farquahr's Point. As one chief speared the other he screamed *Lau-toka* which means 'spear hit' or 'hit to win'. Thus Lautoka acquired a name.

The first sighting of the area was on the dawn of 7 May 1789 when Captain Bligh of HMS *Bounty* sailed by in his launch with loyal crew members – those who had been tossed out as a result of the famous mutiny. Bligh made rough charts of the shores of Lautoka and sketched the mountains in the background.

At the end of the last century the Colonial Sugar Refining Company (CSR) decided to build a mill in Lautoka. Indian indentured

labourers and Solomon Island workers were brought in to do the construction and in 1899 the work began. The mill began crushing in 1903 and still operates today.

Lautoka was proclaimed a city on 25 February 1977 and today is the headquarters for important government and statutory bodies such as the Fiji Electrical Authority, the Fiji Pine Commission and the National Marketing Authority. It is the administrative capital of the Western Division, which contains more than 50% of the nation's population.

Sugar Mill

Queens Rd into Lautoka is lined with royal palms, and railway tracks from the ubiquitous sugar train run adjacent to the highway towards the huge sugar mill looming in the distance. The business of Lautoka is and always was centred around sugar. Tours of the mill are popular during harvest time. For tour information call the Fiji Sugar Corporation (☎ 660 800). The best time of the year to visit is in December during 'crushing season'.

Neisau Marina

Yachties will appreciate the new Neisau Marina on Bouwalu St in Lautoka (☎ 664 858; fax 663 087) – a modern facility that is the first of its kind to be owned and operated by an indigenous Fijian. The complex has berths for yachts needing extensive repair; while for travellers interested in crewing or cooking on a yacht bound for the Yasawas, this is the place to stop. The Neisau complex was conceived by Max Volau, a local who lived for years in Australia and came back as an entrepreneur. Along with his Australian wife, Fiona, they operate the facility which has showers, toilets, lockers and a laundrette where you can wash a load of clothing for F$3, 24 hours a day (as long as you purchase your F$3 token between 9 am and 5 pm).

Other facilities include floating berths, swing moorings, a 63-tonne travel-lift marine hoist, a hard-stand area with cradles, a work shed, tool and machinery hire, a boat refit service, a sewage pump-out service,

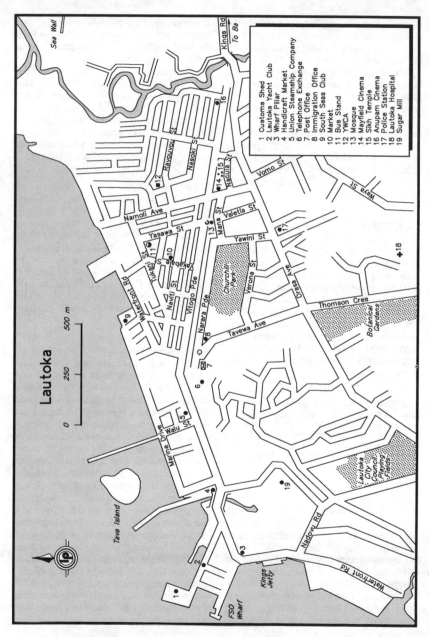

Lautoka

chandlery, as well as supplies of petrol, ice and gas.

Saweni Beach

Saweni, about six km north of Lautoka and two km off the main road, is the largest beach near town and has shade trees. Though a bit shabby and littered compared to an archetypically beautiful beach like Natadola down the coast, it is very popular with the locals, especially for family picnics and beer-drinking bashes. To get there take the Saweni Beach turn-off or the Saweni bus which goes directly to the beach. If you can't get the exact bus, any local bus going north from Lautoka will drop you off on the main road near the turn-off.

Market

Like all Fijian communities, Lautoka has a sizeable market selling produce, yaqona and trinkets, but nothing terribly different from any of the others. Of interest, however, is that this is the largest market in Fiji, renovated in 1992. Some of the artefact sellers are also artisans who make high-quality products (crochet work, for example) that you can watch being made and later purchase.

Other Attractions

Many places north of Nadi – in particular the Garden of the Sleeping Giant, the Guns of Lomolomo, Viseisei and Vuda Point – are also accessible from Lautoka. See the earlier Nadi section for details.

Places to Stay

There are two inexpensive hotels in Lautoka. The *Cathay* (☎ 660 566; fax 340 236) is a massive '50s vintage structure with a whitewashed exterior, restaurant/bar, pool and a total of 44 rooms including a dorm. It is well maintained, clean and has received good reviews from travellers. Prices begin at F$6/18/22 for a dorm/single/double with fan and bath. Rooms with air-con and fridge are F$25/30 for a single/double, F$36 a triple. Meals are reasonably priced in the F$4 to

F$10 range. Note that you can also make arrangements to stay at Robert's Place on Tavewa Island from the Cathay.

The other inexpensive hotel, the 38-room *Lautoka Hotel* (☎ 660 388; fax 660 201), has also received good comments from readers. All rooms are self-contained, and there is a dorm which is becoming more popular with travellers. Prices begin at F$15/20 for a single/double with fan and shared bath; F$40 for a single or double with private bath in the old wing; F$54 in the new wing. A dorm bed costs F$8. The hotel's restaurant, Pizza Inn, has quite tasty pizza, better than any available in Suva. There's also a bar and a bottle shop, plus a pool.

The other major hotel is the 41-room *Waterfront* (☎ 664 777) which is the only semi-luxurious accommodation in town. The architect who designed the building went crazy over plate glass – there is more of it per sq metre in the bar restaurant than any other building in Fiji. The restaurant/bar faces the harbour, making it a sterling place to watch the ships go by. In addition to the plethora of glass, the floors throughout the building are tiled, which is a pleasant change from the ubiquitous cheap linoleum which seems to cover everything in Fiji. Prices for well-appointed singles/doubles are F$80/90. The Waterfront's Old Mill Restaurant, also modern, is considered the most chic in Lautoka. The restaurant has an up-market menu featuring dishes like veal escalopes with a garlic, onion and mushroom sauce and seafood garnish for F$17.

Saweni Beach Hotel Apartments (☎ 661 777) are 11 km north of the airport between Nadi and Lautoka. The F$35 units (single or double) are individual, whitewashed, cement-block houses and though clean, are well worn. The mattresses, linen and bunks have definitely seen better days, and one gets the feeling that the owners do not relish putting money into this place. Each unit has a small stove, refrigerator and utensils. The resort has a bar but no restaurant. There are also two dorm units, one with five bunks the other with two, at F$7 per night. Nearby is a small local store for provisions.

Anchorage Beach Resort (☎ 662 099; fax 665 571) is on Vuda Point, the traditional landing site for the ancestors of the Fijian people. The resort is about 10 minutes by car from Lautoka, and reports have been good. Perhaps the best thing about the resort is its vistas, which are the most spectacular on Viti Levu. From the hotel grounds on the bluff you can see Nadi to the south, the Sabeto Mountains to the east, and the sea and Mamanuca Islands to the west and north. Anchorage Beach Resort is on 2.9 hectares of manicured gardens and has 12 well-appointed rooms (some are self-contained units) and a seven-bunk dorm with cooking facilities. The hotel is very clean and well maintained. There is a large restaurant/bar open to the sea breezes, a pool, gift shop and library where guests may swap books. As the name of the hotel indicates, there is also a beach nearby. Prices are F$70/75 for a single/double, F$85 a triple, and F$15 for a dorm. Self-contained units are F$85 for a single or double, F$97 a triple. Breakfast costs F$4.50 to F$6, lunch is F$5 to F$8 and dinner from F$12 to F$15.

Mediterranean Villas & Restaurant (☎ 664 011), also on Vuda Point, has excellent views. Prices range from F$90/165 for 'standard' singles/doubles, to F$160/280 for deluxe suites. Standard amenities include hair dryer, cassette radio, mini-bar, phone, king-size bed, and in the deluxe suite there's a 'vibrating hot spa bath for your extra relaxation', perhaps the only one in Fiji. There is also a restaurant.

Places to Eat

Even though Lautoka is Fiji's second-largest city, its restaurants do not come close to Suva's in variety. There are, however, some fair, inexpensive eateries. For Chinese cuisine the *Sea Coast Restaurant* on Naviti St is a good bet. Prices range from F$4 to F$8. Indian food enthusiasts can try *Hot Snaxs* on Naviti St, or *Asterix* on Yasawa St, which have curries, Chinese food and European dishes. Prices at both are around F$5. Perhaps the best place to eat is *Gopal's* on Naviti St or Vitogo Parade; first cousin to the

Hare Krishna of Suva, serving first-class vegetarian fare, home-made juices and ice cream in clean surroundings. Prices are in the F$4 to F$6 range.

Entertainment

Club 21 and *Kings Nightclub* on Naviti St are the local dives. They have plenty of action – sometimes in the form of fist fights. Tamer, and a notch or two higher on the socio-economic ladder is the *Great Wall of China*, near the Globe Cinema opposite the market. *Hunter's Inn* (near the Lautoka Hotel on Naviti St) has more of a tourist and local mix, and visitors may consider it the most civilised nightspot in town.

Finally, if you're really bored, there are four cinemas.

OFFSHORE ISLAND RESORTS

There are numerous resort islands off the coast from Nadi and Lautoka, all in the middle to top-end price brackets. Although nightly costs are quoted below for these resorts, the vast majority of people staying here will be on all-inclusive package tours.

Beachcomber Island

Beachcomber Island (☎ 662 600; fax 664 496) which has 17 bures, is the most popular among the young and the unattached. The island is a tiny speck of land (you can walk around it in 10 minutes) a 45-minute boat ride off the Nadi coast. Here you'll find an informal atmosphere, plenty of good food served buffet-style, and a 40-bed dorm. Activities include snorkelling, excursions and dancing. Rates (including all meals) are F$57 in the dorm, F$121/154 for a single/double in lodge-style accommodation, and F$144/190 in a bure. All prices include meals. Snorkelling equipment is provided free of charge but all other water sports will cost you.

Great entertainment and first-class live music are a tradition at Beachcomber. The house band has consistently won top honours in music competitions. Beachcomber has a courtesy bus service from the hotels to

Lautoka Wharf daily to catch the boat to the island at 10 am and 2.15 pm (F$50 one way).

Malololailai (Plantation Island)

Malololailai (which means 'small Malolo Island') is a gorgeous island with a lovely bay, about 16 km off the Nadi coast. The island also has the second-best beach (after Mana) in the Mamanuca group.

Plantation Island (☎ 723 333; fax 790 163), the tourist-brochure name for Malololailai, is one of the finest offshore resorts in Fiji. The clientele includes young couples, singles and families. Overall, the beach and the facilities are better than at Musket Cove, the other resort on the island. There are 104 units, many of them very attractive white-washed bures with thatched roofs and elegant interiors. Aside from the bures there are 43 hotel rooms in a two-storey building, some of which are too close to the action and tend to be noisy. There are also two very nice mixed dorms (that house 17 and 25 respectively) and cost F$71 per night including three meals. There are five 'grades' of single/twin accommodation ranging from F$135 to F$305. There are also large bures which take up to 10 people. The restaurant and band are good. Other amenities include a pool and disco. The resort has a very complete water-sports programme that includes fishing, diving, water-skiing, snorkelling and coral viewing, but the package for this costs extra. There is also a small store with essentials at the restaurant next to the airfield.

Plantation is connected with Nadi by Sunflower Airlines and Fiji Air, and by launch service from the Regent Hotel.

Musket Cove (☎ 662 215; fax 662 878) shares the same air services from Nadi with Plantation Island Resort. It is very informal compared with its neighbour (and most of the other offshore resorts), but accommodation is more than adequate. There are 24 bures (many of which are being upgraded) with kitchenettes that include refrigerator, stove and utensils. Nearby is a general store for do-it-yourselfers, and there is also a bistro where lunch and dinner are served.

Other amenities include a wonderful gift shop on the hill, a pool, bar and Mamanutha Divers where you can hire all the equipment needed for a day's diving or get your PADI open-water certificate.

The advantages at Musket Cove (compared to its neighbour) are that it's cheaper and perhaps more intimate, and that air transport and all water sports are included in the tariff. You can also use the up-market facilities of neighbouring Plantation Island Resort. Because there are units with beds for up to six, Musket Cove might be a good choice for a family. Rates begin at F$120/140 for singles/doubles. Luxury condominiums are also being built, which seem a bit incongruous next to the budget accommodation. The condos are only the beginning of a modern complex which will include a golf course and an entire resort community. Rates for the six condos or 'villas' (which will sleep up to six people) are F$225.

One reader, David Meagher, found a pleasant night stroll along the airstrip to the back beach and then west around the island. There are nice vistas of Viti Levu, and the narrow, rocky beach is usually deserted.

The downside of Musket Cove is that its beach is not as nice as Plantation's and that the low-lying lawns around it can be swampy. Mosquitoes can also be a real problem.

Malolo (Castaway Island)

Malolo is the largest island in the Mamanuca group, and although 'Castaway Island' is the name given by the tourist brochures to Malolo Island, *Castaway Island Resort* (☎ 661 233; fax 665 753) is actually on an 81-hectare island just to the north. The resort, with 66 bures, caters to a yuppie crowd. The thatched-roof main buildings with stone terraces and an indoor-outdoor restaurant, sit on a rocky point overlooking the sea. The resort has recently been refurbished from stem to stern and is now considered one of the premier, if not *the* premier resort in the Mamanucas. The bures are spacious, with various combinations of single and double beds, louvre windows, tiled floors, ceiling fans, rattan furniture, and bathrooms. Prices are F$216 to F$248 a single or double. Amenities include sauna, pool, fine cuisine and free water sports such as snorkelling, water-skiing, sailing, windsurfing and reef fishing. The local band is first class, regularly winning awards in Fiji.

Club Naitasi (☎ 790 192; fax 790 197), actually on Malolo Island, is nestled at the base of a hill and is just metres from a fine little white-sand beach. It has 27 bures and deluxe two-bedroom villas. Definitely upmarket in atmosphere, it has comfortable, well-constructed rooms which are family and couple-oriented; those desiring a cosy, quiet resort will not be disappointed here. Amenities include pool, cooking facilities for guests, an excellent restaurant, a small tennis court, diving, snorkelling and water-skiing. Accommodation is F$175 for a single/twin/triple. There are also luxury two-bedroom villas that accommodate from one to four people at F$275. Children under the age of 16 may stay free of charge. Speedboat transfers from Malololailai to Naitasi or Castaway are available; seaplane transport from Nadi Airport is also possible.

Tokoriki (☎ 661 999; fax 665 292) is one of the newer offshore resorts. It has 19 bures

all with ocean views and beach frontage. Bures accommodate up to six people for F$260.

Paradise Island

Paradise Island (☎ 665 222; fax 665 409) is the newest and closest resort to Lautoka. It is on an island within swimming distance of Lautoka's shore. Run by the Kelly family, the 19-hectare resort has its own generator, and water is barged in from the mainland. It features twin bures with traditional thatched roofs over concrete walls, and full soundproofing between each pair of units. For added comfort there are screened windows, hot water and ceiling fans.

Beyond the two cleared hectares, the native vegetation (including mangrove around the shore) harbours *bici* rails, which are extinct on Viti Levu, and other wildlife, and there are many trails for exploration. Around the island's perimeter is a fitness track. There is also a full gym and fitness programme, horse riding, a pool and facilities for children, plus equipment for many water sports which are rented without time limit. A volleyball net partially in and out of the water invites some interesting games. Tariffs are F$135 for bures, including transfer and continental breakfast. Family-style lunches and suppers are available from F$5.50, and there is also a restaurant with a deluxe menu. A night in a 12-bed dorm costs F$15 (F$45 including meals), plus F$15 for a one-way transfer. A barbecue pit is provided if you bring your own food.

Paradise Island also has day trips for F$25, including lunch, so the best thing a prospective visitor could do is check it out for the day and see if you like it. So far reports have been good.

Tavarua Island

Tavarua, a 12-hectare island off Momi Bay, is one of the few resorts in the South Pacific devoted solely to the sport of surfing. Amenities include 12 double bures plus a restaurant/bar area. Most of the island's power comes from a solar unit, which according to the owner is the largest installation of its type in Fiji. If the waves aren't breaking right for surfing then game-fishing, windsurfing and diving can be arranged. In the event of an accident, the resort has a special fast-transfer system to medical facilities on the mainland. The daily rate is US$125 (including meals, transfers, drinks and other activities). For more information write to Tavarua Island Resort, PO Box 1419, Nadi, Fiji, or call Aquarius Tours in California, USA (☎ 805 683 6696).

Mana Island

A family and couple-oriented resort, *Mana Island* (☎ 661 210; fax 662 713) has more of a formal 'hotel' feel. About 30 km offshore and surrounded by some of the best beaches in the Mamanuca group, Mana, covering more than 120 hectares, is the largest offshore resort. The 120 bures have peaked roofs, each with their own porch, ceiling fans, beamed ceilings, tiled floors, double and single bed, sitting area, refrigerator, radio, coffee pot, bathroom and shower. Hotel rates begin at F$185 for a single or twin. Triples are F$205, while a duplex bure accommodating up to six people costs F$270. Mana is clean and well managed. Amenities include a pool, general store, resident nurse, restaurant, tennis, snorkelling, water-skiing, sailing and jet skiing.

Aqua-Trek, considered one of the best scuba-diving operations in Fiji, has a five-star PADI teaching facility on Mana. Aqua-Trek offers numerous courses including a resort dive for F$75 and a five-day PADI certificate course for F$465. (Bring a doctor's certificate to prove your fitness for diving before you plan to set foot in the water.) A one-tank dive is F$50.

Treasure Island

Treasure Island (☎ 661 599) is owned by Islands in the Sun, the same people who own Beachcomber. Because of hurricanes, the resort underwent F$1 million in renovations. Like Beachcomber, it is a tiny island, but more formal, more luxurious and more family oriented. There are 68 bures with refrigerators and ceiling fans. There is plenty

of snorkelling and fishing, as well as excursions on the water, though activities such as boating and scuba diving cost extra. Singles/twins are F$190/220, boat transfers are extra (F$43 return, F$21.50 for children).

Matamanoa Island

Matamanoa Island (☎ 660 511; fax 661 069), a two-hour boat ride from the Regent Hotel, offers water-skiing, snorkelling, windsurfing, bush treks and picnicking on three nearby uninhabited islands. The 26 bures cost F$150 a single or double and F$260 for a suite which sleeps up to five. Other amenities include a pool, restaurant and bar/lounge.

Sonaisali Island Resort

Sonaisali (☎ 790 411; fax 790 392) which opened in June 1991, is just off the Coral Coast and features 32 rooms and six bures. Single/twin rooms cost F$190 and bures are F$245.

Queens Rd (Nadi to Suva)

UCIWAI BEACH

About 17 km from the airport and two km before the Momi Guns turn-off is Uciwai Rd. The beach is about 5½ km from the highway. The area, in the midst of cane fields, is perfect for a day's outing.

MOMI GUNS

The turn-off for this WW II battery is 24 km from the airport, and should be clearly marked. Follow the signs about 10 km along the dirt road (bearing to the right) to the Momi Guns site which is maintained by the Fiji National Trust. The road to the battery is part of the original Queens Rd. There is a small museum cleverly created inside an old bunker. The walls are filled with historic photos showing Fijian soldiers in WW II battle dress and others illustrating the restoration of the Momi Guns site from decrepitude to its full camouflaged glory.

The six-inch cannon were originally British Naval guns manufactured at the turn of the century and reputedly used in the Boer War and in the relief of Mafeking during WW I. The guns were brought to Fiji with the idea of protecting the capital and were installed in the Suva Battery of Bilo. When Bilo was updated in 1944 the cannon were brought to their current location to protect the strategic Navula pass in Momi Bay. The guns were fired only in practice. The only occasion they were discharged for 'protection' was when a shot was fired off the bow of an unidentified ship which subsequently gave a sharp about turn and identified itself as a New Zealand vessel. The guns had a range of about 19 km.

As one might expect, the Momi Guns are placed on a hill and have a glorious view worthy of a picnic lunch. (Note that in the hills, cane land is beginning to be replaced by pine.) The park is open six days a week and admission is 20 cents. There are toilets, drinking water and plenty of parking space. Unfortunately the site is seldom visited.

Places to Stay

Surftrek Reef Surfing Fiji (☎ 790 435), formerly known as Trekkers Reef Resort, is the other new establishment devoted to hard-core surfers. Other than Tavarua Island Resort, it is the only surf camp dedicated to the breaks at Namotu and Wilkes reefs. Twenty-eight km from Nadi and on 4.8 hectares, it's not a lavish affair but is a notch or two up on the comfort scale when compared to the other surf camp, Club Masa. Accommodation consists of three bures: one a dorm unit with six bunks; another with four beds; and the third with two beds, usually reserved for couples. Toilet and shower facilities are separate. The maximum number of guests is 12.

Surftrek provides three meals a day (usually vegetarian and seafood) and an after-surf snack. A typical evening meal will have three courses; the main course ranging from vegetarian lasagna to fresh peppered fish steaks. A traditional Fijian lovo (food steamed in an underground oven) is featured each week. Drinks at the bar are only F$1. Food is served in two bures which make up the dining/bar/lounge area.

The 'resort' (a term used rather loosely in this case) is very isolated and consequently there is not a lot of entertainment in the evenings. Come to think of it, apart from surfing, there is not much to do during the day. If you plan to stay, make the most of visiting local villages or hop on a bus and go to town. Arrangements can also be made to hire a car and driver as well.

The two main breaks near Surftrek are Namotu and Wilkes reefs. Namotu is a steep left and Wilkes is a fast right. Both are best at five to eight feet but hold up well over 10 feet. The other two breaks utilised by Surftrek are the 'Swimming Pools' (a long wrapping right inside Namotu Island) and 'Desperations' (a peak outside Wilkes which usually has a swell if the others are flat). These two breaks are best at three to six feet. All breaks are very hollow when they are at their peak.

Surftrek operates on package plans – seven nights for surfers are A$560 and A$497 for non-surfers. Tariffs include all meals, and airport/boat transfers. The bar is extra. Group discounts of 10% are available for 10 or more guests and a 5% discount is given for five or more guests. To book, call first and then send dates, flight details and a deposit of 25% to confirm the booking (PO Box 9839, Nadi Airport, Fiji). The balance is to be paid one month prior to arrival. It is recommended that you purchase travel insurance at the time of booking tickets.

SEASHELL COVE

Seashell Cove Resort (☎ 790 100/393; fax 790 294) a family-owned affair, is one of the few places on Viti Levu with both a camping ground and dorm facilities, so it's popular with budget travellers. At first glance the place looks a bit drab and could probably do with a coat of paint, but apart from that aesthetic gripe, it's well maintained. The 'resort' is on about 2.5 hectares of land backed by rolling hills and fringed by mangroves.

There is a swimming pool, and activities such as tennis, windsurfing, snorkelling and day trips to points of interest are offered. Seashell is also one of the few resorts in Fiji to accommodate the needs of surfers by taking them out to the reef. (There are, however, no transfers to Tavarua Island Resort from Seashell Cove.)

Besides camping and dorm facilities, the resort has 10 self-contained bures and six new units with fridge. Rates are F$45/55 for singles/doubles in a whitewashed bure, and F$35/45 in the pink-hued units. The five dorm units (each with five beds) are partitioned by thin wood composite walls, giving them a kind of cheap, flimsy look; they're also painted an institutional green. The nice thing about the dorms is that they are on a second storey and open to the sea breezes. Bunks are F$13 per night (including breakfast) and camping on a fringe of grass is F$6.50. There's also a family bure for F$80/85 (from four to six people) and suites for F$115. Food is about F$3 for breakfast, F$5 to F$7 for lunch and F$9 to F$12 for dinner.

The main complaint I heard about Seashell Cove is that guests in the self-contained units have to go a long way to get groceries (the resort is half an hour's drive south of Nadi). Also, if you plan to stay in a dorm, there are no facilities to prepare food, so you must eat at the cafe which is not outrageously expensive but is not cheap either. Hard-core backpackers may not like that option. For basic needs there is one small Indian grocery store very near the hotel.

Though the resort is on the beach, the term 'beach' might not be quite the right word for this area of Viti Levu – 'coastal tideland' is probably a better description of the shore here and all along the Coral Coast. You can swim inside the reef only during high tide.

H20 Sportz, the dive concession based at Seashell Cove, does a commendable job. It offers a five-day PADI certificate course every week for two or more students for F$275 which is very reasonable. Daily dive

trips are F$60 for two-tank dives, including gear.

Getting There & Away
Seashell Cove is served by the Sam Lal Bus Company from the Nadi bus depot daily at 8 am, 12.15, 2 and 4 pm. You can also get there on Sigatoka buses. There is a limited bus service from the resort, but you can always walk about 1½ km to the main road and catch any of the Queens Rd buses.

If you have your own transport, the road to Seashell Cove runs off the Queens Rd about 17 km from Nadi town or 27½ km from the airport. (Look for the Momi Bay sign, then continue a km further.) From the Queens Rd junction, go about five km and there will be a bright yellow sign. Continue for another 10 km or so to the resort. Seashell Cove will provide free transport from the airport for those who book ahead. For those not wishing to hassle with buses, taxis are about F$15 from the airport and F$12 from Nadi town.

NATADOLA BEACH
This is probably the nicest beach on Viti Levu, isolated from any resorts and thus seldom visited by tourists. There is some surfing here and the beach is also used surreptitiously by campers. Swimmers should be advised that large waves break on the beach, which is great for body surfing but dangerous if you're not a strong swimmer. Hunting for shells and snorkelling here is excellent. In theory you can camp, but there have been problems with thefts by unruly locals and even a recorded instance of rape. I definitely do not recommend that you camp here – better to picnic instead and even picnickers should not turn their back on their belongings while frolicking in the surf. Lock away all valuables.

Natadola Beach is also the terminus for the Coral Coast Railway. Here day-trippers have a chance to enjoy their lunch, sunbathe, hike and return that afternoon via rail.

Getting There & Away
The beach is accessible by public transport

from Nadi or Sigatoka; however, from the bus stop on the Queens Rd to the beach is a three-km hike. If you have your own transport, take the Queens Rd until you reach the large Maro Mosque on the left (45 km from the airport). About 200 metres past the mosque, take the next right (Maro Rd) and follow it to the end (eight km); you'll pass Tuva Indian School and cross two narrow bridges along the way. Turn left at the 'T' junction and follow the road for another 1½ km.

VISTA POINT

This is at the top of the hill, 55 km from the airport, where a road sign warns you of a steep grade ahead. To the left are the green mountains and to the right below is the translucent blue reef. Adjacent to the shore is Yanuca Island. (See later in this chapter.)

CUVU BEACH

Those staying at the Fijian Resort may want to check out Cuvu Beach, 56 km from the airport. Take Cuvu Rd which is sealed and begins about two km west of the Fijian Resort. Then take the first reasonable right-hand turn (which is also sealed) and follow it to the end. Along the way you will pass a railway yard complete with enough narrow-gauge rolling stock to last you a lifetime. Cuvu Beach has long stretches of white sand and plenty of shade trees.

FIJIAN RESORT

This area is roughly the beginning of what is known as the Coral Coast – the part of Fiji that stretches to Pacific Harbour.

The *Fijian Resort* (☎ 520 155; fax 500 402) is a self-contained resort complex constructed on tiny Yanuca Island (not the same island as the one off Beqa), connected to the mainland by a causeway. It is a gorgeous piece of real estate and the hotel is certainly one of the top five in Fiji.

About an hour's drive (59 km) from Nadi Airport, this 364-room resort has all the luxury amenities including two pools, four restaurants, five bars, a general store, a boutique, a duty-free shop, convention facilities, a disco and traditional dance shows and fire-walking exhibitions. Recreational activities are probably the most complete in Fiji, and consist of five tennis courts with professional coach, a nine-hole golf course, horse riding, snorkelling, lawn bowling, sailing, volleyball, scuba diving, deep-sea fishing and water-skiing. The hotel has excellent cuisine – the chef recently won a 'cook-off' competition naming him the best cook in the country. Prices start at F$220/275 for a standard single/double, while individual bures with living rooms cost from F$320 to F$600.

For security and aesthetic reasons, visitors at the Fijian might consider rooms on the second storey rather than on the ground floor. Without picking on the Fijian in particular, rip-offs and petty theft have grown over the years and prudence in this area makes sense. In any case, the top-floor rooms have vaulted ceilings, fewer insects and better views.

All in all, the Fijian is a fine property but expensive unless you take full advantage of the recreational facilities.

SIGATOKA AREA

At the mouth of the Sigatoka River, 69 km from Nadi Airport, Sigatoka town lies in close proximity to rich farmland and some of Fiji's finest hotels. With a population of just over 2000 the town is hardly a metropolis, but instead provides the visitor with a combination of tourist facilities and a genuine 'local' farm-town atmosphere. Sigatoka might be called the 'gateway to the Coral Coast', an area that contains many resorts and stretches from the township approximately 70 km east along the coastline.

Sigatoka is a quiet community marked by a gorgeous mosque and a lengthy bridge that crosses the river. Duty-free stores are abundant here and it's much more pleasant to conduct business with Sigatoka's small-town merchants than with those in Nadi. Outside town there is the river valley road for motorists. Two km north of town are the sand dunes near Kulukulu village – an attraction well worth visiting.

Sigatoka Valley Rd

This valley, the 'salad bowl' of Fiji, ranks

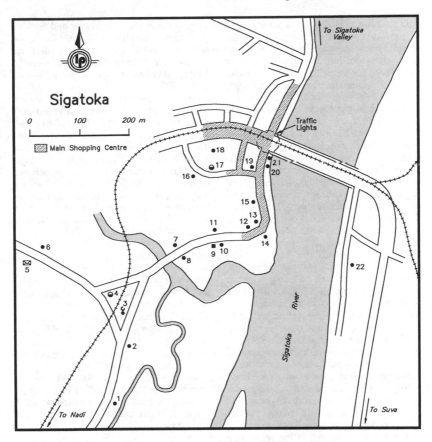

Sigatoka

Main Shopping Centre

1 Mobil Petrol Station
2 Site of Old Victory Theatre
3 Mosque
4 Bus Stop
5 Post Office
6 Police Station
7 Angel Theatre
8 Town Council
9 Sigatoka Hotel
10 Fiji Development Bank
11 Shell Petrol Station
12 Bank of Baroda
13 National Bank of Fiji
14 Sigatoka Club
15 Bakery
16 ANZ Bank
17 Bus Station
18 Market
19 Westpac Bank
20 Taxi Stand
21 Wishing Well
22 School

with the Nausori Highlands as among some of the most magnificent scenery on the island. Follow the main road into Sigatoka town, then turn left and follow the river valley road for about 20 km. The Sigatoka River is second in size and importance among the rivers of Viti Levu. It rises near Nadarivatu in the Nausori Highlands and flows some 136 km to the coast.

The Sigatoka River divides the rich valley into two distinct agricultural areas. The government stipulates that half the valley must be used for growing dalo (taro root), tavioka (cassava), corn, tomatoes, lettuce, green peppers, tobacco, cabbage, passion fruit and other vegetable or fruit crops. At harvest time the crops are transported down the river on handmade bilibili, on small boats or carried by truck to Sigatoka, where they are sent to other markets around the country. The eastern side of the valley is utilised for sugar cane. The government's reasoning is that, if left to the farmers, all the rich valley land would be used to grow cane exclusively, or whatever crop fetches the highest price. Fiji would thus be without other important produce because of the whims of supply and demand. Farmers are restricted to growing no more than six hectares of cane to make sure that no-one crop monopolises the land.

Sigatoka marks the end of the cane-growing region. From here onwards precipitation begins to increase and the foliage becomes greener and denser.

Travelling along the valley road, you should first stop at the agricultural station (about seven km from town) and the nearby pottery village of **Nakabuta**. Continuing for another five km or so, the road takes a turn to the east at **Raiwaqa** and heads towards the Yalavou Beef Scheme, a cattle ranch which makes for an interesting detour. About four km along this route is an accessible **bat cave**. Ask around for directions. Back on the main road there are several other options. You can follow the valley road another 35 km up to a northern junction (a left-hand turn) a few km past the village of **Tuvu**. This will take you to the major junction at Bukuya village. At this point, you can continue north to Ba or

west to the Nausori Highlands and back to Nadi. Give yourself a comfortable five to six hours to travel from Sigatoka to Nadi. Both rides are magnificent. The northern route is a bit rougher and would be better negotiated with a 4WD.

The second option is to continue along the Sigatoka Valley Rd (sticking to your right) to the bridge beyond the village of **Keiyasi**. Past the bridge are two interesting points. The first (and much closer to the bridge) is a **cave** about an hour's hike from the village of **Natuatuacoko**. Ask around and the villagers will probably be happy to show you this cave, which was used as a fortress by local tribes during the Colo Wars of 1876. If they take the time to show you around, you should offer them a suitable gift of money or groceries. The second point of interest is reached by taking the road to the end of the line, beyond the village of Korolevu. From there you walk to **Namoli** – an old-style, thatched-roof community. When visiting the area you should not just barge into the village, but should wait until you're invited and come with suitable gifts. At this point you can simply turn back to Sigatoka or double back to the junction described earlier and continue along the interior.

To get to Keiyasi from Sigatoka take the 9 am bus which arrives in the village around 11 am. The same bus returns to Sigatoka at about 11.30 am, and the next bus comes at about 2 pm.

Coral Coast Railway

The Coral Coast Railway was developed in the mid-1980s by New Zealand entrepreneur David Jones. The service starts at the Fijian Resort with the terminus at Natadola Beach. Not that a railway is new to Fiji at all. The sugar train has been around since the turn of the century, bringing the cane harvest from throughout the western side to the refinery in Lautoka. Up to the 1970s the old train took passengers as well, but this practice was discontinued because it was more trouble than it was worth. It took Jones to utilise the already existing railway infrastructure, add a few stations, rebuild a circa-1911 steam

CORAL COAST RAILWAY CO.

engine, construct carriages from scratch, and *voilà*, the Coral Coast Railway was born.

The first line, which originates at the Fijian Resort, hugs the coastline and passes through rainforest, villages, cane fields and sections of undeveloped countryside which are essentially the same landscape that a rail traveller would have seen at the turn of the century. One hour and 15 minutes later you are deposited on unspoiled Natadola Beach for a barbecue or any number of activities such as hiking, swimming, snorkelling, surfing or windsurfing. Refreshments are served during the ride. The train leaves the beach at 4 pm to return to the hotel. The cost for the ride, which includes lunch and transport from Coral Coast hotels, is F$65 for adults and F$32.50 for children. Tickets can be purchased at any tour desk.

Unfortunately, however, I've heard that the service has gone downhill ever since Jones sold the railway several years ago and I can no longer vouch for its quality.

Sand Dunes

The sand dunes, near Kulukulu village (about two km south of Sigatoka town) rank as among the most beautiful sights in Fiji. Looking like something out of the Arabian nights, the undulating dunes hug the coastline for several km, their soft sand as fine as flour. The tops of these 30 to 45-metre sand hillocks afford a beautiful vista of green mountains to the east and the ocean to the west. Some of them have been planted with vegetation to resist erosion, while others near the roadside are being stripped of their sand for building materials. Occasionally you may see shards of ancient pottery poking through the sand. If you happen to find some, do not remove them from the beach – they are protected by law.

At the foot of the dunes is a new surf camp – Club Masa, a low-budget, no-frills accommodation of interest primarily to surfers. (See Places to Stay later in this section.) Windsurfing, at the mouth of the Sigatoka River, is also excellent.

Ka Levu Centre

The Ka Levu Centre (☎ 50 988), across the highway from the Fijian Resort, provides an interesting, if superficial glimpse of Fijian culture with an emphasis on Nadroga – the local district. 'Ka Levu' is a local chiefly title which, ironically, is being fought over by the local tribe. It is a museum and cultural centre consisting of seven bures built to resemble a traditional Fijian village built before European contact. Each of the structures is devoted to a particular facet of Fijian history or culture. Some display handicrafts and artefacts, while others have canned audio-visual displays. Daily admission is F$10, while on Thursdays it is F$15 for the 'Cultural Show'. There is also a swank Chinese restaurant on the premises.

Kula Bird Park

The Kula Bird Park (☎ 50 505), a combined aviary/botanical garden, is one of the more ambitious tourist attractions in Fiji. Built on four hectares of natural rainforest directly opposite the Reef Hotel, it houses 100 species numbering 500 birds from Australia, Africa, Asia, South America, Papua New Guinea, New Zealand, the Canary Islands, Madagascar and Cuba as well as indigenous species from Fiji. One of the more colourful varieties of local birds that visitors seldom see is the red shining parrot from Taveuni. Of equal interest is the collection of indigenous plants scattered throughout the park.

The park also houses laboratories for ornithological study, a small aquarium, bird hospital, children's playground, picnic area and the obligatory snack bar. Admission costs around F$10.

Other Attractions

The municipal market on the edge of Sigatoka town is worth visiting just to see the abundance of regional produce and a sizeable handicraft selection.

There's also a cruise (for approximately two hours) up the Sigatoka River. The launch stops at a village to let you observe the yaqona ceremony and see a meke. The cost for the trip is F$10.

Korotogo

Korotogo is a small village about seven km east of Sigatoka.

Places to Stay – bottom end

Vakaviti (☎ 500 526) is an excellent bottom to mid-range place 500 metres east of the Reef Resort in Korotogo. Situated on a hillside, with ample vegetation and not too many other residents, it's a great place to take a breather for a few days or perhaps to use as a base to visit Sigatoka or the Sigatoka Valley. There are four self-contained units at F$55, and two family units for F$50. Discounts of 10% are negotiable for stays of a week or more.

All units are squeaky clean and include linen, cutlery and dishes. They are cooled by an overhead fan and the sea breeze. There's also a small pool and a poolside barbecue fired by coconut husks. The express buses coming from Suva or Nadi will drop you at the Reef Resort, from where you'll have to hitch or walk the extra km or so to the

Vakaviti. The local buses will drop you right out in front. The store is a five-minute walk away. For reservations write to PO Box 5, Sigatoka.

Waratah (☎ 500 278) is another barebones, family-run accommodation with five A-frame units that look strangely out of place in Fiji. Each self-contained unit can house up to eight people. Amenities include a small pool, garden and pleasant patio. Tariffs are F$30/40 for singles/doubles. It is on Queens Rd about a km from Vakaviti.

Tubakula (☎ 500 201/97; fax 393 056) continues to be very popular with budget travellers and, in the past, has been highly recommended as an inexpensive accommodation with friendly employees. It's 9½ km outside Sigatoka, about a km east of the Reef Resort on the ocean side, and consists of three rows of monolithic A-frames on a grassy, open expanse. The structures can accommodate up to six people and are self-contained. (There is no restaurant on the premises.) Rates vary according to the location of the A-frames in relation to the water's edge; credit cards are accepted. Staying near the water costs F$37 per night and the poolside accommodation is F$33. The price for an extra person is F$8. There are also family bures which sleep six. Dorm facilities are F$8 per night but you must bring your own blankets and towels. To use the dorm's cooking facilities you must pay for cooking fuel by use of a meter that measures the flow of the gas. Make sure you check out the sand dunes which are nearby. Unfortunately there have been several recent reports of theft at Tubakula; visitors should safeguard their valuables.

There is also the inexpensive *Sigatoka Hotel* in Sigatoka, which is now under new management. The rooms have balconies where you can sit and sip a beer, and there is a garden as well. However, reviews have been mixed since the hotel changed hands. A dorm bed is F$9, singles/doubles F$25/35, and there is a restaurant downstairs. The Sigatoka also provides transport to the Fijian Hotel for guests. (Technically, non-guests are not supposed to use these facilities.)

Club Masa Resort (☎ 800 468 5643 in the USA; 213 473 4591 in California) might be called the poor person's Tavarua – a new, low-budget accommodation primarily for surfers. I say primarily because my hunch is that those outside the surfing cult might find Club Masa's environment a bit psychologically confining. 'The Club' is situated on 36 hectares, a hundred metres or so from the spectacular Kulukulu sand dunes and a vast expanse of cane fields. Consisting of three rough-hewn cabins and a dorm unit, it has the feel of a remote homestead. And remote it is. To get there you must take the Kulukulu bus (available three times daily from Sigatoka). The turn-off is about four km from Sigatoka (just before the Sigatoka River) and another three km off the Queens Rd.

According to my sources, Club Masa is near the only 'beach break' in all of Fiji, thus providing easy access for wave riders. The surfing season is between May and September, when wind patterns kick up a big southern swell. Swimming is OK in the nearby river but not recommended in the sea because of strong currents.

The three cabins each provide accommodation for two people, and one is a self-contained unit. Singles or doubles in a standard cabin are F$20 and F$30 in the self-contained unit. The dorm has 10 bunks at F$9. Beds and dorm bunks are basic foam pads draped in sheets. Camping is also available for F$5.50 per person.

The small bar/canteen sells food at reasonable prices: F$3 for breakfast, F$3.50 for lunch and F$4 for dinner. Guests can also prepare their own dinner at the cook shack. Facilities are acceptable but rudimentary; there is no electricity at Club Masa.

Korotogo Lodge (☎ 500 755; fax 520 182) has been described as a 'very basic' accommodation consisting of four clean rooms, each with four to six bunks. Two of the rooms have a double room-within-a-room making it necessary for guests to pass through a dorm in order to enter their own quarters. Unless your entire family is occupying a unit, this makes for a potentially awkward arrange-

ment. A dorm bed costs F$10, and there are family units from F$30 to F$40; a single is F$20.

The rooms have cooking facilities, consisting of a double gas burner, utensils and a fridge. There's a shabby yard with a dilapidated fence, and also a small restaurant owned by the management. The restaurant serves fish, curries and the like for F$4 to F$6.

In my assessment the Korotogo Lodge is a step down from similarly priced properties such as the Nadi Bay Motel, but is still one of the few budget accommodation places around Sigatoka where you can cook your own food. For reservations, write to PO Box 37, Korotogo, Sigatoka.

Places to Stay – middle

Crow's Nest (☎ 500 230; fax 520 354), near Sigatoka, is a small hillside resort. It is by no means a fancy place to stay, but is comfortable, attractive and well run. The 18 bures are fully self-contained and there is an inexpensive restaurant on the premises serving good food. Prices are F$75 for a single and F$100 for a unit that sleeps up to five. It's a good place to bring children, and is a 10-minute walk from the beach. In addition, the Crow's Nest has one of the best restaurants in the Sigatoka area.

The *Reef Hotel Resort* (☎ 500 044; fax 520 074) was at one time highly rated but I've heard mixed comments of late. It's rather puzzling to hear great things at one time and get very negative comments about food and service a year later. Since I cannot stay in every hotel when I update a book, I must rely on readers' comments and...well, you pay your money and you take your chances.

Free amenities include a nine-hole golf course, tennis, snorkelling, fishing, glass-bottom boat, kayaking and horseback riding. On Tuesday nights guests can visit the nearby village of Malevu and enjoy a traditional lovo (meal cooked in an underground oven). Rooms have balconies or patios with a sea view and are open to ocean breezes. The resort has 72 rooms and prices begin at

F$110 for a single, double or triple and F$140 for a superior suite (which has a sitting area).

Places to Eat

The best place to eat curry in Sigatoka is at an unpresumptuous restaurant called *Rattans* on Market Rd. Meals are F$5 to F$7 and the place is air-conditioned.

The *Crow's Nest*, a small resort a few km east of town, has one of the best restaurants in the region. Specialities are seafood, traditional Fijian food and curries with a dozen condiments or 'chutneys' on the side. For visitors who have never sampled curry before, it is a good place to begin. Curries and fish are moderately priced at F$7 to F$12.

Inexpensive Indian food for F$3 to F$4 can be had at the *Sigatoka* and *Pacifica* lodges, which are both near the market. Adjoining the Casablanca Beach Resort in Korotogo is a pizzeria/general store called the *Hacienda* which reputedly serves good pizza ranging from F$7 to F$14.

Entertainment

There are two cinemas and a theatre in Sigatoka town.

TABUA SANDS RESORT

Tabua Sands (☎ 500 399), about a km west of Hideaway Resort, is on a beautiful beach, with 15 bures dispersed amid coconut palms. The bures are well-constructed, and each has a double and two single beds; none are self-contained. If one wanted a conventional 'honeymoon' hotel with no surprises and plenty of solitude, this would be it. It was

highly recommended by some of the over-60 travellers. Activities include mekes, 'choir night' on Sunday evenings and the yaqona ceremony. As with most accommodation on the Coral Coast, swimming is only possible at high tide. Tabua Sands has a restaurant and a large, tiled breakfast/lunch area facing the sea. Doubles are F$80 per night in a beach bure; F$70 for other bures. Singles are F$60 and children aged under 16 years are free.

HIDEAWAY RESORT

Hideaway Resort (☎ 500 177; fax 520 025) is on the beach 20 km east of Sigatoka, about an hour's bus ride from Nadi. With 48 bures, it is one of the better low to mid-range hotels in Fiji. However, note that the 'bottom-end' facilities here are more expensive compared to those in backpackers' accommodation and that the overall operation is very much aimed at a mid-range clientele. In the last few years the resort has been refurbished, with new bures, a bar, decking and extensive landscaping.

Many come for the surfing, which is excellent and has been featured in a number of Australian surfing publications. The surf has one to three-metre breaks and is a 'right-hander'.

There is a small shop, dive centre, and a high-ceiling, open-air dining facility. A dorm bed costs F$13 per night, including maid service. White stucco bures are priced at F$90 for one to three guests, and F$130 for one to five guests. The dorm accommodates 44 people and those who are Youth Hostel Association (YHA) members get 10% discounts. The 48 bures are well constructed and well maintained. The best bures are on the beach, which is narrow but good for swimming, snorkelling and surfing. There is also a small pool at the water's edge in the midst of a palm grove.

Activities include horse riding, snorkelling, glass-bottom boat trips and excursions to a nearby village. The local village puts on mekes for guests twice weekly, as well as a traditional dance by an Indian group. This entails walking and lying on a bed of nails, firewalking and the performers piercing their

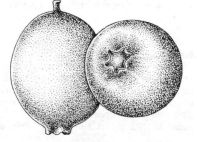

lips and cheeks with copper skewers. To my knowledge, Hideaway is the only property in Fiji offering entertainment that highlights these aspects of Indian culture.

If you are not into self-mutilation, you can dance to the sounds of the house band at a sand-floor disco known as 'Hernando's Hideaway'. The highlight of a stay at the Hideaway is a 4WD trip to a hot spring and waterfall (see under Korolevu). This entails a hike through the rainforest and a dip in the steaming-hot pool or a swim beneath the falls. The trip leaves the hotel six days a week at 9 am. Other good news is that the Hideaway accepts credit cards. The management suggests that unbooked visitors call upon arrival to make sure there is room.

Hideaway's downside is that backpackers on a tight budget will not be able to prepare food because units are not self-contained. Food at the restaurant is not outrageously expensive compared to the higher priced hotels, but this is a resort that happens to have dorms rather than strictly low-end accommodation, so don't expect it to be as cheap as the local restaurants.

KOROLEVU

Near this village is an airstrip and waterfall. The falls, called **Savu-na-Matelaya**, can be reached either on horseback by arrangement with the local hotels, or on foot from Biascvu village, about a km from the airstrip. Villagers charge F$1 per person to guide you to the falls and to the nearby hot spring.

NAVITI BEACH RESORT

The *Naviti* (☎ 500 444; fax 520 343) is a family-oriented resort hotel, roughly halfway between Nadi and Suva. It's on a bay near Korolevu, a 1½-hour drive from Nadi. The 144-room Naviti (which occupies 15 hectares) has all the amenities, but looks like it was designed by a Russian architect whose speciality was Moscow housing projects. The buildings are massive concrete structures that don't really blend in with the environment.

Exterior aesthetics aside, the interior of the hotel and the rooms have been com-

pletely refurbished and are as up to snuff as any in Fiji. Amenities include a duty-free shop, boutique, service shop, restaurant, games room, pool, and activities such as snorkelling, diving, horse riding (donkeys for the kids), canoeing, cycling, hiking, tennis (on a new all-weather court) and nine-hole golf course, live music, local dance shows and firewalking exhibitions. This is a very good place to bring children, as they are well cared for. Prices are F$140 for a single or double, F$155 a triple, and F$260 for a family suite. Car rentals are also available.

WARWICK FIJI RESORT

The *Warwick Fiji* (☎ 500 555; fax 520 010) was formerly the Hyatt and, like the Naviti, is now under the Warwick umbrella. Just two km east of Korolevu, it has 250 rooms and ranks as one of the better resorts in the country. Amenities include four restaurants, four bars, a boutique, duty-free general store, 24-hour room service, convention facilities and local entertainment such as dancing and firewalking shows. Sports include golf on a nine-hole course, tennis (two courts), swimming, snorkelling, windsurfing, scuba diving and canoeing. Rooms, which have a fully stocked bar and refrigerator, start at F$165 for a single or twin and F$185 for a triple. The *Wicked Walu* restaurant serves some of the best seafood on the Coral Coast. The Warwick also provides free transfers from the airport.

VATULELE RESORT

Thirty-two km offshore from Korolevu lies Vatulele, a small island (about 31 sq km in area) which, in places, is honeycombed with caves. In one of these caves, **Korolama-lama**, are large numbers of the creatures Vatulele is best known for – red prawns. Called *ua bua* 'cooked prawns' (after their precooked colour), they are sacred and no-one is permitted to touch them. According to tradition they can be called to the surface by the villagers, much like sharks or turtles can be called in other parts of Fiji.

Vatulele (☎ 790 300; 800 828 9146 in the USA; fax 790 062) is also the name of one of the newest and from all reports, nicest up-market resorts in Fiji. The US$6 million resort is situated on 24 hectares and was developed by Henry Crawford, an Australian film maker whose projects have included the TV miniseries 'A Town Like Alice'. The architecture has been described as a blend of Santa Fe and traditional Fijian styles – 'thick, whitewashed masonry walls and wooden shutters topped by a high Fijian thatched roof producing an airy, sun-washed effect'. The price is US$726 for a double, excluding air transfer.

The 12 individual bures each front onto a white-sand beach, and have a raised, bedroom area, bathroom/vanity, bar, and outdoor terraces on two sides. Food is gourmet quality, prepared by an Australian chef. Water-oriented activities include swimming, snorkelling, windsurfing and game fishing, and there is also tennis and hiking.

Access to the island is via plane; a new airstrip on the island now allows the scheduling of four flights per week. The return flight with Sunflower Airlines costs F$96.

MAN FRIDAY & CORAL REEF RESORTS
Near Somosomo Bay, *Man Friday* (☎ 500 185; fax 303 185) is one of the better, moderately priced hotels on the Coral Coast. About five km off Queens Rd and about 80 km west of Suva, it is at the easternmost extension of the Coral Coast. Units are on the beach or on a hillside (some of these have excellent views). One of its biggest attractions is its isolation and natural beauty. Man Friday has received praise from Lonely Planet readers for its friendliness and value for money. Even if you don't stay here, on a sunny day the drive is worthwhile for admiring the vista.

It has 29 bures with fridge, toaster, coffee maker and utensils, but no stove. The beach bures have thatched roofs, bamboo ceilings, polished-wood floors, ceiling fans, dining/cooking areas with a fridge and hot plate, and bathrooms. Hillside units (reached by a funicular) are newer but not as pretty. Man Friday has a pool, bar, restaurant and badminton court. Activities include snorkelling,

deep-sea fishing, horse riding, tennis, windsurfing, beach barbecue, live band and visits to the local village. Rates start at F$75/80 for singles/doubles; F$85/90 for a triple/quad. There are larger, family-style units as well. You can also negotiate with the manager for discounts of up to 20% depending upon your length of stay. If you go by taxi to Korolevu (to stock up on groceries for example) the fare is about F$15.

Off the same access road as Man Friday (about five km off Queens Rd) is *Coral Village* (☎ 500 807) which is separated from Man Friday by Namaqaqua village. Smaller and more intimate than Man Friday, it is draped on a lush hillside above one of the few decent, sandy beaches on the Coral Coast. At low tide you can walk for miles along the shore, sharing the tranquillity with villagers fishing or searching the tide pools for shellfish. There is also a reef, 100 metres offshore, which is good for diving and snorkelling.

Run by a young, friendly Australian couple, Billy and Wendy Jones, Coral Village bills itself as a mecca for holistic health. Both Billy and Wendy are qualified natural health practitioners with experience in Swedish massage, Shiatsu, Reiki, fitness instruction and nutritional counselling. Billy is also a qualified PADI instructor who offers four-day open-water certificate courses for F$300; two-tank dives for F$80 (including gear) and inexpensive snorkelling equipment rental.

Coral Village also offers a four-day **Matokana trek** into the highlands along an ancient Fijian trail. Trekkers explore caves and hot springs, try bamboo rafting and experience kava ceremonies in remote villages. The trek involves one night in a tent, and two nights in bures. The cost is F$300. Day treks can also be arranged.

Accommodation at Coral Village is in 11 bures, four duplex bungalows (each with queen-size bed and tiled bathroom) and two two-bedroom family units (each with queen beds). There is also an excellent dorm accommodating 12 singles. The rattan furniture lining the rooms has seen better days, but everything is clean and comfortable. Rates are F$98/128 for singles/doubles, F$150 for triples on the first night, and F$76/72/72 on subsequent nights. The dorm rate is F$14 (maid service included), and camping is available for F$6. It is the only camp site on the Coral Coast. The small dining room serves up healthy fare (both vegetarian and non-vegetarian) at moderate prices, ranging from F$4 to F$10.

Management says that they are slowly refurbishing the property (which recently reopened after a five-year hiatus). They suggest calling ahead for reservations. Coral Village is a good value, especially for low-end travellers. Perhaps the only downside is the isolation; Coral Village is far from any large settlement, but you can arrange transport to the bus stop on the Queens Rd (five km from the resort).

SERUA ISLAND
This tiny island, 123 km from Nadi Airport, is on the far boundary of the Serua district, which is the end of the Coral Coast.

QALOA
Near this village (143 km from Nadi Airport) is a famous mission school. The area was also a favourite vacation spot for Fijian statesman Ratu Sukuna. His summer cottage is about a km from the school grounds.

DEUBA
If for some strange reason you wish to spend time in Deuba, there is a whole array of dorm and very inexpensive motel facilities which are clean, comfortable and highly recommended. Across the way is a popular beach – the closest to Suva. You are also within walking distance of Pacific Harbour.

PACIFIC HARBOUR
In contrast to Orchid Island's intimacy, Pacific Harbour's cultural centre and market place (a huge shopping complex) is a slick, megabucks production, and is only one facet of the 500-hectare resort complex, a 45-minute (50 km) drive from Suva. It has recently been purchased by a Japanese

concern and is undergoing some structural renovation. Pacific Harbour has it all, including a golf course (the best in Fiji), an ocean-side pool, game fishing/charter boat, two restaurants (including the fine Japanese Sakura House), an 84-room hotel and 180 villas.

In a nutshell, Pacific Harbour has a lot of things going for it as a dormitory suburb of Suva and is a popular getaway spot for well-heeled locals. However, it is in the middle of nowhere and the weather is similar to Suva's, which may discourage people from spending a lot of time here.

Lake Tour
The cultural centre features a Disneyland-style trip back into traditional Fijian culture. This entails a boat trip around an artificial lake; the boat stops at various 'ports' to watch Fijian actors demonstrate ancient rituals and craft making. All the artisans use genuine implements – stone adzes and coarse brain coral to scrape out logs for canoes; hand-woven coconut fibre to fashion slings and cord; and sea shells to slit broad pandanus leaves which eventually become woven mats. The cost is F$9 for adults and F$5 for children. Bookings can be made through any hotel or travel agency.

The tour begins with the haunting sound of a conch-shell trumpet, perhaps to announce to the gods the arrival of the visitors, who are pushed around gondola-style by a ferocious-looking but very articulate warrior. The boat makes 10 brief stops where the guests may observe demonstrations of old-time crafts such as mat-weaving, masi-making and pottery done by traditionally dressed Fijian women.

However, you must observe all the cultural sights from the vessel: it is taboo for visitors to set foot on the islands. There is really no problem with this as the gondola moors only inches from the islands.

On the islands are traditional bures that include the chief's home, a temple, a storage area for food, a kitchen and a weaving hut. As the boat completes its circuit, it passes near the chief's home which is studded with vicious-looking wooden spikes to keep out uninvited guests and equally vicious-looking warrior guards armed with war clubs. Part of the tour includes a blood-curdling mock battle between opposing warriors that makes you glad you weren't around in those days.

Dance Theatre & Firewalking

The Dance Theatre of Fiji (a troupe that makes regular international tours) and the firewalkers from the island of Beqa are the other daily cultural attractions at Pacific Harbour. The dance theatre, led by a soft-spoken chief by the name of Manoa Rasigatale, is committed to reviving the ancient legends and dances with original choreographed mekes. Though the steps may not be completely traditional, the performances are true to Fijian spirit, right down to the hand-carved war clubs.

The firewalking show is one of those things visitors always want to see and may as well experience at Pacific Harbour. The advantage here is that during the show an announcer explains the steps leading up to the firewalking to help the visitor understand what is going on. Although it seems crass (something akin to a blow-by-blow description of high mass to non-Catholics), it is effective. The cost for the outdoor dance theatre performances and the firewalking exhibitions are F$7.50 for children and F$15 for adults.

Other Activities

You can play golf on an 18-hole Robert Trent Jones-designed course. The fee is F$20 for guests staying at Pacific Harbour accommodation, F$50 for people passing through.

Apart from land-based activities, Pacific Harbour has charters-only, big-game fishing aboard the MV *Marau*, which holds up to 10 passengers. Game fish include marlin, sailfish, wahoo, mackerel, tuna and barracuda. Diving excursions to Beqa Lagoon are organised through Scuba Hire Ltd or Beqa Divers (☎ 361 088), which has several boats at Pacific Harbour. Dive sites are top notch, and beginners are welcome.

Places to Stay

Many of the villas in Pacific Harbour are privately owned by individuals from Hong Kong, the UK and Australia, but others can be rented beginning at around F$100 to F$120 per day for up to four people, which is certainly reasonable. The units have fully equipped kitchens and two to four bedrooms; some even have private pools.

Pacific Harbour International Hotel (☎ 450 011), 50 km from Suva, has a disco, car-rental service, a Bank of New Zealand branch, post office, bottle shop and a host of boutiques. The hotel's restaurant is reportedly below par. Hotel rates begin at F$130 for a single or double.

The *Coral Coast Christian Camp* (☎ 450 178), off Queens Rd about a km past the entrance to Pacific Harbour, has an excellent choice of low-budget rooms and dorm facilities. Prices begin at F$8 per person for rooms with four bunks (including gas stove, fridge and utensils); F$10 for the 'cozy corner' facility which has more 'luxurious' beds and a large communal kitchen; and six motel rooms that cost F$18/30 a single/double. A 10% discount is given for stays of seven nights or more. The motel rooms are clean, have hot water and are self-contained. The camp is an hour's bus ride from Suva, thus is inconvenient if you want to hang around town, but is directly across from the only decent beach in the Suva area. The camp is efficiently run by Mrs McComber, a friendly, no-nonsense woman. Ask for her when you call.

The *Atholl Hotel* is an attractive, newly built structure resembling more a modern public library or university building than a hotel. Located on the grounds of Pacific Harbour it is the dream-come-true of the owners, a couple who wanted to erect a fantasy hotel. Unfortunately they did so without any regard as to whether they could fill the hotel with visitors. It is lavish after a style, built with exotic hardwoods, marble and filled with gleaming brass from Indonesia. Alas, at the time of this writing the hotel was completely empty. Prices may have something to do with this. Tariffs start at

F$195/220 for a single/double (excluding meals) and continue up to F$2100 for the 'penthouse'.

Places to Eat

Sakura House is a 45-minute drive from Suva, but if you crave excellent Japanese food this is the place to go. Meals average F$20 to F$30. Another, less expensive option is *Kumaran's Restaurant & Milk Bar*, opposite the gates to the Pacific Harbour International Hotel. Kumaran's provides simple, yet excellent Indian, Chinese and Western fare (including desserts) at reasonable prices. A typical lunch for two, including fresh fruit juice and tea is only F$20.

Getting There & Away

Pacific Harbour has a regular bus service from Suva and has its own airstrip; there are regular flights from Nadi Airport on Sunflower Airlines.

YANUCA ISLAND

Yanuca is an inhabited island with lush vegetation, fine white sandy beaches and spectacular coral reefs. It is now the location of a new camp site for surfers as well as a yacht charter. These activities are run by Frigates Surf Riders Pty Ltd, a newly formed local company, in conjunction with Rosie Tours, a well respected Fiji tour operator.

The camp site is on the eastern side of the island, about a km from the only village. The operation is reportedly run in the best tradition of Fijian village hospitality – both friendly and informal. One of the managers, Litia, is apparently an excellent cook. Although Yanuca is primarily an overnight camping area, day trips are also available to the island. To reach the surfing locale requires a half-hour boat ride from the island to an area called Frigates Passage, which is on the south-west edge of Beqa Lagoon. The wave is a left-hander and has the advantage of being 'offshore' in the south-east trade wind which makes it a very consistent break. In addition to surfing there is fishing, hiking,

snorkelling, village visits and perhaps a touch rugby game with the locals.

A full day's surfing, including pick-up from Nadi hotels at 8 am and return transport to Pacific Harbour (4 pm) is F$72 for surfers, F$85 for windsurfers. A four-day camping trip including meals, transfers and daily trips to Frigates Passage costs F$312, F$335 for windsurfers.

A live-aboard yacht package is also offered on Yanuca. It's still a surfer's or windsurfer's affair, except you live aboard a 12-metre yacht instead of in a tent, and your speedboat transport to Frigates Passage is provided. The price is the same as the camping package: F$312 for surfers, F$335 for windsurfers. Provisions can be made for extending your stay on the island or the boat.

Finally, there is also an eight-day yacht charter Frigates Passage 'Surfari' which includes all meals and transport to the best surf spots in the area. The cost is F$631 for surfers, F$680 for windsurfers. Contact Rosie Tours in Nadi (☎ 722 755), or write to them at PO Box 9268, Nadi Airport for a brochure.

NAVUA DELTA

The delta is a rich agricultural region 163 km from Nadi Airport, with fields of corn, grazing cattle, and the wooden shacks typical of farming residences. From 1906 to 1922 the area was the site of a sugar mill and the land you see was mostly planted with cane. However, cane farming was stopped when it was discovered that the sugar content was much higher in sunnier areas, and that this was seldom a sunny place. Dairy farming and rice growing have since taken the place of sugar in the Navua region. Inland along the river are spectacular gorges shrouded in mist, and serrated mountains that rise like spires. If you have your own wheels, take a few moments to explore Navua town, it's well worth the effort.

Places to Stay

Dreampoint Lodge (☎ 304 834), on Naqara Island near Navua, is a two-sq km island owned by the Morrells – a family of French and Fijian extraction. The island is studded with coconut trees and has a small beach. Swimming, fishing and snorkelling are good and it is popular with expats from the embassies (which is a very good sign because they always know the best bargains). There are two rooms with two beds at F$12 per person, and a seven-bunk dorm with beds for F$10. To get there call Rose or Bui and they can arrange a boat from Suva for about F$20, or co-ordinate your travel via bus and boat to the island. Because it's popular, the best policy is to call and reserve a space.

Hotel Heartbreak (☎ 460 310) in Navua has four spartan rooms that are reasonably clean, and shared bathrooms. Part of the 'hotel' includes a public bar which is characteristically rowdy and loud. I don't recommend you go out of your way to stay here but it's acceptable if circumstance demands it. Prices are F$19.80/27.50 for a single/double room.

BEQA

Ten km south of Navua Delta is the island of Beqa, best known as the home of Fiji's firewalkers. It is a compact island, seven km in both directions, and is visible for quite a distance along the coastal drive. There are eight villages, but only those from Rukua, on the west coast, are custodians of secrets connected with the firewalking ceremony. Thanks to their unusual skills, Beqans are gainfully employed (at least on a part-time basis) throughout the resort industry as firewalkers. Boats leave regularly from Navua Wharf for Beqa, but with the exception of Marlin Bay Resort, completed in 1992, there are no facilities for visitors. Beqa is approximately a 20-minute boat ride from Viti Levu.

The only show in town, *Marlin Bay Resort* (☎ 304 042; 800 542-FIJI in the USA), caters especially to divers. Owned and operated by Americans Dorothy and George Taylor, the resort has 12 well-appointed bures set near a beach. The centre of the complex is a large bure which houses the kitchen, restaurant, office and lounge area. The food is reportedly good and plentiful.

The diving is equally bountiful off Beqa. Other activities include village visits, hikes to several waterfalls, and kayaking. Four dive boats are available for guests; a two-tank dive is US$65. Doubles cost US$227 including all meals. Transport from nearby Pacific Harbour is US$22 return. For more information write to PO Box 1147, Gresham, OR 97030.

ORCHID ISLAND

Visitors who arrive in Suva with little time on their hands and want to take an excursion may be faced with the choice of visiting Pacific Harbour or Orchid Island. Both are worth seeing, and although both are 'cultural' in nature, they have different slants. Orchid Island, 10 km from Suva, is small in scale compared to Pacific Harbour and is the closer of the two attractions.

It is an island in the sense that it is built in the midst of a mangrove swamp, prone to flooding during calamitous weather. Operated by the very personable Fiji-born Keith Watkins, Orchid Island is basically a museum/zoo with introductory exhibits on Fijian history, culture, flora and fauna. In addition to the museum-like exhibits, there is a replica of an old Fijian village that includes a *bure kalou* (ancient temple) and a chief's house. Local villagers dressed in traditional garb demonstrate handicrafts such as masi-making, pottery and basket-weaving.

Orchid Island is the closest thing Fiji has to a zoo: besides being home to turtles, mongooses, parrots and other birds, it is the only place where you can see the crested iguana, which was discovered as recently as the early 1980s. You can also learn about Fiji's agriculture, geology and natural resources (such as timber). Naturally, there is a handicrafts shop.

Besides the natural sciences, Orchid Island focuses on the heritage of Fiji's ancient religion and its supernatural manifestations. Orchid Island has a kind of 'Ripley's Believe It or Not' element that may be intriguing for some and entertaining for others. Watkins claims that the Fijian temple on Orchid Island, the first to be constructed since the pre-European contact days, has been resettled by the local *vu* or ancestral spirits. It is his contention that sceptics will have difficulty taking a decent photo of the old temple without mysterious fogging of the film or some other strange occurrence. His proof is the countless times this has occurred in the past. He also has photos that have captured on film the essence of these spirits.

In a nutshell, Orchid Island is an intimate, family-run sideshow that is fun and genuinely attempts to educate the visitor about Fiji. It is open six days a week and costs F$9.90 for adults, and is free for children under 15. The island tour (☎ 361 128) begins at 10.30 am and lasts about three hours.

Getting There & Away
You can drive to Orchid Island in 15 minutes from Suva or take a local bus for about 50 cents from the bus station near the municipal market.

Kings Rd (Lautoka to Suva)

The Kings Rd, the route along the northerly coast of Viti Levu, is less often seen by visitors primarily because the road is poorer, the area is less developed for tourism, and the distance to Suva is longer. However, the scenery is beautiful, and there are attractions, so the more adventurous visitor may want to rent a car and drive it. The two main settlements along the way, Ba and Tavua, are primarily agricultural communities but do have small hotels.

There are a few things to know about the road whether you decide to drive yourself or take a bus or hired taxi. The first is that it is much more hazardous than the southern route. The section of Queens Rd from Nadi to Lautoka and the section of Kings Rd from Nausori to Suva are the busiest in the country. These two stretches are paved and well monitored by police, but the accident toll along these roads is staggering, so extra caution is needed.

LOLOLO PINE FOREST
Pronounced Lo-lolo, this picnic area is nestled in a pine forest north of Lautoka on the edge of a large creek. With plenty of picnic tables, it is a good place to get above the heat of the coast in summer time.

From there you could also visit a forest **fire watch station** which offers an incredible view of the north-west side of Viti Levu and the Yasawa Islands off the coast. The trip is worthwhile only on a clear day because the road is very rough and not recommended for small cars or vehicles loaded down with passengers or luggage. To get to there, go past the picnic area to an intersection at the centre of the station. Take a left turn and follow the road to the top of the mountain; the fire tower will be on the left.

Getting There & Away
To get to the Lololo Pine Forest, take the Lololo bus from Lautoka bus station. They run several times a day, but make sure you check the time for the last returning bus, and then get to the stop a few minutes early.

If you're travelling by car or motorcycle head east on Kings Rd about 10 km from Lautoka, and look for the sign on the left side of the road pointing to the right-hand turn-off. Follow the road until you come to the large timber yard at Drasa. Just past the yard the road forks. Bear left down a steep hill and follow the road until you reach the edge of the pine forest. You'll see the picnic area on the right. The distance from the main road to the pine station is about eight km.

BA
Ba is a classic, Indian sugar town 62 km from Nadi Airport that most tourists drive through. While the town's economy has always revolved around sugar, in recent years several small manufacturing firms have started up here. Despite Ba being off the usual tourist track, even here you will find persistent sword sellers, so be warned. A walk through the main shopping area

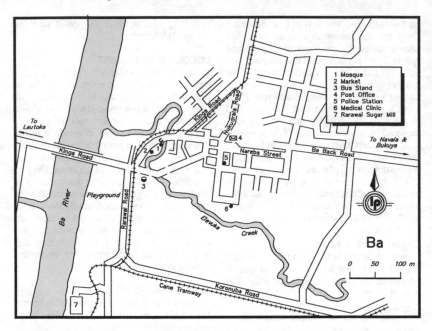

Ba

shows you what a 'blue collar' community this is. The Rarawai Sugar Mill is on the edge of Ba. The most noticeable landmark in town is the large **mosque** near the Ba River in the centre of town.

Places to Stay & Eat

The only place to stay in Ba – indeed one of the few hotels on this side of the island – is the *Ba Hotel* (☎ 674 000). It is a simple 13-room affair with a restaurant and bar. The price for a single/double is F$33/41.80. It's decent, clean and the food is average.

Eateries include an inexpensive Chinese and Indian restaurant on the main street.

TAVUA

This is a relaxed market town 91 km from Nadi Airport where you can catch buses for Vatukoula and Nadarivatu. The Tavua town market is a good place to stock up on fresh fruit. If you plan to spend time in Nadarivatu, this is the last chance to buy supplies.

The *Tavua Hotel* (☎ 680 522) has a classic South Seas hotel feel about it and is far from the beaten tourist track. Recently remodelled, it is one of the best hotels along the Kings Rd in which to stay overnight. It is now a clean, modern 13-room hotel in a colonial shell. It has two tiled pools (one is a shallow children's pool) with an attractive terrace and bar, and a large portico where an elegant breakfast may be had while looking at the hills and distant sea. Tariffs are F$45/50 for a single/double, and dinners in the fully licensed dining room range from F$10.50 to F$15.50 (Indian, Fijian and European cuisines).

Just a two-minute walk from town, there is a public bar, where locals congregated in the hotel's prior incarnations (at this writing, it's too soon to know whether that will continue). Mr M Sharma is the new manager, and brings experience from Nadi's tourist town.

Activities on offer include picnic trips to

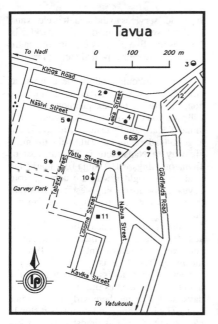

1   Temple
2   Farmer's Club
3   Bus Stand
4   Theatre
5   Tavua Club
6   Courthouse & Post Office
7   Police Station
8   Medical Clinic
9   School
10 Church
11 Hotel

a nearby sandy beach, and to the **Vatukoula gold mines** area, as well as barbecues and lovo with entertainment on the terrace. In nearby Vatukoula, one can play tennis, golf and bowls.

INLAND FROM BA & TAVUA
Navala

The picturesque village of Navala, one of the last in Viti Levu with thatched roofs, is a two-hour, 26-km drive on rough road into the mountains above Ba. Your best bets for transport are a 4WD or a trail bike. The road is passable by ordinary car but the going can be brutal.

From Navala it is possible to continue on to **Bukuya**, where the road forks either to the Sigatoka Valley (it's about 66 km to Sigatoka at this point) or the Nausori Highlands and continues on to Nadi. These are all-day drives, so pack food and be sure to have a full tank of fuel. For motorcyclists it is possible to purchase 'white benzene' from some

of the village shops if needed. Like most villages, it's not a good idea to visit Navala on Sunday. The villagers in this neck of the woods are very religious and most people are in church or in repose most of the day. Even if it's not Sunday, don't simply stroll into a village and begin taking photos. The local chief will not be charmed. Your best bet is to stop short (on the Ba side of the road) and shoot from across the river – which gives you a great perspective.

To get to Navala, from the Ba side of the bridge make a right turn on Rarawai Rd. Turn left at the next junction, just outside the sugar mill. Follow the road about two km where it forks and take the right fork.

An interesting alternative to the Kings Rd to Tavua and Vatukoula is the **Ba Back Rd**. Along this road are sugar cane farms, rural Indian settlements and schools. To find this road, follow the directions to Navala, as far as the fork in the road, and take the left fork.

Vatukoula

Nine km inland from Tavua is Vatukoula, a gold-mining settlement established in 1934 and one of the last bastions of colonialism in Fiji. Here the expatriate still rules the private clubs, bowling greens and golf course. While the colour bar has faded since independence, and even more so since the Emperor Mining Company sold out to Western Mining of Australia, a drive through town quickly reveals the difference between the miners and the bosses.

Gold is mined here both open-cut style

and underground, with one tunnel allegedly extending way out under Tavua Bay. There are excursions to Vatukoula with Rosie Tours, but it is not possible to visit the actual mine. Gold is the country's third-largest source of hard currency, behind tourism and sugar cane.

Nadarivatu

Approximately 30 km from Tavua is Nadarivatu, one of the nicest mountain getaways in Viti Levu. High in the mountains above the heat and surrounded by pine forests, the highlands of Nadarivatu are a far cry from the stereotypical South Seas featured in most brochures. Unfortunately, the pine forest is a commercial concern, and it was clear-felled early in 1992, leaving a shockingly bald landscape in many areas which were formerly luxuriant. The area will be replanted, and in a few years will look like a forest again. But aside from this ugly reminder of economic realities, Nadarivatu is a beautiful and refreshing area.

As the road winds up the escarpment, the views become more and more stunning, until at the top you can see across patchwork hills, beyond Vatukoula and Tavua on the coastal plain to the Yasawa Islands, Ovalau, and on the clearest days even to Vanua Levu. Regardless of how stifling the weather is on the coast, bring a sweater or jacket if you plan to visit Nadarivatu during early morning, late afternoon or evening; it gets very cold, even during summer.

Nadarivatu translates as 'stone bowl'. According to Fiji resident, Peter Taylor, the most convincing explanation of 'the stone bowl' is a rock with a bowl-shaped depression near the forestry station on the road to Navai. It is said that until relatively recent times, a spring issued from that 'bowl' and eventually became the mighty Sigatoka River. Now, however, only a fragment remains. There is an excellent description of the rock and legend associated with it in the *Hill Tribes of Fiji*, Brewster's classic account of life in this area.

Nadarivatu 'village' is actually a government station, and all of its residents are there to provide services to the area. It is clean and neat and well maintained, and it sparkles in the sunshine like the very essence of health. However, a doctor is posted there, in case of need.

From Vatukoula, follow the main road through the town, turn left at the 'T' intersection, then right at the next junction. This road will take you on a dramatic 366-metre climb to the Nadarivatu Plateau. If you decide not to go to Nadarivatu via Vatukoula, the main highway to Nadarivatu is 2½ km east of Tavua on Kings Rd. A large sign marks the road on the right if you are coming from Tavua. If you are coming west from Rakiraki the sign is not so apparent, so keep an eye out.

There is also a Sunbeam bus from Tavua at 2.30 pm. It is the only bus up the mountain and does not return until the following morning. The fare is about F$2 at the Sunbeam office across the street from the market. (Note: the bus fills up quickly some days, so try to get there early for a choice seat.) The bus chugs and grinds as it slowly climbs, but fear not, it almost always makes it. Just enjoy the scenery from the open-air 'windows'. Keep your sweater handy for the often-chilly end of the ride.

On the way to Nadarivatu there is a pleasant **waterfall** worth seeing; look for a culvert crossing a deep boulder-choked gorge about a km before the village of Waikubukubu. The waterfall is about 20 metres above the crossing. In the wet season you can't miss it, as the stream rushes a few cm deep across the roadway.

Hike to Fire Watch One of the nicest short hikes you can take in Nadarivatu is a three-km trek to the fire-watch post on the mountaintop behind the forestry station. The post is easily seen at the sharp corner just after you crest the escarpment. Follow the trail past the training centre to the governor general's swimming hole. From there the trail winds through dense vegetation to the peak. The view from the top is fantastic, but try to make it in the morning before the clouds move in. Don't be tempted to stop at the swimming hole, as it has not been maintained and is no longer usable (anyway, the water used to be unbearably cold). Allow 2½ hours for the climb there and back.

Hike to Tomanivi About 10 km beyond the Forestry Rest House is Tomanivi (Mt Victoria), Fiji's highest peak at 1323 metres. Three large rivers originate in the shadow of this mountain: the Sigatoka, and the Wainimala and Wainibuka, which eventually join to form the Rewa River. The bridge in Navai village (about 10 km past Nadarivatu) is where the trail begins. Do not confuse the bridge in the village with the large bridge about a km before the village proper. (There is now an official marked trailhead about 200 metres before the village so as to avoid confusion.) Follow a wide track about 100 metres and take the trail on the right to the top. Stay on the main trail – markers pointing elsewhere may be misleading. The top is almost continuously cloud-covered, so don't expect a great view. However, you will be able to tell your friends that you hiked to the summit of the highest mountain in Fiji. For the botanically minded, the various layers of vegetation types are fascinating (especially the cloud forest layer). Allow five to six hours for the climb. Guides are available at the village.

Places to Stay & Eat
The nicest place to stay is the *Forestry Rest House* (☎ 661 085, 301 661), which was originally built for expat bosses at the gold mine (so their families could escape the summer heat). This large, rambling structure is now run by the Forestry Department and costs F$5 per person per night. Make sure you book in advance, though if you're told it's fully booked, ask if you can share a room until a vacant one is available. The house comfortably sleeps seven people, cooking utensils are supplied, and there is a small shop nearby for basics. The best idea is to stock up on provisions in Tavua or Ba before you get there. Be prepared to cook on a wood-burning stove (which simultaneously heats your bath water) or a benzene primus.

Nadarivatu is one of the few areas in Fiji where camping is permitted and the pine forest makes quite a nice setting. Make absolutely sure you have a permit from the Forestry Department first, as the district officer ('DO') has been known to be very tough on squatters.

Navai
Currently, Navai is a major agricultural area, producing lettuce, cauliflower, cabbage and carrots which thrive here because of the cool climate. Most are sent to the various town markets, but there is one roadside stand with beautiful fresh vegetables most days. (If there are no vegetables on the stand, ask at the house behind it – maybe they'll pick some fresh from the garden for you.) In 1938, during the colonial era, a potato-growing scheme was established in the Navai area, but the programme failed due to plant disease. New varieties of potatoes have been introduced, and some farmers are successfully growing them again.

Koro-ni-O
Another 25 km down the road from Navai is Koro-ni-O or 'village of clouds', an apt name. Today this area is headquarters for the F$234-million Monasavu hydroelectric scheme, the largest development project ever undertaken by the Fijian government.

Designed to reduce the country's dependency on imported fuels, the project was begun in 1978 and completed in 1983. The most visible part of the scheme is the 82-metre-high earth-filled dam built on the Nanuka River, and its accompanying 17-km-long lake, cradled in the **Nadrau Plateau**, about 1000 metres above sea level in the mountains of central Viti Levu. This lake is the larger of Fiji's two lakes (the other is on Taveuni). Fishing is possible in this lake if Malayan carp *(tilapia)* is to your liking.

About 625 metres below the level of the dam is the Wailoa River power station – connected to the dam via a 5.4-km tunnel which forces water through a series of four 20-megawatt turbines. Overhead transmission lines then carry the relatively cheap electricity to Suva and to Lautoka in the west.

Getting There & Away There are no longer buses from Koro-ni-O to Suva across the interior of the island. If you're thinking of driving this stretch with an ordinary car this is one of the worst roads on the island and the rental agency will not let you near their cars if they catch wind of your plans. Though rough, it is an interesting ride and if you really want to do it, negotiate with a carrier.

YAQARA

Halfway between Tavua and Rakiraki, and 107 km from Nadi Airport is Yaqara, Fiji's biggest cattle ranch – a 7000-hectare estate with 7000 head of cattle. Visitors should not be surprised to see Fijian cowhands in Western hats rounding up cattle.

RAKIRAKI

The road from Tavua to Rakiraki and beyond is now sealed. About 10 km before Rakiraki, watch for **Navatu Rock**. It is a large precipice near the road, at Vitawa village. There is only one access route to the top, making this a very defensible site for a village in hostile olden days. And there is evidence that it was one of the original sites of Fijian habitation. Pottery excavated at the base of the rock dates back about 3000 years. Predictably, there are many legends associated with this rock and with this area.

Also note the small island about 1½ km

from the coast, jutting about 180 metres from sea level. Fijian legend holds that this is the departure point for disembodied spirits journeying into the afterlife. In ancient times there was a village at the top of this peak.

Rakiraki is at a point roughly halfway (about 120 km) along Kings Rd from Nadi, and is a good overnighting spot for those touring the northern coast.

If locals tell you Rakiraki is where you can refuel, get a tyre repaired or buy supplies for your stay at Nananu-i-Ra Island, they are really referring to the town of **Vaileka**, which is a km off Kings Rd. There is a well-marked triangle with a sign pointing toward Suva, and another to Vaileka.

Just prior to the triangle, on the south side of the road, is **Ratu Udre Udre's tomb**. Ratu Udre Udre was a chief famous for his appetite for human flesh, and is said to have consumed over 800 human beings before his death in the mid-19th century. The stones surrounding the base of his tomb are how he kept tally of his grisly meals.

Places to Stay & Eat

The *Rakiraki Hotel* (☎ 694 101) bills itself as the northernmost hotel on Viti Levu basking in the driest and 'deliciously hottest' climate on the island. The 46-room hotel is nothing fancy but is well run and quite comfortable. Amenities include a pool, nine-hole golf course (nearby), local entertainment, tennis court, lawn bowling, bar and restaurant. Prices are F$60/70 for singles/doubles;

all rooms have fridges, and rooms without air-con are cheaper. The large lunches and dinners are well worth the moderate cost of F$5 to F$9.

For eating on the cheap there are also a few curry houses in Vaileka. Meals cost between F$2 and F$4 and are similar in quality.

ELLINGTON WHARF TURN-OFF

This junction is about five km past the Rakiraki Hotel. From the wharf you can catch the boat to Nananu-i-Ra and ferries to the outer islands. See the Getting Around chapter for more information.

NANANU-I-RA

This island has become very popular with visitors who wish to visit a more natural setting and get away from the commercialism of the Nadi area without travelling too far. The island is pretty and has beaches, snorkelling and good shelling. It's five km off the Rakiraki coast, 150 km from the airport along Kings Rd. Three of the places to stay are relatively close to each other, the fourth (Kon Tiki) is on the other side of the island. You need to bring groceries to all of the island's accommodation, except for up-market Mokusiga's, as there is no food available. (Vaileka has a market and several shops which sell groceries, but you'll find a better selection elsewhere, like Tavua or one of the cities.) Linen, a refrigerator and cooking implements are provided at the resorts.

When the first edition of this book appeared I highly recommended the resorts on the island. But now, many readers' letters later, I must slightly temper my enthusiasm. The island is still beautiful and not commercialised in a crass sense, but an awful lot of people come through and sometimes the owners become a little jaded when dealing with travellers. None of the complaints was based on problems with unclean or sanitary conditions. On the contrary, the biggest difficulty seemed to be personality clashes with some of the managers. To be specific, some of my readers and those interviewed felt that at times managers at several of the places to stay were 'controlling' or 'bossy'. In short it was unpleasant enough for them to want to leave.

Another problem was transport to the island. On many occasions the transport companies were 'dumping' travellers on the island without regard for the space available at the accommodation sites. This at times led to overcrowding and less than pleasant circumstances. However, now that all of the resorts have phones, this should not be an issue. If you are in doubt about finding a place to stay, the best thing to do is call and determine if there is room. It is also a good idea to inform the hotelier how many days you plan to stay. Some readers have complained that Bethams, upon learning that visitors only wished to stay one night, wanted nothing to do with them.

Predicament number three was the lack of water on the island. This is just a fact of life. There is only so much water to go around and it is shut off at certain hours of the day, whether you want to bathe or not. Most people can adjust, but if this is too much of an inconvenience, think twice about coming here.

Places to Stay

Bethams Beach Cottages (☎ 694 132) consists of four self-contained bungalows on Nananu-i-Ra. The rooms have anywhere from two to six beds, as well as dorm-style accommodation. The price is F$40 for a double. Bring the supplies you need from Rakiraki and catch the launch (F$20) from Ellington Wharf, 11 km west of Rakiraki, if you are travelling on public transport. For information and reservations write to PO Box 5, Rakiraki.

MacDonald Beach Cottages (☎ 694 633) has the same set-up as Bethams and is under new management. There are two houses with room for five in each, a third house with three beds, and a dorm which sleeps seven people. Prices begin at F$40 for a single or double in a beach-front cottage, and F$45 for a deluxe cottage. Add F$25 a double for return transfer, F$12 each for more than four persons.

Island Divers, run by Ken MacDonald, is a new dive operation based at MacDonald Beach Cottages. Prices are F$40 for a single dive, F$70 for two dives and F$300 for a six-dive package, including all equipment. PADI open-water certificate courses are also available. For more information write to PO Box 140, Rakiraki.

Charlie's Place (☎ 694 676) is a traditional favourite of travellers. Those that stayed here felt comfortable and their needs were taken care of. The manager who runs this must be some kind of saint. This is also the only accommodation on a hill and has a commanding view. To stay in the dorm costs

F$13 per night and there is a deluxe bure for F$50. As usual, bring your own food.

Kon Tiki Island Lodge (☎ 694 290) is a 1½-hour walk from the other budget operations on the island and has perhaps the best beach and the best snorkelling. The wharf, which is used in transporting visitors here is different from the one used by the other island places. It has three self-contained bures that sleep up to six people. Accommodation includes bath and kitchen. The dorms are F$10 per person; a double or twin bed is F$24 per bure. For transfer from the mainland (F$12 return) contact any of the local taxis in Rakiraki. Frankly, in the past I've had mixed reviews about Kon Tiki, but of late, most reports have been very good. The resort will also sell essential food items at a reasonable price.

Mokusiga's (☎ 694 444/9; fax 694 404) is the newest, swankest resort on Nananu-i-Ra. Translated from the Fijian it means 'killing time' – something you're apt to do a lot of in this country. The property has 20 suites, each of which can accommodate up to three people. All have queen-sized beds, large single beds, private balconies, fridges, ceiling fans and terrific vistas. Though small in scale, the resort is well built. Activities include diving, snorkelling, windsurfing, canoeing, fishing and tennis. There's also live entertainment and a gymnasium. Rooms cost F$145 for a single, double or triple. Reports are that Mokusiga's management is not liberal about allowing low-budget accommodation patrons to use the bar, dining room, diving operation or volleyball facilities if the resort is full.

Getting There & Away
Taxi & Bus At the bus station in Rakiraki local taxis will be on the lookout for Nananu-i-Ra-bound passengers. For around F$2 per person the taxi will shuttle you to a grocery store or two to pick up provisions for the island and then directly to a boat (perhaps operated by the taxi driver's cousin) who will take you across for around F$6. The bus fare from Lautoka to Rakiraki is F$2.

Minibus Private transport companies (such as PVV Tours) also run minibuses out to Rakiraki, and will pick you up at any hotel. PVV Tours (☎ 700 600) has the Nadi Town Motel as its booking agent. The one-way fare from Nadi on the minibuses is around F$21 which includes a shuttle boat from the wharf. The trip back to Nadi is F$15. The minibuses leave every morning and stop in Rakiraki so travellers can take care of banking, shopping etc before going to the island.

The problem with PVV and the other transport companies is that they are expensive compared with what you pay for the shared taxi or a bus. Don't let these companies pressure you into going with them if you feel you'd rather take alternative transport. As a matter of fact, many readers say it's preferable to take a taxi or bus, get your provisions in Rakiraki and then call your resort to pick you up by dingy from the appropriate wharf.

NAISERELAGI &
BLACK CHRIST MURAL
Naiserelagi, about 45 km east of Rakiraki, is the home of the church with a mural of the *Black Christ* by French artist Jean Charlot. This is an exquisite work, blending Fijian motifs with the teachings of Christ. Charlot painted the mural in 1962 at the invitation of Monsignor Franz Wasner, the then-caretaker of the mission. (Prior to coming to Fiji Monsignor Wasner was at one time the singing teacher of the Von Trapp family of *Sound of Music* fame.) The mural was painstakingly completed by the dim lamplight of the church – apparently Charlot had a great deal of trouble applying the fresh mortar to the wall.

The central image of the mural is the figure of a black Christ on the cross wearing masi (tapa) cloth around his waist. He is being paid homage to by a number of Fijian figures. In the immediate background are breadfruit leaves and fruit which express his close relationship with nature and, according to Charlot's wife, are a vital symbol in the fresco. The Fijian word for breadfruit, *uto*, is also used for 'heart'. At Christ's feet is a tanoa (yaqona bowl), symbolising the Eucharist. To his right are a child in a mission school uniform, St Peter Chanel (a martyred Saint in the Pacific), Father Mataca (the first Fijian Catholic priest), a Fijian woman bringing Christ an offering of woven mats, and a Fijian man offering Christ a tabua (whale's tooth) – the highest form of respect a Fijian can confer. To Christ's left an Indian woman is portrayed offering a garland of flowers and an Indian farmer is pictured with a pair of oxen. Also shown are St Francis Xavier (whom the church is named after) and an acolyte.

According to accounts, when the mural was complete the entire parish of Naiserelagi held a feast in Charlot's honour. Cows were slaughtered and the traditional yaqona ceremony was observed. As in the mural, women presented the artist with mats.

After visiting what has to be the finest non-Fijian work of art in Fiji, you should not forget to drop some money into the donation box at the door. Proceeds are used to maintain the church.

Getting There & Away

There is no express bus to Naiserelagi, but a local bus will let you off near the church if you ask the driver. Visit in the early part of the day because buses are less frequent in the afternoon. Those driving may find the church easy to miss. Watch for Nanukuloa village; Naiserelagi is the next village to the south. Once there, keep an eye out for the Ra Maternity Clinic. Take an uphill right towards the Navunibitu Catholic Mission School.

SNAKE GOD CAVE

Snakes are rife in Fijian legend. About 23 km west of Korovou (216 km from the airport) is a cave (formerly a meeting place for chiefs) known as the Home of the Snake God. As you approach Korovou from the west, watch for Wailotua village (the first of two villages with the same name) on the left-hand side of the road. Enquire about the cave and someone will show you around, admission is F$2. Ask to be shown a stalactite known as the six-headed snake.

Nine km past the cave, a small bridge crosses a large stream. Keep your eyes open and you'll see a wonderful waterfall here.

KOROVOU

For most of the way between Naiserelagi and Korovou, Kings Rd follows first the Wainibuka River and then the smaller Waimaro River.

There are nine villages named Korovou (including one previously mentioned on Queens Rd) on Viti Levu alone, but for our purposes, Korovou (which translates as 'new village') is in the Tailevu Province, 239 km from Nadi Airport.

Korovou is the centre of Fiji's dairy industry, which was established by several English veterans at the end of WW I. In a magnanimous gesture, the local Fijian chiefs gave the 'European' farmers 4000 hectares of the finest land in the province to 'keep forever'. Some of the descendants of those veterans still run a few of the dairy farms around Korovou. During the period immediately prior to independence many of the farmers began selling their land to the highest bidders, in most cases Indians. This incensed the Fijian chiefs, who said that if the Europeans did not want the land anymore, it should be given back to the villages. The government has since worked out a system whereby, as the original farms come up for sale, the former local landowners have the first chance at purchasing them.

At last report, the only accommodation in town, the *Tailevu Hotel* was closed.

Near Korovou is **Natovi Landing**, a terminus for ferries to Ovalau and Vanua Levu. (There is also a terminus at Ellington Wharf for ferries to Vanua Levu.) From Korovou it's 31 km to Nausori on a recently constructed, sealed road.

NAUSORI

Only 19 km from Suva and 270 km from Nadi Airport, Nausori grew as a city around Fiji's second sugar mill (1881-1959), now the site of the Rewa Rice Mill. The golf course and some of the old colonial homes constructed for expatriates are about all that remain of Nausori's days as a sugar-mill town. The end of the sugar mill marked the final attempt at growing sugar on the eastern side of Viti Levu. Today Nausori is much like

Ba, a working-class town and agricultural centre. The airport which serves Suva is in Nausori, a 20-minute drive from the capital.

Near Nausori are three landings from which you can hire punts or 'water taxis' to explore the Rewa Delta, visit snorkelling areas or visit Toberua Resort. The landings are Nakelo, Wainibokasi and Bau. Buses leave frequently for these points from the bus station in Nausori.

TOBERUA ISLAND RESORT

Toberua Island Resort (☎ 302 356) is actually off the coast, near Suva. Hoteliers consider it the finest island resort in Fiji, and Harper's Hideaway Report rates it as one of the top 12 small island resorts in the world. Host Michael Dennis oversees every aspect of his tiny paradise and there is plenty of snorkelling and day trips to uninhabited islands. The cuisine is fine and there are 14 bures. Singles/doubles are F$229/252. A downside to consider is that the weather at Toberua matches that of Suva – rainy and humid.

Buses leave frequently from the bus station in Nausori for Nakelo Landing, where boats depart for Toberua Island.

BAU ISLAND

Bau Landing is a few metres from tiny Bau Island, to this day the seat of traditional power among Fijians (see the History section in the Facts about the Country chapter). The island is not a place where visitors may casually drop in – it is in fact against the law to visit Bau without permission from someone who lives on the island or from the Ministry of Fijian Affairs. This applies to locals and visitors alike.

Bau has the oldest church in the country, a fascinating cemetery for chiefly families, and an impressive stone nearby that was once used to crush skulls in the days of cannibalism.

If you really want to visit the island, the best way to go about this is to try and befriend someone on the bus ride to Bau Landing in hopes that the person may offer to show you around. Make sure you take a

large bundle of kava root *(waka)* with you and dress conservatively (this applies especially to women). At certain times all non-Bauans are forbidden on the island, so don't attempt to reach it without permission; and if by luck you get there, never walk around unescorted. Some tourists reportedly have tried this but it is a grave insult. Getting on the wrong side of a high Fijian chief is akin to getting on the wrong side of the law. In many remote parts of Fiji the chief is still the one who lays down the law. Even the courts have ruled that a chief's word can in some cases take precedence over the law books.

NAILILILI MISSION

Naililili, 272 km from Nadi Airport, is the largest church in Fiji. It was built at the turn of the century by Father Rougier, who later left the priesthood to become a well-known trader in Tahiti. Apparently Father Rougier accidentally inherited a tidy sum from a down-and-out convict from New Caledonia who was in reality heir to a fortune. At that point he left organised religion to seek a more worldly life. To get to his church take the first left at the junction past the Nausori Bridge. Water taxis cost F$2 to cross the river to Naililili.

Suva

Suva can lay certain claim to being the largest and perhaps the most liveable city in the South Pacific outside New Zealand or Australia. The capital of Fiji since 1883, it is set on 15 sq km of peninsula adjacent to one of the finest naturally protected harbours in the South Seas. It is home for about 80,000 people, with another 30,000 living in the fast-developing corridor along the 25-km stretch from the city limits to the airport at Nausori.

Perhaps the biggest drawback to the town is its weather, which is wet and often muggy. The nicest way to describe Suva is as a changeable town that gleams in the sunlight

Top: Fijian meke night, Matagi Island (TDC)
Left: Clapping in time to the music at a meke (RK)
Right: Fijian warriors (FVB)

Top Left: Swimming at the beach (RK)
Top Right: Idyllic Fijian setting (RK)
Bottom Left: Tom's Campground, Taveuni (RK)
Bottom Right: Savusavu Holiday House, Vanua Levu (RK)

Top: Navala village, Nausori Highlands, Viti Levu (RK)
Bottom: Levuka, the old capital of Fiji, Ovalau (RK)

Top: The cruise ship *Tui Tai*, off Vatulele Island (RK)
Bottom: Village scene in Tailevu, Viti Levu (RK)

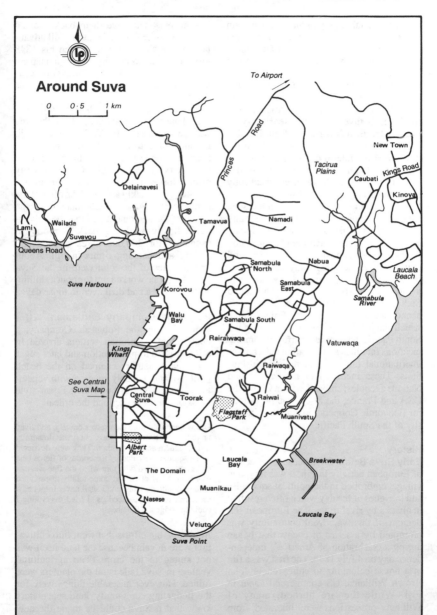

Around Suva

and turns metallic grey in the rain. And rain is not an uncommon occurrence in the capital of Fiji. An average of 3000 mm of precipitation falls annually, and up to 347 mm can shower down in a single day. Historians still ponder the minor miracle of the fair weather one day in 1861 when Colonel W T Smythe, instructed by the Duke of Newcastle, came to Suva to investigate the feasibility of moving the British consulate from Levuka. Had he come during in the midst of the usual downpour, the fateful decision to move the capital to Suva may never have been made.

As Fiji journalist Robert Keith-Reid aptly said, 'Suva isn't a jewel. But on the other hand, what other South Seas town has such a polyglot population?' Suva is a steamy cauldron of Fijians, Indians, Chinese, Tongans, Samoans, Rotumans, Solomon Islanders, Micronesians, Europeans and 'fruit salad' as they are locally called – those of mixed race. In and around Suva there are a variety of Christian churches, Hindu and Sikh temples, Muslim mosques and even an abandoned Jewish cemetery. Fiji's capital, which can justifiably be called the hub of the South Pacific, has a modern array of communications facilities and has attracted a host of international bureaus and regional institutions. These include half a dozen United Nations agencies; embassies from China, the USA and France; the South Pacific Bureau for Economic Cooperation; and the University of the South Pacific.

History
Early Suva Before Suva became the centre of European activity in Fiji, it was a typical village, embroiled in the political squabbles and intrigues of the day which often resulted in attacks by rival tribes. The European settlement of this waterfront community was prompted by a series of events that began during a celebration of America's independence day on 4 July 1848. The first was a fire in a house belonging to entrepreneur John Brown Williams, US commercial agent in Fiji. While the fire burned, many of Williams' possessions were 'liberated' from the burning structure by the villagers, who

saw no reason to give them back. Consul Williams, as he was called, took full advantage of the situation and inflated his 1848 loss of goods looted by the Fijians from approximately £200 (as some have estimated) to nearly £10,000 at the time of his death.

The responsibility for these actions was placed upon Chief Cakobau, who at the time was the self-styled 'Tui Viti' or King of Fiji. Having failed to eliminate the debt by an attempt to cede Fiji to Britain (which took some nerve because Chief Cakobau really didn't have dominion over the entire country), he quickly accepted the offer of the newly formed Polynesia Company to pay the amount. The agreement was that the Polynesia Company would pay back the money in exchange for 200,000 acres of land and trading and banking rights in Fiji. About 23,000 acres of the total were in the Suva area. The price worked out to about a shilling an acre – not a bad deal even in those days.

Polynesia Company Settlement After acquisition by the Polynesia Company, a boatload of Australian settlers arrived in Suva in 1870 to plant cotton and later sugar cane. Early settlers camped on the beach until the land, densely covered with vegetation, was cleared to build their Fijian-style huts. One settler described the ordeal:

Our women folk bore themselves bravely, and lived up to the traditions of our race, but it was dreadfully trying to them and the children. They were devoured by mosquitoes, terrified by the hordes of fierce land crabs and drenched with rain when the fine weather broke up. Most of us had come totally unequipped with mosquito curtains, and I shall never forget how those fell insects punished us...I tried everything I could to dodge the little beasts.

Ironically, the efforts that went into cultivation were in vain because the land itself was not suited to the crops. The agricultural venture in Suva failed and the planters were ruined. However miserable things were for the fledgeling community, land speculators knew that if Suva could be made the new capital, business could be coaxed there, real estate values would soar, and they would be rich. The old capital, Levuka, which had long been the metropolis of the Pacific, was a brawling, prosperous town, but its days as a capital were numbered. Although it was a garden spot, the old capital was hemmed in by 600-metre cliffs which left no room to expand. It became apparent that a new capital was needed.

In the meantime, land in Suva was purchased by two major parties who did their best to promote the area as an ideal spot for a new capital by giving the government ample real estate to build their offices. Thus, in spite of the wet climate, the local government had incentives to establish the new capital in Suva, and in 1882 they did just that.

The New Capital The plan of modern Suva is credited to Colonel F E Pratt of the Royal Engineers, appointed in 1875 as surveyor-general and director of works; and to his assistants W Stephens and Colonel R W Stewart. Despite well-intentioned plans for the capital, Suva's early days saw only gradual improvement – roads were poor, water supply was tenuous at best and not all construction adhered to the city plan. Gradually these deficiencies gave way as the town grew. A few years past the turn of the century Suva was actually a tourist attraction in its own right. The editor of *The Commercial Directory & Tourists' Guide to the South Pacific Islands* observed:

Why Fiji is visited by such a small number of tourists is a puzzle to the writer, for there is not a more interesting or enjoyable trip on the globe. The climate is particularly healthy, and the white settlers being mostly from Australia, vie with each other in extending hospitality to visitors, while the natives, particularly those who live away from the large centres of European population, always extend a cordial welcome to the *turanga papalangi* (white gentleman), or the *marama papalangi* (white lady). Suva is the capital of the colony, and situated on the shores of a fine reef-protected bay of the same name, whose opposite shore is backed by imposing looking ranges of verdure-clad mountains, rising peak after peak until an altitude of probably 1200 metres is attained – they look truly grand, particularly at sunset or during an approaching storm (a frequent occurrence), or

better still when the storm has passed and the white clouds cover their feet, and the picturesque-looking peaks...stand boldly out against the dark-blue horizon, 'tis really a sight to be remembered.

Some things never change.

Information

The Fiji Visitors' Bureau (FVB) (☎ 303 433) is on Thomson St. You can buy maps at the Lands & Survey department in the government buildings complex, at the government bookstore opposite the Fiji Visitors' Bureau, or at other bookstores.

Useful Organisations Some useful phone numbers are:

Colonial War Memorial (CWM) Hospital &
    ambulance (☎ 313 444)
Police (☎ 311 222)
Immigration office (☎ 312 622)
Fiji customs (☎ 302 322)
Early morning wake-up calls (☎ 010)
Directory enquiries (☎ 011)
Overseas calls (☎ 012)

Foreign Embassies Some of the diplomatic offices in Suva are:

Australia
    Embassy, 8th Floor, Dominion House (☎ 313
    844, 312 564)
Belgium
    3rd Floor, Pacific House (☎ 314 188)
China
    Queen Elizabeth Drive (☎ 304 564)
Denmark
    Mr A Dickson, 7th Floor, Air Pacific House
    (☎ 383 142)
Finland
    Mr Swain Christian, Shell Fiji Ltd,
    Prouds Building (☎ 313 933)
France
    1st Floor, Dominion House (☎ 312 925)
Federated States of Micronesia (FSM)
    37 Loftus St (☎ 314 788)
Israel
    5th Floor, ANZ Building (☎ 303 420)
Italy
    Mr R W Warner, Hunts Travel Service, 1st Floor,
    Dominion House (☎ 315 288)
Japan
    2nd Floor, Dominion House (☎ 304 633)

Korea
  8th Floor, Vanua House (☎ 300 977)
Marshall Islands
  8th Floor, Ratu Sukuna House (☎ 302 479)
Nauru
  7th Floor, Ratu Sukuna House (☎ 313 566)
Netherlands
  Dominion House (☎ 313 955)
New Zealand
  10th Floor, Reserve Bank Building (☎ 311 422)
Norway
  3rd Floor, Pacific House (☎ 314 188)
Papua New Guinea
  6th Floor, Ratu Sukuna House (☎ 304 244)
Taiwan
  6th Floor, Pacific House, Butt St; actually the Trade Mission and not a full consulate (☎ 315 922)
Tuvalu
  8 Mitchell St (☎ 301 355)
UK
  Victoria House, 47 Gladstone Rd (☎ 311 033)
USA
  31 Loftus St (☎ 314 466)

Medical Services Aside from the CWM Hospital, of which there has been a plethora of health-care horror stories, a popular clinic with the expat community is the Gordon St Medical Centre (on the corner of Gordon and Thurston Sts) run by Drs Robin & Rosemary Mitchell (☎ 313 555). The clinic is part of Private Hospitals Fiji Ltd, which also includes a paediatrician in Lami town, Dr Rita Vinton (☎ 362 591) who has been recommended by expat doctors at CWM. If in need of a recommendation, call your embassy or high commissioner's office.

Some of the pharmacies in Suva are:

A J Swann & Co – 6 Union Travel Plaza, Thomson St (☎ 302 743)
Central Pharmacy – 109 Cumming St (corner of Waimanu Rd) (☎ 301 877)
Gordon St Pharmacy – 96 Gordon St (☎ 313 355)
Madison Pharmacy – 83 Cumming St (☎ 313 370)
Mouats Pharmacy – Epworth House, corner of Nina and Stewart Sts (☎ 302 363)

Places of Worship Churches where English-language services are held include Wesley Methodist, on the corner of Gordon and Butt Sts; Holy Trinity Anglican Cathedral, McCarthury St; Sacred Heart Roman Catholic Cathedral, Pratt St; St Andrews Presbyterian Church, on the corner of Gordon and Goodenough Sts; and Grace Baptist Church, University of the South Pacific Recreation Centre. Other churches hold services in Fijian, Hindi, Rotuman and various Pacific languages.

Walking in Suva

Suva is a walker's town; most of it can be seen in one day if you have a sturdy pair of shoes and a healthy constitution. You need not be an Olympic athlete to take a walking tour, but the heat – especially for those not used to it – can make a stroll around Suva seem arduous. Visitors to Suva and to Fiji in general should realise that people move slowly for a good reason in this tropical clime – less energy is drained from the body, and it makes sense not to sweat more than is necessary. Aside from a good pair of shoes, an umbrella or at least a hat will shade you from the sun and the rain. If you need to take a breather from the heat keep in mind that all the downtown banks are air-conditioned.

Victoria Parade

Victoria Parade, extending roughly from the post office to Thurston Gardens, is the 'main drag' and the heart of Suva. On it or nearby are most of the finest shops, the airline ticket offices, banks, travel agencies, the best hotel in town (Travelodge), the library, town hall, telegraph office, two of the most popular nightclubs and the classic Grand Pacific Hotel which is undergoing extensive renovation and will be closed until 1994. In the old days, Victoria Parade was a muddy, one-sided street separated from the sea by a row of rain trees (or as they are sometimes called, 'weeping figs'). Some of the original rain trees are still there, although hurricanes have taken their toll.

Suva Municipal Market

Municipal markets similar in style to Suva's can be found in Papeete (Tahiti), Apia (Western Samoa), and all the larger communities in Fiji and the rest of the South Pacific. The Polynesian, Chinese, Indian and Fijian vendors hawk fish, meat, vegetables, fruit, coconut oil and nearly everything else that a Fijian household might need. Although some vendors are farmers who belong to a co-operative, most are intermediaries who receive produce from outlying villages and sell it for a profit to the townspeople.

The newly rebuilt and expanded market provides a colourful and fascinating array of culture. Some sections (upstairs) deal entirely with kava root (both whole and ground). Other merchants sell Indian spices exclusively, display freshly caught shellfish, sell tomatoes or offer bundles of dalo (taro root). A section of new kiosks toward the bus station is the place to try 'Indian sweets', many of which are not sweet at all, but rather are highly spiced and tasty snacks.

There is also a 'yaqona saloon' outdoors at the wharf end of the market dedicated solely to yaqona tipplers. As you walk by, someone may call over, urging you to have a bowl. Should you take them up on it, for a few cents buy a round for the house, which is the customary reciprocal thing to do.

You will no doubt see many strange or exotic fruits and vegetables and should not hesitate to ask what they are. Fijians always have time to talk to a visitor and appreciate the interest shown. Perhaps you might want to sample a passion fruit or purchase an avocado to eat later in your hotel; here is where to buy them. Naturally any fruit should be washed thoroughly. Midnight snackers will be pleased to know that the market is also one of the few places where you can buy takeaway food.

Handicraft Centre

Behind the post office, facing the sea on Stinson Parade, is the handicraft centre. Do not confuse this with the government crafts centre in Ratu Sukuna House on Carnarvon St. Unlike the municipal market which caters to locals, the handicraft market is almost exclusively for visitors. The upshot is that you will be touted continuously. The prices can be cheaper here than at the souvenir shops, but prepare to bargain hard. Items sold are the usual tourist fare: cannibal forks,

tanoa (yaqona bowls), carvings, masi cloth, *gatu* (Tongan-style bark cloth), seashells and necklaces. The market is particularly active on days when ships are in port.

Visitors strolling around the handicraft market area and Suva in general should beware of unusually friendly locals (usually carrying canvas bags) who offer 'swords' with your name carved on them. Sometimes the salesperson will ask your name and before you know it you are not-so-subtly being coerced into buying the custom-made 'artefact'. If you really want the souvenir, the going rate is around F$5 but these swords are by no means genuine Fijian woodcarvings. More accurately, they are someone's clever scam. You are *not* required to buy these swords with your name on them, unless you wish to do so, regardless of what the salesman may tell you. (See also the Things to Buy section in the Facts for the Visitor chapter.)

Cumming St

Cumming St is known for its fine restaurants and duty-free shops. It is crowded and narrow, reminiscent of a Paris or London backstreet. Reclaimed from a swamp, it was developed as a commercial area in the 1920s and was called 'All Nations St' – a place where curry houses, yaqona saloons and houses of ill repute flourished. It was also the original home of the municipal market. Perhaps being the Sodom and Gomorrah that it was, the area was consumed by fire in 1923 and many of the structures were destroyed. During WW II, the tailors, barbers and cafe owners who did business on the street became sellers of artefacts and curios to meet the demand of military personnel with cash to spend. The character of the neighbourhood changed once again in the 1960s when import duties were lowered and entrepreneurs opened up duty-free shops. Cumming St retains this character today. Don't forget to check out the little side alleys and second-storey businesses.

Toorak

Toorak is a residential section built on a

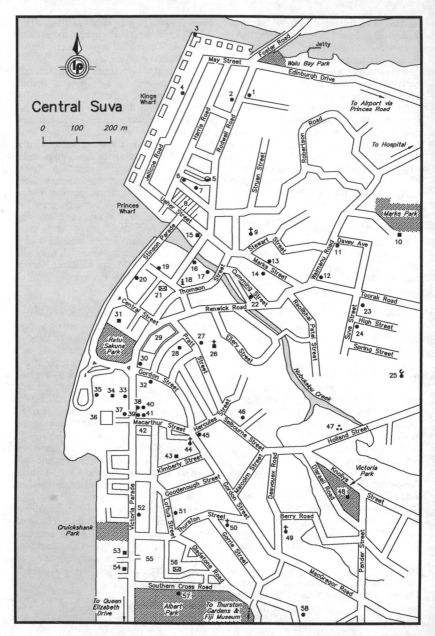

Central Suva

■ PLACES TO STAY

10	Suva YMCA
15	Hotel Metropole
31	YWCA Hostel
43	Coconut Inn
53	Suva Travelodge
54	Grand Pacific Hotel

OTHER

1	Phoenix Theatre
2	Bayly Clinic
3	Fiji Naval Facilities
4	Customs Port Collector
5	Bus Station
6	Main Taxi Stand
7	Public Toilets
8	Markets
9	Methodist Church
11	Alankar Theatre
12	Lilac Theatre
13	Century Theatre
14	Bank
16	Australian Embassy & British Embassy
17	Harbour Centre
18	Fiji Visitors' Bureau
19	Telephone Exchange
20	Handicraft Centre
21	GPO
22	Public Toilets
23	Immigration Department

24	Gospel Hall
25	Mosque
26	Roman Catholic Cathedral & St Anne Primary School
27	Reserve Bank
28	Central Police Station
29	ANZ Bank
30	Fiji National Bank
32	Fiji Times Office
33	Old Town Hall
34	City Council
35	City Council Offices
36	Suva Olympic Pool
37	Suva City Library
38	Fiji Air
39	Lucky Eddie's Nightclub
40	Fiji Air
41	Air Pacific House
42	Government Crafts Centre & New Zealand High Commission
44	Anglican Church
45	Defence Club
46	Fiji Club
47	Temple
48	Tennis Court
49	Mormon Church
50	Anglican Church
51	United States Embassy
52	Golden Dragon Nightclub
55	Government Buildings & Parliament
56	Post Office
57	Kingsford-Smith Pavilion
58	United Club

mildly sloping hillside that affords a fine view of the city. There are two possible origins of the name. The first and most likely is that since the majority of Suva's early settlers hailed from Melbourne in Australia, they named the neighbourhood after that city's most fashionable district. The second possibility is that because *toorak* translates as 'where the chief is' in one of Australia's aboriginal languages, the area was called that because its landowner, C A Huon, was regarded as the chief of the estate.

In its early days the neighbourhood was considered one of the finest in town, and two families – the Joskes and the Huons (both which have streets named after them) – fought bitterly over the property rights. Today Toorak has no pretensions about gran-

deur, but retains touches of its elegant trappings. These are found in massive retaining walls and moulded concrete fences that once surrounded some of the finest homes in Suva – a far cry from the modest dwellings they enclose today. One example of this period is the structure built by Dr Hamilton Beattie on the corner of Toorak Rd and Suva St. Designed with a Graeco-Roman villa in mind, it has freestanding columns in bas-relief and swastikas (for good luck) over the entrance. The home is now divided into flats, and the estate, once adorned with fountains and a garden, is covered by wooden shacks.

Today Toorak is a microcosm of modern Fiji, a scrappy multiracial neighbourhood with many children and the occasional bootleg beer distributor.

The Triangle

The triangle, near the beginning of Victoria Parade, is what Albert Schutz in his fine booklet *Suva – A History & Guide* calls 'the true centre of Suva'. A century ago it was a small lagoon fed by a creek coming down Pratt St; today it is a miniature park usually occupied by several locals sitting on a bench at the foot of an *ivi* tree. At the centre of this triangular park is a concrete historical marker with four inscriptions. The landmark has a special distinction in that three of the four inscriptions set aside for posterity are incorrect:

Suva Proclaimed Capital in 1882.
> This is not quite true. The home government actually approved the move from Levuka to Suva in 1877 and the action was announced by the *London Times* in August of that year. The government's official move from Levuka was made in 1882.

Cross and Cargill First Missionaries arrived 14 October 1835.
> Not quite; according to their diaries, the correct date was 12 October.

Public Land Sales on this spot 1880.
> Wrong location. Apparently the land sales did occur underneath an ivi tree but not this one. In reality the sales were a bit further down the road, near the present-day locale of the Morris Hedstrom & Co store.

British Crown Colony 10th October 1874.
> They got this one right.

Old Town Hall

The old town hall, constructed just after the turn of the century, is one of the finest examples of Victorian architecture. Not only did it serve the duties of government, it was also a centre for the performing arts and a host to concerts, vaudeville acts and amateur shows. In the good old days the upper floor was used as a museum while the government offices were on the ground level. Today the old hall houses an elegant Chinese restaurant and a hairdressing salon. In the evenings the area in front of the hall is a rendezvous point for Lucky Eddie's, on the opposite side of the street.

Swimming Pool & Gym

Behind the town hall is a very fine Olympic pool open to the public. Admission is 50 cents to the pool and 20 cents to the dressing room. From April to September opening hours are 10 am to 6 pm weekdays, 8 am to 6 pm Saturdays; and from October to March, 9 am to 7 pm on weekdays, 6 am to 7 pm Saturdays. There is also a reasonably clean public toilet here.

If you are addicted to a health club back home, you may want to check out the facilities at Olympic Gym (☎ 304 970) at 14 Carnovan St. The gym is in a large quonset hut-shaped building, not far from the municipal pool. The equipment is mostly weight-lifting gear, as well as some older, nautilus-style equipment. The cost is F$2.50 per session.

Suva City Library

Next to the town hall is the Suva City Library, built in 1909. It is a noteworthy landmark in that the money for constructing the edifice (£1000) was donated by the US steel magnate, Andrew Carnegie. Carnegie provided similar donations to other libraries around the world. I have found the librarians a very friendly bunch and the long-term visitor might find it worthwhile to take out a library card. Note that some of the best books are in the Pacific Collection, inside the charge desk, and available on request. (Long-term visitors should also check into the University of the South Pacific Library on the USP campus which has the best books in the country.)

Naiqaqi

About 100 metres down from the library is an area called 'Naiqaqi', which translates as 'the crusher'. This vicinity, which is now occupied by the Native Land Trust Board (NLTB) building and the Fiji Broadcasting Commission building, was once the site of Fiji's first sugar mill, built in 1873. Sugar grows quite well in Fiji but not in the Suva area, where the topsoil is thin and 'the crusher' was never a successful business venture. The only nearby remnant of this exercise in futility is a gear 1½ metres in diameter, on display near the corner of Carnarvon and Loftus Sts.

Government Buildings

The massive government building site is one of the most prominent in Suva, but prior to 1935 the area was a swampy creek bed. Known as part of the greater Naiqaqi district, the area mostly contained tumbledown shacks and many of the neighbourhood's women plied the world's oldest trade.

To support the government buildings, more than five km of reinforced concrete pilings were rooted deep in the creek bed. The foundation stone was laid in 1937 and the building was completed in 1939. The new wing was completed in 1967. There are two statues gracing the grounds – one of Chief Cakobau and the other of Ratu Sir Lala Sukuna.

The government buildings may be of more than passing interest to the visitor. Here the Department of Lands & Survey sells excellent topographic maps and city plans to the public. In the new wing, the Department of Information provides pamphlets such as *Fiji Today*, which offers an overview of the country, statistics and general background information. Nearby, in a barrack-like annex, is the office of the Fiji Dictionary Project.

An impressive new parliament building, offering more space needed by the expanded post-coup government, was opened in 1992 on Ratu Sukuna Rd.

Albert Park

The area that comprises Albert Park was part of the original land grant given by the Polynesia Company to the government as an inducement to move the capital to Suva. Named after the royal consort to Queen Victoria, it is and always has been a general recreational park with a cricket ground and tennis courts.

The pavilion is named after Charles Kingsford Smith, who in 1928 became the first aviator to cross the Pacific. Smith began the journey in Oakland, California and refuelled in Kauai. He flew on to Suva without ever having seen the proposed landing strip, Albert Park, nor realising that a row of palm trees stretched across the middle of his runway, where the pavilion now stands. Fortunately, before Smith arrived the Suva radio station operator thought it might be a good idea to cut down the trees, and persuaded the governor (against the wishes of the city authorities) to raze them and level the field. Aeroplanes were a bit of a rarity in those days and nobody ever thought the aviator need be warned that the field was actually below the level of the street. The *Southern Cross* had no brakes and when the plane landed on 6 June, Kingsford Smith expertly stopped the twin-engine Fokker within a few metres of the field by swinging it almost at right angles before it stopped.

Grand Pacific Hotel

The shoreline adjacent to the Grand Pacific Hotel (or GPH as it is called by locals) was once a landing spot for commoners from the nearby village. It was called Vu-ni-Vesi after a group of vesi trees that grew there. The first hotel built on this spot, the Hotel Suva, was little more than a shack but the GPH, which opened in 1914, was to 'set the standard for the entire Pacific', according to Albert Schutz in *Suva – A History & Guide*.

Constructed by the Union Steamship Company as a base for New Zealand and Canadian shipping services in the northern and southern Pacific, the hotel's design mirrored the 1st-class accommodation found on ships of the day. Like shipboard cabins, the bedrooms opened onto wide decks on one side. On the other, they provided entry to a balcony that overlooked the main lounge. Marine-style plumbing and saltwater baths added to the nautical air of the hotel.

The glamour that this colonial landmark once enjoyed has faded, and a recent addition has failed to maintain the elegant character of the original white-porticoed building. However, a multimillion dollar renovation, estimated to take until 1994 to complete, will try to restore the grandeur and status that the

ARTEFACTS

In recent years some of old Fiji's finest artefacts have been repatriated and are now on display in the Fiji Museum, in Suva's Thurston Gardens. One of the largest collections of Fijian art outside Fiji became available when English collector James Hooper died in 1971 and his collection was sold at a London auction in 1979. Over 60 of Hooper's artefacts were returned to Fiji when Mobil Oil Australia purchased a selection on behalf of the Fiji Museum. The following include pieces from the Hooper Collection, as well as a smattering of other representative Fijian art.

Buli Kula (Golden Cowrie)

One of the finest pieces in the Hooper Collection is the *buli kula* or golden cowrie high chief's pendant, which is attached to a neck cord of plaited black fibres and embellished with light *voivoi* (pandanus) ties. To this day the buli kula is the most esteemed of all ornaments, prized for its beauty and rarity. In the days of sailing ships, sea captains would often ask chiefs for the golden cowries as souvenirs but were nearly always refused them or told that there were none to be had.

Like so many of the finest Fijian artefacts, this pendant was collected and preserved by a Methodist missionary in the 19th century. Missionaries became the recipients of such items because they stayed long enough to win the respect of the chiefs, or were given the artefacts by converts for the purpose of selling them to raise money for the church.

Vunikau Bulibuli (War Club)

This *vunikau bulibuli* would be a typical rootstock club if it were not for the ivory inlaid studs and stars on the business end of the weapon. The inlay work, a Tongan motif, was most likely crafted by a Tongan artisan residing in Fiji, whose primary task was to build a war canoe. In former times it was not unusual for Tongan chiefs to send over boatbuilders to Fiji for years at a time in order to have canoes built.

Making a club involved the work of two men: one to uproot a sapling and season it, and another to do the carving or, in this case the inlay work. This explains why such a classically Fijian weapon bore the earmark of a Tongan. In warfare Fijians seemed to prefer heavy weapons for the purpose of crushing skulls and this club (which weighs six kg) is no exception.

Bui ni Kauvadra
(Old Lady of Kauvadra)

Although not part of the Hooper Collection, the *bui ni Kauvadra* is a recent museum acquisition of great importance. She is a key figure in Fijian mythology – the grandmother of all gods and goddesses. Her uniqueness is that she is a human figure, a rarity in Fijian art.

Her noticeable lack of arms is due to some mythical battle that time has forgotten. The hooks near her feet were probably used to hang offerings and the tattooing on her groin was common among Fijian women prior to the coming of the missionaries. Likewise, both her ears are slit to accept earlobe plugs. Her skirt, which once fell below her waist, has disintegrated with time, as has the human hair which once covered her head and pubic area.

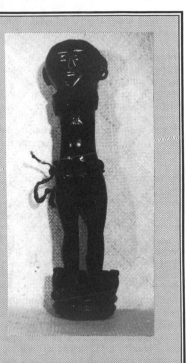

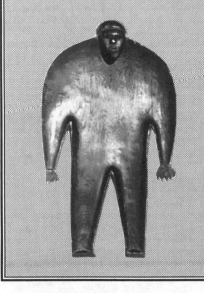

Dave ni Yaqona
(Priest's Yaqona Dish)

The *dave ni yaqona*, carved in the form of a human figure, is one of several still in existence. The ceremonial yaqona dish was used exclusively in Fijian temples and only by the priests. Unlike the normal yaqona drinking ritual, where the brew would be drunk from coconut halves with both hands, the priests placed the dave ni yaqona on the floor of the temple and sucked the contents out of the dish without touching it.

Although most Fijians have long since stopped practising their ancient religion, yaqona drinking remains an important social activity in modern Fijian culture. Like the use of tabua, it is a custom likely to continue.

Both the *bui ni Kauvadra* and the *dave ni yaqona* were collected by the missionary R B Lyth prior to 1854 and donated to the museum by the London-based Methodist Missionary Society.

GPH once knew. Until then, GPH is closed to guests.

Thurston Gardens

These gardens on Victoria Parade contain a large collection of flora from throughout the South Pacific. Named after the amateur botanist and founder, Sir John Bates Thurston, the present site was opened in 1913. The gardens are well kept and almost always uncrowded. They are also an entrance to the Fiji Museum.

Fiji Museum

Founded in 1904, the original site of the Fiji Museum (☎ 315 944) was in the old town hall. After being moved to several locations, the present building was constructed on the grounds of Thurston Gardens in 1954. Despite the multitude of artefacts that were taken from Fiji by missionaries and sailors, the museum has the finest collection of Fijian relics in the world.

Among the exhibits are collections of war clubs, ivory necklaces, cannibal forks, spears, bowls, pottery, tools, cooking utensils, combs and a replica of a huge drua – an ancient, double-hulled canoe. One of the war clubs, which was actually used in battle, has several notches chiselled in it, each representing an enemy slain. The rear of the museum is dedicated to the arrival of European and US sailing vessels, highlighting the bêche-de-mer, whaling and sandalwood eras. There is also an exhibit illustrating the saga of the Indian indenture period and the infamous blackbirding trade that brought Micronesians and Melanesians to Fiji. In addition, you'll see actual relics from the famous *Bounty*. There is a superb collection of old masi (tapa bark cloth) in an air-con room.

Aside from collecting and chronicling Fijian artefacts, the museum is also a research and educational institution. The staff engage in archaeological research, the preservation of Fiji's oral tradition and publication of material on language and culture. Despite the museum's good works, lack of space to showcase the exhibits and chronic lack of funding have always been problems. The museum is open weekdays from 8.30 am to 4.30 pm, Saturday from 9 am to 4.30 pm and is closed Sunday. Admission is F$2 for adults, free for children. There is often a temporary exhibit of some kind going on, and these are usually excellent. Anyone visiting Suva should not miss the museum.

Art Gallery

The only art gallery in Suva is inside the lobby of the Suva Travelodge Hotel. It tends to be pricey, but the art is top-notch and mostly local. Sales hours are from 2 to 7 pm.

President's Residence

Formerly government house, the president's residence was constructed in 1882 as a residence of the then governor, Des Voeux. The house burned to the ground after being struck by lightning in 1921 and the current building was erected in 1928. Today it is occupied by the president and guarded by two sturdy soldiers clad in a scarlet tunic and white sulu. The president's residence is not open to the public. The entrance is directly on Queen Elizabeth Drive.

University of the South Pacific

Established in 1968 on an area that was once a New Zealand seaplane base, USP is a regional institution, jointly operated by 11 South Pacific countries. In attendance are about 2300 full-time students from every South Pacific country except the French-speaking colonies; the majority of the students are from Fiji. The main campus, which is off Laucala Bay Rd, has an excellent library and can be reached by the Vatuwaqa bus. Visitors interested in checking books out of the library need only pay a F$10 refundable deposit. There is also an interesting botanical garden just inside the main gate.

Colo-i-Suva Forest Park

This is a lovely recreational area and nature reserve 18 km north-east of Suva, past the suburb of Tamavua on Princes Rd. The park, which is highlighted by waterfalls, rushing streams and misty canyons, occupies the entire upper drainage of Waisila Creek, once

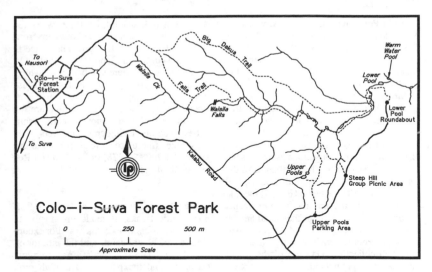

Colo–i–Suva Forest Park

lowland tropical forest. Colo-i-Suva is between 120 and 200 metres above sea level and is therefore cooler and slightly wetter than Suva. (The mean annual temperature in the park is 24°C, which varies an average of only 2°C between February and July, the warmest and coolest months.)

The indigenous forest was selectively cut and replanted with mahogany in the 1950s. Today there are a variety of facilities, including a 500-metre nature trail loop (which begins from the Upper Pools parking area) and more than 3.6 km of other hiking trails. There are also natural pools which have been developed into swimming areas, a rope swing, picnic tables (some of which have bure shelters) and fire grates for cooking.

Visitors are advised to wear good hiking shoes because many of the trails are gravelled, and soapstone makes the surface slippery under the best of conditions. During heavy rains and flooding, crossing the creek can be dangerous and visitors are cautioned to wait in the shelters provided until the water subsides. Swimmers are also advised to carefully gauge the depth of pools before diving.

The big disadvantage is that there have been a few reports of crime (including rapes and robberies) in this secluded area, and hikers should be aware of this problem. A sign at the parking area (if it hasn't been purloined) warns drivers not to leave any valuables in the car. So leave your money (there are no shops anyway) and any jewellery at your hotel. Any questions about the park should be directed to the Colo-i-Suva forestry station (☎ 322 311).

Camera buffs should bring along high-speed film because even on a cloudless day the thick forest allows little light through.

Transport to Colo-i-Suva is easy. Take the Sawani bus from the Suva terminal (about 50 cents) and walk from the bus stop to the clearly marked entrance. Begin your hike on the Waisila Falls Trail.

Beaches Near Suva

Sorry folks, there aren't too many beaches on this side of the island and there really isn't one in the city limits. The closest beach is in the Deuba-Pacific Harbour Resort area opposite the Coral Coast Christian Camp, a 45-minute drive from the capital. It's better to go by car, as it really is a long haul by bus. For the desperate, try dipping into the water at Suva Point, near the University (take a Vatuwaqa bus) or else near the Tradewinds Hotel in Lami (take a Wailekutu or Naboro bus, the fare is 50 cents). There should be local kids at these swimming places, but don't expect sandy beaches.

Mosquito Island, near Lami town is another option. You can walk there at low tide but must arrange a boat for the journey back. (That's where there might be a problem.) Toilets and showers are available. Bring a few pounds of yaqona as a sevusevu (gift) for the caretaker. To get there take the Shoreline Bus to Lami (about 50 cents) and get off near the Tradewinds Hotel. If the tide is high, ask at the marina for any yachts heading in the direction of the island and be prepared to pay them a few dollars for fuel. Activities include swimming, sunbathing and shell collecting. Day use of the island costs 50 cents per person.

Activities
Private Clubs Many of the private clubs have excellent recreational facilities and are great places to meet people. Although private, most will make allowances for visitors with local friends or if you simply call the club secretary.

Originally a spit-and-polish bastion of the empire, the Defence Club (☎ 312 130), at 57 Gordon St, is still very much an 'old boys' type of environment minus the racial exclusivity. There are plenty of magazines to admire in the reading room, an attractive bar, and an all-male environment.

The Royal Suva Yacht Club (☎ 312 921; fax 304 433) is a well-maintained colonial-style clubhouse circa 1930 just outside of Suva towards Walu Bay. It has a tin-roofed dining and bar area open to the sea breezes, and a marina with facilities for yachts. Bathrooms and toilets are ashore. The grounds here are exquisitely manicured and have shaded picnic tables, an outdoor barbecue and a terrific view of the Bay of Islands, Joske's Thumb and the distant mountain ranges of Viti Levu. The RSYC also has a great social scene on the weekend.

Weekly rates are F$20 per yacht with two

or more people aboard, F$10 per week for solo yachts. Weekday office hours are from 8 am to 1 pm and 2 to 5 pm. The office is usually staffed on Saturday as well. On Friday evenings there's a barbecue which includes half-price beer on tap, and on Tuesdays there's a 'happy hour' from 6 to 7 pm. Social functions and use of the club are for yachties only, though honorary membership is bestowed on visiting crew members.

Another fine place to meet people is the United Club (☎ 22 478) on Williamson Rd, especially during their weekend dances.

Other Clubs The Rucksack Club (☎ 322 655, Annie Banks) is made up mostly of expats and offers weekly hikes and/or excursions to the other islands and the interior of Viti Levu. These expeditions are well organised and inexpensive. The club provides temporary membership for visitors (at F$2 for two months), which should be taken advantage of if you are going to be in the Suva area. Write to PO Box 2394, Government Buildings, Suva, for more information.

The Fiji Shell Club (☎ 304 144, Margaret Patel), PO Box 5031, offers excursions to outlying areas for serious shell collectors. Members meet on the first Tuesday of the month at Suva Grammar School.

Suva Orchid & Horticultural Circle (☎ 370 437, Mrs Gul Akbar) meets on the first Monday of each month (except January) at 8 pm. Flower-arranging classes are on the second Tuesday of the month, and cost F$5 for nonmembers.

The Fiji National Trust puts on interesting lectures at 7.45 pm on the last Thursday of each month at St Andrew's Church hall, 75 Gordon St. All are welcome.

News-starved US citizens are invited to the US Embassy on weekdays at 11 am to watch the latest from the USA on big-screen TV. Bring your passport please. The embassy also has a library, open from 8 am to 5 pm, which is full of current magazines and newspapers. Each month the Yanks put on a 'TGIF' party to which all are invited. Evidently, the Australian Embassy has a similar get-together. It's probably a good idea to call for more information.

Tours The Coral Sea cruise (☎ 383 319, 381 570) is a pleasant half-day (9.30 am to 1.15 pm) or full-day (9.30 am to 3.30 pm) trip aboard a motor launch with glass-bottom panels. The launch visits Suva Harbour's barrier reef and tiny **Nukulau Island**. Divers accompanying the vessel bring coral and other specimens aboard for your inspection and you can swim, beachcomb or bake in the sun (assuming the sun is shining). The price of the cruise includes fresh fruit, tea, luncheon, a taste of coconut juice and transfer to Suva Jetty from any local hotel. The price is F$62.

Wilderness Fiji Tours (☎ 386 498; fax 300 584) specialises in boat tours down the Rewa and Navua rivers and has a city tour of Suva. The 'Interior by Boat' tour is a 20-km trip up the Navua River passing through deep gorges and stopping in Fijian villages. The terminus is in the village of **Nukusere** which is 1000 metres above sea level. Navua is famous for its mist-shrouded, precipitous mountains and is generally inaccessible to visitors. This is really the only way to see Navua without chartering a boat or renting a 4WD. The trip leaves at 9 am from Suva hotels and returns at 4.45 pm; the cost is F$41 for adults and F$25 for children.

The Rewa River Delta tour is a half-day journey that explores Fiji's largest river with a local water taxi. The itinerary includes a visit to the Naililili Catholic Mission to see St Joseph's Church, the largest in Fiji. The tour weaves in and out of the huge delta stopping at a Fijian village for the obligatory kava ceremony and souvenir buying. The tour leaves twice daily at 9.30 am (returning at 1 pm) and 2 pm (returning at 4.45 pm). The cost is F$29 for adults and F$18 for children, which includes pick-up from Suva hotels.

Wilderness Fiji also runs a more adventure-oriented, all-day canoe trip (including picnic) down the Navua River. The trip entails a two-hour drive to the upper reaches of the river, swimming and a cooked lunch.

The route passes through rainforest, waterfalls, farmland and villages on the banks. Your day begins with an 8 am pick-up from your hotel and you return by 5 pm. The trip costs $49 per person.

Places to Stay
The hotels listed here are considered good value for their price range. Hotel reservations can be made through your travel agent. For the best hotel in town, the Travelodge, this is certainly a good idea. For most of the other hotels on the 'Suva side' you won't need a reservation, but should you desire one, the hotel can be faxed. Most hotel prices are 'fixed', but some have so-called 'local' rates, especially if they're empty or if you are considering staying awhile. Do not even think about negotiating for prices in the more popular areas.

Places to Stay – bottom end
Coconut Inn (☎ 312 904) is a rock-bottom, dorm-style place two blocks from Victoria Parade on Kimberly St. It's fairly clean, but the dorm area is rather cramped. There is hot and cold water, cooking and washing facilities, and a locker/storage room. This is an excellent place to ferret out information from other travellers. The price is F$7.50 per night for bunks, F$14/20 for a single/double, F$9.50 for B&B.

Hotel Metropole (☎ 304 124), on Usher St is one of Suva's oldest hotels. The four rooms upstairs are clean, the location is excellent and, all in all, the hotel is quite adequate. The rates are F$15/22.50 for a single/twin (a twin has two single beds). There are shared baths, but each spartan room has a washbasin and fan. The clientele is extremely international. A lively Chinese restaurant shares the top floor.

Tanoa House (☎ 381 575), at 5 Princes Rd, is one of the better budget places in Suva. It has more of a 'homey' atmosphere than any other accommodation and the couple that run it are genuinely nice people. It is in a run-down colonial building, a 10-minute bus ride from the centre of town. Amenities include a dining room and bar. Rates for rooms begin at F$15/25 a single/double; F$30 a triple. The food is good and reasonably priced – F$5 for a full breakfast, F$6.50 for lunch and F$8 for dinner. There are no self-contained units here and the 'mix' is half European, half local tourists (such as students). To get there take the Samabula bus at the market and ask the driver to let you off at Tanoa House (near the Fiji Institute of Technology).

South Seas Private Hotel (☎ 312 296), a friendly, well-maintained backpackers' place, is deservedly a perennial favourite. It's a huge, two-storey, colonial-style structure in a quiet residential area on Williamson Rd behind Albert Park. There are 34 rooms, a huge lounge, hot and cold water, laundry facilities and a good communal kitchen with a large fridge. There's also a pleasant garden area and guests are allowed to use the phone. Rooms are clean, and have louvre windows and overhead fans The rate per night is F$7/11 for singles/doubles; F$4 in a dorm.

The *YWCA Hostel* (☎ 315 667), adjacent to Ratu Sukuna Park, is an excellent place to stay if you are a single woman with little money in your pocket. It has hot and cold water, ceiling fans, laundry facilities and a good, inexpensive cafeteria (a great place to sample simple, local cuisine, whether you are a guest or not). Rates at the YWCA are F$16/25 for singles/doubles.

Places to Stay – middle

The *Southern Cross Hotel* (☎ 314 233), a five-minute walk from Victoria Parade on Gordon St, is known by locals for its entertainment in the lounge – a toned-down nightclub where you get revved up before going on to Lucky Eddie's or the Golden Dragon for further nocturnal adventures. The 35-room hotel is an adequate place to stay if you don't mind the nightlife and cigarette smoke pervading the place in the evenings. Prices start at F$48/54 for a single/double. Rooms have a rather worn, lived-in look – some have air-con.

On Robertson Rd, *Tropic Towers Apartment Hotel* (☎ 304 470, 313 855) is a 30-room air-con apartment complex. Modestly furnished rooms sleep two to five people, include self-contained cooking units, refrigerator and laundry facilities, and are inexpensive. It is clean, well maintained and the furniture ꞏnd rugs are only partly run-down. The hotel is usually full of family groups from Australia and New Zealand. Prices begin at F$22/28 for a single/twin. The only downside of this accommodation is the 15-minute walk to central Suva.

Capricorn Apartment (☎ 314 799), at 7 Fort St, is another adequate apartment complex with self-contained units for the do-it-yourself visitor. Amenities include pool, air-con, general store, baby-sitting and a dial-a-meal service. Rooms are F$45/55 for a single/double.

The *Townhouse Apartment Hotel* (☎ 300 055), at 3 Forster St two blocks off Victoria Parade, has one of the best views in Suva but the superlatives stop there. There are 28 self-contained units (many with a fine view of the city), and guests have access to cooking facilities, a restaurant, garage space, and a baby-sitting service. The facilities are run-down but fairly clean. The rooftop bar is one of the undiscovered, quiet places at which to drink in an otherwise boisterous town. You are more likely to see locals at the bar than visitors. Singles/doubles begin at F$34/42.

The *Grand Pacific Hotel (GPH)* (☎ 301 011) is a faded national landmark currently undergoing extensive renovation and expansion. The GPH was opened in 1914 and according to one historian was the trendsetting hotel in its day. In later years it fell into disrepair through mismanagement and neglect. The GPH looks like the kind of place where Somerset Maugham may have tipped a glass. (He never got there but Noel Coward did.) It is currently closed and expected to reopen sometime in 1994 when hopefully it will be restored to its former stature.

Sunset Apartment (☎ 301 799) on Gordon St is about a 10-minute walk from the town centre. It has 11 self-contained two-bedroom units and air-con. Rates for singles/doubles begin at F$28/38.

Suva Peninsula Hotel (☎ 313 711) is known by locals for its semi-civilised nightclub littered with orange plastic stools and drunks. If you don't mind that the entire hotel smells like someone is preparing dinner, you might consider it. Rooms vary in size (either twin or double beds) and are air-con, with kitchenettes, refrigerators, bathrooms and coffee-making facilities. It falls into the acceptable category. Prices start at F$38/42 a single/double.

Outrigger Motel (☎ 314 944; fax 302 944) has single/double units with private bath, cooking facilities and air-con for F$45/55. The rooms also have radio, TV and phone. Given all these amenities, it is not a bad deal. The Outrigger also has dorm units for F$8.80 and is known as one of the few places in town where you can get pizza. An American friend reports that the pizza is good, but an Italian reader tells me it's *mezzo mezzo*.

Places to Stay – top end

The *Suva Travelodge* (☎ 301 600) is the top-rated hotel in Suva. Its 132 rooms have been upgraded and there are convention facilities for about 100 people. Other amenities include piano bar, gift shop, coffee shop, art gallery, hair salon, and tour desk (in the foyer). The restaurant's food is more expensive (F$7 to F$12 for main meals) compared with what you can get in Suva's other eating places, but it's good. The location, on Victoria Parade facing Suva Harbour, is excellent – within walking distance of all the banks and nightclubs you'll ever need. Singles/doubles begin at F$145/160. Friday-after-work jazz and cocktails outdoors at the Travelodge are a new 'tradition' for many Suva expats. The Saturday night buffets for F$14.50 are good value.

The *Suva Courtesy Inn* (☎ 312 300), on Gordon St two minutes' walk from Victoria Parade, is also a fine hotel, and a place you could send your mother-in-law to. It has all the amenities including a pool, 24-hour room service, a coffee shop, fine restaurant and 56 rooms – some with a great panorama of Suva Harbour, and all with air-con. In the evenings the lounge features a cool jazz combo – a

good place for a quiet drink especially if you want to get away from the rowdy nightclubs. Food and service are very good. Rates are F$115 for a single or double. The only disadvantage is that the air-conditioning can be noisy. The barbecue on Saturday evenings is good value for F$9.90.

Places to Eat

Although the quality of restaurants in Suva could never reach the level of Tahiti's French-influenced ones, it has flowered in just the past few years. Fine food is available, most of it very inexpensive, especially when compared to French Polynesia. The price for an average meal for two at a halfway decent restaurant, not including alcohol, ranges from F$10 to F$20. The variety is also good. The basic fare is 'European', Indian, Chinese, Fijian or combinations thereof. Most of the restaurants are in central Suva and within minutes of each other. Wine selection is limited mostly to Australian varieties, but Italian and French wines are now being imported and the quality and variety is getting better every year. The prices quoted don't include alcohol.

Cafes, Takeaways & Cheap Eats The *Suva Wharf* is not the name of a fancy restaurant but the actual market itself, where vendors sell basic Fijian food like fish in coconut milk, chop suey, curry and dalo (taro root) for under F$3 – the cheapest prices in town. Many locals eat here for lunch. To get there, go to the yellow kiosks at the bus station side of the market. This is one of the few places in town where you can get traditional Fijian fare. If you go in the evening, examine what you plan to buy to make sure it hasn't been sitting there for too long.

The *YWCA Hostel* (☎ 313 617) is also inexpensive and features home-style Fijian fare as well as healthy salads. The food is served cafeteria-style and lunch can be had for F$3 to F$5. The food is plain but wholesome, just like the YWCA.

The *Drop-In Lovo Caravan* is a van selling takeaway food near the corner of Loftus St and Victoria Parade, across from the Shell petrol station. It has excellent, traditional Fijian food such as palusami (baked taro leaves with corned beef), fish in coconut cream, roast chicken, rourou (boiled taro leaves), dalo and yams – all cooked in an earth oven. Opening hours are roughly from noon to 2 pm and 6 pm to 2 am. Prices are F$2 to F$3.50. There's a quiet, scenic spot to eat across the street, along the sea wall behind the library.

When you crave a scone, a bun or even a loaf of wholemeal bread, the *Hot Bread Kitchen* (there are many scattered around Suva) is your best bet. The quality is excellent and prices begin at 20 cents. Definitely check it out. If you feel like you just need a quick cookie on the run, the *Nanking Takeaway* makes the best butter cookies downtown, at 20 cents a cookie.

Vanua House Shop No 3 is a small luncheonette smack in the middle of Suva which specialises in sandwiches. You stand in a cafeteria-style line, choose the type of bread, condiments etc and the sandwich is made on the spot. Although it sounds typical of any deli in the world, it's the only one of its kind in Suva. Sandwiches cost around F$3. You can also get steak and kidney pie, and there are some tasty sweets, such as a rich, fudgey brownie which is great with an espresso.

Palm Court Bistro is an open-air cafe in the middle of Queensland Arcade. It features very good sandwiches and an assortment of bakery treats. It's a fine spot to relax, restore your energy and watch the world go by.

Lani's Coffee Shop (☎ 303 530), next to the Regal Theatre, makes the best hamburger in Suva by a wide margin, and also offers first-class fare for the sweet tooth. Fresh coffee and a sweet runs to about F$3, meals are $2 to F$5, and the Fijian Seafood Specials are F$3.75 to F$10. Lani's is open from 7 am to 8.30 pm, and also does outside catering.

The *Curry Place*, on Pratt St, is a luncheonette with several varieties of curry, including vegetarian, goat, beef and chicken. It's not fancy, but the food is consistently good. The small booths are a nice touch. Prices range from F$2.50 to F$6.

The *Old Mill Cottage Cafe Restaurant* on Carnarvon St is a stone's throw from the US Embassy and is run by the same folks who own the Coconut Inn. It has very fine food and clean surroundings and is among the best of the lunch-time eateries. The converted home with bench seating is very popular with government office workers because of its proximity to the Fijian government buildings. Innovative cookery includes Chinese dishes, curries and Fijian delicacies like taro and palusami (baked taro leaves with corned beef) cooked in lolo (coconut milk), and kuita (young octopus) in miti (light coconut milk dressing). The prices range from F$3 to F$5.

You'll pass *Pizza Hut* on Victoria Parade many times, but do not enter if you know what good pizza is. The average price is F$7. For those who crave real pizza, I recommend you take a taxi just a short distance from town (or else take the hospital bus and get out one stop before the hospital) to the *Outrigger Motel* (☎ 314 944) at 349 Waimanu Rd. Climb up the winding staircase (and make a note not to get too drunk: you've got to come back down the same stairs) to the rooftop restaurant. The view is impressive, weather-permitting, and the pizza is considered by some to be Suva's best. Don't expect world-class cuisine, but if you really crave pizza, give it a try.

Restaurants *Lantern Palace* (314 633), at 10 Pratt St, serves some of the best Chinese food in town. Expect to spend F$10 to F$20 per person.

The *Ming Palace* is housed in Suva's old town hall on Victoria Parade. As one might guess, the food is of the Chinese persuasion, and reports are that it is very good. Prices are F$6 to F$10. The building is shared by the *Curry Shop*, which has excellent Indian food at moderate prices. The restaurant is clean and attractive, and serves cold beer which compliments the spicy fare.

Hare Krishna Restaurant (☎ 314 154) on Pratt St is run by adherents of the Hare Krishna sect and offers the best vegetarian food in town. The cafe has a pleasant air-con dining area upstairs that fills up for lunch, so get there early. Prices range from about F$4 to F$5 for a terrific all-you-can-eat meal. The restaurant also has the best ice cream in town; for around F$1 a cone you get a marvellous flavour selection (including fig, almond, ginger and nutmeg, as well as the regulars) and it is the only place to get frozen yoghurt. Even if you do not crave vegetarian food, try the ice cream. There is another branch on Cumming St, in case you need an ice cream, roti or Indian sweet while you're on that side of town.

Just around the corner from the Fiji Visitors' Bureau is *Sichuan Pavilion* (☎ 314 795) on Thomson St, a comfortable and well-run Chinese restaurant (owned by Sichuan Province in the Peoples Republic of China), with delicious food. Prices are a bit higher than at shop-front restaurants, but worthwhile when you want a nice meal rather than just a refuel. You can sit on the balcony overlooking the street, which is quite pleasant in the evenings. Prices range from F$2.50 to F$20. Australian, New Zealand and European wines are featured. Don't let the threadbare entrance mislead you, the upstairs area is clean and pleasant. It's open from 11.30 am to 2.30 pm, and from 5.30 to 10.30 pm – longer than any other restaurant.

The *Castle Restaurant*, in Lami town is a 10-minute drive from Suva on the Queens Rd. This Chinese eatery is owned by the same people as the Lantern Palace and ranks as the best modestly priced Chinese restaurant in the Suva area. If you're in the mood for Chinese food, it's worth the drive. Main courses are priced from around F$6 to F$10.

Upstairs in the Metropole Hotel, the *Ocean Restaurant* is popular with the local Chinese population and with sailors. Of particular interest is its Sunday morning 'dim sum' (a delightful serial meal of assorted savouries and Chinese tea brought around on trolleys. There are usually three of each item per plate, at F$1.50 a plate. The Ocean is open from 9 am to 1 pm daily, and from Tuesday to Saturday for lunch and dinner until 10.30 pm. Prices run from F$4 to F$15.

Moderately priced is *O'Reilly's Brasserie*

(☎ 312 884) on McArthur St around the corner from its cousin the Red Lion. Lunch can be a tasty soup of the day accompanied by home-made bread for F$3, or a selection from an extraordinarily eclectic international menu for F$3.50 to $9.50. O'Reilly's also features a good range of international beers. It's open from noon to 2.30 pm and 6 pm to 12.30 am. In the evenings it's a mob scene filled with the young and the restless.

The *Great Wok*, in Flagstaff, is arguably the best (and one of the more expensive) Chinese restaurants in Fiji. It is equal to any good Chinese Restaurant in San Francisco and that's saying a lot. It has all the touches – white tablecloths, good waiting staff and a great wine list – and is the place to go for a farewell dinner or a place to treat yourself in a moment of indulgence. Try the seafood. Prices are F$9 to F$16 for main meals.

Swiss Tavern (☎ 303 233), at 16 Kimberly St, is an up-market restaurant with good food and a nice atmosphere. Run by Swiss-born Hans Kehrli, former head chef at the Fijian Resort, it has an eclectic range of Continental cuisine including veal, lobster, French onion soup, Hungarian goulash and other dishes. Prices are in the F$8 to F$21 range, and the service, under the stern eye of Hans, runs with the precision of a Swiss chronometer. The downstairs bar is also popular with local cognoscenti.

Tai-Pan and its sibling *Aberdeen Grill* (☎ 304 322) are among the newest high-priced eateries. Both are housed in elegance, in an inn called *Noble House* (formerly Scott's) at 16 Bau St.

For an international novelty, try Malaysian food at *Suva Courtesy Inn* (☎ 312 300), on the corner of Malcolm and Gordon Sts.

Steak and seafood are consistently very good at the *Red Lion*, on Victoria Parade. The restaurant is plush by Fijian standards. Meals average around F$12 per person and include pepper steak, teriyaki steak, burgers, walu (fish) and seafood crêpes.

Tiko's Restaurant is Suva's only floating restaurant. Originally a vessel from the *Blue Lagoon* fleet, it was featured in the version of the film starring Brooke Shields. It is primarily a seafood restaurant – the only one in Suva. Specialities are authentic Fijian dishes such as fish and lolo (coconut milk), prawns, lobster, turtle and clams. They also feature a special Fiji-style bouillabaisse. Prices are in the F$8 to F$20 range and reports have been good. They also have a wine list (mostly Australian) which is fairly extensive for Fiji. It is also a good place to go for a nice lunch for about F$7. Owner Tiko Eastgate, a local, says it's advisable to make reservations (☎ 313 626). The restaurant is anchored in Suva Harbour across from Ratu Sukuna Park, a two-minute walk from Victoria Parade.

Lali Restaurant and *Penny's Coffeeshop* in the Suva Travelodge are comparatively expensive, with entreés in the F$15 to F$20 range at Lali, and meals from F$8 to F$20 at Penny's. Penny's serves meals until 11 pm (10.30 pm at Lali) and thus is worth knowing about.

Entertainment

Suva has plenty of nightlife for the interested. Clubs range from seedy dives to posh discos. Nightclubbing is a popular recreation for urban, single Fijians and is socially quite acceptable – many charitable and social organisations use the clubs as places to hold fund-raising dances. Check the entertainment section of the *Fiji Times* classifieds for special events.

Lucky Eddie's is a nocturnal institution in Fiji. It is modern, tacky, loud, generally safe from violent behaviour and very popular with tourists. Entertainment alternates between live bands and disco, depending on the night.

Next to Lucky Eddie's is *Rockefeller's*, a sort of up-market annex under the same ownership and entered via Lucky Eddie's. Rockefeller's (or 'Rocky's' as it is sometimes called) is more expensive and ritzier in décor with plush seats, a fancier bar and wood panelling. Music here has a slightly lower decibel rating, but like Lucky Eddie's is mostly rock or disco. Admission is about F$5 on a weekend. The club is on Victoria Parade, opposite the old town hall.

Golden Dragon is also one of the most popular nightclubs in Suva, more so with locals than the tourists. On a weekend night the familiar cry 'We go to Dragon!' is often heard. The Dragon is also a booming disco, with no shortage of singles seeking companions. It's on Victoria Parade, opposite the Fiji Development Bank. Admission is about F$5 on weekends.

Though affluent Fijians turn up their noses at the *Bali Hai*, this working-class dive is one of my favourite nightspots. Bali Hai has no pretensions about being upper crust and can be a bit rough. You'd better insure your teeth before entering this place. There's no disco – live Fijian music is the order of the day. Admission is about F$3 on weekends. The club is across from the bus station near the Phoenix Theatre.

The *Galley* is a floating bar, below Tiko's Restaurant which is anchored on Suva Bay opposite Ratu Sukuna Park. It is posh by Suva standards and very chic.

In the hotel of the same name, the *Southern Cross* is usually the most civilised club in town. Music is a mixture of Western standard tunes and Fijian pop. The band is live, but the action is tame compared to the other nightspots, perhaps because the crowd is a bit older and well heeled. It is also popular with 'Europeans' and on a weekend is usually the final stop before heading towards Lucky Eddie's or the Golden Dragon. The Southern Cross closes its doors around midnight and admission is usually free.

O'Reilly's (☎ 312 884) a bar/restaurant (with the emphasis on the bar) has become the premier watering hole in Suva among well-heeled locals. It's off Victoria Parade, literally around the corner from Lucky Eddie's, and the entrance is easily discerned by the presence of a uniformed, broad-shouldered Fijian bouncer. On the weekends, judging by the crowds and ample cigarette smoke, this is the place to be seen. Tastefully done in hardwoods, with a long bar and a number of booths, O'Reilly's is modelled after a prototypical 'fern bar' in the USA.

Trap's (☎ 312 922), at 305 Victoria

Parade, is akin to O'Reilly's: up-market, sophisticated and very popular for people who want to talk or to meet others. The music is usually held down to a respectable level (except when a dance is on). During peak weekend hours and holidays, Traps can be completely packed – a total mob scene. At the time of writing, the management are are experimenting with live Monday night jazz.

Karaoke is a nightly entertainment in the bar of the *Metropole Hotel* – a lively, more-than-rowdy place to pass an evening.

Yasawa Group

Of all the Fiji islands the Yasawas (with a population of about 2000) are perhaps the most archetypically 'South Pacific'. From a distance they suggest a string of blue beads lying on the horizon. Up close they are characteristically precipitous, with long stretches of sandy beaches fringed by azure water. In a word, they are gorgeous and for the most part undeveloped. The beauty of the Yasawas has lured the tourist dollar, and this has been lucky for villagers, as arable land is limited, and some crops difficult or even impossible to grow. The islands are a major attraction for cruise vessels originating in Lautoka (see the Getting Around section of this chapter), and several Yasawa villages derive much of their income from the tourist industry. In the last few years several backpackers' resorts have opened up on the island of Tavewa. To date, the three small properties have received high praise from travellers. On the debit side, transport to the island can be irregular, nocturnal visits from mice are not unknown and since there is no air service, once you're there, you're there (at least until the next boat sails).

History
The Yasawas were sighted by Captain Bligh in May 1789, a few days after he began his legendary voyage after the mutiny on the *Bounty*. It was in Yasawa waters that Bligh's tiny boat was pursued by a drua (canoe), which he miraculously managed to elude. Five years later the islands were visited by Captain Barber in the ship *Arthur*, but little seems to have been known of them until 1840, when they were roughly surveyed and charted by officers of a US expedition under Commandant Charles Wilkes.

In the past, the island's residents had the reputation of making fine sail mats, the dry climate being excellent for the production of the best fibre for this purpose. During the mid-19th century the Yasawans were har-assed by Tongan raiders who levied a tribute of these mats on the islanders or bartered for what they couldn't steal. For the most part, the islands were of little interest to European traders or settlers and for many years they remained one of the most isolated parts of Fiji. During WW II the islands were used by the US military as communications outposts. Paradoxically, today they are probably seen by more visitors than any other of Fiji's outer islands.

Geography
The Yasawa group is volcanic in origin. It comprises six large islands and many smaller ones, and has a total area of 135 sq km. From a point 40 km north-west of Lautoka, the islands stretch for more than 80 km in a north-easterly direction, forming a broken ribbon of land rarely more than five km wide and generally much less. The principal members of the group are high, their summits ranging from 250 to 600 metres in height. Except for the southern end, the land formation is so straight that a line could be drawn through a map of the islands with a ruler.

West of the Yasawas there is an extensive area of unsurveyed water littered with reefs. The only safe passage for ships is between Yasawa Island and Round Island, 22 km to the north-east. This was the route used by Captain Bligh, though how he managed to find it – especially considering that he was being chased at the time by a speedy war canoe filled with cannibals – is a mystery. The maze of barrier reefs lying between the islands and the open sea effectively intercepts ocean currents and prevents the free flow of tidal water into the lagoon, creating unfavourable ecological conditions for the growth of coral. Thus, apart from the few massive formations in the open water there is little coral development except for near the northernmost island. Despite the lack of

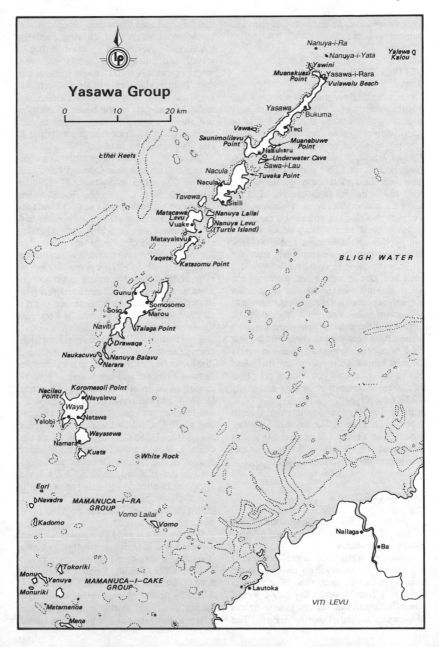

Yasawa Group

0   10   20 km

Nanuya-i-Ra
Nanuya-i-Yata
Yalewa Q Kalou
Yawini
Muanakuasi Point
Yasawa-i-Rara
Vulawalu Beach
Yasawa
Bukuma
Vawa
Teci
Saunimolilevu Point
Muanabuwe Point
Nabukeru
Underwater Cave
Sawa-i-Lau
Ethel Reefs
Nacula
Tuvaka Point
Nacula
Tavewa
Sisili
Matacawa Levu
Nanuya Lailai
Vuake
Nanuya Levu (Turtle Island)
Matayalevu
Yaqeta
Katasomu Point
BLIGH WATER
Gunu
Somosomo
Soso
Marou
Naviti
Talaga Point
Drawaqa
Naukacuvu
Nanuya Balavu
Narara
Nacilau Point
Koromasoli Point
Wayalevu
Waya
Yalobi
Natawa
Namara
Wayasewa
Kuata
White Rock
Eori
Navadra
MAMANUCA–I–RA GROUP
Vomo Lailai
Kadomo
Vomo
Nailaga
Ba
Monu
Tokoriki
Yanuya
Monuriki
MAMANUCA–I–CAKE GROUP
Matamanoa
Mana
Lautoka
VITI LEVU

coral, however, there are plenty of fish, and snorkelling is excellent.

GETTING THERE & AWAY
Boat

The vessels that ply the Yasawas are small 'local' trading or fishing boats, usually without sophisticated navigational gear or safety features such as life jackets. Generally they are safe, but be warned. The fare to Tavewa Island, which has several popular guest houses, is F$60 per person for the round trip. Each guest house operates its own boat, and switching from one vessel to the other is not encouraged. (Incidentally, switching hotels once you are on the island is not a good idea either.) Boats are not equipped with bathrooms and may lack enough seating (as well as shade from the sun) for the three to five-hour voyage. It's not a bad idea to wear a hat, plenty of sun screen and bring water along. If the weather is rough expect to get wet. A better idea is to wear swim suits on the boat. Also, don't be surprised if the skipper lights up a cigarette while sitting near the gas container. It's that kind of a trip. Without sounding overly alarmist I think it's proper to say that when you travel to Tavewa you 'ride at your own risk'. The experience of getting there may not be for everyone.

Boats for Tavewa depart from Queens Wharf in Lautoka on Tuesday and Saturday, returning on Friday and Monday. If you're staying at the Cathay or Lautoka hotels, transport to the wharf is provided.

GETTING AROUND
Cruises

During the past few years, organised cruises around the Yasawas have increased tremendously in popularity.

Although hard-core travellers might scream that 'commercialism' has come to the outer islands, the area that these vessels cover in a four or seven-day cruise would otherwise be difficult for you to see – unless of course you had access to a yacht. The itinerary includes visits to beaches and villages, snorkelling, and viewing partially submerged caverns. An excellent buffet is served, and much of the fare is what you might expect – seafood, caught right on the spot. There is also plenty of alcohol on hand. Locals at some of the villages have set up makeshift markets on the beach where they sell shells, carvings, necklaces, mats and other handicrafts. Prices are generally much less than you'd pay in town.

If a cruise is in your budget, it's hard to go wrong with Blue Lagoon Cruises (☎ 661 622 in Fiji; 231 6755 in Sydney; 77 3790 in Auckland). Blue Lagoon has five 39-metre vessels with 22 cabins on two decks and two 54-metre vessels, the *Yasawa Princess* and the *Nanuya Princess,* which have 33 staterooms on three decks. Prices for the four-day (three-night) 'Popular Cruise' on the smaller boats begin at US$506 per person for a twin cabin and include all transfers, meals, excursions, feasts, visits to villages and beaches, snorkelling, fishing as well as one night's stay at a hotel. The boat leaves at 3 pm and returns at 11 am on the fourth day.

The four-day 'Club Cruise', which covers the same turf as the Popular Cruise (the lower half of the Yasawas), utilises the *Yasawa Princess* and the *Nanuya Princess* instead of the smaller ships. Prices begin at US$614, and the cruise departs on Monday and Thursday at 3 pm. There's also a seven-day 'Club Cruise' on the *Yasawa Princess* priced from US$1119 per person for a twin cabin. It departs from Lautoka on Monday and returns on Sunday. Prices for all cruises exclude bar bills and the 10% VAT, and are always sold outside Fiji as a package with one day's accommodation at a hotel. For information in the USA, contact your local travel agency.

If you want to spend a lot less money and are interested in seeing some of the Yasawa islands in a less conventional manner the Captain Cook Sailing Safari (☎ 701 823; fax 780 045) is worth looking into. It is a relatively new three-day cruise combining the best of several worlds – visiting a Fijian village in the Yasawas and Plantation Island

Resort off Lautoka. See the Cruises section under Tours in the Viti Levu chapter for details.

Around the Islands

WAYA

Forty km north-west of Lautoka, Waya, the highest island in the Yasawas, measures about 6½ km long and almost five km wide and is shaped roughly like an 'H'. There are several singularly sharp peaks on Waya, including a towering bluff directly above the main village of **Yalobi**. This settlement is on the itinerary of many cruise vessels because of its excellent anchorage on Alacrity Bay and its beautiful beach. Those interested in visiting Waya should look into the Captain Cook Sailing Safari or Blue Lagoon Cruises described earlier in this chapter.

NAVITI

Naviti Island lies north-north-east of Waya, the intervening 13 km being bridged by smaller islands. It is irregular in shape, 14½ km long and from several hundred metres to five km wide. It is also steep and rugged, the highest point being Vaturua-yalewa at about 388 metres. The southern bay at **Soso** and the northern bay at **Somosomo** are also regular stops for cruise vessels. Naviti has an important agricultural station.

TAVEWA

Tavewa lies about 1½ km from the island of **Nacula** and is only three km long and 1½ km wide. It is hilly in the centre, with tall grasses and scrub vegetation. There is a bat colony at the top of the hill.

For many years Tavewa was worked as a private plantation and, being freehold land, is the only island in the Yasawas that you don't need a special permit to visit. Lately Tavewa has become a mecca for budget travellers. There are three properties on the island, two of which are aimed at backpackers, the third has two self-contained bures

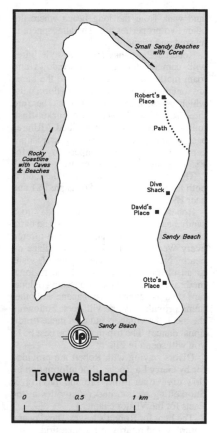

Tavewa Island

which require you to bring your own food. All these places have had good reviews. Note that Robert's and David's are spartan and that the facilities (as in many of the other outlying areas) are often visited by mice. The overly squeamish may find the accommodation too 'primitive'. Be sure to bring your own torch (flashlight) and water-purification tablets.

Robert's Place (☎ 660 566 at the Cathay Hotel), run by father-and-son team Robert and Don De Bruce, is on the northern end of the island and is adjacent to a coral beach with just a fringe of sand. Opened in 1989, the guest house lies on a cove, a short overland walk from the long beach where the other two properties are. The atmosphere is relaxed and friendly.

Robert's Place has six local-style bures with cement floors, screen windows and foam mattresses on cots. Four of the bures are for couples, and there are two dorm units which can sleep up to eight people. There are three saltwater showers, two bucket-flush toilets and one flush toilet in a shed. All bures cost F$10 per person per day, plus F$5 per person for three meals. Campers may stay for F$5 plus another F$5 for meals.

The kitchen is very clean and the food is both tasty and abundant. Sodas are F$1 and beer F$2.

Robert takes guests out every day to a sandy beach on a nearby island for no extra charge. There is also an excursion offered every Wednesday for F$10 to a village on nearby Nacula Island. The trip entails visits to an elementary school and the regional medical clinic, and a meal consisting of local fare such as cassava, fish, banana and other items provided by the villagers. Following the meal, the villagers put on a meke (traditional dance). The trip may be the best F$10 you will spend in Fiji.

Divers staying with Robert are provided for by Garry La Roche. (For information on this dive operation, see the Diving & Snorkelling section under Activities in the Facts for the Visitor chapter.)

The boat for Robert's leaves Tuesday and Saturday and returns to Lautoka Friday and Monday. Write to PO Box 3764, Lautoka for information and reservations at Robert's.

David's Place (☎ 660 388 at the Lautoka Hotel) is on a stretch of white-sand beach shaded by coconut palms. Overall, the facilities are better than Robert's Place and the beach area is much nicer. A new bar/kitchen/dining room is planned in the near future. There are seven bures for couples, and two dorms which can accommodate up to 10 visitors. Two showers and two flush toilets (with tiled floors) are also available for your hygienic needs. Costs are F$20 for a double bure, F$8 for a dorm bed and F$5 for campers. The food is good and

costs F$2 for breakfast, F$3 for lunch or dinner. David's flock is quite religious and grace is said before every meal; there's a small Catholic chapel on the edge of the property. David's is popular with Tavewans and chances are there will be more 'locals' hanging around the premises.

Activities include excellent swimming, and excursions are available at extra cost. Snorkelling gear can be rented for F$8 and diving is provided by Garry La Roche. Boats depart from Lautoka on Tuesday and Saturday, returning on Friday and Monday. For bookings and information write to David and Kara Doughty, PO Box 1784, Lautoka.

One note of caution. I've heard at least one instance where guests showed up at David's and found the place was full. One of the guests had even booked months before. These guests were given a tent rather than being sent to one of the other properties on the island. Evidently the resorts on the island do not co-operate well with each other.

If you are inclined to go it alone, *Otto & Fanny Doughty* (☎ 664 169, 661 175) run two self-contained units. One has a large room with six foam-mattress cots, a dining table for six, rattan couch and chairs and a fully equipped kitchen (with stove, fridge, dishes, pots and pans). The other is similar but set up for a couple. The price is F$20 per person for the large bure and F$45 for the double unit. Electricity is available via generator from 6 to 10 pm. Make sure you bring your own food and beverages. Fanny bakes cakes and serves tea daily at 3 pm for F$2 and everyone is invited. She is very personable – like a favourite aunt. The Doughty's son, Ronnie and his Australian wife, also live on the premises and rent sailboards for F$10 per day. For reservations write to PO Box 1349, Lautoka. The usual stay is from Saturday to Thursday, and the return boat ride from Lautoka costs F$60.

YASAWA

This northernmost island is the largest in the chain, and the one after which the group is named. Yasawa is about 22 km long, less than a km wide, and is shaped much like a closing square punctuation bracket. A steep ridge runs along its length, the two highest points being Taucake in the south (233 metres) and Cololevu in the north (194 metres) near Bukuma village. The most traditional village on the island and the seat of the Yasawa group is **Yasawa-i-Rara**, which is the home of Tui Yasawa (the head chief of the island group).

The villagers are noted for their fishing skills, which have developed from necessity because important staple crops such as taro and cassava cannot be grown on the island. Near the village is **Vulawalu Beach** or 'eight months beach' which is so-named because the sand is so fine it's supposed to take eight months to rid yourself of it. The main village on the island is **Nabukeru**, the inhabitants of which make a good living selling mats, shells and the like to visitors coming off the boats. Sales of these items have made the residents the richest in the Yasawa group, as indicated by the large number of concrete dwellings and the existence of an electrical generator in the village. Nabukeru also has an excellent beach.

Yasawa Island Lodge (☎ 663 364; 800 441 6880 in the USA; fax 665 044) is new, very up-market accommodation on an exquisite beach. The property has eight well-appointed, split-level, thatched bures with king-size beds, double showers, vanities and separate dressing rooms. All the requisite water sports are available, such as fishing, windsurfing, sailing, snorkelling and diving as well as tennis and rainforest walks. The food is reportedly very good.

The price for this type of paradise is not cheap. Rates begin at F$470/650 for a single/double room, and include meals and all activities except scuba diving. Booze also costs extra, and transport to the island via Sunflower Airlines will cost you F$125 per person one way. For more information write to Yasawa Island Lodge at PO Box 10128, Nadi Airport, Fiji.

SAWA-I-LAU
The tiny limestone island of Sawa-i-Lau lies just off Yasawa Island and is famous for one thing – its underwater cave. You step off the boats into the cave, which has a large pool illuminated by the sun. Next you swim with a torch (flashlight) through a small orifice that connects the large cave to a smaller pool, which is dimly lit only by dissipated light from the other cave. Here, according to Fijian legend, a young chief hid his betrothed – a lady of rank whose elders would have married her to someone she did not want. He visited her daily, bringing food and gifts by diving with them through the watery doorway, until at length the couple escaped to friends on another island.

Although normally not shown to visitors, in the main cave are rock paintings of uncertain origin and antiquity. According to historian R A Derrick in *A History of Fiji*, one observer thought that the inscriptions bore a resemblance to Chinese characters;

...and upon this assumption, which at present is no more than an assumption, has put forward the hypothesis that a Chinese junk was at one time blown south and wrecked on Yasawa Island. The possibility that the inscriptions are the work of an itinerant Chinaman suffering from nostalgia is not to be excluded.

According to former Fiji Museum director, Fergus Clunie, similar rock engravings exist on Vanua Levu, Viti Levu and Taveuni, but there is no explanation of their origins. The inscriptions are likewise a mystery to the local Fijian population and presumably are of ancient origin.

TURTLE ISLAND (NANUYA LEVU)
Turtle Island, about two km wide and several hundred metres long, is well known as one of Fiji's most exclusive resorts. It was the backdrop of the most recent version of the movie *Blue Lagoon*. The original *Blue Lagoon* was also filmed in the Yasawas just after WW II.

Turtle Island Resort (☎ 663 889; fax 790 007) bills itself as super-exclusive and has received rave reviews in the US press. For the substantial amount you pay to stay there, it should have. Owned by an American,

Richard Evanson, who struck it big in the cable-TV market, there are 14 units for couples only. The cost for a double is around F$640 per night, substantially less than it was only several years ago. Food and wine are reportedly excellent and guests are free to use sailboats, canoes, sailboards and horses at their leisure.

To get there you must take a 25-minute flight on Turtle Airways.

Ovalau

Ovalau is the principal island of the Lomaiviti group. Lomaiviti, which means 'central Fiji', accurately describes the location of this group of seven large islands and a few small ones in the geographic centre of the archipelago. With an aggregate area of 409 sq km, the group includes the islands of Ovalau, Gau, Nairai, Koro, Makogai, Wakaya and Batiki. Of these, Gau and Koro are among the most important of Fiji's purely volcanic islands, exceeded in size only by Taveuni and Kadavu.

From the standpoint of creature comforts, the group represents Fiji at its best. The islands' temperatures are mild, rainfall is moderate yet ample, and sunshine is plentiful. The villages of Lomaiviti, most of which are on the coasts, stand open to the wind.

On Ovalau there is no shortage of inexpensive accommodation. In Levuka there are a number of hotels and guest houses. On the other side of the island in Rukuruku is a budget resort with one of the few 'legitimate' camping areas in Fiji and the main beach area on the island. And there are offshore resorts on Mystery Island (Naigani), Caqelai, Leleuvia, and Lost Island (Yanuca Levu).

There are plenty of interesting historical sites, and good snorkelling and spearfishing in the harbour or offshore. For anyone with an inclination towards a quiet, bucolic setting, I highly recommend Ovalau.

History
The Lomaiviti group was first recorded by Captain Bligh of the *Bounty* in May 1789, less than a week after the mutiny. In 1792 he revisited the area in the HMS *Providence* to complete the survey that he had begun under less than ideal circumstances three years earlier.

As a historical footnote, Koro, Batiki and Gau were for a short time claimed by the US government, but were never occupied. In July 1867, when the USS *Tuscarora* visited

Levuka, the old capital of Fiji, in an attempt to settle Chief Cakobau's long-standing debt to the US commercial agent, John Brown Williams, these three islands were demanded as security for the promised payment. Two years later the money was paid, although neither on the due date nor by Cakobau himself, and US interest in the islands waned. (See Suva's History section for more details about this incident.)

Ovalau may justly be called the birthplace of modern Fiji. Levuka, the largest settlement on the island, was Fiji's first capital and in the mid-18th century was one of the main ports of call for trading ships and whalers throughout the South Pacific. Today the old capital is a quaint backwater – an archetypal South Seas port looking much the way it did at the turn of the century when Rudyard Kipling visited and wrote, 'The palmgrove's droned lament, Before Levuka's trade'.

Geography
Ovalau is roughly oval in shape, about 13 km in length and nearly 10 km wide; its area is about 100 sq km. Except for the **Lovoni Valley** in the middle of the island, and the areas at the mouths of the various streams, there is little flat land. The Lovoni Valley, covering about 18 sq km, was once a crater walled by naked rock. Today vegetation covers the earth and the valley is home to Lovoni villagers, a fiercely independent tribe who were one of the last peoples in Fiji to be subjugated.

The east coast in particular is rugged, with bluffs rising abruptly from the sea and sharp pinnacles thrusting their way into the skyline. Almost all the surface area is covered with dense vegetation. The highest peak on the island is the 625-metre-high Nadelaiovalau ('top of Ovalau'), which overlooks the east coast near Levuka. The northern end of the island is dominated by

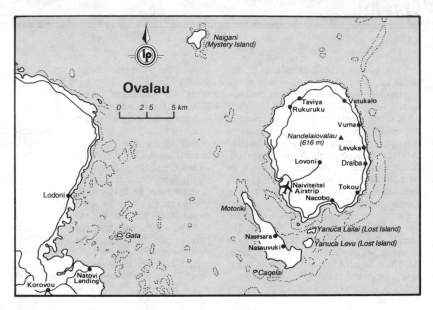

the 526-metre high Tomuna, whose isolated position and sharply conical form are set against the more massive summits of Korotolutolu a short distance beyond.

Activities

Swimming Ovalau's best beach (a black-sand beach) is at Rukuruku. However, there is a rocky beach at the Ovalau Holiday Resort which can be used without charge. Ask permission at their 'Bula Bar'.

Fishing Fishing is permitted from Levuka Wharf. There's no charge, but make sure you ask permission from wharf security as you walk past. Free bait is available from Cafe Levuka, and don't forget to take your hat during the daytime.

Reef fishing (☎ 440 030) can be arranged for four to six people, at F$15 per person, including food from Cafe Levuka. Reef fishing takes place in the evenings, and on Saturdays during the day only.

Snorkelling Ned Fisher (☎ 440 013) has reef tours for snorkellers daily or on request. Reports on the tours have been excellent.

Tours Niumaia Turaganicolo is available to guide visitors to several destinations. He can be located around town in the mornings (check at restaurants during breakfast). Unfortunately, he is reputed to be overly persistent in selling his services sometimes, so you may have to be firm if you don't wish to hire him.

Trekking There is a multitude of hikes around Ovalau, most of which require a guide and are never taken by tourists. The more popular treks are from Levuka to Lovoni, Rukuruku to Lovoni and Ovalau Holiday Resort to Rukuruku.

Peter Taylor, a Fijian resident, recommends walking from the village of **Draiba** to Lovoni. The route was formerly a provincial road, but has been overgrown by weeds since the implementation of the bus service. The track itself is not easy to follow if you don't know the area, and Mr Taylor recommends a guide for first-time trekkers. Start early in the day, in time to take the 3 pm bus back to Levuka. The cost of a guide is around F$5 for half a day.

Mr Taylor also recommends a walk to **The Peak**, near Levuka, for an excellent view of the town, the reef and the islands. Follow Bath Rd (adjacent to Levuka Public School) past the swimming hole to the steel water tank. Turn left through the cassava patch and up the broad gully. The path is faint and you may need some local kids to guide you.

Local history walking tours with a knowledgeable guide, leave from the Levuka Community Centre. A F$3 donation is requested. Guided bush walks (two-person minimum) cost F$3 to The Peak and F$5 to Lovoni (including bus fare). Lunch can be arranged next door at Cafe Levuka. The walk from Levuka to Lovoni takes 3½ to 4½ hours. The path is generally clear but may be overgrown and very muddy in some areas. Bring your own water and provisions. A bus leaves Lovoni at about 2 pm to take you back to Levuka.

Climb the 199 steps behind the Methodist Conference Centre to the top of **Delana Hill** for excellent views (but don't disturb school in session at Delana Methodist High School at the top).

There are also several waterfalls within easy walking distance of town, however, the best is on the opposite side of the island. Make sure you bring your swimming gear on these expeditions. To visit the falls at **Nasosobu**, walk 20 minutes north of Levuka to Waitovu village, and ask for directions there.

Wailailai Falls near Vakadaci village can be accessed by walking 15 minutes north (through the village) and following the river. The best falls are at Rukuruku. Ask for a guide at Rukuruku village to get there.

Lost Island (Yanuca Lailai), between Ovalau and Motoriki, is a good destination for a day trip and is big enough for hiking. It's very quiet, with a simple bure that sleeps four or five people. The owners will prepare a very nice lovo. Book at the community centre before 9 am. Costs are F$1 for the bus

to the boat, F$12 for the boat and lunch, F$3 for a reef trip, F$5 for fishing and F$2 for mask hire. All prices include 10% tax.

GETTING THERE & AWAY
Air
Fiji Air has services from Suva to Ovalau twice a day for F$32 one way, $22 on a stand-by basis (mornings only). The flight is only 10 minutes long. The bus ride from the airstrip into town is about twice as long as the flight and costs F$3. The bus back to the airport departs from the Fiji Air office on Beach St; report to the office 1½ hours ahead of flight departure.

Boat
The Patterson Brothers' *Ovalau* or *Jubilee* depart daily (except Sundays) from Suva for Levuka. The fare is F$18.70 one way. See the Inter-Island Ferry section in the Getting Around chapter for full details.

Schedules are always subject to change, so call Patterson Brothers (the brothers in question are native sons of Levuka) in Suva (☎ 315 644) or in Levuka (☎ 440 125) for information.

Emosi's Shipping has a bus and luggage truck which leave from Suva's GPO daily except Sunday at 11 am, arriving in Bau Landing at noon. The boat from Bau Landing arrives in Leleuvia at 2 pm, then after a half-hour stopover, continues to Levuka, arriving at 4 pm. On the return leg, the boat departs Levuka Wharf at 8 am, and from Leleuvia at 10 am, arriving in Bau Landing at 11.30 am. The connecting bus gets back to the Suva GPO at 1 pm. From either Suva or Levuka to Leleuvia Island costs F$12; Suva to Levuka is F$15. For more information contact Shop No 8 at Union Plaza (☎ 312 445, 304 619) in Suva, or in Levuka, call the Old Capital Inn (☎ 440 057).

GETTING AROUND
Getting around Levuka is no problem. The town is so small that you can walk from one end to the other in 10 minutes at a brisk pace. Since no-one walks briskly in Levuka, figure on 15 minutes. There are always taxis avail-

able, and buses leave four times a day for the outer villages.

Two 10-speed mountain bikes may be rented for F$1.50 per hour from Cafe Levuka.

Those who wish to rent a car should contact Isobel Madhavan at Old Capital Rentals (☎ 440 100). A sedan is available for F$72 a day; cheques and credit cards are not accepted.

Around the Island

LEVUKA

Levuka, nestled at the base of a steep bluff on Ovalau's south-east coast, is a fascinating destination, well off the beaten tourist track. With weatherworn clapboard buildings, narrow streets and ever-friendly residents, it seems to hark back to an earlier time when one knew one's neighbours and life was much simpler. The feeling of the past is palpable in Levuka, so dense it can be smothering.

Levukans are intensely proud of their history and their town. Several years ago the Levuka Cultural & Historical Society was formed with the sole intent of preserving the town's architectural heritage. When one developer from Suva wanted to raze an old building and put up a flashy disco, his plan was bitterly attacked by the members of the society and eventually quashed by the town council. 'If he wants to build a disco,' said one resident, 'let him go back to Suva. We like things here just the way they are'.

Levuka, with a population of around 1500, can be seen in a relatively few hours by the ambitious traveller, but a stay of several days is recommended to really savour its 'lost-in-time' ambience.

History

Its natural harbour and anchorage set the stage for the first traders who arrived in the early 1830s. These early settlers were a mixed bag. Some were honest and industrious and built small sailing vessels for trading in the outer islands, while others were shiftless bounders or opportunists looking for an easy buck. Among the earliest settlers was David Whippy, a Connecticut sailor who jumped ship and eventually became one of the leading citizens of the town. Whippy acted as an adviser to the local chief and served as a translator to Commandant Wilkes during his expedition to the islands. The offspring of these original settlers, many of whom took Fijian spouses, were the beginning of Levuka's part-European, or creole, society.

In 1844 some of the settlers offended the paramount chief, who banished them from his territory; but five years later they were allowed to return and re-establish the settlement. Despite raids and burnings by the Lovoni tribespeople, Levuka grew and flourished. Joining the early traders were cotton growers who came during the brief cotton boom of the 1860s, coconut planters, missionaries and professionals. Soon Levuka's beachfront street (known as Beach St) was crowded with shops, shanties, offices, boarding houses and saloons. The growing number of permanent residents built homes on the hillsides and reached them by steps that were, and still are, Levuka's 'streets'. By 1870 the population exceeded 800.

Ships from every nation crowded the harbour and the bars were bubbling with sailors of every nationality, awash with gin. An early issue of the *Fiji Times* described the atmosphere thus:

We have had rows enough during the last week to satisfy everyone for two fortnights, and if broken heads, black eyes and narrow escapes from a Japanese disembowelling with the broadsword, or a few gentle prickings with a fourteen-inch ham slicer are not sufficient to make us all go about with revolvers in our belts, as many of the more cautious do, yet they make us all wish either for a magistrate that would be a terror to evildoers, or for a beacon to sweep the beach of the drink maddened ruffian.

Unfortunately there was no magistrate in those days because there was no government. In 1871 there was an attempt to form a local government with Chief Cakobau as

Top: Taveuni sunset (RK)
Bottom: Schoolboys (IO)

Top Left: River near Bouma village, Taveuni (RK)
Top Right: Somosomo, Taveuni (RK)
Bottom Left: Fijian fisherwoman (RK)
Bottom Right: Fijian artifacts (JW)

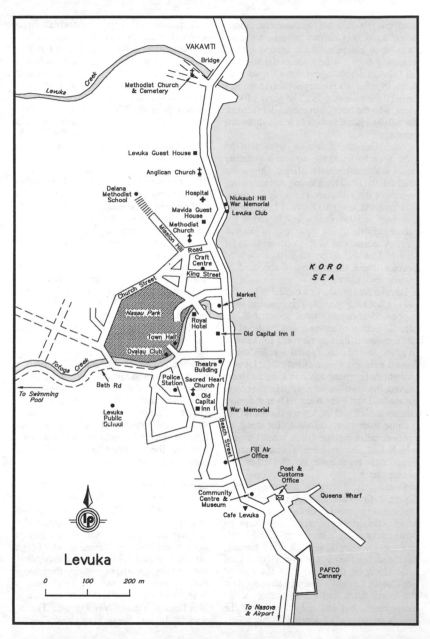

VAKAVITI

Bridge

Methodist Church
& Cemetery

Levuka Creek

Levuka Guest House ■

Anglican Church ✝

Delana
Methodist
School ●

Hospital ✚

Mavida Guest
House ■

Methodist
Church ✝

Mission Hill

Niukaubi Hill
War Memorial ■
Levuka Club

KORO
SEA

Craft
Centre △

Church Street

King Street

Nasau Park

Market ●

Royal
Hotel ■

Old Capital Inn II ■

Town Hall ■

Ovalau Club ■

Totoga Creek

Theatre
Building

Police
Station ■

Bath Rd

To Swimming
Pool

Sacred Heart
Church ✝

Old
Capital
Inn I ■   War Memorial ■

Levuka
Public
School ●

Beach Street

Fiji Air
Office ●

Post &
Customs
Office ✉

Queens Wharf

Community
Centre &
Museum ●

Cafe Levuka ▾

Levuka

0   100   200 m

PAFCO
Cannery

To Nasova
& Airport

head, but this only led to discontent, culminating in riots. Cakobau was under great pressure to compensate for looting claims stemming from a 4 July fire at the home of the US commercial agent, John Brown Williams. (See Suva's History section in the Viti Levu chapter for details.) The grave of Williams, who did not live to see the debt settled, can still be visited in the old Methodist cemetery.

While Cakobau stalled on payment of the debt, anarchy filled the air and a potential race war loomed over the islands. The ageing chief felt the need for a strong outside power to control the situation. His wish for peace was realised on 10 October 1874, when Cakobau and his fellow chiefs ceded the country to Britain and the colony of Fiji was born. A monument to this occasion can be seen in Nasova, the small village south of Levuka where the signing of the deed of cession took place.

Levuka became the first capital of Fiji, but did not last long as such. The founders were concerned about the need to expand the capital. Because the town was confined by cliffs, there really was no room for Levuka to grow. In 1881 the capital was shifted to Suva. Levukans were a chauvinistic lot who thought that even though the capital had been moved, the town would always be the centre for trade. They were wrong. Over the years businesses left and the town's economic life became ever more difficult. The *coup de grâce* came in the late 1950s when Levuka, which had always been a transshipment point for the copra trade, lost that last dribble of commerce.

Fortunately, through negotiations with a Japanese firm, the townspeople brought a fish cannery into Levuka which provided jobs for fisherfolk and workers and kept the community going. The several small hotels and guest houses do provide some income, but the scale of tourism is so small that it has little effect on the welfare of the general population. Levuka's isolation has kept it off the tourist track and out of the economic mainstream, but has helped preserve the town's architectural integrity.

A number of Fiji's historical firsts occurred in Levuka: the first public school was established there in 1879; the first Masonic Lodge in the Pacific Islands was founded there in 1875; Fiji's first newspaper, the *Fiji Times*, was founded there in 1869; and the first bank, the Bank of New Zealand, opened there in 1876. Of these, the school and the lodge still stand, as does the oldest operating hotel in the South Pacific, the Royal Hotel, opened in the late 1850s.

Levuka Community Centre & Museum

This completely revamped storehouse originally belonged to Morris Hedstrom & Co, a trading company established in the early days of Levuka and still in business in Fiji. The first-rate rebuilding was carried out by local craftspeople under the auspices of the Levuka Cultural & Historical Society, financed by donations of time, money, labour and materials from businesses and individuals throughout Fiji. The structure, originally built in 1878, was given by Morris Hedstrom to the National Trust of Fiji in 1980. It was refurbished with salvaged oregon timber from a nearby storage shed and now houses a branch of the Fiji Museum, a public library, crafts centre, kindergarten, squash court and meeting hall. It represents the evident desire of Levuka's residents to have their town remain a living museum. Historical tours of the town can be organised through the museum for F$3 for an hour. Guided treks to Lovoni can also be arranged through the community centre (see the earlier Activities section).

Queens Wharf

Levuka is one of Fiji's three official ports of entry (Lautoka and Suva are the other two) and the wharf has recently been upgraded. It is used by local and sometimes foreign vessels and has a maximum depth of eight metres alongside. The harbour entrance is indicated by a pile light, marking the passage through the barrier reef. In the distance is Wakaya Island, scene of the capture of Count Von Luckner during WW I (see the History section in the Facts about the Country chapter) and now subdivided for expensive homes. To the left is the island of Makogai, which until recent years was a leper hospital.

The entrance to the wharf area, which is adjacent to the Levuka Community Centre, also houses the post office, customs office and the Port Authority of Fiji office. A drinking fountain on Beach St, directly opposite the post office, was once the site of a carrier-pigeon loft which in the late 1800s was the Levuka terminal of a pigeon postal service to Suva. The birds covered the 65-km distance in about 30 minutes. Check out nearby **Patterson Park**, where you can rest, snack and watch the wharf activity.

Pacific Fishing Company (PAFCO)

Founded in 1964 by a Japanese firm, PAFCO is used as a centre for freezing and exporting canned tuna mostly to Europe and Canada. A joint venture with the Fijian government, the cannery was opened in 1976 and is the primary private employer on the island. The deal to bring the facility to Levuka was put together by local citizens when copra shipments were diverted from the port for economic reasons. This act saved the town from economic extinction.

Nasova

A km south of the wharf (towards the airport) is the village of Nasova where Fiji's deed of cession was signed on 10 October 1874. The signing took place in government house, which was below the residence of the district commissioner. On the seaward side of the road, beyond a small creek, is a fence surrounding what are known as the three 'cession stones' (and a flagpole), which commemorate the centenary of that ceremony in 1974 and Fiji's independence on 10 October 1970. The large bure (known as the 'Prince Charles Bure') across the road from the memorial is used for ceremonial purposes and was built in 1970 for Prince Charles' visit. He used it for a headquarters during his sojourn in Levuka. It is built on the site of an earlier bure where King George V (then Duke of Clarence) resided during a visit to Fiji in the 1890s. Two other stones near the

flagpole mark Prince Charles' visits for Fiji's centenary and independence celebrations.

Beach St

In Levuka's early days, Beach St was only 'a narrow strip of shingly beach' between a row of houses, built close to the water's edge – a ramshackle collection of shacks, bars and makeshift businesses. Today the saloons that lined the street are gone, but the peeling, columned storefronts and weatherworn clapboard buildings have somehow withstood the ravages of time. The present sidewalk is the result of linking the verandas of the original buildings. In recent years the town council learned that the title to the walkway it had been maintaining all these years belonged to the owners of the property.

Sacred Heart Church

This was built by the Marist Fathers, who, led by Father Breheret, established themselves in Levuka in 1858. The church boasts a French clock that strikes twice each hour, with a one-minute pause in between. Instead of a chime or a clang the clock produces a most unmusical 'thud'. Note the neon green cross on the church. It is not, as one observer pointed out simply 'bad taste'. Rather, it is used (along with another green neon sign on a building behind the church) to mark the gap in the reef so that ships can navigate this dangerous crossing by night.

Levuka Public School

Opened in 1879, this is the oldest public school in Fiji, and the old school of many of Fiji's leaders. Although it has been maintained in past years, it unfortunately seems to be falling into disrepair.

Totoga Falls

Totoga Creek is the source of fresh water for Levuka. The creek has several swimming holes, one of which is lined with concrete. The concrete pool is now closed due to a huge fallen stone that makes its home there. The other swimming holes are accessible by continuing up the trail known as 'Bath Rd' adjacent to the Levuka Public School.

Nasau Park
This is Levuka's sports field, parade ground and all-purpose grassy area. The rooms to the rear of the Royal Hotel face directly onto the field.

Ovalau Club
The home of one of the oldest social organisations in the South Pacific, this whitewashed clapboard structure surrounded by a white picket fence was once a bastion of White colonials, but the only remnant of that era is a 'Members Only' sign on the entrance. This can be disregarded by visitors, who are genuinely welcomed and will be served perhaps the coldest beer on sale in Fiji. The bar still has a historic letter written by the WW I German sea raider Count Von Luckner, who was captured on nearby Wakaya Island. The story behind the Von Luckner letter is a fascinating piece of historical trivia.

Von Luckner, who abandoned ship after his vessel ran aground elsewhere, landed in a small launch on Katafaga Island in the Lau group. He broke into the home of a trader, 'liberated' some food and wrote a thank you note explaining to the absent owner that he was sorry about the missing food, but that he was on a South Seas sporting cruise and in need of provisions. The conscientious count left some money for the goods and signed the letter 'Max Pemberton'.

Town Hall
Constructed in 1898 in honour of Queen Victoria's jubilee, the town hall is home to the offices of the Levuka Town Council, Fiji's oldest municipality, created in 1877.

Masonic Lodge
This is the home of Lodge Polynesia 562 SC, founded in 1875, and is the oldest lodge in the South Pacific.

Royal Hotel
The Royal is the oldest operating hotel in the South Pacific. Resembling a roadhouse out of the US old west, the 125-year-old hotel is the last remaining one of more than 50 bars and saloons built in Levuka's heyday. It was rebuilt around the turn of the century by

Captain David Robbie, a retired seaman who thickened the walls so they would withstand hurricanes. Atop the roof is a turret-like structure known as a 'widow's watch' or ship's lookout. Just across from the front entrance is Levuka's small municipal market which is open from 6 am every Saturday.

Mission Hill
Atop Mission Hill are some of Levuka's finest old buildings, including Methodist mission homes and the Delana Methodist School. To climb the 199 steps to the top, begin at the historic Methodist church. The vista from the hill is worth the climb. At the foot of Mission Hill is the Levuka Government Hospital.

Niukaubi Hill
Niukaubi Hill is the site of one of Levuka's two war memorials. (The other is on Beach St, opposite the Sacred Heart Church.) The supreme court building and parliament house were on Niukaubi Hill. On the other side of a small boat harbour is an area once occupied by the Levuka Mechanics Institute, Levuka's principal recreational centre before and at the time of cession.

Holy Redeemer Church
The Reverend William Floyd, who came to Fiji in 1870, built the first Anglican church on this spot. The present church was consecrated in 1904. Stained-glass windows commemorate early Levuka residents.

Levuka Fijian Village
This village was home to Tui Levuka, the chief who first befriended early European settlers. On the opposite side of a small creek is a Methodist church, constructed in 1869, where Chief Cakobau once worshipped.

Old Methodist Cemetery
Here lie the remains of at least 135 of Levuka's early settlers, many of them German immigrants. The most famous resident of this graveyard is John Brown Williams, the somewhat unscrupulous US commercial agent whose exaggerated finan-

cial claims helped cause the downfall of the Cakobau government and were a major factor in the cession of Fiji to Britain.

Gun Rock

This point above Levuka village was used in 1849 as a target by the HMS *Havannah* to impress upon Chief Cakobau the power of the warship's cannon. It is said to be where the first Europeans spent their first night ashore. The rock was again battered by naval guns in 1874 by Commodore Goodenough to entertain Fijian chiefs in Levuka. Visitors who inspect the rock can still see the scars left by cannonballs. In a more peaceful vein, Roman Catholic missionary Father Breheret said his first mass beneath the shelter of Gun Rock after his arrival in Levuka in 1858.

Vagadaci

Lying beyond Gun Rock, the village of Vagadaci became headquarters of the Royal Engineers who built the town of Levuka (and later Suva) as well as the roads after cession. The area was also a boat-building centre. The concrete ruins of a large house were once the home of the Palmer family who were boat builders and merchants. King George V (then the Duke of Clarence) and his brother played cricket at Vagadaci, but much of the old sports field is now occupied by the homes of government employees.

Places to Stay

All the places listed here are downright inexpensive compared to most places in Fiji, or anywhere else in the world for that matter. Ovalau has simply not been discovered by the moneyed set and lacks the beaches on the populated side of the island to make it a desirable locale for large-scale resort development.

Places to Stay – Levuka

The *Royal Hotel* (☎ 444 024) is a landmark in its own right and the most up-market of Levuka's accommodation. Constructed in the 1850s, it has been managed by the Ashleys, a local part-European family, for two generations. Never mind that the hot water isn't so hot or an American Express card is an unknown entity there. The 'Royal' is the place to stay in Levuka. It's loaded with atmosphere, found in such particulars as an old-style balcony facing the cliffs, polished brass shell casings for ashtrays, a long staircase, a haunted room and a century-old billiard table in excellent shape. The Ashleys, who are very kind people, do run a restaurant but you must tell them ahead of time whether or not you're eating at the hotel for dinner. Meal prices are moderate (F$6.50 for dinner). Unfortunately, not all of the staff members are equally helpful to visitors, so you might need to seek the 'right' employee to assist you when you arrive. Note that the Royal's bar is reserved for hotel guests only.

The hotel has 14 rooms and two dorms, one each for men and women, with room for 12 in each. Singles/doubles cost F$14/19; triples F$25 and a dorm bed is F$6. A double with a fridge is F$21, and a day room (from 10 am to 3 pm) is half-price.

The Royal is associated with Lost Island Resort, an offshore lodging (see the later section on Lost Island Resort). The hotel also offers day trips to Lovoni village for F$12, which includes lunch.

Also associated with the Royal Hotel are two houses in Levuka: one has three rooms and shared facilities for F$14/19/25 a single/double/triple; the other is an entire self-contained two-bedroom home with a fridge, gas stove and hot and cold water for F$50 a night.

The *Mavida Guest House* (☎ 440 051), run by the Thomas family, is also clean, hospitable and inexpensive, and it oozes with local history and atmosphere. 'Mavida' (pronounced Mavinda) was an elusive night-blooming flower from Verata (in Viti Levu) which a Fijian princess took to Naigani as a remembrance. The current manager, Irene Thomas, delights in sharing stories connected with the various rooms and their furnishings, such as that of Lord Charles Wimbledon Thomas entertaining King George V and many others. She may even entertain you by playing the piano if you're lucky (she used to play professionally). In this graceful old house, with such accoutrements as filigree ceiling vents, what Irene doesn't tell, you can close your eyes and imagine. You can also enjoy the luxury of hot water in the shared bathroom, fans in all rooms, and real beds in the dormitory.

Built in 1869, the guest house is older than the Royal Hotel, and is on Beach St, next to the Thomas' family home. Rates are from F$6.60 in the dorm, and from F$10/16 for singles/doubles, including breakfast. There's also a self-contained unit for F$25. Lunch and dinner are available by pre-arrangement at modest cost. Activities include tours to Lovoni (where you have breakfast in the crater) or to Rukuruku for swimming and snorkelling. Friday nights are for parties – lovo night, tamare night etc – bring yaqona (kava) if you wish. The only criticism of this guest house has been the occasional comment by a guest that Irene's strong personality is too much like their mother's. But would your mother greet you with a cold beer upon arrival?

The *Levuka Guest House* (☎ 440 094), run by Emosi Yee Show's older brother Luna, provides simple accommodation in a single, double or triple room. Reports have been mixed at best; sometimes rooms are rented out to local fishermen who tend to be loud, drunk and generally not the kind of people you dream of spending your holiday with. The guest house is on Beach St, near the northernmost Methodist church. Rooms cost F$3 per person. Unfortunately this house and this section of town have become a bit ramshackle.

The *Old Capital Inn I* (☎ 440 057) is run by Mrs Mary Show whose husband, Emosi Yee Show, runs Leleuvia Island Resort. While it is a place to stay, rooms are often filled with local workers, and travellers are advised to go to Old Capital Inn II. Old Capital Inn I contains a quiet, licensed restaurant which is open for breakfast, lunch and supper and offers tasty Chinese and European dishes at modest prices. The Sunday buffet has 13 items for F$6.00.

The *Old Capital Inn II* (☎ 440 013), on Beach St, is sort of an annex to the original Capital Inn and is run by the Shows' daughter Lela. It has a dorm, plus individual rooms which are more comfortable for couples or families. The shared bathroom has two cold-water showers (bring your own shaving mirror), and there's a video deck in the communal sitting room. The Old Capital Inn II is a quiet and congenial place to stay. Rates are F$6.90 in the dorm, and F$9.90/16.90 for private singles/doubles, and include tax and breakfast (served at the Old Capital Inn I).

Places to Stay – around Ovalau

The *Ovalau Holiday Resort* (☎ 440 329), formerly a copra plantation, is about five km north of Levuka. It has seven chalet-style units, four of which are self-contained. The resort nestles in a shady palm grove at the base of a hill facing a small coral-sand beach and a 100-year-old lighthouse, the oldest in Fiji. Snorkelling equipment is available for F$2 per day (bring reef-walking shoes). Amenities include a pool, shower, toilet, washing machine, refrigerator and gas burner. You can eat at the bar/restaurant in a recently rebuilt 100-year-old whaler's cottage specialising in Fijian food, or fend for yourself. The resort also has a boat for fishing.

Transport by taxi from the resort to town is about F$4, or on foot, it's a 50-minute walk. Rates are F$6.50 in the dorm, F$20/40 for singles/triples, and F$55 in a four-bed room. You may also pitch a tent for F$8 a double, and there is a brand new villa for F$95 per night. Car rental is F$30 a day or F$50 for a weekend.

Rukuruku Resort (☎ 444 329) is on the opposite side of the island, about an hour's bus ride from the booming metropolis of Levuka. It is a beautiful and isolated location, with a beach and rainforest nearby. Lorries also depart from the monument opposite Paak Kum Loong Restaurant on Beach St at 7.45, 11.30 am and 5.00 pm on weekdays. The fare is F$1.20. Taxis are also available.

This modest resort is good for families and has one of the few 'official' camping grounds on the island, complete with shower and toilet facilities. There is a small restaurant on the premises with prices that begin at F$3 for a continental breakfast. The restaurant is reportedly overpriced and the quality is inconsistent, so bringing your own food to supplement the restaurant's may not be a bad idea. There is also a bar on the grounds. Perhaps the nicest thing about Rukuruku is the black-sand beach which is the best on the island. Snorkelling and spearfishing are excellent. Other attractions include good trekking, a lovely waterfall, a boat for hire, and sunbathing. There are six bures (which can accommodate four people) at F$60 per unit, a three-bedroom cottage which costs F$15 per person, and dorm accommodation for F$7 (including breakfast). A camp site and tent costs F$5 per night, F$3 if you have your own tent. A single-burner stove is provided for campers' use.

Places to Eat

The restaurant situation is much better in Levuka than it was in years past, and there are now several excellent and inexpensive eateries, all on Beach St.

Paak Kum Loong, open Monday to Saturday from 8 am to 2 pm and 6 to 8.30 pm, has Chinese, Indian and European dishes for F$2 to F$5. The food is as good as anything served in Suva.

Others include *Deepak's Curry House*, open Monday to Saturday from 8 am to 9 pm, which serves Indian food; *Kim's Restaurant*, which serves Chinese food from Monday to Saturday, 8 am to 2 pm and 6 to 8.30 pm and the *Old Capital Inn I*, which is open daily from 8 am to 10 pm serving Fijian, European and Chinese food (book dinner before 5 pm for best service). There is also *Community Centre Takeaways*, open weekdays from 8 am to 2 pm, which is an outdoor eatery in Patterson's Gardens (adjacent to the community centre) and serves 'local' Indian, Chinese and Fijian dishes.

From all reports, the premier spot in town is *Cafe Levuka*, (☎ 440 095), snuggled modestly next to the community centre. Owner Kathy Hoare escaped here from the highly competitive San Francisco restaurant scene,

bringing all her cooking skills with her. The menu is 'California Cuisine' (lots of fresh vegies and other local ingredients in deliciously creative new combinations) plus breads, juices and ice creams, all lovingly home-made. Kathy insists upon using only local ingredients, often cleverly adapting her favourite recipes to Fiji's food bounty.

The restaurant also contains a book exchange which has some interesting titles, an aquarium with local denizens (like hatchling turtles) in temporary residence, bicycle rental, carefully selected wines, free fishing bait, and travellers' cheque cashing. There's also abundant helpful information about everything there is to see and do in town. The restaurant is open from 7 am to 8 pm daily; a three-course dinner costs F$7. It is also one of the few places in Fiji where people understand how to brew a real cup of coffee. Don't miss it, even if you're not hungry.

Entertainment

Levuka residents have the dubious distinction of consuming more alcohol per capita than people anywhere else in the Fiji islands. During a beer strike several years ago their stockpile of Fiji Bitter held out for the entire duration of the labour dispute, keeping them happy while the rest of the nation ran dry.

Adjacent to the town hall is the venerable *Ovalau Club*, a whitewashed clapboard structure and one of the finest watering holes in the entire South Pacific. Above the dance floor is a portrait of Queen Elizabeth II (circa 1957) and various other members of the British royal family – who Fijians seem to be crazy about. The Ovalau Club, once an exclusively White colonial hang-out, is no longer an austere bastion of the British Empire's faithful servants. Chances are that after one hour in this convivial hang-out you will learn enough about Levuka's inhabitants to last a lifetime. Don't be surprised if bottles of beer suddenly appear at your table. People buy one another quite a bit of beer at the Ovalau Club.

The second drinking establishment is the *Levuka Club*, on Beach St. The Levuka Club is also a fine place to drink, but is a newer structure and doesn't seem to have the character of the Ovalau Club.

OFFSHORE ISLAND RESORTS

Each of the following offshore islands has a different flavour. The party crowd will probably enjoy Leleuvia, while those favouring a more tranquil atmosphere might consider one of the other spots.

Mystery Island

Mystery Island (☎ 440 364; 300 925 for boat pick-up) is the name of an attractive, up-market, out-of-the-way resort on Naigani Island, eight km north-west of Ovalau and about 10 km from Tailevu Point on the main island of Viti Levu. The resort has 12 villas (all with cooking and refrigeration facilities) and a dorm unit with 10 beds and cooking facilities. Mystery Island thus combines comfortable accommodation for older visitors not interested in 'roughing it' and up-market dorm facilities for the younger crowd. Snorkelling here is excellent and there are canoes to paddle about in, big-game fishing, windsurfing and water-skiing. A three-night package, including boat transport and meals costs F$200, a dorm bed is F$15. Singles/doubles in the villas are F$70/90.

Wakaya Island

Wakaya, a private island 20 minutes by powerboat from Levuka, is an exclusive resort and millionaires' retreat. A handful of the rich and famous have built homes here, and there is a modern infrastructure of roads, docking facilities and even an airstrip. Everything works, everything runs smoothly and, aside from the friendly Fijians who work there, Wakaya bears little resemblance to the rest of Fiji. If you wish to stay on the island, the place to visit is the *Wakaya Club* (☎ 440 128; 213 468 9100 in the USA). For a mere US$675 (F$875 a double), you may reside in an exquisite, 1137-sq-metre bungalow with bedroom, living room and deluxe bathroom. Rates cover all meals, alcoholic and non-alcoholic beverages and use of the club's extensive, first-rate sporting facilities.

These activities include golf (played on a nine-hole course), tennis, croquet, scuba diving, windsurfing, glass-bottom boat excursions and fishing.

The Wakaya Club is the brainchild of gold-mining entrepeneur, David Harrison Gilmour, who bought the island in 1973 for a song, and over the last 20 years has put in 22 km of roads, a freshwater reservoir, marina, jetty, village, church, and a school. Indeed, he needed to tap a few ounces of gold dust to build this tasteful eight-bure complex as well. Evidently, a lot of time and scrupulous attention to detail went into Club Wakaya.

Because Wakaya is privately owned, permission is needed before yachts may anchor or visitors come ashore. Guests visiting Wakaya from a yacht must reserve one cottage per night for each couple coming ashore.

Transfers to and from Nadi and Suva are provided by Air Wakaya, the Club's own Britten Norman Islander aircraft. The return fare is US$350 from Nadi and US$200 from Suva, plus the 10% tax. Write to 6525 Sunset Blvd, 2nd Floor, Hollywood, CA, USA for more information.

Caqelai

Visitors with more modest vacation plans should consider *Caqelai*, run by Fijians under the auspices of a Methodist church group from the island of Motoriki. Fringed with very good white-sand beaches Caqelai (Thahn' ghel ai) is yet another option for overnight trippers. Costs (including three meals) are F$14 for a tent, F$16 for a dorm bed, and F$20 for a bure. The food is reportedly very good. Transport from Levuka is F$10; the boat leaves at 10.30 or 11 am, Monday to Saturday. Meet near the Fiji Electricity Authority (FEA) station on Beach St and book at Paak Kum Loong Restaurant. There are 10 bures, whose windows are lined with mosquito netting and two dorms. No beer is sold on the island, but you may bring your own. There is also a small shop. It's a friendly and beautiful place with good snorkelling, and you will be returned to Viti

Levu by boat for F$13. The island has electricity and according to one reader 'real' toilets as well as freshwater wells. Occupancy is limited to 25 people.

Leleuvia Island

Leleuvia Island Resort is a 6.8-hectare islet, shaped entirely of white sand. Emosi Yee Show, an enterprising man of Fijian and Chinese extraction, is the resort's owner and is a most engaging character who will take you out snorkelling or spearfishing, lead you to the eating/partying pavilion or motor you around the island in one of his eight boats. Where Emosi is, the fun is. And after a few days at the island (probably less), you can't help but feel like a member of the family. Indeed, more than one visitor has refused to leave this idyllic refuge until reality (like an expiring visa) has forced them to do so.

The resort consists of five dorm-style bures, plus 17 small private bures. Emosi plans to build several more of each plus upgrade existing facilities to include tiled showers. Perhaps the most intriguing unit of all is the upper room of the two-storey bure. With its veranda overlooking the jewel-coloured lagoon through a big, shady tree (which is visited by several species of birds)

it is very much like being in a tree house. Mosquito nets allow unscreened windows to remain open to the soft sea breeze at night. (Mosquito coils will be provided on request, if you prefer them.) Electricity is restricted to the communal area after dark, so dwellings are lit subtly with hurricane lamps. The island's well pumps brackish water for showers and laundry, but fresh drinking water is brought daily from Levuka. You must supply your own toilet paper for the shared 'bucket toilets' (a bucket of water provides the flush) which are kept reasonably clean. Nevertheless, flies abound. All necessary supplies, and some you'd never have thought of, are available at the canteen. Cold soft drinks and beer and even milk are plentiful. Meals are basic but tasty, with plenty of fresh ingredients, and sometimes there are home-made buns for breakfast. After supper, the employees form a band to get you singing and dancing, or just to serenade your journal writing.

The sea is bath-water warm on one side of the island, more refreshing on the other, and you can sunbathe around the island's entire perimeter. Snorkelling is good (equipment may be rented for F$2.50 a day), and a PADI scuba instructor leads daily boat trips for divers (lessons and gear available) and snorkellers. If water sports are too strenuous, bring a hammock to dream away a warm day or stroll to the 'cannibal pot' through the forest. For a special treat, don't miss the stars on a moonless night or create your own stars by tossing a handful of sand into the water's edge and watching the microscopic noctilucae glitter for a few seconds.

Rates per person (including three meals) are F$15 for a tent, F$17 in the dorm and F$20/25 in a bure/bungalow. Boats from Levuka or Suva cost F$10; see the earlier Getting There & Away section for more details.

Around Leleuvia Island

If you are coming from Suva and take Emosi's Shipping from Bau Landing, the vessel passes very close to chiefly **Bau Island** – as near as one is allowed without a personal invitation from one of its residents. Ratu Sir George Cakobau's tomb and other features are clearly visible, as are nearby fish fences. Several species of sea birds may be viewed during the trip.

For the adventurous romantic, there is tiny white **Honeymoon Isle**, a mere dot of an islet with one tree which looks like a cartoon scene for a shipwreck. By special arrangement with Emosi, you can spend a night there 'al fresco'. This is about as remote as one can get in the modern world!

A Sunday **church service**, for the faithful, is available by taking a boat ride to neighbouring Motoriki Island, and is followed by lunch in the village. Arrange this with Emosi by Saturday night; there is a minimum of six people.

At the full moon in early September, female **hawksbill turtles** lumber onto Leleuvia's beaches to lay eggs. Then in the second week of December, baby turtles hatch and attempt to scamper into the sea before being eaten by sea birds. It's quite an amazing sight.

Lost Island (Yanuca Levu)

There is a third off-island lodging (this one associated with the Royal Hotel) called *Lost Island Resort* (Yanuca Levu is the proper name) and it is the closest offshore island to Levuka. It is owned and operated by Levi Gio, who picks people up at the Royal Hotel and takes them to his island for a round-trip fare of F$2. Reef trips are available for F$3. Given its proximity to Levuka, the island is popular as a day trip.

Accommodation consists of clean and comfortable bures, dorm facilities and tents. Three meals a day are available for only F$7.50 and if there are at least four people interested, Levi will cook a lovo for F$5 each. The bures have thick foam mats and there is a private 'kitchen' if you wish to cook on your own. Prices are F$4 to pitch a tent, F$5 for a dorm bunk and F$6 per person for a bure.

There is also a beach, and activities such as fishing, if you are so inclined. Be sure to bring your own snorkelling gear, however, as none is available. Keep in mind that swimming from the beach is limited to high tide. During low tide it's possible to walk around the island in an hour but there are also trails within the island. The 'resort' includes the home of Levi's middle son, his wife and daughter. There are no other residents on the island.

Lost Island Resort is much smaller than Leleuvia but is also much less crowded. One reader called it more of a quiet 'vacation spot' than Leleuvia which, because of it's popularity, is 'overrun' by 40 to 60 travellers at a time. Information is available by calling the Royal Hotel (☎ 444 024).

LOVONI

Lovoni village is in the crater of an extinct volcano. Early residents of Levuka feared the Lovoni tribespeople, who burned the town down on several occasions and were well known for their ferocity. The tribe was subdued only by treachery. In a peace offering by Chief Cakobau the warriors were invited to Levuka and seized while they were unarmed. They were then forcibly scattered around the Fiji group where they wouldn't present a security risk. Only much later were they allowed to return home.

To this day they are a fierce lot. Several years ago a land dispute caused them to don their war paint and gather their clubs. The dispute was settled peacefully, but not before the tribespeople made their wishes known by blocking the road and forcing the landlord in question (accompanied by a policeman in a jeep) to turn back. You can visit the village by catching a bus or carrier in Levuka (for about F$2) and getting off at the bridge. Be sure to bring some yaqona (there are several grog shops in town) or some food items as a sevusevu. When going to the village it's best to get a youngster or another resident to take you across the bridge and lead you into the community. Many of the villagers come into town during the day and chances are that you will meet someone if you ask around.

Vanua Levu

Vanua Levu, with a population of approximately 130,000, is the second-largest island of the Fiji archipelago and is only 64 km north-east of Viti Levu. Although very near Viti Levu geographically, it is a long way from there in its development – particularly that of its tourism infrastructure – and is little-known to the average visitor. This is changing, however, because the introduction of ferry services has made it easy and inexpensive to commute to and from the capital. An added advantage of having a ferry service is that the visitor can rent a car in Suva, take it across on the boat and then drive along the very beautiful (and mostly sealed) road from Savusavu to Labasa or along the Hibiscus Highway, which follows the southern coast from Savusavu.

Because the island is such virgin territory for the visitor and the local economy does not totally rely on tourism, residents are particularly friendly and interested in strangers. Vanua Levu offers the guest an ideal opportunity to observe relatively untarnished island life. Compared to the range of accommodation on Viti Levu, there are fewer places to stay on Vanua Levu. Most of the island's resorts are in the old copra port of Savusavu in the south and in the Taveuni area. The sugar-mill town of Labasa, though the largest metropolitan area in the north, has few places to stay. The offshore islands of Taveuni, Qamea, Matagi and Laucala also have small hotels.

History

The first European to visit the Vanua Levu region was Abel Tasman, who in 1643 navigated off the eastern portion of the island's coast. Captain Bligh was the next explorer to visit, dauntlessly sailing past the southwestern portion of Vanua Levu in 1789 following the mutiny on the *Bounty*. Captain James Wilson, skippering the missionary ship *Duff*, added to the discoveries of Bligh

and Tasman when he explored the region in 1797, narrowly escaping the reefs that had nearly ended Tasman's journey.

Vanua Levu did not receive much attention until sandalwood traders began exploiting sandalwood thickets in the Bua Bay area around 1805. Ten years later the island's sandalwood resources were depleted and only the occasional whaler or bêche-de-mer trader came looking for supplies.

The first European to make it into the hill country of Vanua Levu was a young sailor by the name of Jackson, who late in 1840 jumped ship at Somosomo, leaving a crew of 'freebooters' he evidently did not trust. He was adopted by the local chief and accompanied a war party to Maucata. In doing so, he explored the northern and eastern arms of the island. Jackson, however, seemed more interested in making inroads into the lives of some of the young women than in taking notes about the countryside. Despite these distractions, much of what was known about these areas up to 1850 was due to Jackson's descriptions.

Most of the settlers who arrived from the Australian and New Zealand colonies in the 1860s went to Ovalau and Viti Levu. Those who settled on Vanua Levu usually went to the Savusavu area, which became a centre for coconut plantations. The planters in this area mixed with the local population to create a creole society, and many became wealthy from copra sales. Their riches were lost in the crash of the 1930s, which depressed the price of copra and from which they never recovered. Meanwhile, the industrious Indian community to the north created the thriving sugar town of Labasa – an area that shows the most promise for economic growth today.

Geography

Vanua Levu is about half the size of Viti Levu, with an area of 5538 sq km. The squiggly, irregularly shaped island is up to 180 km long and from 30 to 50 km wide. Geologically, it is a complicated structure, evidently having been formed by the amalgamation of several volcanic islands whose coasts melded during successive stages of uplift. A rugged mountain range runs from one end of the main part of the island to the other, but it is discontinuous and does not divide the land symmetrically. On each side of the island are equally precipitous parallel ranges with lowlands in between. The highest point on the island is Batini (Nasorolevu), which is 1111 metres high and about 13 km from the southern coast. It is followed by Dikeva (Mt Thurston), which is 1030 metres high and about 16 km to the north-east of Batini.

The principal ranges stand near the windward (southern) coasts, causing most of the rain to fall on that side of the island. Like Viti Levu's western side, the north of Vanua Levu is dry eight months of the year, making it ideal for growing sugar cane, the area's major agricultural product.

Between Bua (the south-west portion of the island where sandalwood was harvested in the 1880s) and Lekutu to the north is an area the Fijians call *talasiga*, which means 'sunburnt land'. This rain shadow is barren, with desert-like vegetation and arid soil. Just east of this region is the Seatovo Range, which was once said to have been the home of albinos.

To the south-west, in the hilly area known as Dradramea, is Nasavunimuku Falls, which Fijian folklore says was a favourite suicide spot. The Dradramea region was used as a mountain stronghold during the ancient Fijian tribal wars, and the remains of a fortification can still be seen 91 metres from the summit of Dradramea, the highest peak in the chain.

The rivers of Vanua Levu are short and second-rate when compared to those of Viti Levu. None are navigable by large vessels.

The most important bay in the south is Savusavu, an early European settlement ringed by high mountains. The area is known for its hot springs (some of which send their steam directly over the main street). Savusavu's hot springs are among more than 20 distributed throughout the island.

The main city in the north, Labasa, with a population of approximately 5000, is built on a delta formed by three rivers – the Wailevu, the Labasa and the Qawa. The Labasa and the Qawa are joined by a short canal about eight km from the sea where the town is built. Shallow-draft vessels can enter the canal but the larger freighters, many of which come to load sugar, must anchor on the coast.

GETTING THERE & AWAY

Air

Fiji Air has a twice-daily service from Suva to Savusavu for F$67 one way and Suva to Labasa for F$73. Sunflower Airlines has flights twice a day from Nadi to Savusavu and Nadi to Labasa for F$96 one way. Sunflower can be reached in Savusavu (☎ 850 141), at Savusavu's airport (☎ 850 214), in Labasa (☎ 811 454) or at Labasa's airport (☎ 812 121). Fiji Air, which has its Savusavu offices at the Copra Shed, can also be reached at the Savusavu airport (☎ 850 538/173).

Boat

Consort Shipping's *Spirit of Free Enterprise (SOFE)* sails twice a week to Savusavu from Suva, departing Wednesday and Saturday. Return voyages depart on Monday and Thursday. See the Inter-Island Ferry section in the Getting Around chapter for more details.

Patterson Brothers has a daily bus/ferry service from Suva to Nabouwalu, Labasa and Savusavu. The bus leaves Suva GPO at 5 am for Natovi Landing. The ferry departs at 6.30 am and arrives in Nabouwalu at 10.45 am. The bus continues to Labasa, arriving at 2.30 pm. The daily service back to Suva from Labasa departs at 6.30 am and arrives in the capital at 5 pm. (See the Getting Around chapter for more information.)

The Patterson Brothers' *Ashika* also serves Savusavu once a week from Suva.

If you are interested in getting to Taveuni

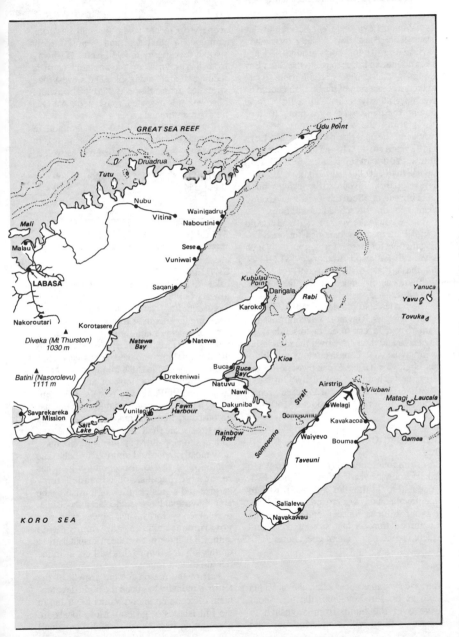

from Vanua Levu there is a service to that island from Buca Bay. A daily bus leaves Savusavu at 10 am, costs around F$3 and takes about two hours to get to the Buca Bay terminus. This is a very scenic route (try to sit on the ocean side of the bus) and could be a wonderful way to soak up a little 'local colour' for those who have time. It stops often along the way and may be very crowded. The boat ride between Vanua Levu and Taveuni costs F$10 and takes about three hours. You can also take SOFE from Savusavu to Taveuni at midnight on Wednesdays or go from Taveuni to Savusavu at noon on Thursdays. See the Getting Around chapter for the full schedules and fares.

Before you make your plans it's advisable to call Patterson Brothers or Consort Shipping in Suva for more information. On Vanua Levu, call Patterson Brothers (☎ 812 444/7 in Labasa, 850 161 in Savusavu) for schedules; you can buy tickets at the Takia Hotel lobby in Labasa.

The ferries also provide a roll-on/roll-off service for cars. The more adventurous may want to rent a car in Suva, disembark in Savusavu and then drive over the mountains from Savusavu to Labasa or along the Hibiscus Highway. To book car passage on the ferry, call Thomas Cook Travel in Suva (☎ 301 603). The price for three-day rental including the ferry trip is about F$150.

GETTING AROUND
Bus

Buses run four times a day from Savusavu to Labasa and vice versa; the fare is about F$3. Buses also make the six-hour run to Nabouwalu on the western side of the island. It is an arduous journey and there is no accommodation on that side of the island except for the government guest house.

Car

The road system is not as extensive on Vanua Levu as on Viti Levu, but the three-hour drive over the hump from Savusavu to Labasa is filled with wonderful mountain

scenery. In recent years the road has been improved a great deal and is now largely sealed. Likewise, the Hibiscus Highway from Savusavu along the southern coast is scenic and quite navigable. The newest road stretches from Savusavu to Nabouwalu, however, it is unsealed, rough and a 4WD is highly recommended.

Budget (☎ 850 265) has cars available in Labasa and there is an Avis agent in Savusavu (☎ 850 184) with 4WD as well as standard vehicles for rental.

The taxi fare from the airport to town is about F$4.

Around the Island

SAVUSAVU

Like Suva to the south, Savusavu is a pretty town when it doesn't rain. On gorgeous Savusavu Bay, set against a backdrop of towering green, mist-shrouded mountains, it consists of one main drag about half a km long, which faces the water. **Nawi Island** sits directly offshore, and there are usually a few yachts anchored in the harbour.

Savusavu has the look of an archetypal 'wild west' town, but in pastels. It is definitely a little rough around the edges and has an outback, frontier kind of feeling. Lining the streets are half a dozen Chinese and Indian shops, painted in blue and pink hues, now mostly faded and dingy. This belies the condition of the local economy which has rebounded because of expanded ferry service and a greater influx of tourists to the area. Savusavu has been declared an official port of entry for yachts, however in true government fashion, the immigration authorities have not yet been dispatched to do the job. It is hoped this will occur in the not too distant future.

Part of the reason for the growth of the tourism industry has been the rapid development of scuba diving on Vanua Levu and in the Fiji Islands in general. More locals are also getting into the act, establishing small

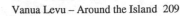

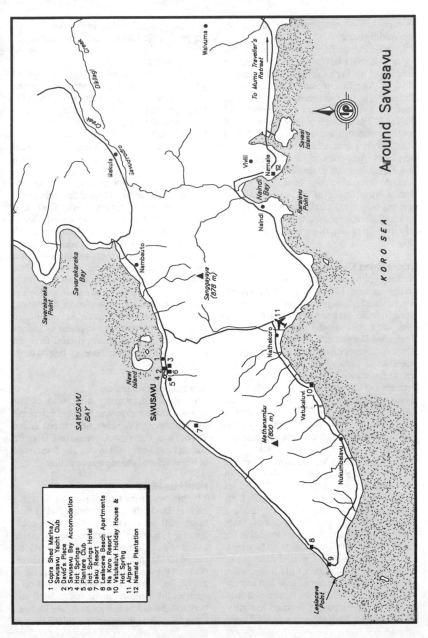

Around Savusavu

1 Copra Shed Marina/
    Savusavu Yacht Club
2 David's Place
3 Savusavu Bay Accomodation
4 Hot Springs
5 Planters Club
6 Hot Springs Hotel
7 Daku Resort
8 Lesiaceva Beach Apartments
9 Na Koro Resort
10 Vatukaluvi Holiday House &
    Hot Spring
11 Airport
12 Nemale Plantation

rooming houses, restaurants and other entrepreneurial ventures.

Despite the decline in importance of the copra industry, planters are also reaping the benefits of having a fairly new copra mill in the area. An efficient planter can make up to 75% profit from each tonne of copra, depending on the workers and the quality of the land. The average planter has about 16 hectares and can make about F$10,000 a year. This is a quite a bit of money by Fijian standards when one considers a staff doctor at a Fijian hospital makes about F$8000 a year. Another advantage of the new mill is that a by-product of the copra-milling process is coconut meal, which planters can now buy cheaply and use to help them diversify into the raising of pigs and chickens.

Copra Shed Marina

Nothing epitomises Vanua Levu's new entrepreneurial spirit like the Copra Shed Marina, a renovated storage shed on Savusavu's waterfront, in the heart of town. Built in the 19th century, it is the oldest building in Savusavu. Despite its historical significance, it sat in a semi-dilapidated state for many years, an all too applicable metaphor for the rest of Savusavu. That is, until Geoff Taylor, perhaps the foremost geologist in Fiji and a Savusavu resident, decided to renovate the decaying building. Working with his sailing buddy, entrepreneur Tony Philp, he started from the pilings up, and worked intensively for nearly a year to complete the job.

The Copra Shed Marina is now home to the Hot Bread Kitchen, Captain's Cafe, Fiji Air offices, Sea Fiji Travel (a dive travel specialist), H20 Sportz dive shop, two boutiques, two self-contained rental units, a geologist's office, and the Savusavu Yacht Club. There are also moorings available for yachts, as well as shower and toilet facilities.

The Copra Shed is a terrific example of what can be done with a little imagination and the right investment of time and money.

It is indeed ironic that the newest and most successful development in town has risen like a phoenix from the ashes of what once was the storage building of the most important product in 19th-century Fiji – copra.

Hot Springs

Visitors should not miss the hot springs for which the town is famous. Most are near the elementary school grounds, across from the Hot Springs Hotel. The bubbling holes are lined with rocks on which locals often leave pots of dalo or tavioka to cook while they attend to shopping or visiting. As you walk from the hotel to the main part of town you'll see a steaming spring just a few metres from the sidewalk, sometimes covering the ground with vapour. The sad thing about the bubbling springs that made Savusavu famous is that they are so ill-tended. One is apt to find plastic bags and other rubbish strewn around the environs which is a big turn-off. The city fathers could really turn this into a first-rate attraction with a little imagination and very few dollars.

Interestingly enough a recent geological survey found that there was enough potential for geothermal energy in the Savusavu area to provide power for the entire island of Vanua Levu. Don't be surprised if over the next decade geothermal energy begins to be tapped.

Savarekareka Mission

The most noteworthy attraction is the mission at Savarekareka. A 10-km ride north of Savusavu, the venerable chapel (circa 1870) was the first Catholic mission on Vanua Levu and is still in use. The compound is beautiful and the view spectacular.

Hibiscus Highway

The highway runs from Savusavu to land's end at **Darigala** and is delightful. Local buses will get you there but it's more comfortable to hire a driver (a three-hour taxi ride to the end of the road is about F$40). Along the roadside, nestled among the numerous coconut groves, are some of the oldest homes in Fiji. Some are well preserved while others, such as the Simpson home (circa 1850 and perhaps the oldest European house in Fiji), have fallen into disrepair, a result of the ups and downs of the market and of family fortunes. The highway, which runs along the coast, is unsealed but is generally in good condition. The ride offers some quintessential South Pacific vistas – cobalt-blue waters lapping at a shore studded with palm trees.

Activities

Water Sports The Savusavu Yacht Club (☎ 850 457; 351 087 or 361 796 in Suva; fax 679 351 010), upstairs at the Copra Shed Marina, is the headquarters for all yachting activities in the area and is a great source of general information about Savusavu. The club, replete with pennants and other nautical décor, has a small bar and T-shirts for sale. The Copra Shed Marina provides stern-to berths for F$40 per week including toilet and shower facilities, water, electricity, a mail holding and forwarding service, security, and courier links to Suva for chandlery and spare parts on a daily basis. Hurricane-season term discounts are available for any yachts wishing to sit out the season in Savusavu.

Visitors should note that sailboards can be rented at the Copra Shed as can 'Optimist' dinghies for children. Water-skiing can also be arranged. Advanced windsurfers and wave jumpers should contact Geoff Taylor (whose geology office is at the Copra Shed).

Emerald Yacht Charters (☎ 850 440) has four vessels (from 11 to 14 metres) moored in Savusavu. Each is well equipped with food, beverages and linen. For more information, write to them c/o the post office in Savusavu.

Diving Diving is dominated in the Savusavu area by H20 Sportz, an Australian operation that runs the dive concessions at Na Koro, Namale, Matani Kavika and Seashell Cove (on Viti Levu). The man in charge is a capable Kiwi named Rick Mansbridge who can often be found at H20's local dive shop/office at the Copra Shed Marina. The shop does have basic equipment such as masks, snorkels and fins but is primarily used to book guests. H20 also offers water-

skiing at Na Koro and from the jetty near the Copra Shed.

The H20 operation has a five-day PADI certificate course which is usually held at Na Koro. Courses begin every Monday when two or more people are available and there is free pick-up anywhere in Savusavu. Rick notes that classes usually have only four to six people, which is very much advantageous to the neophyte. Daily dives cost F$85 for two dives including all gear.

Dive enthusiasts might also consider visiting Sea Fiji Travel (☎ 850 345; fax 850 344) at the Copra Shed Marina. Operated by long-time Savusavu resident Curly Carswell, this is a travel agency that specialises in putting custom diving packages together. Carswell has clients fill out a questionnaire that helps him pinpoint the interests of the diver (and the non-diver). For visitors interested in diving in other parts of Fiji, Sea Fiji Travel can be quite helpful.

Places to Stay – Savusavu

The *Hot Springs Hotel* (☎ 850 294) at one time was the best (and really the only) place to stay in town. However, those days are long gone. Perhaps the nicest thing about the hotel is its spectacular view – on a bluff facing Savusavu Bay. The hotel terrace is a terrific spot to swill Fiji Bitter and watch the sky turn crimson. Formerly a Travelodge, the hotel has gone through many incarnations. It has been on the trading block for years but there don't seem to be any takers. There are 48 rooms, a pool, a dreary bar and a mediocre restaurant. Singles/doubles cost from F$45/55 but I've been told that people have wandered in and negotiated rooms for as little as F$25.

The *Savusavu Holiday House* or *David's Place* (☎ 850 216/149), near the Hot Springs Hotel, is a cheap B&B with 10 bedrooms (doubles and triples) and shared bathrooms. It also has a new seven-bunk dorm which is airy and clean, and there are communal cooking facilities. The accommodation has received good reviews from readers. Singles/doubles are F$12/17 and triples F$22, including breakfast. A dorm bunk costs F$8.50. Home-cooked meals are also available. Incidentally, some of the food is prepared the old-fashioned way – steamed in the nearby hot springs 100 metres from the motel. For reservations write to PO Box 65, Savusavu.

Savusavu Bay Accommodation (☎ 850 100), on Savusavu's main drag, is a clean but faded, well-maintained two-storey building with an average restaurant (the Seabreeze) that serves Indian, Chinese and European dishes. There are four air-con rooms at F$25, and seven fan-cooled singles/doubles for F$10/15. There is also a communal kitchen upstairs with a refrigerator, utensils and a gas stove. On the roof there is a terrace with a view, and a place to wash clothing.

Hidden Paradise Guest House (☎ 850 106) is the newest low-budget accommodation on the Savusavu scene, and it is a winner. In downtown Savusavu in a fenced compound (behind a yellow storefront) it has six spotless rooms each with a double and single bed. Cooking facilities include a double burner and fridge, and laundry facilities are available. The owners, Harry and Vida Chan, are good natured, and the place has received favourable reviews. The guest house's clientele include local as well as foreign guests. Singles/doubles are F$10.80/16.20, triples F$27 and prices include tax and an excellent breakfast. The owners state that beer, pork or hard liquor are barred from the premises.

Copra Shed Marina (☎ 850 457) has two well-appointed, self-contained units, each on a different level of the complex. The bottom unit has a large double bed with cooking facilities, louvre windows, and bathroom. It is clean, airy and spacious. In the evening you can doze off to the sound of the water lapping below the decking. Prices are F$42/53 for a single/double. The upstairs unit is equally attractive, but larger, with two singles and a double at F$30 per person.

Places to Stay – outside Savusavu

Vatukaluvi (☎ 850 143) run by Geoff Taylor is an excellent option for those who want to be isolated and near the sea. Honeymooners who like to fend for themselves might seriously consider this option. About 15 minutes from town by taxi, it is on a gorgeous point of land on the Koro Sea. There is, however, no beach. This sturdy, very comfortable guest house costs F$45 per night and accommodates up to six people, although I think it's best suited for a couple or a small family. It is self-contained and is very clean and well maintained. Geoff, whose family house is next door, has lived in Fiji for 15 years and is a great source of local lore. It is wise to book in advance, and Geoff will consider long-term rentals.

Mumu Traveller's Retreat (☎ 850 416), a private estate 40 minutes east of Savusavu, caters for budget travellers and is the only facility on the island that provides camping. It's set into a wooded hill and offers spectacular views of the coast. There is one 'main' house with a single/double/triple room for F$12/25/35, and a 'dream house' that accommodates up to five people for F$60. Camping costs F$5/7 for a single/twin. Three-meal plans are available for F$19. Reports on Mumu's have been good. Divers who wish to use the facilities at Matani Kavika might consider Mumu's, which is five km away.

Lesiaceva Point Beach Apartments (☎ 850 250; fax 850 350) are five km from Savusavu and 15 minutes from the airport, and have a spectacular view over Savusavu Bay. The building is a two-storey affair – the proprietors, Glenn and Rhonda Mulligan live on top and the guests stay in the two units below. Each unit is fully furnished, accommodates up to six people, and has a fridge, a three-burner stove, utensils, a lounge, bathroom, a double bed in one room and two sets of bunk beds in other rooms. Singles/doubles cost F$45/60, triples F$70. These prices only apply if tariffs are paid 'up-front', otherwise standard rates increase by F$5 per night.

Guests should also pay a deposit of one day's rate for a stay of up to three days if bookings are made more than two weeks in advance. Write c/o Savusavu post office for reservations. Credit cards are accepted and transport to and from the airport is provided. A private cook can be arranged for guests for F$2 an hour, and a laundry service for F$3 an hour. This would be an option for divers on a budget. One guest summed up the accommodation by saying 'everything works', which in Fiji is quite a statement. There is good snorkelling offshore, but no beach.

Matani Kavika (☎ 850 262), formerly 'Kon Tiki', is about 30 minutes by car from Savusavu, and is once again under new management. A mid-range resort specialising in diving, Matani Kavika now has luxury dorm facilities in addition to its bures. What are luxury dorms, you might ask? They are more comfortable, come with hot water and have a housekeeping and linen service. The downside is that they only accommodate a maximum of four guests and have no cooking facilities. Dorms are F$15 per person.

In addition to a PADI dive operation run by H20 Sportz, there is a nine-hole golf course on the property which is free for guests. The bures cost F$90/125 for singles/doubles and include a mini-bar, fridge and satellite TV. There are also two all-weather tennis courts, a marina, 60 hectares of grounds, a children's playground and rental cars (including 4WD) available.

Prices for meals range from F$3 to F$8 for breakfast, F$5 to F$10 for lunch and F$6 to F$20 for dinner. Manager Peter Marks claims that Matani Kavika has the best chef on the island. There are special reduced rates (subject to availability) for walk-in guests.

Peter can be found playing croquet daily at 4 pm. Finally, there is a happy hour at the bar from 5 to 7 pm every day.

Namale Plantation (☎ 850 435) is one of the more popular places to stay in the Savusavu area. Surrounded by a working plantation (complete with cattle and goats), it consists of three 'family' bures and four double bures, some of which are built adjacent to huge volcanic outcrops and conform to the terrain. There are nature walks, garden tours, copra plantation tours, snorkelling and 4WD land tours, fishing, windsurfing and yacht cruises. Bure accommodation (with meals) costs F$220/260 a single/double.

Na Koro (☎ 850 188) which means 'the village' in Fijian, is the largest development to date in the Savusavu area. Of all the hotels in the area the word 'resort' applies most aptly to Na Koro, especially to its design and layout. Most of its 15 bures are in a shady coconut grove only several metres from the beach, which has nice sand, but becomes the usual disappointing tidal flat when the tide goes out. Singles/doubles, including meals, cost F$170/190 per day. (Divers should add F$60 per person.)

Probably the best thing about the resort is the excellent diving. The local operation is run by H20 Sportz, from Hamilton Island. They have a 13.7-metre dive boat, photo lab and new equipment. The resort also operates in conjunction with the 58-metre *South Pacific Explorer* (formerly a cruise vessel known as the *Matthew Flinders*), which has been converted into a dive/cruise boat. It can accommodate up to 40 divers and another 24 guests. It costs F$150 per day, and there is a decompression chamber and doctor on board.

Daku Estate Resort (☎ 850 046; fax 850 334) has been around for years and I have been remiss in not mentioning it in earlier editions. Owned and operated by the Anglican church, it caters primarily to church groups and is popular with 'local tourists' from Suva, but is open to the public.

The resort is perched on a grassy knoll 10 minutes' walk from Savusavu, and there is a breathtakingly beautiful view of Savusavu

Bay. The environs are spacious and the gardens, dotted with coconut palms, fruit trees and hibiscus, are immaculately tended. The gardens are also decorated with huge millstones taken from a long-gone copra mill. The management is friendly, and the resort is often full.

Daku has seven bures, two small duplex-style lodges which are self-contained, and two very well-appointed, self-contained villas. The bures have traditional thatched roofs, which adds a quaint quality to the setting. All units are spotlessly clean and have tiled floors.

Guests in the self-contained units have the choice of preparing their own food or eating at the restaurant. Prices are F$43 for a single or double in the bures, F$75 with meals. Triples cost F$104, or F$198 with meals. Singles/doubles in a villa (without meals) cost F$75/100, triples are F$115 and a quadruple is F$125. Prices for breakfast/lunch/dinner are F$6.50/10/15. All the above prices do not include tax.

Overall, Daku is good-value for a mid-range place. The only thing it doesn't have is a proper beach, and alcohol isn't served, though you can BYO. Reservations need to be made way in advance.

Places to Eat

The *Captain's Cafe* (☎ 850 511), at the Copra Shed Marina, is the premiere spot in town. Serving passable pizza, it is an indoor/outdoor affair decorated with a nautical flair. Cold drinks and coffee, notably cappuccino, are served. The glass fishing floats on the ceiling suspended by nets are a nice touch. The best thing about it is the outdoor deck overlooking spectacular Savusavu Bay. The deck is a great place to watch the sunset and sip a cappuccino – especially on a Sunday when there is not much else to do. Pizza starts at F$6.

Wing Yuen on the main street next to the bank, has the best Chinese food in town. Not that it will win gastronomical awards, but you take what you can get in Savusavu. Prices range from F$4 to F$8 per person. Down the street, opposite the town market,

is *Ping Ho's*, which serves more or less the same thing from F$4 to F$7. There are also two curry houses side by side, *Soni's A-1 Restaurant* and *Lilly's* on the main drag, though they are noted more for their quantity of bones than curry. Another curry shop is in the same building as the Hidden Paradise Guest House. Prices for Indian food are in the F$3 to F$5 range. *Ah Kee's Coffee Shop*, also on the main street, is a good bet for curries, chop suey, snacks, sandwiches, and meat pies. A meal will cost from F$3 to F$4.

Entertainment

Savusavu is a quiet town in the evenings, but on the weekend there just may be a dance at the *Planters Club*, down the street from the Hot Springs Hotel. The Planters Club, not unlike a grange hall in the USA, is a turn-of-the-century clapboard building with a long bar and a friendly crowd. At least, the crowd is usually friendly until the end of a dance, when it is not unusual for a fight to break out among the drunks. The club was built by the once-prosperous community of plantation owners and is still the heart and soul of the 'part-European' community of Savusavu.

Planters is the place to drink, gossip and discuss the depressingly low price of copra. Although it's a private organisation, visitors are made to feel very welcome by the locals, who are more than likely to buy a stranger a beer. This is one place you don't want to miss.

The only other significant place to drink is the *Hot Springs Hotel*, which has a modern lounge facing the bay. Dances are occasionally held there but also often end in brawls.

OFFSHORE ISLAND RESORTS
Namenalala Island

Moody's Namenalala Island (☎ 813 764) is a 44-hectare resort and nature reserve, 24 km south of Vanua Levu (off Wainunu Bay) and 32 km north-west of Koro. Because in the past there was no constant supply of fresh water, the island never supported a permanent human population. Consequently the flora and fauna remain undisturbed. The owners state that only a quarter of the island has been developed and the rest of it is left as a wildlife sanctuary. Turtles lay their eggs on the beaches and other fauna such as flying foxes, small colonies of red-footed boobies and other bird life can be seen.

The island has superb diving and snorkelling, windsurfing, shelling and fishing. Transport is either via Turtle Airways seaplane from Nadi to Namena, or by scheduled Fiji Air and Sunflower Airlines flights to Savusavu, then by speedboat (1¾ hours) to the island.

The resort has five double bures, which cost F$176 each, plus F$70 for three meals. A deposit of F$400 is required. Scuba equipment is provided for F$42 per dive. Write to Moody's Namenalala Island, c/o Private PO Box, Suva for more information.

BUCA BAY

Buca Bay is 72 km (three hours by bus) east of Savusavu and is the terminus for the ferries that ply the waters of the Somosomo Strait between Vanua Levu and Taveuni. The area will soon become the newest tourist site with the opening of the *Buca Bay Resort* in mid-1992. The resort will be a budget affair with camping, dorms and guest houses with private bedrooms. Prices will be F$3 for camping and F$10 for dorms. Tariffs for rooms will be F$20/33 a single/double, F$45 a triple. Activities will include gold panning in the Natuvu River, trekking, horse riding, swimming, diving, fishing and boating. The resort will have a capacity for 36 people. Though it's now being developed in a small way, the owners wish to greatly expand the operation and establish a writers' colony with annual seminars featuring guest authors from throughout the English-speaking world.

Opposite Buca is the island of **Kioa**, which is leased by displaced Kiribati islanders whose home island became uninhabitable.

Places to Eat

Currently there is only one reliable place to eat in Buca Bay and that is at the recently established *Garden Cafe* (☎ Tukavesi 6). Run by American Lisa Blanton, the Garden Cafe is open to serve passengers waiting for the ferry, as well as for breakfast, lunch and dinner. Sandwiches are F$1, hamburgers F$3, and complete dinners of filet mignon, lobster or walu steak are around F$17.95.

LABASA

Labasa is a hot, dusty sugar mill town, pure and simple. Although growing in importance economically as an agricultural community, the town is still very quiet and provincial. The surrounding countryside is beautiful (much like on Viti Levu's western side), with golden, sunburnt hills and miles of green cane fields. In general, one would have to agree with a recent article that appeared in the Fiji Times with the headline 'Tourism is Dead in Labasa'.

However, that does not mean that there is nothing to see or do. For instance, visitors might want to look at the **Floating Island**, the most famous attraction in the Labasa area. To get there take a bus to Kurukuru (in Daku), about 50 km east of Labasa. The island, replete with pandanus palms and reeds, floats in a lake surrounded by cane fields. There are many legends associated with the genesis of the island, but it's believed that it was formed when a chunk of land broke away from the shoreline.

On the way back to Labasa, about five km from Kurukuru, you may want to stop at the **Chand residence** to examine the Chand brothers' handiwork. The brothers spend their time carving large stones in the likeness of dogs, turtles, Hindu deities, and people. The objects are painted bright colours and given to the local Hindu temple as offerings. In case you are thinking of taking one home, they do not sell them. Incidentally, the Chands quarry the stones from a hill about two km from their home, dragging them with the help of bullocks.

If you are interested in still more curious stones, you may want to look at what is known locally as the **Growing Stone** in Vunika, 11 km west of Labasa. Local legend has it that this stone actually grows in size. It is housed under a Hindu temple and attracts hundreds of devotees every year.

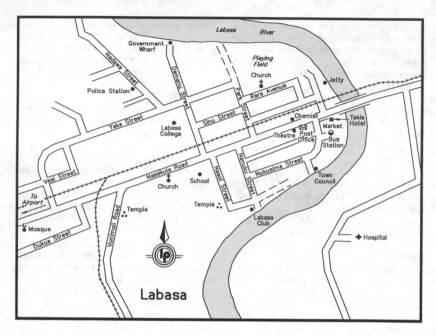

Labasa

True believers say the temple roof had to be elevated several times over the years to accommodate the stone. You will recognise the temple by the inscription 'Shree Sanatan Dharm' on the façade.

While in the neighbourhood you also might want to check out the **Blackbirders Track**, about nine km out of Vunika, where a 40-metre-high hillock was excavated right down the middle to make way for a sugarcane railroad. The job was done by slave labourers from the Solomon Islands who worked with simple spades. (Blackbirders were 19th century 'entrepreneurs' who kidnapped islanders throughout the Pacific and sold them to plantation owners in Fiji and elsewhere.)

If you actually want to do something more conventional, about five km from the Chand's stone sculptures and a total of 15 km from Labasa, is **Korovatu Beach** – a terrific place for a picnic. The white-sand beach is about 400 metres long and has a plethora of coconut palms to shade you from the sun. The owner, Durga Chand, charges F$5 per car to enter. He maintains the beach and the access road.

Places to Stay

The *Grand Eastern* (☎ 811 022) is a venerable 18-room classic roadhouse affair with a restaurant/bar and pool. It's about a five-minute walk from the bus station, and used to be one of the great old hotels in Fiji, but for several years fell from grace. However, reports I get lately are more favourable. Some rooms come with air-con and private bathroom, others with fan and shared bathroom. The rooms are clean, the food is good and the prices reasonable. Singles/doubles cost from F$12.50/17.50 (no air-con) to F$48/54 for the top units.

The *Takia Hotel* (☎ 811 655) is the most modern of the Labasa-area hotels. That's not to say that it's a truly great hotel. It has 34 rooms, and amenities such as a refrigerator, air-con, a bar and a restaurant. Prices for singles/doubles begin at F$30/40 (fan-cooled) to F$45/55 for rooms with air-con. You can also purchase tickets for the Patterson Brothers' ferries at the hotel.

The *Riverview Private Hotel* (☎ 811 905/367) has rooms at F$11/16.50 a single/double. Reports are that it is clean, quiet and has a great view of the river. It's in Namara, a few hundred metres past the police station, opposite a church.

The *Labasa Guest House* (☎ 812 155), on Nanuku St, is another low-budget alternative. Singles/doubles go for F$10/11.

Places to Eat

Labasa will not overwhelm you with its gourmet restaurants, but there are several decent places to dine. *Isa Lei*, on Sangam Ave, has good Indian cuisine from around F$5 to F$8, and a bar. *Nanyang*, at the Takia Hotel, and *Wun Wuh*, on Nasekula Rd, both have good Chinese food from around F$3 to F$8.

NABOUWALU

The Fijian government has several guest houses scattered throughout the country. One of them is in Nabouwalu (☎ 84 010), one of the westernmost points of Vanua Levu and a six-hour bus ride from Labasa. It can also be reached by commercial boat from Suva or Savusavu. Visitors may stay if there are no government officials occupying the bunks. Accommodation is spartan, but the price is only a few dollars per night. Ring to see what the space situation is. As mentioned above, there is now a road from Savusavu to Nabouwalu but it is negotiable by 4WD only.

Taveuni

Taveuni, the garden island of Fiji, is extremely rugged, wet and verdant. Only seven km off the coast of Vanua Levu, it has excellent air and sea transport from Viti Levu and Vanua Levu but compared to other parts of Fiji, still remains relatively 'untouristed.'

What is new on the island? Taveuni has always held an interest for divers but of late, has become popular with backpackers and budget travellers. Local entrepreneurs have responded by opening up new camp grounds, guest houses, restaurants and even a bakery. The Garden Island Resort, the largest accommodation on the island, has finally been refurbished after years of neglect under a series of different owners. A new low-end resort, Susie's Plantation, has also opened in Vuna, on the opposite side of the island from Matai Airport. In short, the island is bustling as never before.

Taveuni's primary attraction (other than diving) is its landscape – virgin rainforest, an array of rare flora and fauna, two waterfalls and a legendary lake.

History

The first European to sight Taveuni was Abel Tasman in 1643. Tasman was north-east of Taveuni in the stretch of water that now bears his name, and though visibility was poor he glimpsed points of land which he took to be separate islands and which were probably the peaks of Taveuni and islands to the north.

Taveuni's inhabitants were feared throughout the Fiji group as fierce warriors who relished the taste of human flesh. In prehistoric times the village of Vuna was the most important settlement on the island, but it eventually lost this status to the more northerly village of Somosomo in a series of tribal wars. Perhaps the most memorable battle in Somosomo occurred when the Tongan warlord Ma'afu was defeated by Chief Cakobau in a skirmish that took place several years before Fiji's cession to Great Britain. Somosomo currently holds the title

of 'chiefly village' and is also the burial site of one of Fiji's most important missionaries, William Cross. The **William Cross Memorial Church**, established in 1839, suffered a great deal of damage during a 1979 earthquake and has been rebuilt in Somosomo.

Except for tribal struggles and later settlement by planters, Taveuni remained out of the historical spotlight. Perhaps the most interesting visitor to come along was Commandant Charles Wilkes of the US expedition, who visited Somosomo in 1840. (See the History section in the Facts about the Country chapter for more information about this expedition.)

One of the more fascinating historical incidents concerns the villages of Lovonivonu and Kanacea. Both are populated by descendants of inhabitants of several other islands which were sold by Chief Cakobau, to Europeans. The inhabitants were deprived of their land as punishment for taking sides with the Tongans against Chief Cakobau during a war.

Linguistically, the island is characterised by a local dialect that has eliminated the consonant 'k', which has become a glottal stop. Everyone on the island (including the Indians) speaks this distinct Fijian dialect.

A little-known fact about Taveuni is that it is one of the few places in the archipelago with traditional surfing. Because ancient surfers were here long before the sport ever reached Tahiti or Hawaii, Taveuni may actually be surfing's original home. Surfing may once again become popular on this island as a new company 'Return to Blue Lagoon Cruises' plans to construct a surf camp at Lavena Point.

Geography

Taveuni more or less ties with Kadavu as the third-largest island in the Fiji archipelago. It is still a fraction of the size of Viti Levu or Vanua Levu, but is triple the size of Gau, the next island in order of size. Taveuni is about

42 km long and an average of 10 or 11 km wide, and covers 435 sq km. The island is wholly volcanic in origin (the most recent volcanic activity was 2000 years ago) and has a uniform backbone of volcanic cones forming a 900-metre-high ridge which stretches for more than 16 km. Among the four summits contained in this ridge are two of the highest mountains in Fiji: Uluigalau (1241 metres) at the southern end; and Des Voeux Peak (1195 metres) in the centre. Uluigalau, the highest point in Taveuni, also has the distinction of being directly under the 180th meridian (the International Date Line) and therefore 12 hours east and west of Greenwich. Though the date line no longer officially runs through Taveuni (it was changed for the sake of convenience), the marker can still be seen on the beach near Waiyevo and visitors can purchase T-shirts commemorating the landmark.

The high ridge of Taveuni lies directly in the path of the prevailing winds, in a perfect position to intercept moisture, and much of the time is hidden in a cloud. The higher slopes on the windward side can receive more than 1000 cm of rain per year and, as you might expect, are smothered with dense forest.

The 'Garden Island of Fiji' possesses some of the nation's best coconut planta-tions, and its rich, reddish soil is ideal for agricultural development such as vanilla cul-tivation. It was on this land that high-grade cotton was raised and exported to Europe during the American Civil War. Later, sugar cane was grown. Although coffee and tropi-cal fruit grow in profusion, and sheep, cattle and poultry have been raised, the staple of the island's economy has always been copra.

Flora & Fauna

Taveuni is especially noteworthy for its diversity of bird life. It is the home of the orange dove (the males of the species have green-speckled plumage that changes in season to flaming orange).

Years before Europeans arrived, the island was famous for its kula – a species of parrot endemic to the area. In ancient times trading parties of Tongans would journey to Fiji to barter for the brilliant maroon feathers of this bird, which they then took to Samoa to exchange for fine mats. Taveuni is also one of only two islands in the Lau group (the other is Cicia) where the Australian magpie was introduced to control coconut pests. Now a conspicuous part of the fauna, it is admired for its curiously melodic song.

Perhaps the main reason for the variety of bird life is the absence of the mongoose, which was introduced on other islands to

---

Logging on Taveuni

Sadly, parcels of Taveuni's magnificent natural birthright, its rainforest, are being cut down. Deep within the mountains a Korean firm is logging parcels of Taveuni timber stands at a rapid rate. This activity, which was approved by the highest levels of government, has raised the ire of local environmentalists and dive operators. They fear that without proper ground-cover, the soil will be washed into the lagoon thus ruining the delicate ecology of the reef system. However, their fears may be overblown. A European forester I spoke to on the island said he didn't think the logging would interfere with the reef ecology. Just the same, he did not approve of the logging operation because he felt it set a 'bad precedent'.

Despite the logging operation there is reason for hope. The inhabitants of Bouma village, where a waterfall has been a major tourist attraction in Taveuni, have a different tale to tell. They too were offered money to log their communal land. Instead, at the behest of the New Zealand government, they were offered a F$60,000 grant to improve the land and thus continue to utilise the waterfall as a tourist attraction and of course earn revenue from it. They weighed their options and came down on the side of conservation, rather than the lure of easy money from logging. Bouma villagers have since improved access to the falls and done a moderate amount of landscaping, extensive trail building and constructed barbecue pits, benches and picnic spots. When you visit and pay your F$5 admission, think of it as a contribution to the village. There is, after all, (as we say in the USA) 'no free lunch'. ■

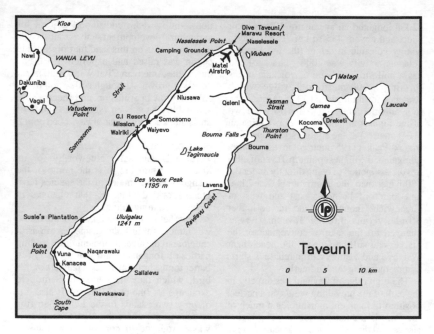

control rats. Additionally, Taveuni's relatively inaccessible mountains and abundant food supply have made it a haven for many species once found throughout the Fiji group. For example, several types of dove proliferate, and Pacific boa snakes are still fairly common in the rainforest. The mountains also harbour several known species of palms and other plants not found elsewhere on earth, and much of the forest still remains unexplored.

Information

Taveuni's administrative centre is in Waiyevo, north of the the Garden Island Resort. Nearby are schools, a hospital, a dock, a police station and drinking establishment called the Taveuni Country Club, which is a good place to meet the locals. (Don't expect denizens of the Taveuni Country Club to be dripping with expensive jewellery – in this case the term 'country club' has an entirely different meaning.)

When visiting Taveuni (or any of the outer islands for that matter) it's a good idea to bring cash rather than travellers' cheques, as banks are few and far between. On Taveuni the only place to bank is with Westpac at the general store next to the Garden Island Resort (Wednesdays only).

The home of the president of Fiji is near the administrative centre. You'll know he's around if you spot his yacht at the dock or see his 4WD about town.

Activities

Sport For sporting types, Soqulu Plantation offers golf, tennis and lawn bowling for 'moderate' fees. The golf course is maintained at a very minimal standard but is fun to play. There is also an informal tennis club which meets on Saturday afternoons (visitors would be welcome I'm sure) at Soqulu. The oldsters have bowls earlier in the afternoon and it's fun to watch. For information ask Frank at Lesuma's, or else just show up.

Those who like a beer after nine holes would be interested to know that the clubhouse at the course has reopened, and provided you have transport down there in the first place, it's a nice place to relax. Enquire at any of the hotels for more information.

Water Slide There is a great water slide on the Waitavala Estate, owned by Carpenters Ltd. The water slide is actually on private land, accessible through Waitavala. Make sure you ask permission to pass through the estate from the manager; notice the coffee bean processing facilities on your way through. If you have trouble locating the slide, ask one of the local kids to show you, or follow these directions: look for a turn-off about 150 metres north of the Garden Island Resort. Follow the narrow dirt road (up the hill), bearing right and then left until you see the coconut palms with orange trunks and turn right down a narrow track. Fifty metres further on you'll see the water slides carved into the rock face.

Diving Diving in Taveuni is world class. Rick Cammick of Dive Taveuni (☎ 880 441) is the dean of Taveuni divers – he dives solely in the Somosomo Strait, which has the now famous Rainbow Reef (an unusually brilliant collection of soft corals) and the Great White Wall (a marine canyon with a spectacular soft white coral wall). The Somosomo Strait is known for very strong currents, a characteristic that promotes the growth of soft coral. You had better be experienced when diving with Rick – Somosomo Strait is no place for amateurs.

Rick has two boats, one measuring 10 metres and the other a 13-metre aluminium catamaran designed specifically as a dive vessel. At no charge, Rick will transfer a diver staying anywhere on the island for a day's dive, which includes lunch, two tanks, buoyancy vest and weight belt for US$75. For longer stays, the price is US$114 per person per night.

Garden Island Resort (☎ 880 286) has a full range of activities as well as its own diving operation. Rates are F$90 for two

dives, F$255 for a six-dive package or F$400 for 10 dives. An introductory resort course is F$90, a resort dive is F$75 and a night or dawn dive is F$60 (reputedly a mystical experience). A five-day PADI open-water certificate course is F$400 and a three-day PADI advanced course is F$325.

Taveuni's reefs offer some of the best shelling spots in the world. The island is currently under government study as a source of shells for commercial sales.

Tours Maravu Plantation Resort (☎ 880 555) provides tours of its 22-hectare plantation, which has cattle, pigs, goats, chickens, vanilla, cocoa and coffee. Visitors can see the stages of copra production, from collecting the nuts all the way to bagging and weighing. Other activities include nature treks (with guides available), fishing, snorkelling, tennis, windsurfing, and 4WD excursions. Rental cars are available.

The family owns four horses and there are a multitude of trails nearby. Treks and tours are made to the **Wainibau River** and the Des Voeux Peak in search of the *tagimaucia* flower (see the Lake Tagimaucia section later). There are also visits to some of the unoccupied islets nearby, where you can be left alone for the day with a fresh fish to barbecue in an open pit.

Visitors interested in seeing the **Ravilevu Coast**, which includes some of the most scenic real estate in the Fiji Islands, might want to arrange a boat trip with villagers. Among the attractions is the magnificent **Savuleveavonu Waterfall** that cascades into the sea. It was featured in the sequel to the most recent remake of the film *Blue Lagoon*. The best way to set up transportation to this little-visited area is with your hotel.

Those interested in exploring other areas of the Taveuni coast and some of the offshore islands (in a sea-going kayak) should contact Keni Madden and TC Donovan at Ringgold Reef Kayaking (☎ 880 083). They run overnight kayak/camping tours from June to September, as well as renting kayaks for day use all year-round. (See the Activities section in the Facts for the Visitor chapter for more details.)

Accommodation

Accommodation on Taveuni is as follows: one large (35-room) moderately priced hotel (Garden Island Resort); a smaller up-market establishment (Maravu); two inexpensive guest houses (Kaba's and Kool's); four camping grounds (Beverly, Tom's, Lisi's and Lavena); several locals who rent out rooms in their homes to visitors; and a luxury housing development/country club known as Soqulu Plantation, which is always in search of a cash infusion. At the time of writing, another camping ground near Vuna (Namoli Beach Club) is also under construction.

GETTING THERE & AWAY

Air

Both Fiji Air and Sunflower Airlines serve Taveuni. Fiji Air flies twice daily from Nausori Airport for F$88 one way. Sunflower has two daily flights from Nadi to Taveuni for F$116. Both carriers have flights between Savusavu and Taveuni for F$45 one way. Sunflower also has a Labasa to Taveuni flight five days a week for F$45 one way. Make sure you telephone the airport (☎ 880 062/461) to confirm your flights.

While you're at Matai Airport, look for Audrey Brown – a delightful lady with a basket of baked goodies. Audrey bakes some of the very best sweets in the South Pacific. If you have a birthday, she will deliver your beautifully embellished cake to your hotel.

Likewise, keep on the lookout for Margaret Peterson, another charming woman, who sells home-made snacks at her small booth at the airport. Margaret is also a first-class cook – try her roti curry.

Boat

Consort Shipping's *Spirit of Free Enterprise (SOFE)* and the Patterson Brothers' *Ashika* both have services to Taveuni. As it is an overnight trip, the less adventurous (or those who value a night's sleep) should consider booking a cabin, which is available only on *SOFE*. *SOFE* also has hot showers (for 1st-class passengers) and good meals consisting of rice, cassava and curries for around F$3. Economy passengers can sleep on long, soft seats which are quite comfortable. The vessel is often crowded as many locals travel back and forth to Suva to attend the markets. The worst thing about *SOFE* (and most vessels of this variety) are the awful restrooms – you should definitely bring toilet paper with you.

If you happen to be on the *SOFE* when it stops at Koro Island be sure to get off the boat and buy one of the excellent, inexpensive, freshly cooked local meals. They are sold on the wharf by women from one of the nearby villages – even if the boat docks at 2 am.

There is also a service to and from Buca Bay in Vanua Levu and Taveuni which costs F$10. It connects with a bus to Savusavu. There is some gorgeous scenery en route (try to get a window seat on the ocean side of the bus).

See the Getting Around chapter for full details of schedules and fares.

GETTING AROUND

A good (although not wholly sealed) highway runs the entire length of the western side of Taveuni. It starts at Vuna in the south and runs around the northern end of the island to Lavena Point midway around the opposite side. There is also a cross-island route from Vuna to Salialevu on the southern side. There is a local bus service throughout the island, which leaves Waiyevo three times a day at 9 am, 12.30 and 5 pm. Taxis are always available, but are expensive for long jaunts.

Rup Narayan, a young taxi driver, has a very good reputation and is quite knowledgeable. He will provide an excellent commentary on the way to your destination. Ask the local operator for Rup – he lives in Somosomo. The main problem with Taveuni is the lack of frequent, inexpensive transport to and from both sides of the island. You can usually hitchhike if scheduled transport cannot be found, but getting from point A to point B involves some planning. Thus, if you decide to stay at a particular guest house or hotel, most of your time will probably be spent arranging transport

Keep in mind that curtailed commercial activities may inhibit your travels, so ask about buses or taxis on Sundays. Some taxis will run only by previous arrangement.

Around the Island

SOMOSOMO

Three km or so from the dock at Waiyevo is Somosomo, the largest settlement in Taveuni and the site of a famous battle. Its most imposing structure, a modern community centre, was built within the last few years to accommodate the Great Council of Chiefs, a traditional, quasi-governmental body made up of the most important chiefs in Fiji. The council meets periodically in various locations around Fiji to discuss the important issues of the day and participate in one of Fiji's national pastimes – politics.

Kaba's store, just across from Kaba's Guest House, is the largest store on the island, and accepts plastic. It's also a rental agency for cars and 4WDs, and for the Westpac bank.

Places to Stay – Somosomo area

Kaba's Guest House & Motel (☎ 880 058, ask for the Taveuni operator) has a three-room guest house with communal kitchen, as well as motel rooms with fully equipped kitchenettes, radio, fridge, telephone,

laundry service and hot and cold water. Both facilities are spotlessly clean. Prices for the guest house are F$12/20 a single/double, F$28 a triple. Motel rooms start at F$25/30 for a single/double; F$32 a triple.

The largest accommodation on the island is the *Garden Island Resort* (☎ 880 286), formerly Castaway Taveuni. The 30-room hotel fronts the sea three km south of Somosomo, and has its own dive centre. It's now under the ownership of American expat, Lela Prym, who, at the time of writing, is in the final stages of revamping the hotel. All rooms have been tiled and painted, and the hotel looks better than it has in years. Rooms cost F$48/65 a single/double, F$75 a triple.

In addition to conventional rooms, Garden Island Resort has 17 'backpacker' bunks available for F$16 per person; these are spread out in four standard hotel rooms, each room having a shower, toilet, lockers and fridge. A nice plus is that the bunks are 'modular', meaning they can be stacked, or placed on the floor.

Food at Garden Island is good and reasonably priced. Breakfast is F$3 to F$6, lunch $6.50 and dinner around F$12. If you get a chance, try the home-made apple pie. Optional meal plans starting at F$25 for buffet breakfast and dinner are also available.

There is no beach, but the hotel is close to dive sites. Also, because the resort is so close to Somosomo, many travellers drop in for a beer, lunch, dinner or a dive. Unlike many hotels, Garden Island Resort does not discourage budget travellers from using its facilities or participating in activities. For divers on a budget or for backpackers who don't mind spending more for better accommodation, Garden Island Resort is excellent value.

Kool's (☎ 880 395) is a ramshackle yellow building 100 metres or so down the road from Kaba's (away from the airport). It has six rooms that resemble a row of box-like barracks. The communal kitchen is small, clean and has all the utensils. Units are well maintained but very spartan; each has two simple beds, and bathrooms are shared.

Singles/doubles cost F$8/12, triples F$15. Meals are not provided, but you can wander up to Kaba's supermarket for groceries, or go to several takeaway eateries in the area. The main complaint I've heard regarding Kool's is that security is poor – it's easy to break into a room. One visitor reported two thefts within four days, and when I dropped in for a visit, the place was completely unattended – no-one was around to keep an eye on the rooms.

In Somosomo there is a villager called *Serua Ledua* who will put up visitors for around F$10 per night including meals. Mr Ledua's operation has been called 'safe and courteous' by one reader. Enquire in Somosomo, or look for him meeting visitors at the nearby ferry dock.

Places to Stay – Matei area

Bibi's Hideaway (☎ 880 443/365) is an eight-hectare property with a private home and three cottages about half a km from the airport, four km from the beach and a 15-minute walk from the store. The house is well maintained, airy and has two bedrooms (one with a double and single bed, the other with a single), a full kitchen, a large toilet, an outdoor shower and a phone. It is ideal for a family or for a gang of divers. It costs F$75 per day for the home, F$25/35 for a single/double. Directly across the road is a beach. Two of the self-contained cottages have two double rooms and cost F$30 per room or F$60 for the whole cottage. The third cottage has a single bedroom with a double bed and costs F$35/50 for a single/double. All the cottages have a shower and toilet.

Good home-cooked meals can be arranged through neighbour Margaret Peterson (☎ 880 171) who lives a two-minute walk away. What more could you want? For reservations, write to James Bibi, PO Box 80, Waiyevo, Taveuni.

Margaret Peterson (☎ 880 171) is an easy person to find because she runs the food concession at the airport. She also has two rooms, each with a double bed, to rent at her homestead which is a short walk from the airport. Margaret is a terrific cook and three meals are included in the F$25 room rate. To find her place, after rounding the turn from the airport (towards Somosomo) walk up the third driveway on your left which is marked by a telephone pole. Staying with Margaret will give you a good taste of life on the outer islands with a part-European family.

Audrey's (☎ 880 039) is an excellent bet for honeymooners on a budget. In the village of Naselesele, on a hillock overlooking the sea, Audrey's is a modern, self-contained bungalow in a secluded spot. The one-bedroom unit, with all kitchen and bathroom facilities, is for two people only – no children are allowed. The price is F$55 plus tax. Audrey's is a 10-minute walk from the airport, 50 metres from the beach and two minutes' walk from the grocery store. To find the property walk to Naselesele village, pass the Indian shops and look for a modern home on the mountain side of the road.

Your hostess, the lovely and gracious Audrey Brown, is an American who hails from California. She can also be found at the airport selling her famous chocolate chunk cookies or other goodies.

Narajan's Budget Accommodation is a new bottom-end place two minutes' walk from the airport, and next to Prasad Brothers' shop. Though building was not complete at the time of writing, rooms will cost F$35 a single or double, F$45 a triple.

Coconut Grove Cafe, on the waterfront opposite the airport, has a cottage for rental on a weekly and monthly basis. At the time of publication I do not have details on tariffs or amenities.

Beverly Beach Camping also has bures, each with a double bed, mosquito net and Fijian mat on the floor. The units are well built and cost F$10 per person per night. (See under Camping for more details.)

Maravu Plantation Resort (☎ 880 555) is the up-market resort in Taveuni. It's a working plantation with eight large bures and is owned and operated by Ormand Eyre, who was born on Taveuni but spent years in Europe and was a Qantas flight attendant. The resort is perched on a gentle slope in a grove of coconut trees, about a km from the airport, and has the advantage of having a small beach within walking distance. Rates are F$150/180 per day for singles/doubles; F$207/230 a day for triples/quads. The 'honeymoon' bure costs F$205. Meals are F$14 for breakfast, F$18 for lunch, F$32 for dinner or F$60 per day for all three. The food is good, the atmosphere is very pleasant and Ormand is a true gentleman. Travellers with plenty of cash should give Maravu serious thought.

The *Garden of Eden* (☎ 880 252; 370 571 in Suva), Taveuni's newest top-end accommodation, is best described as a tropical villa. If you have a reasonable amount of discretionary income, you might consider spending your honeymoon or dream vacation here. Perched on a bluff overlooking the sea and a small rocky outcrop called Honeymoon Island, the home is surrounded by manicured tropical gardens, mango trees and coconut palms. There's a lawn tennis court, a pool and a one-of-a-kind Fijian art collection. Fifty metres away is private beach frontage. The home, large by Fijian standards, is built with local hardwoods and has wooden floors polished to mirror-like perfection. There are two large bedrooms that can sleep a total of four adults, and an attic-like second storey that sleeps several children.

A cook, maid and laundry service is provided, and fresh fruit, wine and freshly baked pastry from Audrey Brown is also available. Ah yes, I almost forgot the yacht. Included in the price is the use of the owner's speedy 10-metre motor yacht *Purple Haze*. The daily tariff (excluding yacht fuel and the captain's wage) is F$1250. The minimum stay is one week, and reservations are accepted upon receipt of full payment. Write to Peter Madden (Estate Manager) c/o Postal Agency, Matei, Taveuni. The Garden of Eden is easy to find – it's directly across from Matei Airport, though if you have trouble locating it, ask for Peter Madden.

Dive Taveuni (☎ 880 441), near Matei Airport (just across the road from Maravu), is one of the oldest dive operations in Fiji. It

has four bures for rent for US$114 per person per day. Amenities include solar-generated electricity and solar-heated water. The bures are well constructed, comfortable and stylish, and compare favourably with any outer island resort in Fiji. The resort is situated on a bluff overlooking the sea and the vista is absolutely spectacular; the view from the outdoor patio is especially memorable. The food is good but no booze is served on the premises so you must bring your own. Note that Dive Taveuni is only for top-notch divers; there are no lessons here.

Camping Of the three camping grounds near Matei Airport, the best is *Beverly Beach*, about a km from the airport. It's run by Bill Madden, a friendly chap who will rent tents to the tentless. Beverly Beach is the only camping ground actually on the beach, which is great unless there are too many people and things get a bit crowded. Facilities here are good – there is a shower, a toilet and good snorkelling. A tent site costs F$5 per person, F$7 if you need a tent as well.

Bill often brings fresh fruit and distributes it free to campers. Campers can also buy supplies from several stores in Naselesele village, which is about a 15-minute walk from the camping ground. The stores are also a good place to meet the locals and swap gossip.

Horseback riding is available nearby at F$20 for four hours. Next door to Bill's camp ground, his brother Keni and wife TC provide sea kayaks for day rental, as well as guided, overnight tours. Call them (☎ 880 083) for more information.

Just down the road (heading away from the airport) is *Tom's Campground* (formerly Valentine's), a grassy plot facing the beach which is in fact the family's front yard. Run by Selau Celau and his wife Nisi, the facilities include a laundry, shower, toilets and a small cook shack with two burners and utensils. There's also a comfortable room attached to the family house which is available for F$7. Camping costs F$4/6 for a single/double site. Selau will take you fishing or bushwalking if that is your pleasure.

Lisi Camping, next to Tom's, has a slightly larger camping area on the same grassy expanse. Run by a charming couple (Loti and Mary), there is also one room in their home which is available for F$10/15 a single/double. It has mosquito netting and is open to the sea breezes. Lisi Camping also has simple laundry and shower facilities (call it a tin shack) and a single toilet. A tent site costs F$5.

At the time of writing, a camping ground is planned for *Lavena Beach*, and may be in operation by the time this book is published. Lavena, known for its beach and nearby waterfall, is on the opposite side of the island from Wairiki. You can get there by bus (it's the end of the line), or by taxi (F$15 from Matei).

Susie's Plantation, on the opposite end of the island from Matei, has camping facilities in addition to houses and bures. (See following description.) Groceries are available within walking distance of the grounds.

Places to Stay – other areas

Susie's Plantation (☎ 880 125), one of the newer places to stay on the island, is actually an old homestead, first settled in the 1850s. It's in Vuna, at the southernmost end of the island (about an hour by car from the airport and two hours by bus) and is both a dive operation and a funky travellers' resort. The homestead consists of three rambling structures near the sea amidst a profusion of fruit trees, coconut palms, and old copra mill paraphernalia. In addition to the family home there are two houses for rent. The houses are comfortable and fully equipped with kitchen and bathroom facilities. One, the *Seaside Guest House* can accommodate up to seven people at a single booking and has a suite (F$35), a double room (F$25), a single room (F$12.50) and a double annex (F$20).

The *Guest House* can sleep up to eight people and has two double rooms (F$22), a single dorm (F$10) and a double annex (F$20). Though units are self-contained, owners Susie and Brian also offer a F$25 per

day meal package including breakfast, lunch and dinner. Guests are also welcome to the mangoes, bananas and avocados which grow on the property. Four self-contained bures are also planned, some of which will rent for F$25 and house up to three people. The others will be luxury waterfront bures accommodating up to six guests at F$65.

Sunset Accommodation (☎ 880 229) in Lovonivonu, is another new bottom-end place. The two self-contained bures cost F$8/12 a single/double. Write to PO Box 15, Lovonivonu, Taveuni for more information.

Namoli Beach Resort, just outside Vuna, was under construction at the time of writing and will be aimed at the budget market. It is situated on white sandy Namoli Beach and offers swimming and snorkelling in Vuna Lagoon, fishing from a small boat, and nature hikes in the hills of western Taveuni (or a trip to the shoreline blowhole). A unique activity here is exploration of adjacent ruins of ancient (pre-European) war fortifications, where many pottery shards are buried in the accumulated soil. You can't keep these shards, of course – they are part of the heritage of Fijians and are protected by law. (I don't know of any other resort in Fiji that offers an activity like this.)

Guests at Namoli will stay in bures at the edge of the beach, with part of a huge old copra plantation behind them. Nearby is an old stone house where the plantation boss used to live. Host Paul Masirewa is a native Taveunian, and he'll help you to discover the venerable but unknown Vuna area.

Also new is *Wailevu Lodge* in the village of Bouma. The lodge has two bure-style dorms at F$10 per person, and four bures at F$40 or F$50. Canoeing and other activities are available, and there is a minimarket. For information and bookings, enquire through the Nadi Bay Motel (☎ 723 599; fax 790 092).

Places to Eat – Somosomo area

In Somosomo village, an Indian family sells takeaway food in the F$2 range a few doors down from Kool's. There is also the *Central Restaurant* which is cheap but not good; and

Raj's, opposite Kaba's store, which doubles as a hairdressing salon. You can also try eating at the home of Semi Waqa. Known locally as *Semi's Place*, it is recommended that you bring kava with you. He charges F$8 to F$12 per person, and the food is reportedly very good. Perhaps the best cheap food is at *Lesuma's*, near the Garden Island Resort, where you can have inexpensive, wholesome food (and icy beer) at a table by the sea wall.

Places to Eat – Matai area

You can buy ice, fresh fish, and fish & chips in Waiyevo at a roadside stand (the site of a former market) just across from the Lesuma Store. Opening hours are very flexible, so keep an eye out for the 'fresh fish' sign at the roadside to see whether the stand is open for business.

Maravu Plantation Resort serves some of the best food on the island; the cuisine includes Indian, French, Italian and local dishes. Despite the rustic environment, the resort lends a definite air of refinement to the Taveuni hotel scene. Ormond Eyre has done what the large hotels cannot do – provide excellent food, good service and a personal touch in an intimate atmosphere.

If you are in Matei, a much less expensive alternative is to visit the home of *Margaret Peterson* (☎ 880 171), who also runs the food concession at the airport. It's a good idea to call her before you pop over so she can prepare. Keep in mind it is her home, not a restaurant. Meal prices are around F$5. See under Places to Stay for directions to Margaret's home.

A third option in the Matei area is the *Coconut Grove Cafe*, a new eatery run by American expats Ronna Goldstein and Steven Cohen. It is on the waterfront property, just opposite the airport. Prices range from F$5 to F$10 for lunch and F$15 to F$20 for dinner. Meals are served on a veranda overlooking the sea.

If you are in the same neighbourhood as the Coconut Grove and you crave home-baked desserts, check out *Audrey's Sweet Somethings*. Audrey Brown serves home-made goodies every day (10.30 am to 5.30 pm) from her porch in Naselesele village, a 10-minute walk from the airport. She is famous for her chocolate chunk cookies, Fijian fudge cake and lime tarts. She also serves a home-grown Taveuni blend of coffee, cold drinks and other goodies.

WAIRIKI CATHOLIC MISSION

A few km past Waiyevo there is an old church at Wairiki Catholic Mission with beautiful stained glass which, according to local legend, came from a cathedral that was demolished during the French Revolution. The glass was supposed to have been used in several churches throughout the Pacific but somehow all ended up in Wairiki. In addition to the stained glass there is a painting of the famous 19th century battle between the Tongan Ma'afu and the *kai Taveuni* (the locals) in the mission presbytery. Not coincidentally, the battle took place in the vicinity of the mission.

Surrounding the mission is a classic coconut plantation. You are also quite near where the International Date Line used to pass through and the sign is still on the roadside.

SALIALEVU PLANTATION

This is the island's largest copra/beef plantation, about 35 km from the Garden Island Resort. On the plantation grounds are the ruins of the 100-year-old **Billyard Sugar Mill**. There are also freshwater pools and a beach, but avoid swimming in the ocean – it's treacherous here. Ask permission from the plantation manager before entering because it is private property. Keep your eyes open, and you may see some lovely Monarch butterflies on orange milkweed in the pastures.

Nearby is **Dolphin Bay**, where you can water-ski and picnic. Arrange transport with a taxi or take a rental car.

LAKE TAGIMAUCIA

Perhaps the most famous geographical landmark on the island is Lake Tagimaucia, which is in an old crater 823 metres high in the mountains. The lake is filled with floating masses of vegetation and is home to Fiji's most famous and beautiful flower, the tagimaucia, which produces red blooms with white centres. Contrary to popular mythology which suggests that the tagimaucia flower grows nowhere else but on the shores of the lake, the epiphytic plant does, apparently, flourish at one other site. It is believed to be the sole surviving species from a related group that used to inhabit its mountain habitat. Still, any attempt to transplant the flower at a lower altitude has failed.

There are at least two legends attached to this lake.

The first relates to the greenish hue imparted to its perimeter by the submerged vegetation. The legend asserts that the fat of all turtles killed on Taveuni is taken by spirits to the lake.

The more famous tale (or at least one version of it) is attached to the flower and concerns a small girl who lived above the shores of the lake. One day she was playing when she should have been attending to her chores. Annoyed by her behaviour, her mother spanked the daughter and chased her out of the home. She ran sobbing and blundered into a tree full of thick vines in which she became entangled. As the tears rolled down her cheeks they turned to blood, which fell on the vine and turned to flowers. The girl did manage to free herself and lived happily ever after.

According to historian R A Derrick, the derivation of the name is as follows: the child of a local chief, having seen the flower, cried *(tagi)* for it; but as it could not be transplanted, crying was useless *(maumau)*, for there was nothing that resembled it *(ucuia)* to put in its place.

Getting to the lake is no easy task and necessitates hiring a guide for anywhere from F$10 to F$20. Leave yourself a full day for the arduous trek, which begins near the Mormon church in Somosomo. A guide can be recruited from the village, or enquire at the nearby hotel. This is not for the faint-hearted; trekkers should be in above-average condition for the journey. Please use all of your conservation ethics: this ecosystem is particularly fragile, and footsteps in the swampy lake side take years to disappear!

If you want to see the lake from a distance,

as well as some other great vistas, a hike up to **Des Voeux Peak** is worth the effort. Walk three km south from Garden Island Resort to the Catholic Mission. Just before the mission, a road to Des Voeux Peak branches to the interior. From the mission to the top is about six km which can comfortably be covered in three hours: two hours up and an hour back down. From the peak you can also see Tagimaucia but it's not possible to hike to the lake's shores.

Another option is to take a 4WD vehicle from Kaba's (or other places to stay) to Des Voeux Peak, through the rainforest; this is a popular trip for bird-watchers.

BOUMA FALLS

Bouma Falls, 36 km from the Garden Island Resort and on the island's east coast, are definitely worth seeing. To get to them, wait at the hotel at 9 am for the local bus heading north; you can also take a taxi, but the round-trip fare is F$25. When you reach the village of Bouma, walk 100 metres past it, and take the track inland 200 to 300 metres (past stands of wild ginger) to the falls. They cascade more than 24 metres into a cold-water pool in which you can swim, or you can walk on the ledge behind the falls and look out through the plunging water. There are several levels of the falls to explore.

Admission is now F$5. Though comparatively steep, the price is worth paying when you consider that the Fijian tribe which owns the property decided to forego logging the land in exchange for the opportunity to keep the falls as a tourist site. (See the introduction to this chapter for details.) It would be bad karma to avoid paying and, according to local lore, spirits have been known to punish those who don't pay. I was recently told that a family of four who sneaked into the falls was killed in a car accident on the way home. Pouring beer into the pool and rowdy behaviour are strictly taboo.

LAVENA

Near Lavena village (south of Bouma Falls), another waterfall plummets off a cliff directly into the sea. During WW II, ships requiring fresh water could actually go beneath the falls and fill their tanks with ease. A few km past the falls is Lavena Beach, a gorgeous white-sand beach with fine snorkelling and swimming. Admission is F$2. You can take the local bus here as well, or a taxi for about F$15 from Matei. Combining the falls and the beach for a day's outing is an excellent idea. This is a location where *Return to the Blue Lagoon* was filmed – a 'B' movie with stunning scenery.

BEACHES

Near Matei Airport is **Prince Charles Beach**, a white-sand beach with lots of shade. Swimming is great there, with plenty of shallow areas for kids. **Barbara Carrera Beach**, named after the sultry actress, is near Prince Charles Beach. Ms Carrera spent some time in Taveuni several years ago filming a TV mini-series based on the life of Queen Emma, a Samoan woman involved in turn-of-the-century political intrigue.

Lavena Beach, at the end of the paved road (past Bouma Falls) is also good, though there's a F$2 charge for day use. Unfortunately some visitors have found evidence that the beach may be used as a latrine by some members of the nearby village. Let's hope this practice stops.

Qamea, Laucala & Matagi

Qamea, Laucala and tiny Matagi are volcanic islands grouped immediately to the east of Thurston Point, Taveuni. Qamea and Laucala are surrounded by one barrier reef. Until a decade ago these islands were never visited by tourists because there was no accommodation on them. Today Qamea has one small resort, and Laucala, which is owned by US financial publisher Malcolm Forbes, has the most exclusive resort in Fiji. Matagi, the newest development in the area, caters for up-market divers.

Around the Islands

QAMEA

Qamea, 2½ km from Thurston Point, is 10 km long and varies in width from several hundred metres to five km. Its area is 34 sq km. Like its large island neighbours, Qamea is rugged and covered by dense forest. Steep-sided valleys divide high hills, some of which approach 300 metres in height. Qamea's **Naivivi Bay** is known geographically as a 'hurricane hole' – in other words, it is sheltered naturally from hurricanes. During these periods many vessels anchor offshore.

For its size, Qamea is a populous island, having six villages (Kocoma being the largest) and a population of around 550. Both Qamea's and Laucala's original populations were displaced during the 19th century by Chief Cakobau, who was angry with the original inhabitants for having taken the side of his enemy, Ma'afu, during a tribal conflict.

Like Taveuni, Qamea is of interest to naturalists because the mongoose was never introduced there; thus the indigenous fauna, especially bird life, was never interfered with. For some reason (unknown to me), natives of Qamea are referred to as *kai-Farani* (Frenchmen) – not a compliment.

They prepare a local food called *paileve* – a concoction fermented in a pit.

There's only one place to stay, *Qamea Beach Club* (☎ /fax 880 220), an eight-bure resort on 17 hectares of land. All of the bures face the beach, and have verandahs, overhead fans and hammocks. Singles/doubles cost F$240/270, triples F$295. The food is excellent and meals cost F$60 per person per day; island transfers are F$30.

Activities include water-skiing, fishing, windsurfing, snorkelling, sailing, shelling, canoeing, a waterfall tour and crab hunts. Qamea is a comparatively big island compared to the Mamanucas (offshore from Viti Levu) so you don't feel claustrophobic. There is plenty of room for nature walks and there are organised visits to the local village of **Vatusogosogo**, which has traditional thatched bures and is quite beautiful. The hotel also has two dive masters, two dive boats and all the equipment. Reefs in the area are reportedly magnificent.

Getting There & Away

Clients of Qamea Beach Club are picked up by boat from the airstrip at Taveuni, which is only a 15-minute, four-km ride away.

LAUCALA

Laucala lies east of Qamea, separated by a strait just several hundred metres wide. It is five km long and from 1½ to three km wide, with an area of 12 sq km. It was sold by Chief Cakobau – who was once kept a prisoner on the island – to Europeans who turned it into a copra plantation and later sold it to the Carpenter Group, an Australian corporation.

In 1972 the owners sold the island to the late Malcolm 'Capitalist Tool' Forbes for a cool US$1 million. When Forbes purchased Laucala, the workers' houses – ramshackle tenements – were in a sorry state of repair. The US millionaire then spent an undisclosed fortune constructing more than 40 modern homes for his workers, all of which have water-seal toilets, piped-in spring water for washing, individual cisterns for drinking water, modern kitchens and electricity. He also built a home for himself, four guest houses, a school complex, a copra plant, store, workshop, dormitory, boathouse, refrigeration plant, airstrip and other facilities. Primary education is free on Laucala (unlike in the rest of Fiji) and 'Fiji Forbes' will pay for up to half a youngster's secondary education, including the university level.

Workers' paradise? Perhaps. However, although Laucala has all the trappings of a Fijian community, there are fundamental differences. Because it is a private estate one of many owned by Forbes around the world – the traditional authority of village government is nonexistent there. In some instances, as in cases where people are removed from the island, the manager has even more power than a chief might.

The lack of traditional authority accounts for other differences between Laucala and more typical communities. As a University of the South Pacific student whose father lives on Laucala told me:

Dress is different on the island. For example, some women wear pants, which they would never do in a village. Also, church attendance is much poorer than you would expect in an average community. There is no chief or village elder to watch over you, which is a sort of unnatural situation for villagers.

Roughly half the workers on the island are native Laucalans, while the other half come from neighbouring villages on Qamea or elsewhere. The plantation supplies jobs to people in an area where outside employment is nil and people live largely in a subsistence economy. Cash filters down to the non-resident relatives of those who work on Laucala, and in this way wealth is spread.

Because copra farming is not the most profitable enterprise, Fiji Forbes has invested money in the island's future by diversifying industry through the introduction of animal husbandry (cattle and goat farming) and the establishment of a small-scale resort for high-rolling tourists.

Laucala Resort

Laucala Resort (☎ 880 077; 780 040) has been dubbed 'the ultimate tropical paradise' by several travellers. Certainly on Laucala, which specialises in game fishing, Robinson Crusoe never had it so good.

The resort has four air-con bures that sleep up to eight people. Two are equipped with two bedrooms and a bath, and two have one bedroom and a bath. All have a living room, kitchen and fully-stocked bar including wines. A chef makes your dinner in your own home, and reports are that he knows how to cook pretty damn well. Prices begin at US$2400 per person (all inclusive) for seven days and eight nights, the minimum stay. A 10% deposit secures your reservation and the balance must be paid at least four weeks prior to arrival.

In the USA contact Fiji Forbes Inc, c/o Forbes Magazine, 60 Fifth Ave, New York, 10011 (☎ 212 620 2461), or in Fiji write to Fiji Forbes Inc, Laucala Island, Waiyevo PO Box 41, Taveuni.

Since fishing is the main attraction, a fishing boat (with skipper) and tournament-quality tackle are provided. You apparently need the tournament quality because fishing is superb. You can expect to hook black Pacific sailfish up to 90 kg, yellowfin tuna up to 45 kg, barracuda up to 45 kg, mahimahi up to 45 kg, and even black marlin up to 225 kg.

The coves and inlets around Laucala also offer great fishing, especially for those using light spinning tackle and lures. There is a great reef for snorkelling and scuba diving 22 km from Laucala. Near the reef is also a small sandy island for picnicking or diving excursions. Naturally Forbes 'throws in' amenities such as scuba tanks and water-skiing gear so you can dive or ski to your heart's content. For those who want to travel around Laucala itself, there is even a jeep with which to explore.

Other amenities include jet skis, windsurfing, a VCR with a supply of movies, tennis, volleyball and a swimming pool.

Getting There & Away

When Forbes' clients disembark from their

scheduled flight in Nadi, they are met by their own personal pilot who skippers a twin-engine green-and-gold Navajo Chieftain (with 'Capitalist Tool' inscribed on the side). They are whisked to Laucala, 90 minutes away by air.

There are also local boats which ferry people to and from Qamea.

MATAGI

Matagi (☎ 880 260; fax 880 274) is the name of a horseshoe-shaped, 71-hectare private island 10 km off the north-east coast of Taveuni. It ranks as one of the finest small resorts in Fiji, and is owned and operated by Noel Douglas, the man who successfully ran Malcolm Forbes' island for years. Douglas stresses that Matagi is still a working plantation and he will show guests how a plantation is run.

Matagi Resort has 10 round 'Polynesian-style' bures that are exquisitely crafted and can withstand 160 km/h winds. I have no doubt that Mr Douglas supervised every nail being banged in! The bures have tile floors, bamboo and rattan cane walls and overhead fans. The area around the bures is landscaped and the beach front, only metres away, is excellent. There is also a great view of Qamea. Prices in the standard bures begin at F$140/187 a single/double, F$220 a triple. Deluxe bures are F$180/235 a single/double, F$280 a triple. Meals are F$60 per person per day.

Matagi is primarily suited to divers and fishing enthusiasts. Diving in the area is superb, as is light-tackle sport fishing. There is also deep-sea fishing from September to December, and saltwater fly fishing. Other activities include windsurfing, sailing, water-skiing and snorkelling. The island has nature trails, bush walks, caves, inlets and great bird-watching. The daily rate for a two-tank dive begins at F$99 per person per day (from one to four days). Divers are provided with a dive boat (the *Matagi Princess)*, a guide, a weight belt, tanks and tank refills. Transfer to and from Taveuni costs F$45. For more information, write to PO Box 83, Waiyevo, Taveuni.

Getting There & Away

You can fly to Taveuni with Fiji Air from Suva or with Sunflower Airlines from Nadi. The Matagi Resort people will shuttle you on a speedboat to the island. Transfer is free going over, but costs F$30 going back.

Kadavu Group

The Kadavu group lies between 88 km and 96 km south of Suva. Aside from the main island of Kadavu, which is the fourth-largest in the Fiji archipelago, the group includes the island of Ono and a number of smaller islands lying within the Great Astrolabe Reef and making up its northern extension.

Kadavu, with a population of approximately 9000, is not one of the tourist hot spots and retains a conservative, traditional culture. It is an island known for its head strong, independent thinkers: its chiefly system is different from other parts of Fiji, allowing affairs to be run by stronger local chiefs rather than by a few 'big chiefs'.

In the last few years the number of places to stay in the Kadavu group has grown. The oldest is Reece's Place, on Galoa, formerly a whaling station. The newer properties are Albert's Place, a few km to the east of Galoa; Dive Kadavu Matana Resort, a 10-minute boat ride from Vunisea; Nukubalavu, at the eastern tip of Kadavu (near Albert's Place) and Kini's Bure Resort on Ono Island. There is one other resort, Kenia, but due to family squabbles its operation has only been intermittent.

From the visitor's viewpoint, the main problem with Kadavu has been a lack of transport around the island, as well as between Kadavu and the rest of Fiji. However, sea and air links between Kadavu and the rest of Fiji have improved. It's best, especially where catching international flights are concerned, to make certain your air reservations to and from the island are firm. Flights to Kadavu are still not as frequent as those to other destinations.

The island is best known for its fantastic diving in the Great Astrolabe Reef, considered one of the finest dive destinations in the world. Some villagers of Kadavu are also known for their ability to call turtles up from the depths of the sea. Other, more arcane facts about the island are that it's the home of a rare parrot; it's famed for raising goats;

the local yaqona is very strong; and fishing between Kadavu and Beqa is excellent.

History

Kadavu was first sighted by Captain Bligh on his return voyage to Fiji aboard HMS *Providence* in 1792. Seven years later, the US vessel *Ann & Hope*, skippered by Captain C Bently, touched on Kadavu while on a voyage from Australia. In 1827 the French commander Dumont d'Urville brought the *Astrolabe* to the island, nearly running it onto the great reef that envelopes the northern extension of the Kadavu group. He named the reef after his ship. In later years, Tavuki Bay on the island was frequented by bêche-de-mer traders and by whalers from Sydney (Australia) and from the New England ports of the USA. By this time whale teeth (primarily those of the cachalot species) had replaced the ancient form of tabua in religious ceremonies and become an important item of barter with the whalers. The teeth were in such demand that on one occasion a Fijian chief kidnapped a mate and ship's crew of the *Nimrod* from Sydney in exchange for whale teeth he had seen on the ship.

As years passed and overseas shipping increased, Galoa Harbour in Kadavu became a regular stop for mail ships from San Francisco, Sydney and Auckland. At Galoa (which was once considered as a possible capital for the Fijian colony), passenger cargo and mail were transshipped to the steamers of the branch line running to New Zealand, and to the small vessels plying the waters between the port and Levuka. Galoa was not a busy port, even though the anchorage was spacious and well protected, and was only used for about three years. The shore accommodation, according to historian R A Derrick, was 'wretched', consisting of a few huts, several small shops and a whisky store. After this brief flurry of activ-

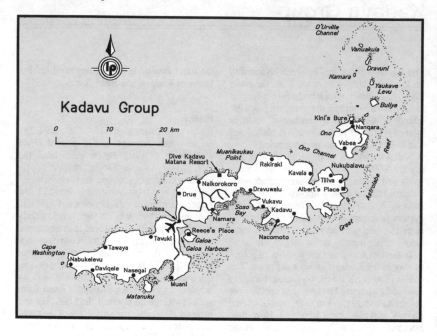

ity the island reverted to its former sleepy nature.

Geography

The Kadavu group is volcanic in nature, the main island being Kadavu, which is 93 km long and varies in width from several hundred metres to 13 km. It has an area of 408 sq km. All its coasts are deeply indented, some bays biting so far into the land that they almost divide the island. One geographer has suggested that the shape of Kadavu resembles that of a wasp, with the head, thorax and abdomen linked by narrow waists. Thus Vunisea (where the administrative centre is), Namalata Bay and Galoa Harbour are separated by only a sandy isthmus standing a few metres above sea level; and at Vunisea the heads of Daku Bay and Soso Bay are within 1100 metres of each other, with only a low ridge between. This same characteristic occurs elsewhere on the island to a varying degree; the shape and arrangement of these bays suggests that they may be drowned valleys.

Kadavu is rugged and its mountains are high for so narrow an island. Several peaks rise more than 600 metres, while many are half that size. Coasts are generally fringed with coral reefs, the most famous being the 48-km loop of the Great Astrolabe Reef on Kadavu's northern extension.

The island can be divided into several main areas. The western end is 24 km long and dominated by **Nabukelevu** (Mt Washington), 822 metres high. Flanking the mountain on the southern side are lovely crescent-shaped beaches. From this peak a spur runs west to Cape Washington – a rocky bluff crowned by a lighthouse – and continues in a range terminating in a steep cross range overlooking Galoa Harbour. One of the most beautiful villages in Fiji, **Daviqele**, is in this area. The northern part of this region is called Yawe, known for its large earthenware cooking pottery still made by the women of Nalotu village. Most of the northern coast extending to the Sanima and Yale districts further east is dry and sheltered by reed-like vegetation and scattered reefs offshore. Much of the goat raising is done here.

The link between the island's western end and its centre is Namalata Isthmus, known to Fijians as Na Yarabale (literally, 'the place where the canoes are dragged across'). In the same area is the village of **Namuana**, home of the people who can call turtles from the sea.

Opposite the isthmus on the southern side is Galoa Harbour, and in the harbour is 2½-km-long Galoa Island (after which the harbour was named). On the southernmost point of this part of the island is a tiny islet, **Tawadromu**, which was once home to an American Indian – the sole representative of his race among the mixed population of the period. Why he stayed and what he was doing there is anyone's guess. Further along the southern coast is the Naceva area, perhaps the most untouched and primeval in nature, with forests, mangrove swamps along the water's edge, many waterfalls and an ever-present mist hanging over the mountains.

The Ono Island group, enclosed by the Great Astrolabe Reef, has wonderful fishing and diving. Cruise ships sometimes stop at **Dravuni Island**, perhaps because there are great white-sand beaches. There is also a fisheries station. Yachts find the area appealing, but must first get a permit to stop there.

Information
On Namalata Isthmus are Vunisea, the government station, a high school, a hospital, the island administration and an airstrip. There are a few small stores and a public market in the vicinity.

Travellers should bring cash as there are no banks on Kadavu.

GETTING THERE & AWAY
Air
Air transport is available from Suva and Nadi. Because there are fewer flights between Kadavu and Viti Levu than other outer island destinations it may be advisable to make your reservations way ahead of time.

Fiji Air has flights on Monday, Tuesday, Thursday and Saturday for F$47 one way. Sunflower has three flights (Wednesday, Friday and Sunday) for F$66. Those disembarking at the airport and heading towards Reece's Place should realise that they will have to lug their baggage about a km to catch a boat to the 'resort'.

Boat
The MV *Gurawa* (☎ 340 015; 312 426; 320 308) sails twice a week (Monday and Thursday morning at 6 am), dropping travellers off at Albert's Place for F$20. The *Princess Ashika* (☎ 315 644) sails on Thursday at midnight, dropping passengers at Vunisea for F$34.10. If you need boat transfers from Vunisea to Albert's Place, contact the resort (☎ 302 896) to arrange transfers. I'm told it's preferable to take the *Gurawa* rather than the *Ashika* because you see more (the vessel stops in several villages along the way) and you are dropped off directly at Albert's Place in Nukubalavu. See the Inter-Island Ferry section in the Getting Around chapter for more details.

There are also other boats going to Vunisea and it is easy to catch one to Galoa.

Around the Islands

KADAVU

Vunisea

Vunisea is the largest settlement on the island, and is a government station with stores, a hospital, school, post office and jetty. There are several beaches in the vicinity. Nearby also is Biana, an 'off-licence' store where the only beer on the island is sold. West of Vunisea is the traditional turtle-calling stone where the Namuana villagers have called turtles from the depths of the sea for generations.

Beaches

There is a good beach north of Vunisea's jetty (on crown land) and another (with a waterfall after it rains and great swimming) at **Udulevu**, just around the western corner of Vunisea Bay. The beach at Udulevu is actually on village land, but it's OK to visit if you wade along the shore and stay away from nearby Namuana village.

Waterfalls

About two km south of the airport and a short hike off the road is **Waikana Falls**, which has two nice pools for swimming.

Better yet is another wonderful, more secluded waterfall and pool five to six km east of Vunisea – probably on village land, but far enough from any settlement generally to be considered public. The second fall is better for wildlife viewing – you may see one of the local parrots.

Places to Stay

Albert's Place (☎ 302 896), on the south-eastern edge of Kadavu, is one of the newest places to stay in Fiji's outer islands. Situated on a crescent-shaped beach several hundred metres in length, it is an attractive proposition both for divers and non-divers. Beaches and snorkelling here are superior and there are accessible tide pools in the area. There are also several villages nearby which makes it an excellent scene to meet locals and learn about Fijian culture.

Albert's Place has 15 clean, spartan thatched-roof bures, some of which sleep up to four people; a dorm that sleeps six; a dining hall; a recreation bure; plenty of camping sites; flushing toilets and ample drinking water. Fishing, snorkelling and diving (run by Naiqoro Divers) is excellent. There is no electricity but kerosene lamps are provided. Meals can be purchased at the resort, or you can cook your own. If you plan to cook, bring plenty of food, as there is only one small local shop nearby with few provisions. If you can afford it it's probably better to let Albert take care of the cooking. Prices are F$12 per person to share a double bure within spitting distance of the beach. Add another F$18 per person for three huge meals. Campers are charged F$3.

Diving at Albert's Place is reportedly superb, and dive sites at the famous Astrolabe Reef are only a five-minute boat ride from the resort. Fish are huge, as is the soft coral. One dive costs F$35, two dives are F$65, which is reasonable by Fijian standards. Equipment such as tanks, weights etc, are available. You are required to bring your PADI certification.

If you let Albert know of your arrival, arrangements can be made for visitors to be picked up from the airport by boat at a cost of F$50 for the first one or two people and F$23 each for the next three or more. The boat ride takes about 1½ hours from the airport. The MV *Gurawa* (a commercial trading boat) departs Suva's Kings Wharf on Monday and Thursday at 6 am and returns on Tuesday and Friday. The trip takes six hours, and people can be dropped off at Albert's Place. The fare is F$20. For more information, see the Getting There & Away section earlier in this chapter.

It is also possible to travel by boat to Albert's Place from Reece's Place. Write to the O'Connors, c/o Naleca Post Office, Naleca, Fiji.

Nukubalavu Resort (☎ 520 089; 311 075 in Suva), has undergone management changes and is now run by two Australians,

Dave Miller and Mark Hinton. It is set well off the beaten track at the eastern tip of Kadavu, on a long beach near the village of Waisalima. The resort provides for basic needs and in keeping with this theme, is strictly 'no frills'. One flush toilet and a cold-water shower serve up to 24 guests and there is no electricity. Most construction is traditional thatch or woven palm fronds with all its romantic associations and practical disadvantages. When you explore the area, you may also find yourself fording a thigh-deep river.

Without electricity, beer is only lukewarm but food is simple, hearty and nicely prepared, using primarily local ingredients. (Guests may learn to actually like taro after a few days.) Given the 'hardships' associated with staying at a remote locale like Nukubalavu there is also a camaraderie among the guests built upon shared experiences and adventures.

The hills around Nukubalavu, which have terrific views, are inviting for day treks. There are waterfalls and rainforests as well as steep climbs through native gardens known as 'plantations'. For the ornithologically inclined, there are many species of birds found nowhere outside of Kadavu. The beaches are empty and you can follow connecting narrow tracks along the shoreline cliffs.

As in all of Kadavu, snorkelling and diving is excellent. PADI instruction is available. Diving costs range from F$25 for a shore dive to an offshore two-tank dive for F$65.

Accommodation prices range from tent sites for F$3 per day (supplied by the resort), to dorm beds, private bures, and family bures which run to F$24 per day. Optional, reasonably priced meals are charged separately. There is no store nearby so it's probably easiest to rely on the resort for food.

Transport can either be provided from the airport by transfer (previously arranged) or by the *Gurawa* which will drop you directly at the resort. For more information, write to PO Box, Naleca, Kadavu.

Dive Kadavu Matana Resort (☎ 311 780; fax 303 860) is close to Vunisea and the airstrip and is also the most luxurious accommodation on the island. In this case 'luxurious' should not be confused with plush or ostentatious; 'comfortable' is perhaps a better adjective, as the resort is one of two properties on Kadavu with electricity. Cleverly designed to blend in with the landscape as one approaches via boat, it is constructed with a blend of traditional and modern materials. There's a lovely beach just metres away, and the property is immaculately maintained. The maximum number of guests is only 20, so the feeling is very intimate.

Amenities include hot showers, flush toilets and ceiling fans (which take over when the sea breeze quits). There are also clam-shell footpaths along the bures which eliminate tracking dirt into your room. Food is good and ample, and is usually served buffet-style which encourages guests to mix. Wine and beer are available.

Tariffs begin at F$100 for budget accommodation; F$115/165 for a single/double with private ocean view; and F$100/140/200 for a single/double/triple with private beach front. All tariffs include meals.

Diving is the primary activity, with Namalata Reef at the front door. There are so many dive sites that the underwater explorer will probably not return to the same area twice. Full PADI certification courses are available and Dive Kadavu has a good reputation. Boat dives are F$50 each, night dives F$60 and shore dives F$25.

Snorkelling is also possible a few steps from your bure. Hiking in the nearby hills will yield spectacular seascape vistas, a look at wild orchids and perhaps a glimpse of several species of parrot endemic to the island. Swimming, beachcombing and sunbathing are also possible for non-divers. In the evenings, one can hang out in the lounge reading a paperback or listening to a CD available from the 'library'. As most of Matana's guests will arrive by air, make sure you arrange transfer from the airport ahead of time. Write to PO Box 8, Vunisea, Kadavu for more information.

Places to Eat

There is a minuscule coffee shop at the airstrip, but short of that and the resorts, there really is no formal eatery.

Getting Around

There are a few buses on Kadavu that will get you to the outer villages, but the island lacks a good road system. The best way to get around is by foot or boat. Vavu in Murani village has a boat and is willing to take people fishing or on excursions for a fee. Boats are also for hire in Vunisea. Check with the local police or government station for information.

GALOA ISLAND

Reece's Place on Galoa Island, off the southern coast of Kadavu, is a F$5, 20-minute boat ride from the administrative centre at Vunisea. There is electricity from 7 am to 8.30 pm, and a dive operation called Sun & Sea Dive.

Reviews of Reece's Place have been mixed, but are generally favourable. On the positive side, the Reece's are friendly people and the price is reasonable. However, there have been reports of less than great food, rats and (guest) overcrowding. Because there is no phone, and communication is only by mail, the place is popular with those who want to get away from it all. Bunks are F$12 per person per night in bure-style accommodation or F$4 for campers.

Food is 'home-style' family cooking and is reportedly OK, but is often bereft of vegetables, and portions can be small. Some travellers recommend bringing snacks to liven things up. Breakfast is F$2, lunch F$3 and dinner F$6.

The biggest drawback with Reece's is that there is no nearby beach. Snorkelling is good but you have to take a boat to get to the reef. At Reece's Place one dive costs F$35, two dives are F$60, and a shore dive F$15. Prices include tanks and weights. A PADI-approved open-water course is F$295, which includes all equipment, tank refills etc. Those wishing to hire gear can rent a regulator, buoyancy vest, fins, mask, wet suit and gloves for F$15 a day, F$25 for two days and F$75 per week. Underwater attractions include caves, chasms and plenty of fish. There is also a so-called 'House of Sharks'. Write to Joe and Mona Reece at PO Box 6, Vunisea, Kadavu for more information. For bookings and information in Australia contact Sea Life International Travel (☎ 02 665 6335), 27 Alfreda St, Coogee, Sydney, NSW 2034.

ONO

The Ono Island group, north-east of Kadavu, is enclosed by the Great Astrolabe Reef, an area renown for its spectacular diving and fishing. Locals on Ono still practise an ancient ritual of fermenting stored foodstuffs (breadfruit, plantains and dalo) underground. A hole is dug in the ground, the food is placed in it and is stored up to several years as an insurance against times of need. This used to be done throughout Fiji but is now rare.

On Ono you can stay at *Kini's Bure Resort* a reportedly beautiful spot on the beach run by Fijians with simple, bure-style accommodation. Diving in the area is operated by Astrolabe Divers (☎/fax 302 689). The price is F$50 per person per day including meals. An open-water certificate course is F$350 and two-tank dives are F$90. For more information write to Astrolabe Divers PO Box, Naqara, Kadavu.

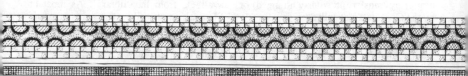

Lau Group

The islands and atolls of the Lau (Eastern) group are scattered over an area of 114,000 sq km to the south-east of Viti Levu. The main islands of the Tongan group extend in a parallel chain less than 320 km to the east; in fact, southern Lau is closer to Tonga than it is to Suva. Tongan influence in Lau has been important for as many as 1000 years, and during the mid-19th century it was dominant. Students of the South Pacific will note that Tongan place names are common throughout the area; and on many of the islands, Tongan was spoken as freely as Fijian. Likewise, material culture, customs and traditions were all modified by Tongan contacts.

The total land area of the Lau group is about 461 sq km, which exceeds that of Taveuni or Kadavu; but since one-third of this is composed of the three islands of Moala, Lakeba and Vanuabalavu, and there are five others of more than 26 sq km in area, the majority of the 60-odd islands that make up the group are very small.

Tourism to the Lau group has been relatively insignificant, but this may change with the construction of a new property, Yanuyanu Island Resort in Vanuabalavu. At the time of writing the project is still under construction.

History
European discovery of the Lau group was piecemeal, being spread over nearly 50 years, from Cook's visit to Vatoa in 1774 to Bellingshausen's discovery of the Ono group in 1820. As early as 1814 there existed charts of the archipelago that contained more reliable information about the area than about any other part of Fiji. The names of the islands, however, were unrecognisable because the written Fijian language had not been developed and the European discoverers had scarcely any contact with the islanders.

Although the islands are classified for administrative purposes as one group, until the middle of the last century they comprised three different territories: northern Lau, Lau proper and the Moala group.

Northern Lau extended as far south as Tuvuca, and paid tribute to the chiefs of Cakaudrove (Vanua Levu) until about 1855, when the Tongan warlord Ma'afu acquired the right of sovereignty over the area and established his headquarters at Lomaloma in Vanuabalavu.

Lau proper, which extended from Cicia to Ono-i-Lau in the extreme south, was under the authority of Tui Nayau, the paramount chief of Lakeba. (This title, incidentally, is now held by Ratu Sir Kamisese Mara, the prime minister.) With the advent of Ma'afu, however, the Tui Nayau's influence waned; and although he kept the title of 'king' of the region, he was dominated by the Tongans.

The Moala group historically had affiliations with Lomaiviti and Bau, rather than with Lau; but shortly after Ma'afu established himself at Lomaloma he extended his influence over the Moala area as well.

Under Ma'afu's control during the mid-19th century, the Lau group was united and attained a degree of prosperity and peace unknown before. Ma'afu created a title for himself, Tui Lau (King of Lau), encouraged the settlement of Europeans, and developed a constitution and set of laws. His Lau Confederation proved to be the most successful of the early attempts at constitutional government in Fiji.

GETTING THERE & AWAY
Fiji Air has two flights a week at F$89 one way to Lakeba, or you can travel the old-fashioned way on a copra boat or government vessel. Contact the government Marine Department in Suva (☎ 315 230) for schedules.

Around the Islands

LAKEBA
Lakeba, with a population of about 2000 in eight villages, is the largest island in the Lau group, and politically the most important. It is one of the few places in Lau that has accommodation. Lakeba is also the home island of Ratu Sir Kamisese Mara, the prime minister. The main source of income on the island is copra production, which is expedited by the presence of a coconut mill four km outside the government station at Tubou.

Geography
Lakeba is irregularly oval in outline, shaped somewhat like a shark's tooth, with a tongue of land jutting out from the south coast. The island is about nine km long and nearly as wide, covers 57 sq km, and is the 10th largest island in the archipelago. The central mass of Lakeba is volcanic in origin, the highest point rising to 219 metres. On the west and north-west slopes are masses of coralliferous limestone forming steep bluffs, cliffs and several major caves near the village of Nasaqalau. The soil of Lakeba is fertile and the once bare hills have been planted with pine trees. Of late Lakeba has been the subject of a thorough archaeological excavation which has revealed the presence of a massive fortification, built perhaps a thousand years ago as a defence against Tongan invaders. The fortification was believed to have been large enough to house 2500 people, the entire population of the island.

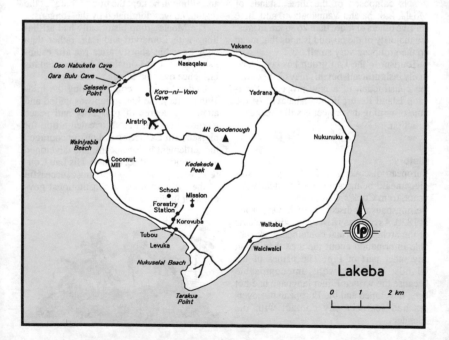

Culture

As has frequently been mentioned, Tongan influence in language and culture is strong in Lakeba. The cultural manifestations of Tongan culture even appear in the shapes of the houses, which are rounded like those in Samoa and Tonga rather than square-ended like those in the rest of Fiji. Even when homes are constructed with wooden materials, the ends are sometimes rounded. Church services also exhibit Tongan origins: a special evening service called *polotu* features many Tongan hymns; on formal occasions Tongan clothing including a mat tied around the waist is worn; and Tongan mekes (dances) may also be performed.

Shark Calling There is one clan in the village of **Nasaqalau** where the only people in Fiji who can call sharks live. They do this annually in October or November, though generally not for the benefit of visitors. The power comes from the village of Wainikeli in Taveuni, where some of the settlers from Nasaqalau originated. Not only are these folks imbued with the power to call sharks, but according to tradition, the same force serves as a protection from sharks if a boat capsizes.

About a month before the ceremony, a post is stuck in the reef with a piece of masi (tapa cloth) attached to the end of it (something like a pennant) in the area where the sharks are to be called. No-one is allowed in the vicinity of the post. A bete (a traditional Fijian priest) performs a daily yaqona ceremony nearby and checks the area daily to make sure no-one fishes or trespasses.

When the big day comes, the caller (a man or woman) wades in the water, neck high, and begins chanting. Within between 30 minutes and an hour a school of up to 50 sharks, led by a white shark, will circle the caller. The sharks are then led to the shallows where all of them (except the white shark) may be killed and later eaten.

In former times many sharks were killed as part of the annual event, but it has been about 40 years since their slaughter has been part of the ceremony. Currently, the prime minister is encouraging the revival of the complete ritual. Visitors lucky enough to attend should be prepared to offer donations to a charitable Fijian institution. No money should be offered as payment for this ceremony: according to my source, villagers believe that the 'leader shark' was formerly incarnated as a young man and would dislike commercialisation, which would be sacrilegious. Should the villagers not respect tradition, it is believed the sharks may decide not to show up one day.

There is no scientific explanation for the seemingly obedient sharks. One theory is that the arrival of the sharks may be connected to an annual migration.

Stopping the Sun As if calling sharks wasn't challenging enough for the villagers of Nasaqalau, I am told they also have the power to stop the sun, if just for a few minutes. Galu Veitokiaki, an old friend and native of Nasaqalau, told me that if someone is on the way to the village around dusk and wants a little extra daylight to get home in time for dinner, the villager can go to

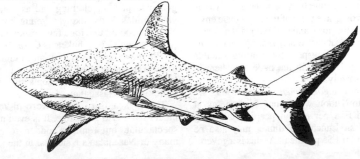

Saubukbuki (near the village), pick a certain type of reed and call to the sun to let it know what's going on. The reed is tied into a knot while simultaneously hidden in the fist, out of the light. The villager then runs home quickly (with light to spare) and upon returning, opens the hand. At this very moment darkness closes in like a tidal wave.

Bat Balolo Up to the early 1960s fruit bats were also herded like cattle to one end of the island and then clubbed and eaten. This was a very involved process requiring that some of the village women from Nasaqalau don special costumes and live in the bush for three months. The practice was stopped because someone in the village died mysteriously: it is believed that the reason for the death was an incorrect following of the ceremonial procedure.

Tubou

The main village on the island is Tubou, which is on the south coast and is the home of the prime minister. The village has a government station that includes a telephone exchange, a hospital and a post office. The lovely Methodist church beside the village green is cross-shaped, an unusual feature of Methodist churches in Fiji. In Tubou are also the graves of perhaps two of the more influential personalities in Fiji during the last century – the Tongan leader and warlord Enele Ma'afu, who conquered much of Fiji; and Ratu Sir Lala Sukuna, who helped transform the colony into a nation. Behind the village is a church compound where many of the early missionaries are buried. A climb to the Catholic church on the hill west of Tubou gives you a nice view of the immediate environs. To the north and the south of the village are good beaches. When visiting them or the village, show respect by wearing suitable clothing. Bathing in the nude anywhere in Fiji is strictly taboo.

There is a *government guest house* (☎ 42 090) in Tubou which has four rooms at around F$8 per person per day including breakfast. Lunch and dinner may also be bought for F$5 per meal. As this is a govern-

ment facility, you should book ahead to ensure that room is available. If you can't get a room there, do not go to Lakeba unless you are invited ahead of time to stay in a village.

Levuka

Adjacent to Tubou is the village of Levuka (not to be confused with the old capital of Fiji). It is home to a fishing tribe who, according to legend, came from Bau.

Caves

Near Nasaqalau are several caves, the most famous being **Oso Nabukete**, known as the 'Pregnant Women's Cave'. It is called this because legend has it that a woman hiding her pregnancy will not be able to slip through the cave's opening.

To visit this marvellous cave, see Nautogumu, Nasaqalau's *turaga-ni-matagali* (chief of the clan), who will provide a guide for a fee of approximately F$5. The guide should have a benzene lamp, but you should still bring a torch (flashlight) to really appreciate the size of the caverns and the many stalagmites and stalactites therein. There are many narrow passages to squeeze through and plenty of bat guano around, so wear your grubbiest clothing and oldest tennis shoes. In the cave is a stream with icy cold water, so you may want to bring a bathing suit for a refreshing swim. The entire tour takes from one to 1½ hours. Outside the entrance is the grave of Sapuga, the Tongan who, according to local legend, brought fruit bats from his homeland to Lakeba. Once outside the cave, you are several metres from the beach. This might be the opportunity to wash the bat guano from your clothing and ask one of your guides (most likely a young boy) to climb a coconut tree for a few drinking nuts.

Adjoining Oso Nabukete is **Qara Bulu**, a smaller cave once used as a jail in times of tribal war, but generally not shown to visitors. You may see this by contacting Tiko Veitokiaki in Nasaqalau.

There is a third cave, **Koro-ni-Vono**, inland from Oso Nabukete. It is even more spectacular, but remains hidden to even many of Nasaqalau's residents. In the good old days those who acquired the dreaded *lilabalavu* disease (tuberculosis) were shunted inside and left to perish while the cave was sealed. To this day villagers say that the moaning of the victims can be heard when you go near the entrance. If you want to find out for yourself (and see the old bones), talk to Tiko Veitokiaki and he will arrange a guide to take you there for F$5.

Getting Around
There is a 29-km road circling the island but little traffic, except for a few carriers that are generally unscheduled.

KAIBU
Kaibu is the name of a small, privately owned island (four km long and a km wide) with a jewel of a resort called Kaimbu Island Resort. (The added 'm' makes it easier for those unaware of the idiosyncrasies of the Fijian language to pronounce.) Encompassing Kaibu and the neighbouring island of Yacata is a spectacular 22.4 km long reef. The two islands are separated by a lagoon, ideal for snorkelling and other water sports. As it is in the midst of the Lau group, about 56 km west of Vanuabalavu, there is no worry that one would suffer from overcrowding. Because of its isolated setting the island is pristine. Beaches are untouched and shelling is excellent.

Kaimbu Island Resort (☎ 880 333; 1 800 473 0332 in the USA) is an ultra-exclusive lodging that is as remote from the world as one could want it to be. It has only three octagonal bures, but each of them is exquisitely constructed from imported and local materials. The octagonal motif, which features eight-metre ceilings, is said by the owner to resemble a high chief's dwelling. The roof is buttressed by massive hardwood beams from trees on the island, wrapped in *magi magi* (coconut fibre) rope. The bure also has floor-to-ceiling sliding glass doors that feature a 180-degree view of the beach and the neighbouring islands. Each two-room suite is furnished with a king-sized bed, onyx bathroom, fully stocked fridge and bar.

Fresh food comes from Kaimbu's own vegetable 'plantation' and of course the sea. Meals are served in a clifftop dining room on the premises. As if it weren't enough there is also a masseuse on staff, and the resort can perform weddings and renewal of vows.

In addition to water sports, activities include tennis, golf, hiking, volleyball, badminton, croquette, shuffleboard, table tennis, water-skiing, sailing, and deep-sea fishing (in an 8.5-metre boat). The ocean around Kaibu is full of game fish including sailfish and black marlin up to 400 kg. Diving gear is also available for those who wish to explore the virgin reefs.

Needless to say, Kaimbu is not for everyone. The price is US$995 per couple per night (plus 10% tax), and includes air transfer (on Kaimbu's own private plane), all meals, booze, diving, deep-sea fishing – in short, everything. The island can also be hired by private groups for US$2500 a day for up to six guests. Once again, all expenses are included in the price.

For reservations and information write to Brenda McCrosky, PO Box 10392, Newport Beach, CA 10392 (fax 714 730 0827).

Rotuma

Rotuma Island, 386 km north-north-west of the Fiji archipelago, has an indigenous population of Polynesians (as opposed to the Fijians, who are Melanesian), related most closely to the Samoans. Rotuma is governed as a dependency of Fiji, and its people follow a life style as traditional as that of the Fijians.

Measuring 13 km long and about four km wide, the island has rich volcanic soil that will grow just about any type of tropical fruit. The best oranges sold in Fiji are grown in Rotuma.

The first visit by Europeans was in 1791, when the crew of HMS *Pandora* landed in search of *Bounty* mutineers. Later contact with the European world came in the form of runaway sailors and escaped convicts, who eventually killed each other off or were killed by Rotumans. In 1842 Tongan Wesleyan ministers found their way to the island, followed by Marist Catholics five years later. The result was actual warfare between followers of the two groups.

Weary from the chaos caused by the fighting, Rotuman chiefs ceded the island to Britain in 1881. Rotuma became a province when Fiji gained independence, and today some 3000 Rotumans live on the island while another 8000 live in the Fiji archipelago.

The main attractions on Rotuma are the beaches and reefs, which are a fishing enthusiast's paradise. The drawback for potential visitors is that there is no accommodation on the island. As recently as 1985, the leaders on the island voted seven to one against opening up Rotuma to tourism. For the determined traveller with plenty of time, it is possible to see Rotuma; but you had better have a Rotuman friend on the island

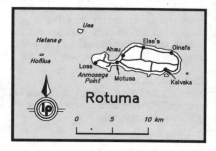

because without an invitation you will be told to leave.

GETTING THERE & AWAY
Air
Fiji Air flies twice weekly to the island for F$184 one way, but the flights are frequently booked out in advance.

Boat
The most frequent visitors arrive by yacht. Permission for anchorage can be obtained from the government station at Ahau on Maka Bay. Government ships and a couple of commercial vessels make monthly visits to Rotuma, but getting passage can be difficult. Even if the Marine Department or a private shipping firm says there is a berth, the captain has the final say. Your best bet is to talk to the skipper ahead of time, or to have a Rotuman friend make the arrangements. Keep in mind that if you depend on a ship for transport, your stay on the island may be a month or more, depending on space availability.

Glossary

bete – a priest-cum-master of ceremonies
bilibili – bamboo raft
bure – home or residence
bure kalou – ancient temple
bulumakau – cattle or beef

dalo – taro
drua – large double-hulled canoe

ibe – woven mat

kai colo – hill people; almost always used as a colloquial term to describe unsophisticated 'country' people
kai loma – part-Europeans, usually people of mixed European/Fijian heritage
kanikani – white, scaly skin blotches associated with excessive amounts yaqona consumption

lolo – coconut milk
lovo – underground oven

masi – bark cloth (tapa)
meke – traditional communal dance/theatre

polotu – an evening church service devoted to singing or chanting
puaka – pig

sevusevu – gift from a guest or visitor, bestowed as a token of respect
sulu – rectangular piece of cloth (national costume)

takia – Fijian canoe with sail
tabua – whale's tooth, given as a token of respect
talanoa – conversation or story-telling, often while drinking yaqona
tanoa – bowl for drinking yaqona
tavioka – cassava

vanua – political confederation
vu – ancestral spirits

walu – fish

yaqona – another word for kava, the Fijian national beverage derived form the *piper methysticum* plant

Index

248 Index

PLANET TALK
Lonely Planet's FREE quarterly newsletter

We love hearing from you and think you'd like to hear from us.

When...is the right time to see reindeer in Finland?
Where...can you hear the best palm-wine music in Ghana?
How...do you get from Asunción to Areguá by steam train?
What...is the best way to see India?

For the answer to these and many other questions read PLANET TALK.

Every issue is packed with up-to-date travel news and advice including:

- *a letter from Lonely Planet founders Tony and Maureen Wheeler*
- *travel diary from a Lonely Planet author - find out what it's really like out on the road*
- *feature article on an important and topical travel issue*
- *a selection of recent letters from our readers*
- *the latest travel news from all over the world*
- *details on Lonely Planet's new and forthcoming releases*

To join our mailing list contact any Lonely Planet office (address below).

LONELY PLANET PUBLICATIONS
Australia: PO Box 617, Hawthorn 3122, Victoria (tel: 03-819 1877)
USA: Embarcadero West, 155 Filbert St, Suite 251, Oakland, CA 94607 (tel: 510-893 8555)
TOLL FREE: (800) 275-8555
UK: 10 Barley Mow Passage, Chiswick, London W4 4PH (tel: 081-742 3161)
France: 71 bis rue du Cardinal Lemoine – 75005 Paris (tel: 1-46 34 00 58)

Also available: Lonely Planet T-shirts. 100% heavyweight cotton (S, M, L, XL)

Guides to the Pacific

Australia – a travel survival kit
The complete low-down on Down Under – home of Ayers Rock, the Great Barrier Reef, extraordinary animals, cosmopolitan cities, rainforests, beaches ... and Lonely Planet!

Bushwalking in Australia
Two experienced and respected walkers give details of the best walks in every state, covering many different terrains and climates.

Bushwalking in Papua New Guinea
The best way to get to know Papua New Guinea is from the ground up – and bushwalking is the best way to travel around the rugged and varied landscape of this island.

Islands of Australia's Great Barrier Reef – Australia guide
The Great Barrier Reef is one of the wonders of the world – and one of the great travel destinations! Whether you're looking for the best snorkelling, the liveliest nightlife or a secluded island hideaway, this guide has all the facts you'll need.

Melbourne – city guide
From historic houses to fascinating churches and from glorious parks to tapas bars, cafés and bistros, Melbourne is a dream for gourmets and a paradise for sightseers.

New South Wales & the ACT
Ancient aboriginal sites, pristine surf beaches, kangaroos bounding across desert dunes, lyre-birds dancing in rainforest, picturesque country pubs, weather-beaten drovers and friendly small-town people, along with Australia's largest and liveliest metropolis (and the host city of the year 2000 Olympic Games) – all this and more can be found in New South Wales and the ACT.

Sydney – city guide
From the Opera House to the surf; all you need to know in a handy pocket-sized format.

Outback Australia
The outback conjures up images of endless stretches of dead straight roads, the rich red of the desert, and the resourcefulness and resilience of the inhabitants. A visit to Australia would not be complete without visiting the outback to see the beauty and vastness of this ancient country.

Victoria – Australia guide
From old gold rush towns to cosmopolitan Melbourne and from remote mountains to the most popular surf beaches, Victoria is packed with attractions and activities for everyone.

Hawaii – a travel survival kit
Share in the delights of this island paradise – and avoid some of its high prices – with this practical guide. It covers all of Hawaii's well-known attractions, plus plenty of uncrowded sights and activities.

Micronesia – a travel survival kit
The glorious beaches, lagoons and reefs of these 2100 islands would dazzle even the most jaded traveller. This guide has all the details on island-hopping across the Micronesian archipelago.

New Caledonia – a travel survival kit
This guide shows how to discover all that the idyllic islands of New Caledonia have to offer – from French colonial culture to traditional Melanesian life.

New Zealand – a travel survival kit
This practical guide will help you discover the very best New Zealand has to offer: Maori dances and feasts, some of the most spectacular scenery in the world, and every outdoor activity imaginable.

Tramping in New Zealand
Call it tramping, hiking, walking, bushwalking or trekking – travelling by foot is the best way to explore New Zealand's natural beauty. Detailed descriptions of over 40 walks of varying length and difficulty.

Papua New Guinea – a travel survival kit
With its coastal cities, villages perched beside mighty rivers, palm-fringed beaches and rushing mountain streams, Papua New Guinea promises memorable travel.

Rarotonga & the Cook Islands – a travel survival kit
Rarotonga and the Cook Islands have history, beauty and magic to rival the better-known islands of Hawaii and Tahiti, but the world has virtually passed them by.

Samoa – a travel survival kit
Two remarkably different countries, Western Samoa and American Samoa offer some wonderful island escapes, and Polynesian culture at its best.

Solomon Islands – a travel survival kit
The Solomon Islands are the best-kept secret of the Pacific. Discover remote tropical islands, jungle-covered volcanoes and traditional Melanesian villages with this detailed guide.

Tahiti & French Polynesia – a travel survival kit
Tahiti's idyllic beauty has seduced sailors, artists and travellers for generations. The latest edition of this book provides full details on the main island of Tahiti, the Tuamotos, Marquesas and other island groups. Invaluable information for independent travellers and package tourists alike.

Tonga – a travel survival kit
The only South Pacific country never to be colonised by Europeans, Tonga has also been ignored by tourists. The people of this far-flung island group offer some of the most sincere and unconditional hospitality in the world.

Vanuatu – a travel survival kit
Discover superb beaches, lush rainforests, dazzling coral reefs and traditional Melanesian customs in this glorious Pacific Ocean archipelago.

Lonely Planet Guidebooks

Lonely Planet guidebooks cover every accessible part of Asia as well as Australia, the Pacific, South America, Africa, the Middle East, Europe and parts of North America. There are five series: *travel survival kits*, covering a country for a range of budgets; *shoestring guides* with compact information for low-budget travel in a major region; *walking guides*; *city guides* and *phrasebooks*.

Australia & the Pacific
Australia
Australian phrasebook
Bushwalking in Australia
Islands of Australia's Great Barrier Reef
Outback Australia
Fiji
Fijian phrasebook
Melbourne city guide
Micronesia
New Caledonia
New South Wales
New Zealand
Tramping in New Zealand
Papua New Guinea
Bushwalking in Papua New Guinea
Papua New Guinea phrasebook
Rarotonga & the Cook Islands
Samoa
Solomon Islands
Sydney city guide
Tahiti & French Polynesia
Tonga
Vanuatu
Victoria

South-East Asia
Bali & Lombok
Bangkok city guide
Cambodia
Indonesia
Indonesia phrasebook
Laos
Malaysia, Singapore & Brunei
Myanmar (Burma)
Burmese phrasebook
Philippines
Pilipino phrasebook
Singapore city guide
South-East Asia on a shoestring
Thailand
Thai phrasebook
Vietnam
Vietnamese phrasebook

Middle East
Arab Gulf States
Egypt & the Sudan
Arabic (Egyptian) phrasebook
Iran
Israel
Jordan & Syria
Middle East
Turkish phrasebook
Trekking in Turkey
Yemen

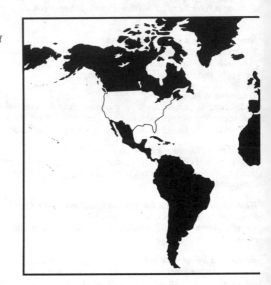

North-East Asia
China
Beijing city guide
Cantonese phrasebook
Mandarin Chinese phrasebook
Hong Kong, Macau & Canton
Japan
Japanese phrasebook
Korea
Korean phrasebook
Mongolia
North-East Asia on a shoestring
Seoul city guide
Taiwan
Tibet
Tibet phrasebook
Tokyo city guide

Indian Ocean
Madagascar & Comoros
Maldives & Islands of the East Indian Ocean
Mauritius, Réunion & Seychelles

Mail Order

Lonely Planet guidebooks are distributed worldwide. They are also available by mail order from Lonely Planet, so if you have difficulty finding a title please write to us. US and Canadian residents should write to Embarcadero West, 155 Filbert St, Suite 251, Oakland CA 94607, USA ; European residents should write to 10 Barley Mow Passage, Chiswick, London W4 4PH; and residents of other countries to PO Box 617, Hawthorn, Victoria 3122, Australia.

Indian Subcontinent
Bangladesh
India
Hindi/Urdu phrasebook
Trekking in the Indian Himalaya
Karakoram Highway
Kashmir, Ladakh & Zanskar
Nepal
Trekking in the Nepal Himalaya
Nepali phrasebook
Pakistan
Sri Lanka
Sri Lanka phrasebook

Africa
Africa on a shoestring
Central Africa
East Africa
Trekking in East Africa
Kenya
Swahili phrasebook
Morocco, Algeria & Tunisia
Arabic (Moroccan) phrasebook
South Africa, Lesotho & Swaziland
Zimbabwe, Botswana & Namibia
West Africa

Central America & the Caribbean
Baja California
Central America on a shoestring
Costa Rica
Eastern Caribbean
Guatemala, Belize & Yucatán: La Ruta Maya
Mexico

North America
Alaska
Canada
Hawaii

South America
Argentina, Uruguay & Paraguay
Bolivia
Brazil
Brazilian phrasebook
Chile & Easter Island
Colombia
Ecuador & the Galápagos Islands
Latin American Spanish phrasebook
Peru
Quechua phrasebook
South America on a shoestring
Trekking in the Patagonian Andes
Venezuela

Europe
Baltic States & Kaliningrad
Dublin city guide
Eastern Europe on a shoestring
Eastern Europe phrasebook
Finland
France
Greece
Hungary
Iceland, Greenland & the Faroe Islands
Ireland
Italy
Mediterranean Europe on a shoestring
Mediterranean Europe phrasebook
Poland
Scandinavian & Baltic Europe on a shoestring
Scandinavian Europe phrasebook
Switzerland
Trekking in Spain
Trekking in Greece
USSR
Russian phrasebook
Western Europe on a shoestring
Western Europe phrasebook

The Lonely Planet Story

Lonely Planet published its first book in 1973 in response to the numerous 'How did you do it?' questions Maureen and Tony Wheeler were asked after driving, bussing, hitching, sailing and railing their way from England to Australia.

Written at a kitchen table and hand collated, trimmed and stapled, *Across Asia on the Cheap* became an instant local bestseller, inspiring thoughts of another book.

Eighteen months in South-East Asia resulted in their second guide, *South-East Asia on a shoestring*, which they put together in a backstreet Chinese hotel in Singapore in 1975. The 'yellow bible' as it quickly became known to backpackers around the world, soon became *the* guide to the region. It has sold well over half a million copies and is now in its 8th edition, still retaining its familiar yellow cover.

Today there are over 140 Lonely Planet titles in print – books that have that same adventurous approach to travel as those early guides; books that 'assume you know how to get your luggage off the carousel' as one reviewer put it.

Although Lonely Planet initially specialised in guides to Asia, they now cover most regions of the world, including the Pacific, South America, Africa, the Middle East and Europe. The list of *walking guides* and *phrasebooks* (for 'unusual' languages such as Quechua, Swahili, Nepali and Egyptian Arabic) is also growing rapidly.

The emphasis continues to be on travel for independent travellers. Tony and Maureen still travel for several months of each year and play an active part in the writing, updating and quality control of Lonely Planet's guides.

They have been joined by over 50 authors, 90 staff – mainly editors, cartographers & designers – at our office in Melbourne, Australia, at our US office in Oakland, California and at our European office in Paris; another five at our office in London handle sales for Britain, Europe and Africa. Travellers themselves also make a valuable contribution to the guides through the feedback we receive in thousands of letters each year.

The people at Lonely Planet strongly believe that travellers can make a positive contribution to the countries they visit, both through their appreciation of the countries' culture, wildlife and natural features, and through the money they spend. In addition, the company makes a direct contribution to the countries and regions it covers. Since 1986 a percentage of the income from each book has been donated to ventures such as famine relief in Africa; aid projects in India; agricultural projects in Central America; Greenpeace's efforts to halt French nuclear testing in the Pacific and Amnesty International. In 1993 $100,000 was donated to such causes.

Lonely Planet's basic travel philosophy is summed up in Tony Wheeler's comment, 'Don't worry about whether your trip will work out. Just go!'.